KU-379-639

Contents

Writers and artists in the Lake District colour section following p.160

Out and about in the Lakes colour section following p.208

3

◄◄ Above Glenridding ◄ The view from Cat Bells

△ Skipton & Leeds

Settle

Slaidburn

YORKSHIRE

A65

LANCASHIRE

▷ Manchester & Liverpool

Lancaster

M6

A586

Sedburgh

Kirkby
Lonsdale

Oxenholme

Kendal

Minthorpe

River Kent

Troutbeck
Orrest Head
Staveley

Sizergh
Castle

Levens
Hall

Arnside

Morecambe

Heysham

Lyth Valley

Bowness

Blackwell

Winster Valley

Grange-
over-
Sands

Windermere

Sawrey

Newby
Bridge

Cartmel

Cark

Tarn
Hows

Brantwood

GRIZEDALE
FOREST

Holker
Hall

Fleetwood

Hawkshead

Esthwaite
Water

Lakeside &
Haverthwaite
Railway

Windermere

Old Man of
Coniston

Coniston

Coniston
Water

Ulverston

Dalton-in-Furness

Furness
Abbey

A590

River Duddon

Broughton-
in-Furness

A595

A5087

Ravenglass &
Eskdale Railway

Boot

Eskdale

Muncaster
Castle

Duddon Bridge

Black
Combe

Swinside

Barrow-in-Furness

River Irt

Whicham

Millom

Ravenglass

Silecroft

Haverigg

A595

N

Lake District National
Park boundary

10 miles

Feet	
3000	
2000	
1500	
1000	
500	
250	
0	

0

© Crown copyright

5

Introduction to the

Lake District

The Lake District is England's most celebrated, most visited and most hyped scenic area. Tucked into a bulge between the industrial cities of northwest England and the Scottish borders, the small region – just thirty miles across – is irresistible to the twelve million visitors a year who pour in to experience its famous lakes, picturesque villages and alpine landscape. To many, the lure is of a misty-eyed English past – quiet country lanes, ivy-clad inns, agricultural shows and sheepdog trials – while others seek to tick off English superlatives, including the country's highest mountain (Scafell Pike), and its largest and deepest lakes (Windermere and Wast Water respectively). The sundry pastoral images could hardly be better known, whether bolstered by the siren words of the Lake Poets or embedded in the minds of the nation's children who grow up with the lakeland tales of Beatrix Potter, Arthur Ransome and John Cunliffe's *Postman Pat*.

▲ Sea wall, Ravenglass

It's hard to think of a region in Britain with a similar breadth of scenery in such a small area – wild fells to walled grazing land, glacial lakes to forested valleys, steeply pitched mountains to tumbling waterfalls. Tourist numbers are concentrated in fairly specific areas and even on the busiest of summer days it's relatively easy to escape the crowds by climbing to the higher fells or exploring more remote valleys. There are parts of the region, particularly in the north and west, where tourism is still decidedly low-key. Choose to come in the early spring, late autumn or winter – when magical crisp, clear days often enhance the natural backdrop – and even the most beaten paths and over-visited sights can be refreshingly uncluttered.

The scenery is, of course, the major attraction, and if **hiking and the great outdoors** isn't your bag, it's tempting to say that you're on the wrong holiday. The central lakeland crags – the birthplace of British rock-climbing – still lure climbers from far and wide, while the lakes, paths and valleys support an entire industry of adventure activities, from kayaking and windsurfing to pony-trekking and off-road biking.

The region's **literary connections** are justly famous, though you may be surprised to find that it's not all Wordsworth, Coleridge, Southey and De Quincey: writers and poets as diverse as Sir Hugh Walpole, Norman Nicholson and John Ruskin have left their mark, and their houses, haunts and places of inspiration form the backbone of many a lakeland literary trail. There's a long **industrial history**, too, which manifests itself in scattered mining works, scarred quarry sites, surviving mills (one still working at Stott Park) and a couple of old railway lines – Ravenglass to Eskdale, and Lakeside to Haverthwaite – now converted to tourist use.

Fact file

- The Lake District National Park was established in 1951 and covers 885 square miles (half a million acres).

- Most of the land within the park (59 percent) is privately owned. The rest is owned by the National Trust (24.8 percent) and water and forestry concerns (12.4 percent), with 3.8 percent owned by the National Park Authority itself.

- There are 42,000 people living within the National Park. Up to fifty percent of all jobs are attributable in some way to tourism.

- Farming accounts for just ten percent of the Park's working population – and the National Trust alone owns 91 farms.

- The highest mountains are Scafell Pike (3210ft), Scafell (3162ft), Helvellyn (3118ft) and Skiddaw (3053ft); the deepest lakes are Wast Water (243ft), Windermere (204ft) and Ullswater (200ft).

▲ Scafell

The Lake District has one of the country's highest concentrations of classic rural **pubs and inns**, many of them former coaching inns dating back several hundred years. Locally brewed beer is widely available, and a circular walk and a pint in front of a roaring fire at the end of it takes some beating for an afternoon out. Stay overnight and you can experience another Lake District speciality, the **country-house hotel**: some of the grandest specimens in England occupy exclusive lakeview positions. Finally, in summer the region hosts many of its annual **sports, festivals, shows** and **events**, providing a fascinating snapshot of traditional rural life.

◄ Foxglove

Where to go

t's easy to see a great deal of the Lake District in just a few days, even if you are travelling by public transport or getting around on foot. If you're pushed for time, you could tour around most of what's detailed below in a week, but you'd be doing precious little hiking or relaxing. It's far better to pick a base and see what you can from there, walking rather than driving between villages, and building in time for doing nothing more strenuous on occasion than taking out a rowboat or picnicking in a meadow. **Windermere** is the longest and largest lake, featuring a cruise service which calls at all points north and south. Two late Victorian mansions on its shores provide must-see attractions: the National Park's Lake District Visitor Centre at **Brockhole**, and **Blackwell**, whose restored Arts and Crafts interior is one of England's architectural gems. The lake's towns – Windermere, Bowness and, especially, **Ambleside** – have populations of just a few thousand but are among the region's busiest settlements and, given their choice of accommodation, cafés, restaurants and pubs, they make obvious bases. Even if they don't plan to stay there, most people at least pass by Windermere on the way to **Grasmere** and the famous Wordsworth houses of **Rydal Mount** and **Dove Cottage**, or to pretty Hawkshead and Beatrix Potter's house at **Hill Top**.

Nearby **Coniston** sits at the head of Coniston Water which boasts the big draw of **Brantwood**, comfortably endowed home of the critic and essayist John Ruskin. Nearby natural attractions include **Grizedale Forest**, where you can cycle or hike the shaded trails, and **Tarn Hows**, many visitors' favourite splash of water in the entire Lakes. Away from the literary trail, there are renowned hikes, peaks and tarns in central **Langdale** – and, arguably, the finest hikers' inn in the region (the *Old Dungeon Ghyll*) from which to explore them. Less dramatic rural pockets in the hills and dales south of Windermere and Coniston offer easy rambles, village visits and pub lunches in the **Duddon**, **Winster** or **Lyth** valleys.

On the whole, the scenery is more dramatic in the north, where four peaks – **Scafell Pike**, **Scafell**, **Helvellyn** and **Skiddaw** – top out at over 3000 feet, and several other equally famous mountains (including **Great Gable** and **Blencathra**) don't lag far behind. The quite different lakes of **Derwent Water** and **Ullswater** provide superb backdrops for a day's cruising and walking. **Keswick**, the main town in the north (with a population of around 5000), is the one major lakeland settlement with real year-round character, and it makes a handy base for exploring: south through the precipitous delights of **Borrowdale**, a valley for which the word picturesque might have been invented; west over the forested **Whinlatter**

Lakeland place names and terms

Many lakeland place names, geographical features and dialect words have origins which go back to Norse, Saxon or even Celtic times. The most common are appended to features you'll see every time you stride out into the countryside – like "fell" (hill, mountain, or high common land), "mere" (lake), "holme" (island), "beck" (stream), "force" (waterfall) and "tarn" (small mountain lake). With other names, it helps to know the derivation in order to figure out exactly what you're looking at, thus place names ending in "-thwaite" (signifying a clearing), or those incorporating the words "ghyll" or "gill" (narrow ravine or mountain stream), "hause" (summit of a pass), "how" or "howe" (rounded hill), "pike" (peak), "raise" (summit of a ridge), "rake" (natural rock passage) or "wyke" (bay). Farming language is deeply rooted in the past – words like "heaf" (grazing area), "garth" (enclosed land or field) or "lath" (barn) have ancient roots – and there was once an entire counting system for keeping tabs on sheep (yan, tyan, tethera, or one, two, three . . .). That's not to mention scores of dialect words, many still in use, for describing traditional skills and pastimes, from basket-weaving to wrestling.

▲ Langdale

Pass; or north around the little-visited region known as **Back o' Skiddaw**.

The summer crowds thin out in the western side of the Park. Although **Buttermere** and **Crummock Water** see a fair amount of traffic, **Wast Water**, **Ennerdale Water** and **Loweswater** lie further off the beaten track. All these lakes provide supreme walking opportunities, from simple lake-circuits to fell-top clambers, and anyone looking for typical rural accommodation – whether a room above a pub, a farmhouse B&B or lakeside hotel – will find the western lakes and fells irresistible. Keep heading west and you find the only part of the Cumbrian **coastline** that lies within the National Park. This stretches twenty miles south from **Ravenglass**, an undistinguished village with a Roman past, but which provides a bucolic route into the heart of dramatic **Eskdale** by either following the snaking road or the Ravenglass and Eskdale Railway.

This book concentrates on the natural attractions, towns and villages within the National Park, but people's itineraries and interests don't always follow the somewhat arbitrary Park boundaries. Outside the National Park, most visitors make time for **Kendal** and its excellent museums, the revitalized Georgian port of **Whitehaven**, and the peripheral historic market towns of **Ulverston**, **Penrith** and **Cockermouth**, the last also famous as the birthplace of Wordsworth. These are bigger settlements than anywhere in the National Park, so they make useful bases; and they're also rainy-day boltholes of sorts,

Kendal Mintcake

You'll see blocks of **Kendal Mintcake** on sale throughout the Lake District, though "cake" is perhaps a misleading term for such a solid confection of molar-shattering properties. It does come from Kendal, though – first produced in the town in 1869 – and it is undeniably minty. As is the way with many great inventions, its initial production came about as a mistake made during the process of combining sugar and peppermint oil for clear mint sweets. It was quickly apparent that the grainy, energy-giving "mintcake" would go far in a region where you often needed a quick boost if you were to scale the local fells and crags. **Romney's of Kendal**, established 1919, is still the biggest producer, famous since Sir Edmund Hillary carried their mintcake up to the top of Everest in 1953. Stick some in your backpack and there's not a Lake District peak you can't knock off before breakfast.

offering a varied set of attractions, including the startling **Rheged** visitor centre near Penrith, fashioned to blend in with the local fells. More reflective destinations lie on the southern flanks of the National Park where **Furness Abbey** and the priory church in the highly attractive village of **Cartmel** provide a glimpse of the erstwhile religious influence on the Lakes.

When to go

▲ Ullswater

High **summer** may be the warmest season – usually – but it isn't the ideal time to visit the Lakes. July and August can see accommodation (and the roads) stretched to capacity as the bulk of the annual visitors descend. If you're thinking of swimming in the lakes, it's worth knowing that late August and September see the waters at their warmest, as they've had time to soak up the summer sun. To be honest, though, you'll barely notice the difference: the inland waters are pretty cold, at best, year-round. Other busy periods include **Easter week**, the few days around **New Year**, and school **half-term holidays** (Feb & Oct). Fewer people visit the Lakes in the **late autumn**, **winter** and **early spring**, so if you're looking for relative peace and quiet, these are the seasons to choose. Many of the indoor sights and attractions remain open year-round, so you shouldn't be unduly inconvenienced, and while some hotels, guesthouses and campsites are closed, those that do stay open tend to offer reduced rates. Spring usually arrives a little later than in the south of England, though in mild seasons you sometimes get the famous **daffodils** flowering as early as February. Mostly, though, before May you might get bright, blue days, but you can also expect chilly mornings, overnight frosts and cold conditions (snow can linger on north-facing slopes as late as June). December has the shortest and rainiest days; November and January aren't much better.

Average daily temperatures and rainfall in the Lake District

	Jan	Feb	Mar	Apr	May	Jun	Jul	Aug	Sep	Oct	Nov	Dec
°F	38	42	45	50	58	62	65	63	60	52	44	42
°C	4	5	7	10	14	17	19	18	15	11	7	6
inches	2	1.75	1.75	1.75	1.9	1.8	2.2	2.2	2	2.1	2.3	1.9
mm	50	44	44	44	48	45	55	55	50	53	58	48

18

things not to miss

It's not possible to see everything that the Lake District has to offer in one trip – and we don't suggest you try. What follows, in no particular order, is a selective taste of the highlights of the region. They're arranged in five colour-coded categories, which you can browse through to find the very best things to see and experience. All entries have a page reference to take you straight into the guide, where you can find out more.

01 Hardknott Roman Fort Page **180** • The finest Roman remains in the Lakes stretch across a blustery hillside.

02 Great Langdale Page **106** • For the best rugged walking in the central fells, head for the glorious Langdale valley.

03 Stylish lodgings Page **69** • Contemporary style meets traditional England in the *Punch Bowl Inn* at Crosthwaite, one of the Lake District's most fashionable lodgings.

04 Dove Cottage, Grasmere Page **98** • The most famous literary house in the Lake District – the early home of William and Dorothy Wordsworth, containing a wealth of memories.

05 The #79 bus ride in Borrowdale Page **155** • The Lakes' most scenic bus ride flanks Derwent Water and runs through the stunning valley of Borrowdale, with rustic stops at packhorse bridges, waterfalls, crags, woods and hamlets.

06 **A walk on the fells** Page **35** • Some of Britain's best hikes meander across the lakeland mountains (or fells, as they're known in these parts).

07 **Tarn Hows**
Page **128** • The most beautiful spot in the Lake District? Many people think so, but you decide as you stroll the undulating paths around this most serene of tarns.

09 **A cruise on Windermere**
Page **59** • Cruises and boat trips depart all year round from Bowness piers on Windermere, England's largest lake.

08 **Farm life** Page **26** • Staying in a farmhouse B&B is the best way to learn something about rural life in the Lake District.

10 **Townend** Page **79** • Get close to the life of a yeoman farmer in one of the Lake District's best-preserved domestic houses.

11 **Wild ospreys, Bassenthwaite Lake** Page **164** • A viewing platform above Bassenthwaite allows you to see these majestic birds at close quarters.

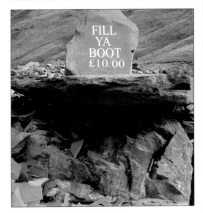

13 **Honister Slate Mine** Page **159** • Don a hard hat and explore the caverns and tunnels of the historic slate mine on Honister Pass.

12 **Aira Force** Page **206** • The sparkling waterfall with a seventy-foot drop is a cherished location – Wordsworth "wandered lonely as a cloud" among the neighbouring daffodils.

14 **Ravenglass & Eskdale Railway** Page **178** • A ride on "La'al Ratty", as the train is known, makes a great family outing, with easy walks possible straight off the platforms of the tiny Eskdale stations.

15 **Castlerigg Stone Circle** Page **143** • The dramatically sited standing stones at Castlerigg, above Keswick, are the most prominent reminder of Lakeland's ancient inhabitants.

17 **Pubs** Pages **26 & 30** • The Lake District has some of the best old inns and pubs in the country, many dating back hundreds of years and still offering a hearty welcome, rooms for the night, local beer and filling bar meals.

16 **Grizedale Forest** Page **130** • The remarkable sculptures lurking in Grizedale Forest are the backdrop to an adventurous day's walking or cycling.

18 **Furness Abbey** Page **233** • The beautiful Cistercian abbey ruins provide a contemplative corner in an unsung region.

Basics

Basics

Getting there

The Lake District is in the county of Cumbria, in the northwest of England, 80 miles north of Manchester and 270 miles from London. The M6 motorway gets you within a few miles' drive of the eastern side of the region, while public transport links are good, with trains or buses providing reasonably direct access from most major British cities (and from Manchester Airport). The major points of access are Lancaster, Kendal and Windermere to the south, and Penrith and Carlisle to the north.

This section tells you how to reach the Lake District by bus, train or car, and gives all the contact details you'll need for planning routes and booking tickets. The government-sponsored website ⓦwww.transportdirect .info also has a useful door-to-door journey planner for all public and private transport in the country. Touring around the Lakes by either public transport or car is covered in the next section, "Getting around".

A number of operators offer **organized holidays** in the Lakes for those who'd rather someone else made the day-to-day arrangements. Large-scale package-tour operators tend to concentrate on whirlwind trips through the region, bussing passengers in en masse to see the famous lakes and literary sites. Generally speaking, you can do much better than that on your own – either using public transport or booking local minibus tours (covered in "Getting around"). But if you're interested in a residential outdoor activity or pastime-based holiday – from cycle-touring to art appreciation – in the Lakes you may prefer to let the specialists take charge. We've picked out some of the more interesting options in the "Walking and climbing" (p.35) and "Organized holidays, courses and outdoor activities" (p.39) sections.

For more guidance on holidaying in the Lake District, contact **Cumbria Tourism**: ☎01539/822222, brochure line ☎0870/513 3059, ⓦwww.golakes.co.uk, ⓦwww.gocumbria.co.uk.

By bus

National Express (ⓦwww.nationalexpress .com) buses from London's Victoria Coach Station run once daily to Windermere, via Birmingham, Preston and Lancaster, an eight-hour ride (£37.50 return; £29.50 if

Getting there for overseas visitors

Overseas visitors heading straight for the Lake District should consider taking a connecting **flight** from London, or flying directly to Manchester Airport, northern England's major airport, from where there are direct train services to Kendal and Windermere. Other services from or via Manchester sometimes require a change of trains either at Lancaster or at Oxenholme, the station for the Lakes on the west-coast main line.

Travelling from Ireland by **ferry**, the most logical port to use is Liverpool (sailings from Belfast and Dublin), from where it's an easy train ride to Manchester and on to the Lakes. Using the Belfast service to Stranraer in Scotland, you'll need to travel first by train to Glasgow and on from there; arriving in Holyhead from Dublin, take the train via Crewe to Oxenholme. From the rest of Europe, using the North Sea crossings makes most sense. Docking at Hull (from Rotterdam and Zeebrugge), take the train to York and Manchester, changing for the onward service to the Lakes; from Newcastle (Hamburg, Amsterdam, Norway and Sweden), take the train to Carlisle, changing for the service south to Penrith and Oxenholme.

booked seven days in advance). This service continues from Windermere on to Ambleside (15min), Grasmere (30min) and Keswick (45min). From Manchester's Chorlton Street Coach Station there's one National Express bus a day to Windermere, via Preston, which takes up to four hours (£21.50 return; £18.50 if booked seven days in advance) and which also stops in Ambleside, Grasmere and Keswick. There's a connection to this service from Manchester Airport. From Birmingham, the once-daily service to Windermere takes under five hours (£34.50 return; £30 if booked seven days in advance). National Express services from York, Newcastle and Scotland all route via Manchester to the Lakes; from the south, east and west you'll have to change in London or Birmingham. A £3–5 supplement is charged on all routes for travelling on a Friday (as well as on Saturdays in July and Aug).

Regional bus operators provide other services to the Lake District, though these are often limited to weekend departures in summer from towns and cities in northern England. Stagecoach (ⓦwww .stagecoachbus.com) has the most useful year-round, direct regional service (#555/556), from Carlisle (three daily) to Keswick and points beyond, or from Lancaster (hourly) to Kendal, Windermere, Ambleside, Grasmere and Keswick.

By train

Access is via Virgin Trains' west-coast main-line service between London and Glasgow. For the Lake District, you change either at Lancaster or **Oxenholme** for the branch-line service to Kendal (3min from Oxenholme) and Windermere (20min). The only other places in the region directly accessible by train are Penrith (also on the west-coast main line) and Carlisle (west-coast main line, plus connections from Newcastle upon Tyne). There are also direct services from Manchester to Kendal and Windermere; and from Manchester, Preston and Lancaster along the Cumbrian coast to Ulverston, Barrow-in-Furness, Ravenglass and the coastal towns to Carlisle, providing a leisurely approach to the south and western Lakes. Various train operators are responsible for the services but you don't need to know specific details as **National Rail Enquiries** (☎08457/484950, ⓦwww.nationalrail.co.uk) can give you all the timetable, route and service information – the website has a journey planner and links to ticket-sale sites.

From London (Euston Station) there are up to ten departures a day to Windermere, and it's usually around a 3hr 30min trip. There are some good deals if you book in advance (by 6pm the day before travel), with one-way fares starting at £17.50. If you buy your ticket on the day, expect to pay more like £70 return, and a lot more if you intend to travel on a Friday or during peak commuter hours. To reach Keswick and the northern Lakes, either take the train from Oxenholme to Windermere and continue from there by bus or stay on the main-line service to Penrith or Carlisle, from where buses also run to Keswick.

From Manchester (Airport, and both Piccadilly and Oxford Road train stations), the quickest trains to Windermere take 1hr 40min (advance return fares from £15). Coming **from Yorkshire**, a longer, more scenic approach is provided by the famous **Settle to Carlisle Railway** (connections from Leeds and Bradford), which runs through stunning

Distances in miles from major cities

	Windermere	Keswick	Penrith
London	270	305	290
Birmingham	150	190	175
Manchester	80	115	100
York	100	115	95
Newcastle upon Tyne	90	80	75
Edinburgh	145	135	115
Glasgow	140	135	115

Yorkshire Dales countryside. At Carlisle, you'll have to switch to local buses to get you to Keswick, Penrith or Cockermouth. The best deal on this route is the Settle to Carlisle Round Robin (£35), which gives unlimited travel between York, Leeds and Carlisle. Anyone seeing the Lakes as part of a wider northern England trip might consider buying a **North Country Rover** ticket (any 4 days in 8; £65), valid for unlimited rail travel in a region which stretches between Carlisle, the Cumbrian coast and Lancaster east into Yorkshire and northeast to Newcastle.

Services from **Glasgow Central** (2hr 30min–3hr 30min) and **Edinburgh** (3hr–3hr 30min) run to Oxenholme for connections to Windermere, with stops en route at Carlisle and Penrith. Advance return fares to Windermere from either city start at £23, though cost up to £71 if you buy on the day, or travel on a Friday or at peak times.

By car

The Lake District lies to the west of the M6 motorway, which – as it approaches the hills

and troughs of the Lakes and the Eden Valley – displays one of the best feats of road engineering in the country: the section between Kendal and Penrith is as impressive as major highways get in England. Where you come off the motorway depends on your ultimate destination – for Keswick and Penrith, take junction 40; for Kendal and Windermere, take junction 38 (north) or 36 (south); for Cartmel and Ulverston, take junction 36.

Count on a **driving time** of five hours from London and the southeast, an hour and a half from Manchester or Newcastle, two and half hours from York or Birmingham, and three hours from Glasgow or Edinburgh. Once you leave the motorway, the nature of the roads and the summer traffic can slow you right down, so allow plenty of time if you're aiming for the central fells, Borrowdale or the western Lakes. Local radio stations (see p.43) carry regular traffic and weather reports. Both the AA (ⓦwww.theaa.co.uk) and RAC (ⓦwww.rac.co.uk) have useful **route-planning services**.

Getting around

Too many people bring cars to the Lake District and, as a consequence, once-quiet valleys and villages can be adversely affected by the amount of traffic. However, over the last few years – recognizing the damage that's being done to the environment – the local authorities have made great improvements to the public transport network within the National Park to encourage people to leave their cars at home. As well as providing public transport information, this section also recommends local minibus tours, which are a good way of seeing the region quickly. There are also full details about getting around by car, and a section on cycling in the Lake District (though for cycling holiday operators, see p.40).

The southern, central and northern band – from Windermere and Coniston through Ambleside and Grasmere to Keswick – is the easiest section of the Lakes to tour by public transport. In summer especially, when services are at their peak, there's no longer any real excuse not to use public transport

for at least some journeys. In the western Lakes and valleys, and in the far north beyond Keswick, getting around by bus becomes trickier, though nearly everywhere is connected by some sort of service, however limited.

Timetables and information

Major bus routes and frequencies of the services on them are listed at the end of each chapter in "Travel details". For extensive coverage of all public transport services – bus, rail and ferry – get hold of a copy of the free *Getting Around Cumbria and the Lake District* timetable book, available twice a year from Traveline (see below), tourist information centres and National Park offices. It's complemented by a County Council public transport map, available from the same offices.

For all public transport enquiries in Cumbria – bus, coach, rail and ferry services – call **Traveline**. The website gives access to a searchable database of all public transport services in the area; the office can send out timetables on request.

Public transport information

Traveline ☎0870/608 2608, ☯www.traveline.org .uk. Telephone enquiries service available Mon–Fri 7am–8pm, Sat & Sun 8am–8pm.

By bus

Stagecoach (☎0870/608 2608, ☯www .stagecoachbus.com/northwest) is the biggest bus operator in the Lakes, though many of its routes are subsidized by Cumbria County Council, the Countryside Agency or the National Parks Authority to ensure coverage of areas that wouldn't otherwise be economically viable. Dozens of routes connect every major town and village, and although travel frequencies vary you can usually count on being able to reach most places at least once a day throughout the year. The most frequent services on all routes are between Easter and the end of the school holidays in August, though some peak-period timetables continue into September and October (often at weekends only). Local services connect with express routes at Windermere, Ambleside and Keswick to places outside the National Park, such as Cockermouth, the Cumbrian coast, Carlisle, Penrith, Kendal, Ulverston and Barrow.

You can buy tickets on the bus as you go, though the best deal is the Stagecoach **Explorer Ticket** (one-day £8.50, four-day £19, seven-day £26.50), which is valid on the entire network and available on any bus from the driver. For a week's unlimited travel within Cumbria (and beyond, to Lancaster and the northeast) there's the **Cumbria Goldrider** card (£21, available on the bus), while other special Stagecoach **day-rider tickets** offer hop-on-hop-off transport between Bowness and Grasmere, and bus-and-boat combinations for Windermere, Coniston and Ullswater – specific details are included in the Guide.

Current Stagecoach routes and ticket details are spelt out exhaustively in the invaluable free *Lakesrider* magazine, published twice a year and available on board buses in Cumbria, and from tourist offices and visitor attractions. Most tourist offices also have individual route timetables available.

Other services in the Lakes are run by a partnership of agencies and operators, most notably the useful **Cross-Lakes Shuttle** (operates Easter–Oct; timetable information from Mountain Goat ☎015394/45161 or see ☯www.lake-district.gov.uk). This runs under the slogan "Two lakes, one ticket, no problem" since it combines two boats and two minibuses to connect Bowness-on-Windermere with the Beatrix Potter house at Hill Top (£7.35 return), Hawkshead (£8.55), Grizedale Forest (£10.80) and Coniston Water (£14.60). The boats-and-minibus service can also carry up to five bikes. In addition, the **YHA** operates a shuttle-bus service from Windermere train station to the Ambleside, Hawkshead, Coniston, Elterwater, Langdale and Grasmere hostels (Easter–Oct; £2.50 a journey; information from Ambleside hostel on ☎0870/770 5672).

If you're short on time, a **minibus tour** through the lakes can show you an awful lot quickly. Most day tours are in small vehicles, which means that, compared to the big tour buses, you get much more time at the sights and share them with fewer people. The specialist operators listed below have some interesting itineraries and can arrange pick-ups from most of the major towns. Prices usually start at around £20 for a half-day to £30–35 for a full day out on the road. As well as calling the contact numbers given, you can book most bus tours at local tourist information offices.

Specialist bus tour operators

Fellrunner ☏01768/88232, and at the Penrith tourist office ☏01768/867466, ⓦwww .fellrunnerbus.co.uk. Community-run minibus service offering bargain-priced summer-holiday day tours (selected days, mid-July to mid-Sept) of Cumbria, concentrating on the Eden Valley and Ullswater.
Lakes Supertours ☏015394/42751 or 88133, ⓦwww.lakes-supertours.com. Eleven- and sixteen-seater, all-day minibus tours – lakes and mountains or literary themes – with some cruises and house entries included.
Mountain Goat ☏015394/45161, ⓦwww .mountain-goat.com. Minibus tours that get off the beaten track: Duddon Valley and Back o'Skiddaw as well as the usual lakes and passes. Daily departures from Windermere, Bowness, Grasmere, Ambleside and Keswick. Also offers themed four- to seven-night touring holidays (such as the five-night "Spring gardens of the Lake District", £440).
Touchstone Tours ☏017687/79599, ⓦwww .touchstonetours.co.uk. Small (maximum eight people) Keswick-based historical tours – lakeland legends, Romans in Cumbria, prehistoric stone circles – that involve some walking and are a bit pricier than the rest but include a country pub lunch and admission fees. Also tailor-made tours, and walking and weekend trips.

By train

The only place actually in the Lake District National Park you can reach on a regular train service is Windermere town, on the branch line from Oxenholme (on the London–Manchester–Glasgow west-coast main-line route) via Kendal and Staveley. Outside the National Park, but still a handy approach to the northern Lakes, Penrith is also a stop on the west-coast main-line route, while the Furness and Cumbrian Coast branch line from Lancaster runs via Ulverston, Ravenglass and the Cumbrian coastal towns to Carlisle.

Various regional multi-day rover tickets cover the north of England, but you're unlikely to get much use out of them if you're just visiting the Lake District. However, the **Cumbria-Lake District Rail Rover** (7 days, from £52.50) covers rail travel anywhere in Cumbria and the northwest between Carlisle and Lancaster – it also includes the Settle to Carlisle Railway and gets you a discount on a one-day Stagecoach Bus Explorer ticket.

There's also the **Lakes and Furness Day Ranger** ticket (adult £11.20, child £5.60, family £21.50), on services from Lancaster to the Cumbrian coast, and between Oxenholme and Windermere; and a **Cumbria Round Robin** (£23, child £11.50), valid for a circular journey in either direction from Barrow-in-Furness via Whitehaven, Carlisle, Penrith and Lancaster. The latter two tickets are valid after 8.45am Monday to Friday, and all day at weekends and on public holidays – you can buy them at the stations or from conductors on board trains. All timetable and ticket details are available from National Rail Enquiries (☏08457/484950, ⓦwww .nationalrail.co.uk).

What the Lakes lack in a regular train network is made up for in a couple of scenic steam-train lines. Both **Lakeside and Haverthwaite** (southern end of Windermere) and **Ravenglass and Eskdale** (western fells and valleys) lines are covered in the guide. The former is the more popular (and easiest to access); the latter provides the more enjoyable ride and operates a year-round service.

By ferry

Of the lakes themselves, Windermere, Coniston Water, Derwent Water and Ullswater have ferry or cruise services of varying degrees of usefulness, all covered in detail in the Guide. Windermere and Ullswater are the most popular choices for a round-trip cruise, while the Windermere boats also run from Bowness and Ambleside to the main National Park visitor centre at Brockhole. The service on Derwent Water is extremely useful for hopping around the lake and accessing Borrowdale walks, while the Coniston launches and Gondola steam yacht are used mainly as a means of reaching Ruskin's house, Brantwood.

By car

While driving around the Lakes might seem convenient, it soon loses its attraction on July and August weekends when the roads are busy, it takes ages to get from village to village and you can't find anywhere to park once you arrive. Leave the car at home, or at your hotel or B&B, whenever you can and you'll get more enjoyment out of the region.

Parking can be difficult throughout the Lakes, especially in the towns and villages. There is free on-street parking in Ambleside, Windermere, Bowness, Coniston, Grasmere and Keswick, but there's not very much of it and it's usually limited to thirty minutes or an hour. Most towns have also introduced a **disc parking** scheme, so to park on the street you'll have to nip into a local shop or tourist office and pick up a disc for your dashboard. For longer stays, the best advice, every time, is to follow the signs to the official car parks and pay up. All car parks mentioned in the Guide – and marked on our maps – are **pay-and-display** unless otherwise stated, so a supply of change is a necessity. Expect to pay £1.50–3.50 for up to four hours' parking, and up to £6 for a full day, even in car parks on National Park Authority and National Trust land in out-of-the-way places. Most town and village hotels and some B&Bs have private parking, mentioned in the reviews where available – if the accommodation is rural, you can take it as read there'll be somewhere free to park.

Most A and B **roads** in the area are in good condition, though single-track driving is common – don't park in passing places. Surfaces on high ground and off the beaten track tend to deteriorate rapidly, being little more than unmetalled tracks in places: many routes can be adventurous at the best of times and downright treacherous in winter or bad weather. The steepest road gradients and most difficult driving are on the following **lakeland passes**: Blea Tarn Road (between Great and Little Langdale), Hardknott Pass (Eskdale and Duddon Valley), Honister Pass (Buttermere and Borrowdale), Kirkstone Pass (Ullswater and Windermere), The Struggle (Ambleside and Kirkstone Pass), Whinlatter Pass (Braithewaite and Lorton Vale) and Wrynose Pass (Duddon Valley and Little Langdale).

Any of the national **car rental** outfits can oblige, but if you'd prefer to rent locally there are rental agencies in the main towns of Kendal, Keswick, Penrith, Ulverston and Windermere, as well as in the county capital of Carlisle. **Taxis** are widely used, as a sort of backup to the public transport network, and there are local taxi firms in the same towns plus Ambleside, Cockermouth, Coniston and Grasmere. All the relevant contact details are given in each town and village's "Listings" section.

By bicycle

Off-road cycling is becoming increasingly popular in the Lakes, though walkers and environmental organizations are concerned by the detrimental effect that mountain biking can have on ancient bridleways. Local cycle businesses do much to promote responsible cycling within the National Park, and by following agreed routes, exercising caution and respecting walkers' rights of way you'll help to ensure continued cooperation.

Bike-rental outfits are detailed throughout the Guide and can kit you out with all the gear. The going rate is around £18 for a full-day's rental of a mountain bike, with helmets, locks and route maps usually included in the price. Children's bikes, trailer bikes and tandems are also often available. The YHA also has a fleet of budget-priced "Budgie Bikes", available from fifteen Lake District hostels, with rental starting at £1.50 an hour (maximum is around £10 per day).

Long-distance tourers have the choice of several national and regional routes that cut through Cumbria and the Lake District, including the 72-mile **Cumbria Way Cycle Route** and the well-known **Sea-to-Sea (C2C)** cycle route, a 140-mile trip between Whitehaven/Workington and Sunderland/Newcastle (ⓦwww.c2c-guide.co.uk). Other parts of the National Cycle Network – like the Hadrian's Wall Cycleway or the Reivers Cycle Route – also pass through the region; route details are available from Sustrans (ⓦwww .sustrans.org.uk). For **mountain-bike routes** and information on off-road cycling in the Lakes, check out ⓦwww.mountain-bike -cumbria.co.uk. If you'd like someone else to make all the arrangements, then contact one of the specialist **cycling tour operators** (listed on p.40), who offer fully inclusive cycling holidays in the Lakes.

Accommodation

The Lake District has no shortage of accommodation, though it sometimes seems like it at peak periods. At New Year, Easter, public holidays and school holidays (particularly the six-week summer break from late July to the end of August) it's always wise to book ahead – though tourist information centres will always be able to find a room for anyone arriving without a reservation. Accommodation listed in the Guide is open year-round unless otherwise stated, though note that, even so, many places close for a few days over Christmas and New Year.

Cumbria Tourism has a **Booking Line**, ☎0845/450 1199, for short breaks, special offers and late bookings. Otherwise, local information offices all offer a free room-booking service where you'll be charged a deposit (usually ten percent) that's then deducted from your accommodation bill. For full **lists of Lake District accommodation** you'll need the following four annual publications: *Great Places to Stay in the Southern Lake District*, *Keswick and the North Lakes Visitor Guide*, *Western Lake District Visitor Guide* and *Where To Stay in Eden* (covers Ullswater, Penrith and the Eden Valley). All are available from information offices in the Lakes, or by mail if you call local tourist offices.

Hotels, guesthouses and B&Bs

Bed-and-breakfast (B&B) rates in the Lake District start at around £18 per person per night. Even in the most basic of places, you should get a sink, a TV and a kettle in the room, and the use of a guest lounge. These days, most B&Bs and guesthouses have added en-suite shower and toilet cubicles to their rooms, for which you'll pay from £20–25 per person – don't expect a great deal of space (or indeed a bath) in these "bathrooms". Once above these prices – say from £30–35 per person – you can expect a range of services and facilities that you won't get in a standard B&B, from fresh flowers and gourmet breakfasts to king-sized beds and quality bathrooms. Many B&Bs and small guesthouses have raised their game in recent years – some are truly excellent – and we've highlighted the best choices in every area.

Hotels in the Lakes tend to charge what they can get away with, and, as location is everything, lakeside or isolated fell-side retreats can get away with an awful lot – you can easily spend £150–200 for a room in one of the famous country-house hotels, like *Miller Howe*, *Sharrow Bay* or *Gilpin Lodge*. There's a lot of choice in the £70–110 range, though it pays to pick and choose – a classy, personally run B&B often has the edge over a traditional hotel. Again, though, overall standards are slowly improving, as contemporary style, designer fabrics and new technology make inroads into the Lakes. Several places have had makeovers,

---

Accommodation price codes

All **hotel** and **B&B** accommodation in the guide is priced on a scale of ❶ to ❾, indicating the **average price** you could expect to pay per night for a **double/twin room** in high season. **Breakfast** is included, and rooms are **en suite**, unless otherwise stated.

❶ under £40
❷ £41–50
❸ £51–60
❹ £61–70
❺ £71–90
❻ £91–110
❼ £111–150
❽ £151–200
❾ £201 and over

adding fancy linen, marble and slate detailing, and flatscreen TVs and DVD players to rooms – Ambleside's townhouse-style *Waterhead* hotel is the most dramatic example, while Grasmere's *Moss Grove* takes a seriously stylish yet organic, environmentally friendly approach.

Rooms are also available in many town-centre and country **pubs and inns**. Often this is traditional B&B in old-fashioned or modernized rooms, starting at around £25 per person, rising to £50 in the best-known traditional hikers' inns (like Langdale's *Britannia Inn* and the *Old Dungeon Ghyll,* and Wasdale's *Wasdale Head Inn*). However, several country inns in particular have gone contemporary, with sharp styling, snappy service and good food now the norm at places like the *Drunken Duck Inn* outside Hawkshead, the *Punch Bowl Inn* at Crosthwaite and Loweswater's *Kirkstile Inn*.

Prices in all establishments are often higher at weekends, during summer and over public holidays: conversely, it's always worth asking about off-season **discounts**, which might shave a couple of quid off a B&B room, or up to forty off a hotel.

At weekends, many places insist upon two- or (over public holidays) even three-night **minimum stays**. There again, staying more than a couple of nights in many places brings the standard price down a pound or two a night. There aren't a great many **single rooms** available, and solitary hikers or holidaymakers won't often get much knocked off the price of a double room if that's the only option. Finally, many guesthouses, inns and hotels offer a discounted **dinner, bed and breakfast** (D,B&B) rate which – provided you want to eat there in the first place – is often a better deal than the standard B&B rate: the guide picks out those D,B&B places where the cooking is particularly good. Note, though, that some hotels *only* offer stays on a D,B&B basis while others are so remote that there's nowhere else to eat anyway.

At all the establishments listed in this book, **payment by credit card** is accepted unless otherwise stated. However, even where credit cards are accepted, American Express cards often aren't – pack another card, just in case.

Farm stays

Not surprisingly, one of England's most rural regions offers plenty of opportunity to see country life at close quarters by staying on a farm. At its most basic this might be simple farmhouse B&B, offered on many farms as a way of boosting income. Accommodation might be in the farmhouse itself or in cottages on the farm, and you can expect to pay standard bed-and-breakfast rates. Sometimes accommodation is on a self-catering basis and then the price depends on the property and length of stay. You'll see signs advertising rooms on farms all over the Lake District, and while it helps to have your own transport (because of the isolated nature of many farms), some farms sited on the edge of villages are easy to reach on foot. Although there's no obligation, many farms provide a more in-depth experience and, where it's appropriate, you'll have a lot more opportunity to muck in, either feeding the animals or finding out more about farming life.

Around twenty farms on **National Trust** land in the Lakes offer B&B. Some of the best are reviewed in the Guide, though the full list and booking details are on the NT website (𝕎 www.nationaltrust.org.uk; click on "Holidays" and then "Bed and breakfast"). Or contact **Farm Stay UK** (☏0247/669 6909, 𝕎 www.farmstayuk.co.uk) for more farmhouse options in Cumbria, including a group of superior farmstays marketed as "Luxury in a Farm" (𝕎 www.luxuryinafarm.co.uk).

Youth hostels and backpackers' accommodation

There are nineteen Youth Hostel Association (YHA) **youth hostels** in the Lake District, four more just outside the park boundaries and a summer-only hostel in the county capital of Carlisle. Several, including those in Ambleside, Keswick and Grasmere, are amongst the most popular in the country, so advance booking is a good idea at any time of the year. Gone are the days of tasks and sackcloth comforts: many hostels have rooms with just two, three, four or six beds, all bed linen is provided, and nearly all are well equipped with kitchen, laundry and drying-room facilities; some have licensed bars and cafés, bike rental and Internet access. A YHA shuttle bus runs between the major Lake District hostels (see p.22); alternatively, buy a copy of *The Lake District Youth Hosteller's Walking Guide* by Martin Hanks (Landmark Publishing), which describes walks between every hostel.

You no longer have to be a member to use a YHA hostel, though non-members pay a £3 supplement (under 18s, £1.50) for accommodation and aren't eligible for any other hostel discounts or benefits. **Joining the YHA** (☎0870/770 8868, ⓦwww.yha.org.uk) costs £15.95 per year, £22.95 for joint/family, or from £9.95 for under-26s. However, overseas visitors who belong to any **International Youth Hostel Federation** (IYHF) association in their own country have automatic membership of the YHA; and if you aren't an IYHF member, you can join the YHA in person at any affiliated hostel on your first night's stay.

YHA **hostel prices** are grouped into bands, and vary according to age, season and demand, but in the Lakes they start from £10.95 per night for an adult bed at simple, remote establishments such as those in Ennerdale, rising to £20 a night at the flagship Ambleside hostel. Breakfast is included in the price only at Ambleside, Keswick, Kendal and Buttermere hostels, and otherwise costs an extra £4.20; packed lunches (£4.80) and a three-course dinner (where available, £8.40) can usually be provided too. Many hostels have **family rooms** available, and some will let couples stay in rooms or have specific **twin rooms** (usually with bunk beds) available. Couples will pay the current overnight bed price, while a typical family room sleeping four to six people costs between £50 and £70. You can book any YHA hostel by calling the **central reservations number** (☎0870/770 8868; Mon–Fri 8am–8pm, Sat 9am–1pm) or the hostels direct. The major YHA hostels are open daily, year-round, though many others have restricted **opening periods** in the winter, which are detailed in the Guide. You can usually check in before 1pm and again after 5pm, though smaller hostels tend only to open their reception at 5pm.

The few **independent backpackers' hostels** in the Lakes (in Ambleside, Windermere, Grasmere and Keswick) have similar facilities and are pitched at roughly the same prices as the higher-grade YHA hostels. On the whole, they have a more laid-back feel than the YHA hostels and tend to attract a more international crowd. There are no membership requirements for backpackers' hostels and they are usually open year-round, with someone generally on hand throughout the day.

Holiday property rental

The dream of renting a pretty rural holiday property in the Lakes is easily accomplished. The hardest thing is deciding what you want, with choices ranging from simple stone cottages to large country houses, by way of barn conversions, former mills, town houses and shooting lodges. There are lots of companies out there vying for your custom but all offer the same kind of basic deal. The minimum rental period is usually a week, though outside the summer season and especially in the winter you may be able to negotiate a three-day/long-weekend rate – except, that is, at Christmas, New Year and Easter when prices are at their highest and demand at its most intense. All properties come with a fully equipped kitchen and many (but not all) provide bed linen and towels. Prices vary dramatically – from around £200 a week for the smallest properties to as much as £1000 for a week in a large, luxury property with admission to the local pool and health club thrown in.

The list of **agencies** on p.28 should help in finding the property you want, but it's worth scanning accommodation brochures and notices in local shop windows for other choices. Throughout the guide we've also picked out recommended individual self-catering properties, while an advance-booking service based at Windermere tourist information centre (☎015394/46499) can provide up-to-date information about lots of other self-catering properties, mainly but not exclusively in the southern and central Lakes.

Holiday property agencies

Coppermines and Coniston Lakes Cottages
☎015394/41765, ⓦwww.coppermines.co.uk.
Specialist in the Coniston area, with unique properties in Coppermines Valley as well as around Coniston Water.

Cumbrian Cottages ☎01228/599960, ⓦwww
.cumbrian-cottages.co.uk. A wide range of over 600 cottages and apartments in the Lake District and Cumbria.

Goosemire Cottages ☎01539/731801, ⓦwww
.goosemirecottages.co.uk. Thirty-five barn conversions or traditional cottages, some with lake views, in the Ullswater, Haweswater, Bassenthwaite and Wast Water regions.

Heart of the Lakes ☎015394/32321, ⓦwww
.heartofthelakes.co.uk. Excellent choice of over 300 quality properties in all corners of the National Park.

Holidays in Lakeland ☎0870/078 0162,
ⓦwww.holidays-in-lakeland.co.uk. Anything from modern studios to traditional cottages in the southeastern area of the Lakes.

Keswick Cottages ☎017687/78555, ⓦwww
.keswickcottages.co.uk. A good selection of cottages in and around Keswick, Braithewaite and Portinscale in the northern Lakes.

Lakeland Cottage Co. ☎015395/38180, ⓦwww
.lakeland-cottage-company.co.uk. Southern Lakes specialist – from simple cottages to large country houses – with outdoor activities, babysitting and catering services offered too.

Lakeland Cottages ☎017687/76065, ⓦwww
.lakelandcottages.co.uk. Period cottages and farmhouses in the northern Lakes, from the Keswick area, through Borrowdale, Lorton Vale, Bassenthwaite and Cockermouth.

Lakeland Hideaways Cottages
☎015394/42435, ⓦwww.lakeland-hideaways
.co.uk. Cottages, barn and farm conversions in Hawkshead, Sawrey and around Esthwaite Water.

Lakelovers ☎015394/88855, ⓦwww.lakelovers
.co.uk. A large range of quality properties mainly in the western and southern Lakes, with accommodation generally on the chintz-free side.

National Trust ☎0870/458 4422, ⓦwww
.nationaltrustcottages.co.uk. Eighteen lakeland properties, lakeside cottages to remote farmhouses – mainly around Ambleside, Little Langdale, Eskdale, Loweswater and Penrith.

Wheelwright's ☎015394/37635, ⓦwww
.wheelwrights.com. Best starting place for cottages in and around Elterwater, Chapel Stile, Langdale, Grasmere and Ambleside.

Windermere Lake Holidays ☎015394/43415,
ⓦwww.lakewindermere.net. Water-edge apartments and luxury houseboats available on the Windermere shore, sleeping up to six people.

Campsites, bunkhouses and camping barns

The Lake District has scores of **campsites**, though in the Guide we've tended to recommend those that favour tents over the large family-style caravan-RV parks. Many sites close between November and March, while in July and August it's always worth booking a pitch in advance. Prices vary considerably, from a couple of quid to stick your tent in a farmer's field (and possibly the use of a toilet and cold tap) to £10 a night for the use of all the facilities in one of the big caravan sites, complete with shop, bar and hot showers. Tourist offices can tell you about sites in their area, while Cumbria Tourism puts out a free annual *Caravan and Camping Guide*. Or consult ⓦwww.lakedistrictcamping.co.uk, a really useful site giving more in-depth details about Lake District campsites. The National Trust (ⓦwww.nationaltrust.org.uk/campsites /lakedistrict) also maintains three popular campsites – Great Langdale, Low Wray and Wasdale Head (all featured in the guide) – in fantastic locations and moderately priced at £4.50 a head per night.

The number of **bunkhouses** in the Lakes is slowly increasing, as farms, pubs and individuals make good use of old barns and other buildings to provide simple accommodation for hikers and backpackers. At its most basic, a bunkhouse might provide a mattress on the floor and a shower room, though others provide bunk beds, kitchens, lounges and other comforts. You'll have to provide your own sleeping bag and prices usually run to between £6 and £10 per person per night. In a similar vein, there's a series of twelve **camping barns** in and around the National Park, mostly self-catering converted farm buildings with communal facilities. The cost is £6 per person per night, and although mattresses are provided you'll need your own sleeping bag, foam mat and other camping equipment (not all have cooking utensils available) – some of the farms offer breakfast. To check availability and make reservations, you need to contact the **Lakeland Camping Barn Booking Office** (☎01946/758198, ⓦwww.lakelandcamping barns.co.uk); you can also book online.

Food and drink

Few people come to the Lakes purely for the gastronomic experience, but many are pleasantly surprised by the range and quality of food on offer. Pub and café meals have improved immeasurably over the last few years, while in restaurants right across the region there's good lakeland cooking in abundance, using local ingredients – fish, lamb, locally grown vegetables, home-made bread – and a dash of flair. Those with more cosmopolitan tastes will be relieved that cappuccino machines have made steady inroads into lakeland cafés, and though there aren't yet any sushi bars in the Lakes there are decent pizzerias, Modern-British and Thai restaurants, gastro-pubs and gourmet vegetarian places. There just aren't very many of them.

Traditionally, fine dining in the Lakes – as in the rest of England – was very much a silver-service roast-and-veg affair, or heavily Anglo-French in character, a state of affairs that still survives in many old-fashioned lakeland hotels. But some regional chefs have married contemporary flavours and trends with well-sourced local ingredients to produce something slightly different: if not a specific lakeland style of cuisine then at least a welcome change to old-school menus. At the more adventurous places expect to see plenty of pan-searing and char-grilling of local meat and fish, together with seasonal vegetables and fruit given ethnic and fusion twists. The Lake District also offers a dozen of the finest **country-house dining** experiences in England, notably the Michelin-starred *Holbeck Ghyll* and *Gilpin Lodge*, as well as traditionally renowned foodie locations like *Sharrow Bay* and *Miller Howe*. However, for sheer style and panache, nothing beats Cartmel's *L'Enclume* restaurant-with-rooms, also Michelin-starred, which has few peers in Britain, never mind the Lakes.

You're as likely to come across good food in a tearoom or café as in a restaurant or hotel. As a rule, meals in **pubs and inns** are a bit more hit and miss, though many in the Lakes are carving out a reputation for their food as much as for their beer. In the Guide we've picked out our favourite choices for pub meals, whether it's a good sandwich in a town-centre hostelry or gourmet food in a rural gastro-pub, of which there are increasing numbers.

All cafés, restaurants and pubs listed in the guide serve **lunch and dinner** daily unless otherwise stated. Winter opening hours are notoriously fickle, so a phone call before you set out never does any harm. Listed places all take **credit cards** unless otherwise stated (though this often doesn't include American Express, except in the more expensive hotels and restaurants).

Local specialities

It's pretty much as you would expect in farming and fishing country. Beef and pork tends to be overshadowed by the local **lamb**, particularly by Herdwick lamb, the traditional lakeland breed which finds its way onto menus across the county. It also forms the basis of dishes such as "tattie pot", a traditional lamb stew topped with potato. The region's biggest **organic meat** producer is the 3000-acre Lowther Park Farm, which supplies restaurants and shops across the

Restaurant price codes

Restaurants listed in this Guide have been assigned one of four price categories:

Inexpensive under £15
Moderate £15–25
Expensive £25–40
Very expensive over £40

This is the price you can expect to pay per person for a three-course meal or equivalent, excluding drinks and service.

district. In the south, Holker Hall estate specializes in producing home-reared venison and saltmarsh lamb (reared on the saltmarshes of Morecambe Bay). Menus also often feature **local trout** (farmed on Ullswater and elsewhere, as well as found wild), Morecambe Bay shrimps and, on occasion, the lake-caught **char**, a trout-like fish peculiar to the Lake District.

Bread is at its best from the organic, artisan-style Village Bakery, Melmerby, near Penrith (ⓦwww.village-bakery.com), while **cheese** from the Thornby Moor Dairy, in Thursby (near Carlisle), is well regarded too, either made plain (a smooth, creamy variety), smoked, or flavoured with garlic and herbs. The Old Smokehouse at Brougham Hall (near Penrith) **smokes** everything from garlic to goose, and supplies Fortnum & Mason as well as local outlets – try its award-winning smoked Penrith Pepperpot sausage.

Howbarrow Organic Farm (ⓦwww.howbarroworganic.co.uk), near Cartmel, is the region's leading distributor of **organic fruit and vegetables**. You should also keep an eye out at roadside stalls, craft outlets and village shops for locally made honey and preserves – the Lyth Valley's **damson** harvest, for example, ends up in jams, ice cream, chocolate, even beer, gin and vinegar, and there's a celebratory Damson Day each spring (ⓦwww.lythdamsons.org.uk). The Hawkshead Relish Company (ⓦwww.hawksheadrelish.com) and others supply locally made **chutneys and pickles**, often served as part of a ploughman's lunch, and Alston in northern Cumbria provides many outlets with speciality Cumberland mustards.

In many places, **breakfast** is the best meal of the day – no surprise in England. Even the humble B&B makes an occasional outstanding effort (the best are noted in the Guide), with home-made bread and muesli, yoghurt, muffins, pancakes, rissoles and other delights appearing alongside the ubiquitous fry-up. And on that subject, the Lake District is the best place to try **Cumberland sausage**, a thick, spicy, herby pork sausage (traditionally made in a spiral shape); the supreme example is that made by Woodall's of Waberthwaite, near Millom (ⓦwww.richardwoodall.co.uk), suppliers by Royal Warrant to the Queen, and purveyors, too,

of fine dry-cured hams and bacon.

No rundown of local treats would be complete without **Kendal Mintcake** (ⓦwww.kendal.mintcake.co.uk), a brutal peppermint confection made by Romney's of Kendal and favoured by strong-toothed hikers and mountaineers – the proud boast is that it was carried to the top of Everest on Hillary's ascent of 1953. There are plaudits too for Cartmel Village Shop's **sticky toffee pudding** (ⓦwww.stickytoffeepudding.co.uk) and **Penrith fudge and toffee**, while creamy lakeland **ice cream** is increasingly available in local shops and cafés – Windermere Ice Cream (ⓦwww.windermereicecream.co.uk) is made with organic milk from Low Sizergh Barn (where you can see the cows being milked daily) and comes in over thirty flavours.

Vegetarians

Vegetarians are increasingly well catered for in the Lakes. Most B&Bs these days at least make a stab at a non-meat breakfast, while if you want a true **vegetarian guesthouse** you can choose between (among others) the *Beech Tree* in Coniston, *Yewfield* at Hawkshead and Ulverston's *Walkers' Hostel*. There is also a fair number of vegetarian/wholefood **cafés and restaurants** in the Lakes, notably in Keswick, Kendal, Grasmere, Ambleside and Cockermouth. The best places are all reviewed in the Guide, and there are more details about veggie and vegan cafés, restaurants, pubs, wholefood shops and accommodation in the useful *Vegetarian Lake District* booklet (ⓦwww.vegetarianguides.co.uk), available in local bookshops or for purchase online.

Pubs and beer

There's a fine selection of country pubs and former coaching inns throughout the region, many dating back several hundred years. Those tied to the major breweries feature the same range of drinks you'll find all over England, but it's worth seeking out those owned by the main regional breweries and other independent (ie free house) pubs for the best selection of local beer.

Jennings (ⓦwww.jenningsbrewery.co.uk) has the main lakeland stranglehold and offers brewery tours at its base in Cockermouth. You'll come across its beers everywhere – both a Bitter and Cumberland Ale, and the stronger Cocker Hoop and Sneck Lifter ales. Meanwhile, the **Bitter End Brewery** (ⓦwww .bitterend.co.uk), based at the *Bitter End* pub in Cockermouth, bravely brews a range of beers on Jennings' home soil.

Elsewhere there's been a renaissance in Cumbrian brewing and independent breweries abound, one of the most established being **Yates Brewery** (ⓦwww.yatesbrewery .co.uk), from Westnewton, Aspatria, whose assorted bitters, ales and seasonal beers are widely available. Several other small craft brewers started as single-pub outlets but now sell their beers at increasing numbers of pubs across the region. Ones to keep an eye out for include: the **Coniston Brewing Company** (ⓦwww.conistonbrewery.com), which produces its award-winning Bluebird bitter, Old Man Ale and Bluebird XB pale ale at the village's *Black Bull*; **Barngates Brewery** at the *Drunken Duck Inn* (ⓦwww .barngatesbrewery.co.uk) near Hawkshead, serving beers (Cracker Ale, Tag Lag, Chester's Strong and Ugly) named after dogs that have lived at the inn; and the **Hesket Newmarket Brewery** (ⓦwww.hesketbrewery.co.uk; tours available), based at the community-owned

Old Crown, Hesket Newmarket. The **Hawkshead Brewery** (ⓦwww.hawksheadbrewery .co.uk) was founded by former BBC journalist Alex Brodie, and now has a second brewery in Staveley near Windermere as well as in Hawkshead. There's also the **Tirril Brewery** (ⓦwww.tirrilbrewery.co.uk), based at Long Marton (near Appleby) but with its main outlet at the *Queen's Head Inn* gastro-pub at Tirril near Penrith. Three classic inns with their own **microbreweries** are the *Wasdale Head Inn* (ⓦwww.wasdale.com), the *Kirkstile Inn* (ⓦwww.kirkstile.com) and the *Woolpack Inn* (ⓦwww.woolpack.co.uk), while the *Mason's Arms* (ⓦwww.strawberrybank.com) at Strawberry Bank, Cartmel Fell, produces a strong fruit-based Damson Beer. Cumbria even produces **cider**, and many of the pubs mentioned here stock stonkingly strong brews by local producers Cock Robin Cider (ⓦwww.cockrobin.org) and Solway Cider.

The local branches of the **Campaign for Real Ale** (CAMRA) have useful websites listing real-ale pubs and carrying news about breweries and beer festivals: ⓦwww.camrawest morland.org and ⓦwww.westcumbriacamra .org.uk.

Festivals, shows, sports and annual events

In addition to the traditional annual festivals and shows, there are hundreds of other events held throughout the year in the Lake District – guided walks, exhibitions, lectures, craft demonstrations, re-enactments, concerts and children's entertainments. The month-by-month festival and events calendar below picks out the annual highlights: many traditionally take place on fixed days (often fairly convoluted), so for exact annual dates either check the websites or contact local information offices or Cumbria Tourism (☎01539/822222, ⓦwww.golakes .co.uk). The National Park Authority (☎015394/46601, ⓦwww.lake-district.gov .uk) also sponsors scores of annual events, many held at the Lake District Visitor Centre at Brockhole – there's something on somewhere nearly every day between March and December, listed in the NPA's free *Out & About* magazine.

Festivals and events calendar

February

First and second week Word Market Literary Festival, Ulverston ⓦwww.word-market.co.uk.

Third week Keswick Film Festival ⓦwww .keswickfilmfestival.org.

March

Second week Words By The Water, Literature

Festival, Keswick Ⓦ www.wayswithwords.co.uk
/cumbria.

Third or fourth week (Sat & Sun) Daffodil and
Spring Flower Show, Ambleside
Ⓦ www.ambleside-show.org.uk.

April

First week Ulverston Walking Festival
Ⓦ www.ulverston.net.

May

First and second week Ulverston Flag Fortnight
Ⓦ www.ulverston.net.
Second week Ullswater Walking Festival
Ⓦ www.ullswater.com.
Second or third week Keswick Jazz Festival
Ⓦ www.theatrebythelake.com.
Third week Keswick Mountain Festival
Ⓦ www.keswickmountainfestival.co.uk.
Fourth week (bank holiday weekend)
Cartmel Races Ⓦ www.cartmel-steeplechases
.co.uk.

June

First week Holker Garden Festival, Holker Hall
Ⓦ www.holker-hall.co.uk.
First week (Sat & Sun) Keswick Beer Festival
Ⓦ www.keswickbeerfestival.co.uk.
Second week Boot Beer Festival, Eskdale
Ⓦ www.bootbeer.co.uk.
Third week (Sat) Cockermouth Summer Festival
and Carnival Ⓦ www.cockermouth.org.uk.
Fourth week (last Sun) Ullswater Country Fair,
Patterdale.

July

First week (Sat) Ambleside Rushbearing
Festival.
First week (Sat) Ulverston Carnival
Ⓦ www.ulverston.net.
First week Coniston Water Festival
Ⓦ www.conistonwaterfestival.org.uk.
Second or third week Furness Tradition Folk
Festival, Ulverston Ⓦ www.furnesstradition.org
.uk.
Third week (Sat) Cumberland County Show,
Carlisle Ⓦ www.cumberlandshow.co.uk.
Fourth week (Thurs before first Mon in Aug)
Ambleside Sports.
Fourth week (Sat) Cockermouth Agricultural
Show Ⓦ www.cockermouth.org.uk.
Fourth week (Sun) Coniston Country Fair
Ⓦ www.conistoncountryfair.com.

August

First week (Wed) Cartmel Agricultural Show
Ⓦ www.cartmelshow.co.uk.
First week (Thurs before first Mon in Aug)
Ambleside Sports.
First week (Thurs) Lake District Sheepdog Trials,
Ings, Staveley.
First week (Fri–Sun) Lowther Horse Trials and
Country Fair, Lowther Castle, Askham
Ⓦ www.lowther.co.uk.
First week (Sat) Grasmere Rushbearing.
First and second weeks Lake District Summer
Music Festival Ⓦ www.ldsm.org.uk.
Second week (Thurs) Rydal Sheepdog Trials.
Third week (Wed) Gosforth Agricultural Show.
Third week (Wed) Threlkeld Sheepdog Trials.
Third week (Sat) Skelton Agricultural Show,
Penrith Ⓦ www.skeltonshow.com.
Third week (Sun) Langdale Country Fair,
Great Langdale.
Third or fourth week (Sun) Grasmere Lakeland
Sports and Show Ⓦ www.grasmeresportsandshow
.co.uk.
Third or fourth week (penultimate Tues)
Hawkshead Agricultural Show
Ⓦ www.hawksheadshow.co.uk.
Fourth week (last Wed) Ennerdale and Kinniside
Show.
Fourth week (Sat before bank holiday Mon)
Millom and Broughton Agricultural Show,
Broughton-in-Furness
Ⓦ www.millomandbroughtonshow.co.uk.
Fourth week (Sat before bank holiday Mon)
Patterdale Dog Day Ⓦ www.patterdaledogday.co.uk.
Fourth week (bank holiday weekend) Cartmel
Races Ⓦ www.cartmel-steeplechases.co.uk.
Bank holiday Mon Keswick Agricultural Show and
Sports.
Bank holiday Mon Muncaster Country Fair,
Muncaster, Ravenglass.

September

First week Wasdale Head Inn Beer Festival.
First week Ambleside Summer Flower Show and
Craft Fair Ⓦ www.ambleside-show.co.uk.
First and second week Ulverston Charter Festival
Ⓦ www.ulverston.net.
Second week (Thurs) Westmorland County Show,
Crooklands, Kendal Ⓦ www.westmorland-county
-show.co.uk.
Second week (Fri) Kendal Torchlight Carnival
Ⓦ www.kendaltorchlightcarnival.co.uk.
Third week (Thurs) Loweswater Agricultural
Show.

Third week (Sat) Egremont Crab Fair and Sports Ⓦ www.egremontcrabfair.org.uk.
Third week (Sun) Borrowdale Shepherds' Meet, Rosthwaite Ⓦ www.borrowdaleshow.org.uk.
Fourth week (last Thurs) Kentmere Sheepdog Trials.
Fourth week (last Sat) Eskdale Show, Eskdale Green.
Last weekend (biennial, odd-numbered years) Lakeland Festival of Storytelling, Staveley Ⓦ www.taffythomas.co.uk.

October

First week (Sat & Sun) Taste District Food and Drink Festival, Rheged Ⓦ www.tastedistrict.com.
First and second week FRED Art Invasion, across Cumbria Ⓦ www.fredsblog.com.
Second week (Sat) Wasdale Head Show and Shepherds' Meet.
Second or third week (Sat) Buttermere Show and Shepherds' Meet.

November

Second week Kendal Mountain Film Festival Ⓦ www.mountainfilm.co.uk.
Third week (Thurs) Biggest Liar in the World Competition, Santon Bridge, Wasdale Ⓦ www.santonbridgeinn.com/liar
Fourth week (Sat & Sun) Ulverston Dickensian Christmas Festival Ⓦ www.ulverston.net.

December

First week (Sun) Keswick Victorian Fair.

Festivals and events

The oldest festivals – dating back to medieval times – are the annual **rushbearings**, harking back to the days when church floors were covered in earth rather than stone. The rushes, or reeds, laid on the floors (on which churchgoers knelt or stood) would be renewed once a year. Now the rushes are fashioned into crosses and garlands and carried in symbolic procession around the village and into the church: the most famous rushbearing festivals (with accompanying bands and hymns) are held at Grasmere and Ambleside.

Towns such as Kendal, Keswick, Cockermouth and Ulverston host a variety of annual festivals concentrating on music, dance, film and drama. **Ulverston** in particular – the self-billed "Festival Town" – has a really strong annual events calendar, with

something on every month, from flag parade to folk festival, while **Cockermouth** follows its spring Georgian Festival with a varied annual Summer Festival. Keswick's renowned **Jazz Festival** turns the whole town into a carnival for five days of gigs and street performances, and there's also the Lake District-wide **Summer Music Festival** which brings together an international line-up of talent at venues across the region. Winter, meanwhile, sees popular **Christmas and Victorian fairs** in Ulverston and Keswick featuring period costumes, carol-singing, street stalls and Santas.

Lake District literary and film festivals are starting to acquire an international reputation, notably Keswick's early spring **Words By The Water**, which offers ten days of writers' and readers' events with some high-profile names. Kendal's autumn **Mountain Film Festival** is one of the leading festivals of its kind, with screenings, lectures, events and activities all related to films and books about the mountains and mountainous regions. Meanwhile, the local landscape has fostered a ten-day **walking festival** in Ulverston, with walks and events for all tastes and abilities; a newer walking festival also now takes place around Ullswater.

Cumbria's independent breweries have promoted a growing attendance at local **beer festivals** – the longest running is the Keswick Beer Festival, but for an example of a smaller event that typifies a real community spirit it's hard to beat Eskdale's Boot Beer Festival.

Some annual events defy categorization. **FRED** is a two-week autumn "art invasion" across Cumbria (Europe's largest such event), showcasing cutting-edge exhibitions, shows, workshops, artist-led walks and all sorts of other funny goings-on, from roadside haikus to twilight forest installations. In the west, there are a couple of even more peculiarly Cumbrian affairs. The **Egremont Crab Fair**, held annually since 1267, features such arcane events as greasy-pole-climbing and pipe-smoking competitions and the World Gurning Championship (where contestants stick their head through a horse collar and pull faces). And at a pub in Santon Bridge, Wasdale, the **Biggest Liar in the World Competition** attracts porky-tellers from all over Cumbria (indeed, the world) to a century-old event that celebrates the tallest of tales – see the feature on p.186 for more.

Shows, meets and sheepdog trials

Many of Cumbria's most loved annual events take the form of **agricultural shows**, featuring farming equipment, trade and craft displays (including dry-stone walling), food stalls, vegetable-growing and sheep-shearing competitions, and prize-winning animals. The separate Cumberland (Carlisle) and Westmorland (Kendal) shows are the largest examples – relics of the days when they were the annual county shows – but the smaller shows in places such as Gosforth, Coniston, Loweswater and Ennerdale are highly enjoyable affairs where it's still very much a case of local communities coming together.

Some very traditional shows (at Buttermere, Borrowdale, Wasdale and Eskdale) are termed **shepherds' meets**, since that's what they once were – opportunities for shepherds to meet once a year, return sheep belonging to their neighbours, catch up on local gossip and engage in competitions, sporting or otherwise. The mainstays of these events are sheep- and dog-judging competitions, bouts of hunting-horn blowing and displays of decorated shepherds' crooks. In addition, there are several annual **sheepdog trials**, the main ones at Rydal and Patterdale, where border collies are put through their paces, rounding up sheep into pens at the call and whistle of their owner.

Sports, races and traditional pastimes

Some annual shows specifically announce themselves as **Sports**, such as those at Grasmere and Ambleside, the two most important gatherings. At these (but in practice at all of the agricultural shows and meets too) you'll encounter a whole host of special Cumbrian sports and activities, as well as bicycle and track events, carriage-driving, gymkhanas, ferret- or pigeon-racing and tugs-of-war.

Cumberland and Westmorland wrestling is the best-known of the local sports, probably dating back to Viking times: two men, dressed in embroidered trunks, white tights and vests, grapple like Sumo wrestlers and attempt to unbalance each other – the first to touch the ground with anything except their feet is the loser, and if both men fall, the winner is the one on top. It's a best-of-three contest that is hugely technical, yet strangely balletic, and has its own vocabulary of holds and grips, like the "hype", the "hank" and the "cross buttock". The winner is declared "World Champion".

Fell-running is basically cross-country running up and down the fells. It's a notoriously tough business, dominated by local farm workers and shepherds who bound up the fells like gazelles. The famous Joss Naylor of Wasdale is typical of the breed: in 1975 he raced over 72 peaks in under 24 hours; in 1986 he ran the 214 Wainwright fells in a week; and to celebrate his 60th birthday he did the sixty highest lakeland peaks in 36 hours. The sports show races are shorter than these trials, but no less brutal. In a similar masochistic vein is the challenge known as the **Bob Graham Round**, named after Bob Graham of Keswick who in 1932 completed a traverse of 42 Lake District peaks within 24 hours (starting and finishing at Keswick's Moot Hall); around 1300 other people have completed the round since records started being kept in 1960, while the most extreme competitors have extended the round to include as many peaks as possible in 24 hours (the current record is 77).

Hound trailing dates back to the eighteenth century and is derived from the training of fox-hounds for hunting. A trail is set across several miles of countryside using a paraffin-and-aniseed-soaked rag and the dogs are then released, with the owners calling them in across a finish line at the show. Trailing (and the heavy betting that accompanies it) occurs most weeks during spring and summer outside the shows – the season runs from April to October, with five main events a year (starting on May Day) and scores of smaller meetings. As in other English rural areas, **fox-hunting** proper was long a Cumbrian pastime (on foot in the Lakes, not on horseback), though the government's controversial 2005 ban on hunting with hounds is supposed to have put paid to the practice. However, the traditional Lake District hunts still meet throughout the autumn and winter, all now claiming to work within the restrictions – ie, the hunts gather for trail-hunting, rather than pursuing foxes (though see "History", p.256, for more on this).

Walking and climbing

The Lake District was the birthplace of British fell-walking and mountaineering, and hundreds of thousands of people still come to the Lakes every year to get out on the hills. An almost unchartable network of paths connects the lakes themselves, tracks the ridges of the fells, or weaves easier courses through the valleys, around the flanks and onto the tops. So whatever your level of fitness or expertise, you can find a Lake District walk to suit – from an hour's stroll up to a local waterfall to an all-day circuit, or "horseshoe" route, around various peaks and valleys. If you're not confident about being able to find your own way, or simply want someone else to do the organizing, then it's probably best to join a guided walk or a tour. Various operators run Lake District walking holidays, while local schools and instructors can also introduce you to the arts of rock climbing, mountain navigation and winter hill walking.

Footpaths and walks

Of the long-distance paths, Wainwright's **Coast-to-Coast** – which starts in St Bees, near Whitehaven – spends its first few sections in the northern Lakes, and the Dales Way finishes in Windermere, but the only true Lake District hike is the seventy-mile **Cumbria Way** between Ulverston and Carlisle, which cuts through the heart of the region via Coniston and Langdale. The fifty-mile **Allerdale Ramble**, from Seathwaite (Borrowdale) to the Solway Firth, spends around half its time in the National Park area, running up Borrowdale and across Skiddaw, while the 150-mile **Cumbria Coastal Way** runs from Silverdale on Morecambe Bay, all round the Lake District peninsulas and Solway Firth to the Scottish border town of Gretna.

The **walks detailed in this Guide** – often in special feature boxes – aim to provide a cross section of lakeland experiences, from valley bottom to fell top. Some of the most famous mountain ascents are included, as well as gentle round-lake perambulations.

It's vital to note that the brief descriptions in the Guide are not in any sense to be taken as specific route guides, rather as providing start and finish details and other pieces of local information. The colour feature "Out and About in the Lakes" also includes the Rough Guide choice of the **ten best all-round walks** in the Lake District. For routes specifically designed for those in **wheelchairs or with strollers**, consult the excellent "Miles Without Stiles" section of the National Park Authority (NPA) website (ⓦ www.lake-district .gov.uk).

There is any number of local **walking guidebooks** and national trail guides on the market: the best are reviewed on p.260.

Walking equipment, skills and support

Experience isn't always necessary but for any walk you should have the proper equipment. It's no cheaper in the Lakes than anywhere else, but there is a wider selection available – Ambleside and Keswick are the best places to shop for outdoor gear. Wear strong-soled, supportive walking shoes or boots – you can turn your ankle on even the easiest of strolls. Colourful, warm, wind-and-waterproof clothing, a watch, water (two litres each on hot days) and something to eat are all essential on longer hikes. If you don't have your own, outdoor stores can often rent you a pair of boots, a day-pack and some waterproofs.

Bad weather can move in quickly, even in the height of summer, so before starting out on the fells you should check the **weather forecast** – many hotels, all hostels and most outdoor shops post a daily forecast, or check with one of the weather forecasting services listed below. Above all, **take a map** (reviewed on p.42) and, for up on the fells, a compass – they're not fashion accessories, so know how to use them. If you're uncertain or inexperienced, you might want to join a guided walk or attend a map-and-compass course – the NPA runs both in spring and summer, while any of the climbing schools and instructors listed in the next section offer instruction courses on all aspects of mountain skills and safety.

The NPA also does a huge amount of work in the Lakes on **improving access to the countryside**, repairing paths and maintaining rights of way. The NPA website (@www.lake-district-gov.uk) carries the latest news and details, and you can also contact the **Ramblers' Association** (@www.ramblers.org.uk), a campaigning organization dedicated to promoting walking in the UK.

Hiking support services

Adventure Network @www.adventurenetwork.com. An invaluable American website – nowhere else can you access so much expert, esoteric advice about surviving the great outdoors, from caring for your binoculars to choosing a sports bra.
Coast-Coast Packhorse ☎017683/71777, @www.cumbria.com/packhorse. Daily, door-to-door baggage service on the Coast-to-Coast route, plus left-luggage storage for overseas visitors. Service operates Easter until end of Sept.
Sherpa Van ☎0871/520 0124, from abroad ☎00-44-1748/822460, @www.sherpavan.com. Daily, door-to-door baggage service for walkers and cyclists between overnight stops on the Coast-to-Coast, Sea-to-Sea, Cumbria Way and Dales Way. Service operates from the week before Easter until mid-Oct.

Weather forecasting services

Lake District National Park Weatherline ☎0870/05 50575, @www.lake-district.gov.uk/weatherline. One-day advance forecast for fells and valleys, including hiking conditions.
Met Office @www.met-office.gov.uk. Three-day regional forecasts, plus specific Lake District mountain forecast and five-day town (Kendal, Keswick, Penrith and Whitehaven) forecasts available.

Walking holidays

Whatever your level of experience, the tour operators listed below are a good place to start looking for an organized walking holiday in the Lakes – all are either locally based or have specialist knowledge of the area, and are happy to entertain questions about their holidays. Trips run year-round unless otherwise stated, though there's most choice between Easter and October. Some holidays are self-guided (ie the arrangements are made for you, but you're given a map and walking instructions to follow), while others are fully guided, but there are always baggage transfers and emergency back-up services provided where appropriate. The prices below give an idea of what you can expect to pay for certain types of holiday, but note that transport to and from the Lake District is not included (though some operators may be able to arrange it, if requested).

Specialist walking-tour operators

Contours Walking Holidays ☎017684/80451, @www.contours.co.uk. Large variety of self-guided walking holidays along the Cumbria Way, Dales Way and Coast-to-Coast, starting at £210 for four nights' B&B, walking from 10–12 miles a day.
Curlew Guided Walking ☎01524/35601, @www.users.globalnet.co.uk/~curlewgw. Small walking groups tackle six- to twelve-mile hikes a day on seven-night tours (five days' walking) in the southern and northern Lakes. Trips cost around £420 B&B, with packed lunch and guide services included. Shorter two- and three-day breaks also available (£150–230).
Discovery Travel ☎01904/766564, @www.discoverytravel.co.uk. Self-guided walking tours, following the Cumbria Way (seven nights, from £395) or a Lakeland Round circuit (eight nights, £440), though Coast-to-Coast (fifteen nights, £745) or a single-centre Keswick walking holiday (seven nights, £325) are also available. Prices include B&B

accommodation, maps and guides, baggage transfer and emergency support.

Knobbly Stick ☎01539/737576, ⊛www .knobblystick.com. "The easy way to take a walk on the wild side" – fully guided four- to seven-night (three to six days' walking) holidays, based in comfortable hotels at Ullswater, Keswick, Wasdale, Grasmere and south Lakes, from £385 to £835, including dinner, bed and breakfast, guiding and transport. All are available as self-guided options too. Operates all year.

Walking Women ☎08456/445335, ⊛www .walkingwomen.com. Women-only guided walking trips to suit all abilities in Borrowdale, Grasmere, Derwent Water and the western Lakes. Two- to four-night tours (£150–300) on a B&B or full-board basis. Trips run from Feb to Nov.

Rock climbing and mountain skills

There's probably no better place in England to learn some rock climbing and mountain skills, and certainly no better pool of climbing talent available to teach, at either introductory or advanced level. The schools and instructors listed below offer sessions or courses to individuals, families and groups – it's always best to call first to discuss your requirements. Prices can vary wildly, depending on the number in the group, the level of training and length of the course, but for a guided walk in the company of someone hugely experienced in the mountains you might pay £15 per person. For a day's rock-climbing instruction or abseiling for beginners, you can expect to pay £35–50, while two-day residential courses start at around £150. If all you want is a climbing taster, then the indoor climbing walls at Kendal and Keswick, and at Cockermouth and Penrith Leisure Centres, can offer an hour's unsupervised fun for around £5, or £15 for an introductory training session.

Above the Line Wasdale Head Inn, Wasdale ☎019467/26229, ⊛www.wasdale.com. The birthplace of British mountaineering (see feature on p.273) offers a full programme of courses, including hill-walking for softies, guided ascents, mountain navigation courses, mountain first aid, and snow and ice techniques. Women's courses (with women instructors) available too, plus accommodation at the inn.

Carolclimb Low Gillerthwaite, Ennerdale ☎01946/862342, ⊛www.carolclimb.co.uk. Carol Emmons and Richard Sagar offer beginners' courses, guided climbs, ghyll scrambles, winter skills training and kayaking. Beginners, children and families welcomed. Accommodation also available.

Harold Edwards Mountaineering Wham Head Lodge, Hutton Roof, Penrith ☎017684/84465, ⊛www.whamheadlodge.com, ⊛www .haroldedwardsmountaineering.co.uk. Individuals and families of all ages can learn climbing, hill-walking, navigation, abseiling and winter skills, plus introductory and classic rock-climbing courses. Self-catering accommodation available.

Highpoint ☎017684/86731, ⊛www .mountainguides.co.uk. Weekend and five-day courses throughout the year (March to November) based at Patterdale YHA, concentrating on hill-walking, navigational skills and rock climbing – suitable for beginners and improvers.

Keswick Climbing Wall Southey Hill, Greta Bridge, Keswick ☎017687/72000, ⊛www .keswickclimbingwall.co.uk. Indoor climbing wall, as well as abseiling and ghyll-scrambling days out around Borrowdale. For individuals, families and groups.

Lakeland Climbing Centre Kendal Wall, Mint Bridge Rd, Kendal ☎01539/721766, ⊛www .kendalwall.co.uk. Sessions on the indoor wall for adults and children, plus a full programme of outdoor climbing courses, from introductory sessions and weekend scrambles to five-day in-depth courses.

Boating, water sports and swimming

There's plenty of water in the Lake District and plenty of ways to get out onto it. Apart from the ferry and cruise services on Windermere, Derwent Water, Coniston Water and Ullswater, a dozen or so outlets and operators rent out all sorts of craft, from rowboats to sailing boats, kayaks to windsurfers. Most places offer instruction as well as rental.

Rowboat piers are detailed in the Guide and prices start at around £3 per person per hour; boats usually aren't available in the winter. The main **boating and water-sports centres** are listed below. Most offer canoes and kayaks (from around £7 an hour), dinghies and sailing-boats (from £50 half-day, £75 full-day), and small, self-drive motorboats and electric boats (from £50 half-day, £80 full-day). At most places you can expect to pay around £50 for a couple of hours' windsurfing instruction, or £100 a day, and around £70 for an introductory two-hour sailing lesson, or from £150 for a two-day sailing course.

Windermere, Coniston Water, Derwent Water and Ullswater have an overall 10mph **speed limit** (6mph in certain clearly marked zones on Windermere). Powerboats are allowed on the lakes (with the exception of Bassenthwaite), but operators must stick to the speed limits. Any boat with an engine (including an outboard motor) also needs to be registered with the National Park Authority (NPA). For more information about what you can and cannot do on the lakes, call the **Lake Wardens** (☎015394/42753) who enforce the restrictions on Windermere, or the NPA for the other lakes.

The water craft and reservoirs put some areas off-limits for bathers – Loweswater, for example, might seem very tempting but it's classed as a reservoir so there's no swimming allowed. Even where **lake swimming** is permitted, it can be very dangerous, owing to the extremely cold water and steeply shelving sides – people do drown, even on the sunniest, calmest days, most recently on Ullswater in the summer of 2006 when four young men lost their lives in a bathing accident. You might want to stick to local **swimming pools** instead, listed in the town accounts in the Guide (in Windermere, Keswick, Kendal and Ulverston).

Boating and water-sports facilities

Coniston Water

Coniston Boating Centre Lake Rd, Coniston ☎015394/41366, ⓔ conistonbc@lake-district.gov .uk. Rent electric boats, dinghies, rowboats, kayaks and Canadian canoes – there are also sailing lessons and two-day sailing courses available, and a lakeside café. Closed mid-Oct to Feb.

Derwent Water

Derwentwater Marina Portinscale, Keswick ☎017687/72912, ⓦ www.derwentwatermarina .co.uk. Sailing, kayaking, canoeing, windsurfing – rental and tuition (and lakeside apartments available too).
Nichol End Marine Portinscale, Keswick ☎017687/73082, ⓦ www.nicholendmarine.co.uk. Windsurfing, sailing, canoeing, motorboats and rowboat rental.
Platty Plus Lodore Boat landings, Borrowdale office ☎017687/76572, waterfront ☎017687/77282, ⓦ www.plattyplus.co.uk. Canoeing, kayaking, sailing and dragon-boating. Closed Nov–Feb.

Ullswater

Glenridding Sailing Centre The Spit, Glenridding ☎017684/82541, ⓦ www.lakesail.co.uk. Canoes, kayaks and dinghies; introductory sailing lessons, plus weekend and five-day tuition courses. Closed Nov– March.
St Patrick's Landing Glenridding Pier ☎017684/82393. Rowboats, motorboats and electric boats. Closed Nov–Feb.
Ullswater Marine Rampsbeck Boatyard, Watermillock ☎017684/86415, ⓦ www .ullswatermarine.co.uk. Motorboat rental. Closed Nov–March.

Windermere

Lakes Leisure Rayrigg Rd ☎ 015394/447183,
🌐 www.lakesleisure.org.uk. Canoe, kayak, sailing
and windsurfing lessons.
Low Wood A591, Windermere, a mile south of
Ambleside ☎ 015394/39441, 🌐 www.elh.co.uk
/watersports. Rowboat rental plus sailing, kayaking
and motorboat rental or tuition. It's also the only
surviving waterski/wakeboard centre on Windermere
(within the 10mph limits), suitable for beginners.
Windermere Canoe & Kayak Ferry Nab Rd,
Bowness-on-Windermere ☎ 015394/44451,
🌐 www.windermerecanoekayak.co.uk. Canoe and
kayak rental; instruction also available.

Organized holidays, courses and outdoor activities

Once you've been out on the fells, climbed the mountains and splashed on the lakes, there's still plenty of scope for an eventful day out. Local tourist offices have details of all sorts of outdoor activities, from horse riding and pony trekking to fishing and go-karting. Individuals and small groups are always welcome, though bear in mind that some of the activity days are aimed at the corporate or group market, so you may have to fit in around larger groups. Some operators, such as Outward Bound and Summitreks, are particularly good for family days out and can tailor their activities to most ages and levels of experience.

Prices vary wildly, though you can expect to pay from around £20 for an hour's pony trekking, £35 for a half-day's activity session, £50–70 for a full-day's activity, and up to £160 for a balloon flight over the Lakes.

Many of the same operators offer residential courses, for those who fancy more than a day's activity, while other businesses offer all-inclusive organized holidays based around various themes, from cycle touring and sketching to cooking and pottery. Note that the prices for organized holidays don't include transport to and from the Lakes, which you'll usually be expected to arrange for yourself.

Arts, crafts and cookery

Bill Birkett Photography Courses
☎ 015394/37420, 🌐 www.billbirkett.co.uk. The
respected lakeland writer and photographer runs
small-group photography courses throughout the year
in Langdale, based at local inns and involving daily
walks, mountain photography, technical assistance
and slide shows. Prices vary according to length of
course but start at around £260 for an all-inclusive
two-night course (bring your own camera equipment)
– latest details are on the website.

Gosforth Pottery ☎ 019467/25296, 🌐 www
.potterycourses.co.uk. Formal instruction in pottery
making (wheel-throwing, handwork and decoration),
followed by working at your own pace, or opportunities
for local rambling and exploring. The pottery – based
in Gosforth, in the western Lakes – runs two-night
weekend courses (from £210) and one-week courses
(from £485) on a full-board basis, tuition and
materials included.
Higham Hall ☎ 017687/76276, 🌐 www
.highamhall.com. Residential and day-courses at an
adult education centre on Bassenthwaite Lake. A huge
variety of courses on offer, from local history or art
appreciation talks (£12) to two-day wine-tasting
seminars.
Lucy Cooks ☎ 015394/32288, 🌐 www.lucycooks
.co.uk. An offshoot of Lucy's deli and restaurant in
Ambleside, this is a purpose-built cookery school
based in the Mill Yard at Staveley (near Kendal). The
emphasis is on locally sourced food and ingredients,
with subjects taught ranging from bread- and
preserve-making to vegetarian or Aga cookery. Full-
day courses from £130, evening demos from £30.
Miller Howe ☎ 015394/42536, 🌐 www
.millerhowe.com. One of the country's top country-
house hotels, on Windermere, offers a four-day, all-
inclusive, residential cookery course every November
(and perhaps other months too), for between £450

and £675 per person (more for single-room occupancy). Also three-day art courses (each spring, summer, autumn and winter) from £125 (rooms and food extra), and occasional needlework and embroidery courses.

Rothay Manor Hotel ☎015394/33605, ⊛www .rothaymanor.co.uk. Two- to five-night themed activity breaks at this agreeable Ambleside hotel include landscape photography, painting (oil and watercolours), music appreciation, gardening, antiques and bridge. Available mainly in winter, spring and autumn, from around £250 to £550 per person on a dinner, bed and breakfast basis.

Cycling tour operators

Country Lanes ☎0845/370 0622, ⊛www .countrylanes.co.uk. Bike-touring specialist offering group tours, day-trips and various inclusive multi-day tours, like the "Taste of the Lakes" self-guided circuit (from £340).

Discovery Travel ☎01904/766564, ⊛www .discoverytravel.co.uk. Self-guided cycle tours, including a seven-night Lake District circuit (from £425, B&B basis).

Holiday Lakeland Cycling ☎016973/71871, ⊛www.holiday-lakeland.co.uk. Two five-night cycling tours (including hotel accommodation and baggage transfer): "Nine Lakes Tour" (£370), "Sea to Sea Adventure" (£395; includes two nights in the Lakes). Also tailor-made single-centre cycling breaks based around Keswick or Ambleside, where you choose how long to stay and where to cycle. All tours May–Sept only.

Spinoff ☎01539/822176, ⊛www.spinoff.co.uk. Guided mountain biking for individuals, families and groups, with courses, rides and tours for all abilities. Prices vary, as you can take your own bike or hire one, and go for just a day ride or make a trip of it (accommodation bookings also available).

Equestrian centres

Holmescales Riding Centre Holmescales Farm, Old Hutton, near Kendal ☎01539/729388, ⊛www .holmescalesridingcentre.co.uk. Riding instruction, pony trekking and hacking at a 350-acre riding school with indoor and outdoor facilities.

Lakeland Pony Trekking Limefitt Park, Troutbeck Valley ☎015394/31999, ⊛www .lakelandponytrekking.co.uk. Short rides (one- to three-hour) in Troutbeck Valley, near Windermere, plus a daily pub ride, full-day excursions and two- and three-day trail rides.

Park Foot Trekking Pooley Bridge, Howtown Rd, Ullswater ☎017684/86696, ⊛www .parkfootponytrekking.co.uk. One- or two-hour treks

on the northeastern fells, longer trips on request. April–Oct only.

Sockbridge Pony Trekking Centre Sockbridge, Penrith ☎01768/863468, ⊛www .sockbridgeponytrekking.co.uk. One- and two-hour treks in the northeastern fells, near Ullswater.

Fishing

Esthwaite Water Hawkshead Trout Farm ☎015394/36541, ⊛www.hawksheadtrout.com. Boat-fishing on Esthwaite Water, with tuition for beginners (free on certain days), equipment rental/ purchase, BBQ and picnic areas (cook your own catch), rowboats, bird-watching, a farm shop and café.

⊛www.lakedistrictfishing.net A useful resource for all aspects of fishing in the Lakes, with links to courses, clubs and information.

Other activities and holidays

Country Adventures ☎01254/690691, ⊛www .country-adventures.co.uk. A varied programme in the Lakes, from a day's scenic walking or cycling in like-minded company to sailing weekends, gorge-scrambling/climbing and multi-activity sessions. Many holidays are youth-hostel-based in places like Ambleside, Elterwater and Borrowdale.

Kankku ☎015394/47414, ⊛www.kankku.co.uk. Off-road 4WD expeditions on rough and rocky terrain in Grizedale Forest, Tarn Hows, Langdale and Coniston, with an emphasis on promoting sound driving skills and techniques. Individuals and families welcome – a full day out costs from £150 per vehicle (for up to 4 people), or bring your own 4WD (from £79 a day). Based in Windermere, pick-ups available.

Lake District National Park Authority @ events@lake-district.gov.uk, ⊛www .lake-district.gov.uk. Organizes a huge programme of day events throughout the year, mostly free though charges are made for some activities. Highlights include mountain biking with the park rangers, falconry displays, dry-stone-wall building and water sports weekends. Contact the events team or check the events diary on the website.

Outward Bound centres at Watermillock, Ullswater; and Eskdale Green, Eskdale; reservations on ☎0870/513 4227, ⊛www.outwardbound-uk .org. Half- or full-day adventures – canoeing, rafting, zip wire, abseiling – with experienced instructors; especially good for families (children must be over 8) who qualify for family tickets.

Pleasure in Leisure ☎015394/42324, ⊛www .pleasureinleisure.co.uk. Huge range of activities organized across the region – archery, ballooning, go-karting, climbing and abseiling, paragliding, kayaking, clay-pigeon shooting, caving and 4x4 driving, to name but a few.

River Deep Mountain High ☎015395/31116, ⓦ www.riverdeepmountainhigh.co.uk. Multi-activity holidays (weekend/week-long, self-catering or fully inclusive) incorporating guided walking, canoeing and mountain biking, plus activity days, river trips and instruction.

Rookin House Farm Troutbeck, A5091, Penrith ☎017684/83561, ⓦ www.rookinhouse.co.uk. Go-karting, quad-biking, horse riding, pony trekking, archery and clay-pigeon shooting, not forgetting "human bowling" (one person strapped into a ball, while the others roll it at pins).

Summitreks ☎015394/41212, ⓦ www .summitreks.co.uk. Established adventure company offering a year-round programme of activities, from

climbing to canoeing, aquasailing (abseiling down waterfalls) to canyoning (descending gorges). Children's multi-adventure days in the school holidays usually incorporate mountain biking, gorge scrambling and canoeing; adults can learn orienteering or join guided walks.

Youth Hostel Association ☎0870/770 8868, ⓦ www.yha.org.uk. One of the biggest organizers of holidays in the Lakes, the YHA uses its hostels for weekend breaks or longer holidays, with the emphasis on activities such as hill walking, rock climbing, kayaking, mountain biking and orienteering – though Pudding Nights and Murder Mystery weekends also feature. Accommodation is in bunk rooms (twins and family rooms often available) and most hostels serve budget meals, though self-catering is also available.

Travel essentials

Costs and discounts

Generally speaking, you're unlikely to spend less than £35 a day travelling around the Lakes, even if staying in a B&B, buying a picnic or café lunch, hiking or taking the bus, and eating and drinking in a pub. Camping, hostelling and self-catering shaves a few pounds off this figure. Upgrade to a better room, or eat in a restaurant, and you can double it easily. Meanwhile, dinner, bed and breakfast alone in one of the region's celebrated country-house hotels or restaurants-with-rooms can run to well over £100 per person.

If you're counting the cost, there are plenty of ways to keep to a more moderate budget. Nearly all accommodation options – from simple B&Bs to luxury hotels – offer special **off-season deals** or discounts or even free nights for longer stays. It always pays to ask when booking. **Youth hostels and self-catering cottages** – the Lakes has the most extensive network of either in the country – mean you can save money by cooking for yourself. **Children and senior citizens** get discounts on most forms of transport in the

Lakes, and on entrance to the sights, museums and historic houses. **YHA members** qualify for discounts and special deals on all sorts of activities and at attractions and retail outlets.

As far as **events and activities** go, many of the traditional festivals or local attractions are free, while the National Park Authority organizes free or low-cost activities, courses, walks and events throughout the year. And if you join the **National Trust** (denoted in the Guide by the suffix "NT"; membership enquiries ☎0870/458 4000, ⓦ www.nation altrust.org.uk) or **English Heritage** ("EH"; ☎0870/333 1182, ⓦ www.english-heritage .org.uk), you have free entry to all relevant sights and attractions.

Hospitals and pharmacies

There are accident and emergency services at the hospitals listed on p.42. For dealing with minor complaints there are pharmacies in the main towns and villages (all listed in the Guide). These are open standard shop hours, though local newspapers and all pharmacy windows list the pharmacies that stay open an hour or two later on some nights of the week (usually on a rota basis).

Hospitals

Barrow-in-Furness Furness General Hospital, Dalton Lane ☎ 01229/870870.
Carlisle Cumberland Infirmary, Newtown Rd ☎ 01228/523444.
Cockermouth Cockermouth Community Hospital, Isel Rd ☎ 01900/822226.
Kendal Westmorland General Hospital, Burton Rd ☎ 01539/732288.
Keswick Keswick Cottage Hospital, Crosthwaite Rd ☎ 017687/72012.
Penrith Penrith New Hospital, Bridge Lane ☎ 01768/245300.

Internet

There are Internet points in all the major towns and villages and we've listed the most useful places in the Guide. It's rarely cheap (around £2 for 30min is standard), though local libraries now all have broadband Internet access, too, which can be free for short periods or inexpensive. Most youth hostels, B&Bs, guesthouses and hotels in the Lakes are also online these days, and even if they don't have specific Internet access for guests you might be able to persuade them to let you check for mail. An increasing number of hotels, guesthouses and cafés in places like Ambleside and Keswick now also offer wireless Internet access; if you're taking your own laptop make sure you've got insurance cover for it.

Laundry

Most youth hostels have washing and drying facilities of some sort, and B&B owners can sometimes be persuaded (or offer) to help out. There are self-service laundries in Ambleside, Keswick, Penrith, Windermere and other towns (though none in Grasmere or Coniston), with details included in the relevant listings sections.

Left luggage

Hotels, B&Bs and hostels will all mind guests' luggage for the day (or longer), but there's a distinct shortage of places where you can simply turn up in town and leave your bag or pack for the day. Tourist offices

are understandably reluctant to help, given the number of visitors; the only railway stations in the Lakes (at Kendal and Windermere) don't have the facilities; and bus stations are usually little more than roadside stops. A couple of willing cafés – in Windermere and Kendal – are picked out in the Guide. Otherwise, your best bet is to ask nicely at local shops, cafés or hotels – buying something first sometimes helps.

Mail

Each town and major village in the Lakes has a single post office where, apart from the usual postal services, you can usually exchange travellers' cheques and foreign currency. Normal opening hours are Monday to Friday from 9am to 5.30pm and Saturday from 9am to 12.30pm, though smaller offices may have restricted hours. It's worth noting that not all post offices are stand-alone businesses – the smaller ones, especially, are often housed in village stores. For information about postal services in Cumbria and the Lakes, or to find a post office address, contact the post office enquiry line on ☎ 0845/722 3344, ◍ www.postoffice.co.uk.

Maps

The best general map of the National Park area is the Ordnance Survey (◍ www.ordnancesurvey.co.uk; OS) Tour Map no. 3 (1:100,000), with hill shading and principal footpaths illustrated. For more detail of Cumbria as a whole (including Carlisle and the coast), you'll need the (1:50,000) OS Landranger series of maps (nos. 85, 89, 90, 96 and 97).

Essential for hikers are the orange (1:25,000) **OS Explorer** series – four maps (nos. 4, 5, 6 and 7) which cover the whole Lake District National Park. There are more rugged, plastic-coated versions available of these too. Some prefer the **Harvey Superwalker** (◍ www.harveymaps.co.uk) series of six waterproof maps (also 1:25,000) covering north, east, west, central, southeast and southwest Lakeland. There's also a good, compact, ring-bound Harvey Lake District **National Park Atlas** (1:40,000), useful for cyclists and general walkers, as well as detailed (1:40,000) fold-out Harvey **route maps** for the Cumbria Way, Dales Way and

Coast-to-Coast long-distance paths that all pass through the Lake District.

Most bookshops, outdoors stores and tourist information offices sell the full range of maps, as well as various **local walk map-leaflets**. Recommended series include the packs of *Lakeland Leisure Walks* (five assorted walks in each of the major areas), local fell expert Paul Buttle's various walking booklets, and the National Park Authority's *Walks in the Countryside* leaflets. For **hiking guides** for the Lake District, see p.260.

Markets

Local markets are held on: Monday, Cockermouth and Kendal; Tuesday, Broughton-in-Furness and Penrith; Wednesday, Ambleside and Kendal; Thursday, Ulverston; Saturday, Kendal, Keswick, Penrith and Ulverston. The best regional **farmers' market** is that at Orton in the Eden Valley (🕸www.orton farmers.co.uk), two miles off the M6 (junction 38; 17 miles north of Kendal), held on the second Saturday of the month. The Orton farmers are also at Pooley Bridge in the summer (April–Sept last Sun) and Rheged visitor centre in the winter (Oct–March last Sun), and there are other farmers' markets at Keswick (second Thurs of the month, plus fourth Thurs April–Sept), Ulverston (third Sat), Kendal (last Fri), Whitehaven (first Sat), Cockermouth (July–Sept & Dec first Sat) and Penrith (third Tues).

Media

Local newspapers (published weekly) are a good source of information about lakeland events, politics and personalities. Look for the *Westmorland Gazette* (which covers eastern Cumbria and the southern and central Lakes); the *Lake District Herald* (Penrith, Keswick and the northern Lakes); the *Keswick Reminder* (covering just Keswick); and the *Cumberland News* (Carlisle, Keswick and Penrith). Two daily evening papers carve up the region between them: the *North West Evening Mail* (southern Cumbria) and the *Evening News and Star* (northern Cumbria).

Cumbria (🕸www.dalesman.co.uk), the small-format monthly **magazine**, and the bigger, glossier, bi-monthly *Cumbria Life* (🕸www.cumbrialife.co.uk) concentrate on the history, culture and social and natural fabric of the Lakes. The quarterly *Lakeland Walker* is a chatty periodical aimed at hikers and lakeland lovers, featuring walks, news, reviews and equipment-testing. Finally, the National Park Authority details all the region's annual activities, events and festivals in its *Out & About* magazine, available free in information offices across the Lake District.

Local radio stations

BBC Radio Cumbria North Cumbria 95.6 FM/756 AM; West Cumbria 104.1 FM/1458 AM; South Cumbria 96.1 FM/837 AM; Windermere 95.2 FM/104.2 FM.
The Bay North 96.9 FM; Lakes/South 102.3 FM; Cumbria 103.2 FM.
Lakeland Radio South Lakes area 100.1/100.8 FM.

Money

Banks are fairly plentiful, in the towns at least, and the reciprocal use of cash dispensers (ATMs) means you are unlikely to be stuck for money, whoever you bank with. Normal banking hours are Monday to Friday from 9.30am to 3.30pm, with some branches in the major towns open on Saturday morning too. Conversely, in smaller lakeland villages, bank branches sometimes only open a couple of days a week. At least one of the major banks (Abbey, Barclays, Halifax, HSBC, Lloyds-TSB or NatWest) has an ATM in each of the main settlements (Ambleside, Bowness, Cockermouth, Kendal, Keswick, Penrith, Ulverston and Windermere) and addresses for each are listed at the end of town accounts in the Guide. In addition, stand-alone ATMs are increasingly found in village shops and petrol stations, though note that these nearly all charge a fee for withdrawing cash with your card. Apart from at the banks, you'll be able to exchange travellers' cheques and foreign currency at major post offices.

Credit cards are widely accepted in shops, hotels, restaurants and service stations, but don't count on being able to use plastic in B&Bs, guesthouses, pubs and cafés: we indicate all those that don't accept credit cards in the Guide. Be aware, however – even those that do accept credit cards often don't accept American Express.

Opening hours and public holidays

Full opening hours are given in the Guide for sights, attractions and tourist offices. Church opening hours vary considerably, though most of those mentioned open daily between 9 or 10am and 4 or 5pm, but you can't count on it. Shops and businesses follow the standard pattern for the UK (Mon to Sat 9am to 5.30pm or 6pm), though you'll find some village stores and local shops open an hour or so earlier or later than these times. Early closing day (when the shops shut for the afternoon) is still observed in many towns and villages, usually on Thursday in the Lakes.

Public and bank holidays in the UK

January 1
Good Friday (late March or early April)
Easter Monday (as above)
First Monday in May
Last Monday in May
Last Monday in Aug
December 25
December 26
Note that if January 1, or Dec 25 or 26 falls on a Saturday or Sunday, the next weekday becomes a public holiday.

Phones

There are public telephone boxes all over the Lake District, even in isolated rural areas, and most take phonecards and credit cards, which is just as well because you'll sometimes find that coverage from your mobile phone network is patchy to say the least. The nature of the terrain means you sometimes can't get a signal (though you're usually all right in the main towns and villages), which is one reason why it's not recommended that hikers rely solely on their phones – rather than their navigational skills – to get them out of trouble on the fells. Local telephone codes are included for all numbers listed in the Guide.

Police and emergencies

Dial ☎999 for all emergencies: in relevant circumstances ask for Mountain Rescue. If you want to speak to the police but it's not an emergency, call ☎0845/330 0247. The addresses of local police stations are given in the relevant town listings and most are only open for limited weekday hours – you'll have to call the non-emergency number above for telephone assistance. There's more information about stations and services at ⓦ www.cumbria.police.uk.

Tourist information

For information before you go, contact Cumbria Tourism or the Lake District National Park Authority (NPA), both of which also maintain useful websites. In the Lake District itself, a series of visitor information offices provides help on the ground – all are listed in the Guide – with the main National Park Visitor Centre located at Brockhole on Windermere. The other offices are funded and run by the tourist board and the NPA, or by local councils and volunteers: opening hours vary, though in the summer most of the main offices are open daily from 10am to 6pm, sometimes an hour earlier in the morning and an hour later in the evening. Opening hours are reduced in winter and, in some offices, may be restricted to weekends only (usually Fri to Sun) from 10am to 4pm. Local budgetary constraints also sometimes restrict hours and services, but at each office, when it's open, you'll be able to book accommodation, check on local weather conditions, and buy guides and maps.

Visitor information

Cumbria Tourism Windermere Rd, Staveley, Kendal, Cumbria LA8 9PL ☎01539/822222, brochure line ☎0870/513 3059, ⓦ www.golakes .co.uk, ⓦ www.gocumbria.co.uk.
Lake District National Park Authority Murley Moss, Oxenholme Rd, Kendal, Cumbria LA9 7RL ☎01539/724555; for events and visitor information contact the NPA at Brockhole, Windermere, Cumbria LA23 1LJ ☎015394/46601, ⓦ www.lake-district .gov.uk.

Websites

Travel and tourism

ⓦ **www.cumbria.com** Cumbria on the Internet: a useful searchable database of Cumbrian tourist resources (from information offices to accommodation lists) and businesses (from fish suppliers to quarry companies).

ⓦ **www.thecumbriadirectory.com** Guide to Cumbria and the Lakes, with useful round-ups of towns, villages, people, attractions, books, news and traditions.

ⓦ **www.golakes.co.uk, www.gocumbria.co.uk** Official website of Cumbria Tourism, with an interactive map, accommodation and restaurants databases, events diary, webcams and more.

ⓦ **www.lake-district.gov.uk** Official website of the National Park Authority – all you need to know about National Park work, services and events.

ⓦ **www.lake-district-peninsulas.co.uk** Official website for the Lake District peninsulas region – information, accommodation and events for Broughton-in-Furness, Lakeside and Newby Bridge, Ulverston and Cartmel.

ⓦ **www.lakesnet.co.uk** Leisure, travel and business resource, with plenty of useful links and searchable databases.

ⓦ **www.western-lakedistrict.co.uk** Website of the Western Lake District Tourism Partnership, covering events, accommodation and attractions in the lakes and towns west of Keswick to the coast.

Regional news, features and services

ⓦ **www.cumbria.gov.uk** Cumbria County Council site – the place to come for local community, social, government and business information, with useful links to other sites.

ⓦ **www.cumbria-online.co.uk** The online presence of a local newspaper group, with daily news and features from the *Evening Mail*, *Cumberland News* and *Cumbria Life* among others. This is the best one-stop site for Cumbrian news, sport, entertainment, property, classified ads, message boards, photographs, webcams and so on.

ⓦ **www.gonmad.co.uk/cumbria** Learn to talk like a native with the excellent A-to-Z Cumbrian slang dictionary, plus the "Babel Sheep" Cumbrianator translation engine.

ⓦ **www.madeincumbria.co.uk** Dedicated to Cumbrian crafts, gifts and food, with over five hundred craftspeople and local suppliers offering everything from handmade baskets to furniture.

ⓦ **www.thisisthelakedistrict.co.uk** Official site of the *Westmorland Gazette* – daily updated news and features, plus full coverage of everything to do with eastern Cumbria and the southern and central Lakes.

Walking and the mountains

ⓦ **www.bassplace.freeserve.co.uk/wildcamp** Backpacking, camping and walking in Britain, with particular emphasis on the Lake District – click on any of the 214 Wainwright fells for a full description, or check out the pictures, routes, trip reports, camping tips and more.

ⓦ **www.bonington.com** Official site for the grand old man of British climbing, Chris Bonington, born in London but based for many years in Caldbeck in the northern Lakes. There's more in his biography, plus expedition details, Lake District views and signed copies of his books.

ⓦ **http://homepages.enterprise.net/ldsamra** Cumbria's Search and Mountain Rescue Association site, packed full of useful advice for walkers and mountaineers, and a forbidding tally of accident stats.

ⓦ **www.lakedistrictoutdoors.co.uk** Cumbria Tourism site featuring walks and cycle rides, water sports and hang-gliding, together with safety advice, weather information and other useful bits and pieces.

ⓦ **www.lakedistrictwalks.com** John Dawson's incredibly detailed Lake District hiking site features over forty classic walks, complete with route descriptions, photos and a distance calculator.

ⓦ **www.stridingedge.net** Sean McMahon's stunning photo diary of fell walks gives a useful first look at the 214 Wainwright and 541 Birkett fells, from route descriptions to summit photos.

ⓦ **www.ukclimbing.com** Mountaineers should go straight to this site, the definitive online climbing resource – walls, climbs and crag summaries, photos, features, news and events, online shop and message forums.

Lakeland scenery

ⓦ **www.billbirkett.co.uk** Renowned lakeland climber, writer and photographer Bill Birkett shares his distinctive view of the Lakes.

ⓦ **www.keswick.u-net.com** Ann Bowker's site claims she's "Mad About Mountains" – and she certainly is. Digital pix, routes and ascents of Skiddaw, her local mountain, plus an incredibly comprehensive photo-gallery of ascents and views of each of the 214 Wainwright peaks.

ⓦ **www.lakelandcam.co.uk** Beautiful shots of lakeland scenery and the weather in all seasons and conditions from the roving digital camera of Tony Richards.

Guide

Guide

1

Windermere

CHAPTER 1 # Highlights

✳ **The view from Orrest Head**
The summit of Orrest Head, a short climb from Windermere town, provides stunning views up and down the lake. See p.53

✳ **A cruise on Windermere**
Spend the day on England's largest lake using a go-as-you-please "Freedom of the Lake" ticket. See p.59

✳ **Lake District Visitor Centre at Brockhole** The National Park HQ, set in acres of gardens, makes a great family day out. See p.64

✳ **Blackwell** Stunning Arts and Crafts house overlooking Windermere, with a handcrafted interior of immense style. See p.65

✳ **A night out in Ambleside** A romantic dinner at *Lucy*'s, or a meal, a movie or a jazz gig at *Zeffirelli's* – Ambleside is the best place in the Lakes for a big night out. See p.70

✳ **Armitt Collection, Ambleside**
The lowdown on lakeland literary and artistic life – from the writings of John Ruskin to watercolours by Beatrix Potter. See p.72

✳ **Overnight at the Waterhead**
Waterfront designer style at the sharpest contemporary hotel in the Lake District. See p.77

✳ **Kentmere** This quiet corner of the southern Lakes boasts some dramatic walking on the Kentmere Horseshoe trail. See p.82

△ Blackwell, Arts and Crafts house

Windermere

The elongated comma that is **Windermere**, England's largest and most famous lake, rarely fails to impress. Its rocky inlets, secluded bays, grassy banks and wooded heights form the very core of most people's image of the Lake District. And on bitingly cold winter days, or in the dappled spring and autumn sun, there are few finer places in England to soak up the scenery. Hardly surprisingly, its manifest attractions make it far too popular for its own good and you're unlikely to find real solitude in any of the three settlements – Windermere, Bowness and Ambleside – which group together on its northeast shore. However, the southern and western reaches of the lake are still remarkably underdeveloped, and their small hamlets, low-key rural attractions and local fells provide some of the most inviting destinations in the southern Lakes.

Windermere town itself (a mile inland of the lake) has been the largest engine of change – it was the coming of the railway in the mid-nineteenth century that brought the first mass influx of tourists. Even today, most people approaching the central lakes and fells from the south at least funnel through the town, getting their first glimpse of the lake at nearby Bowness – formerly a medieval lakeside village, though now the National Park's largest resort and boating centre. This also has the pick of the local cultural attractions, most notably the Steamboat Museum, just to the north of Bowness, and Blackwell, a restored Arts and Crafts mansion to the south.

Wordsworth himself thought that "None of the other Lakes unfold so many fresh beauties" and it makes sense to get out on the water as soon as possible. The cruise-boat ride south from Bowness provides access to **Lakeside** and its aquarium, and to the picnic lawns of **Fell Foot Park**, while combined boat-and-train tickets are available for trips on the popular **Lakeside and Haverthwaite Railway**. Heading north from Bowness there are landings at **Brockhole** – whose magnificent gardens form the backdrop for the Lake District Visitor Centre and National Park Headquarters – and at Waterhead for nearby **Ambleside**. This is the northernmost settlement on Windermere, and is a handily sited hiking and touring base with a terrific local museum and a couple of other diverting entertainments.

Away from the lake, the quiet hamlet of **Troutbeck** is strung along a gentle valley that lies between Windermere and Ambleside. There's good walking from here, as there is from the neighbouring **Kentmere** valley, where the River Kent tumbles down through the old mill village of **Staveley** – only four miles east of the hubbub at Windermere but refreshingly unvisited.

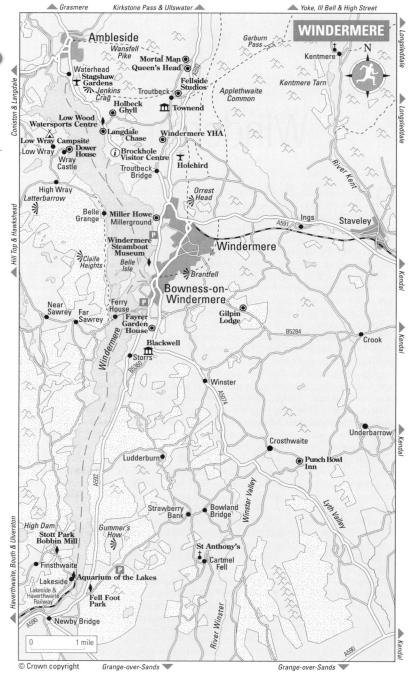

WINDERMERE

N

Grasmere Kirkstone Pass & Ullswater Yoke, Ill Bell & High Street

Ambleside
Wansfell Pike
Mortal Man
Queen's Head
Waterhead
Stagshaw Gardens
Jenkins Crag
Troutbeck
Fellside Studios
Holbeck Ghyll
Townend
Low Wood Watersports Centre
Langdale Chase
Windermere YHA
Low Wray Campsite
Dower House
Low Wray
Wray Castle
Brockhole Visitor Centre
Troutbeck Bridge
Holehird
High Wray
Latterbarrow
Orrest Head
Belle Grange
Miller Howe
Millerground
Ings
Staveley
Windermere Steamboat Museum
Claife Heights
Belle Isle
Windermere
Brantfell
Near Sawrey
Far Sawrey
Ferry House
Bowness-on-Windermere
Fayrer Garden House
Gilpin Lodge
Crook
Blackwell
Storrs
Winster
Underbarrow
Crosthwaite
Punch Bowl Inn
Ludderburn
Strawberry Bank
Bowland Bridge
Winster Valley
Lyth Valley
High Dam
Stott Park Bobbin Mill
Gummer's How
St Anthony's
Cartmel Fell
Finsthwaite
Lakeside
Aquarium of the Lakes
Lakeside & Haverthwaite Railway
Fell Foot Park
Newby Bridge

Garburn Pass
Kentmere
Kentmere Tarn
Applethwaite Common
River Kent
Longsleddale
Longsleddale
Kendal
Kendal
Kendal
Kendal
Kendal
Coniston & Langdale
Hill Top & Hawkshead
Haverthwaite, Bouth & Ulverston

A592
A591
A591
B5284
A5074
B5360
A592
A590
A590

Windermere

0   1 mile

© Crown copyright   Grange-over-Sands   Grange-over-Sands

Windermere town

The completion of the railway from Kendal in 1847 changed the face of Windermere for ever, providing direct access to the lake for Victorian day-trippers and holiday-makers. The hillside hamlet of Birthwaite, lying a good mile from the water, was entirely subsumed within a newly created town, soon named **WINDERMERE** to emphasize the link with the lake itself. Not everyone welcomed the development. William Wordsworth, ever more conservative in his old age, feared the effects of the railway (while conveniently forgetting that his own *Guide to the Lakes* had done much to popularize the district in the first place). The poet attempted to keep out the hordes by means of a sonnet – "Is then no nook of English ground secure from rash assault?" – and by penning rambling broadsides which must have sorely tested the patience of their recipient, the editor of the *Morning Post*. Wordsworth's defence of the "picturesque" had reason behind it, and he can hardly be said to have been wrong in fearing the "railway inundations [of an] Advance of the Ten Thousand". But (like most gentlemen of his day) his real fear was that of the great unwashed, the "imperfectly educated", sullying his back yard with their "wrestling matches, horse and boat races ... pot houses and beer shops".

Most of the villas and guesthouses built for the Victorians still stand, and Windermere town remains the transport hub for the southern and central Lakes, but there's precious little else to keep you in the slate-grey streets. Instead, all the traffic pours a mile downhill to its older twin town, lakeside Bowness, and the only reason for not doing the same is to take time to climb the heights of **Orrest Head** (784ft), just to the north of Windermere town. The bare summit gives a famous 360° panorama, sweeping from the Yorkshire fells to Morecambe Bay, the Langdale Pikes to Troutbeck valley. This was the very first lakeland climb made by a young Alfred Wainwright (see p.221), on his earliest visit to the Lake District in 1930 – one that, in his own words, cast a spell that changed his life. It's an easy twenty-minute stroll up through shaded **Elleray Wood**: the signposted path begins just to the left of the large *Windermere Hotel* on the A591, across from the train station. Ten minutes up the path, in Elleray Wood, you'll pass the cottage-studio of **blacksmith** Steve Hicks, where on most days you can grab a cup of tea and browse his creative, handcrafted ironwork.

Practicalities

The A591 between Kendal and Ambleside runs across the northern side of town, past the **train station**. There's a **car park** inside the train station yard and another down in the town on Broad Street; otherwise on-street parking is usually limited to thirty minutes. Windermere is a major **bus terminus**, with National Express and all local services stopping outside the train station – useful routes include the open-top #599 (to Bowness, Brockhole, Ambleside and Grasmere), the #555/556 (Kendal, Ambleside, Grasmere and Keswick), the #618 (Lakeside, Newby Bridge and Ulverston), the #505 (Brockhole, Ambleside, Hawkshead and Coniston) and the #517 (Troutbeck and Ullswater). A one-day **Central Lakes Day Rider** ticket (buy from the driver; from £5.95) gives unlimited travel on any service running between Windermere/Bowness and Grasmere, while the **Windermere Bus and Boat Rider** (from £7.50) combines the #599 bus service with a Windermere lake cruise.

A hundred yards away from the station, in the wooden chalet opposite the NatWest bank, stands the **tourist information centre** at the top of Victoria

ACCOMMODATION				CAFÉS, PUBS & RESTAURANTS	
Applegarth	**J**	Coach House	**E**	Brookside	**2**
Archway	**L**	Haven	**M**	Darryl's	**3**
Ashleigh	**K**	Holbeck Ghyll	**C**	First Floor	**1**
Boston House	**H**	Lake District Backpackers' Lodge	**G**	Jericho's	**7**
Brendan Chase	**I**	Langdale Chase	**A**	Lamplighter Bar	**4**
Broadlands	**D**	Meadfoot	**F**	Lighthouse	**6**
		Miller Howe	**B**	Queen's	**5**
				Renoir's Coffee	
				Shop	**8**

Street (daily 9am–5pm, possibly open later July & Aug; ☎015394/46499, ⓦwww.lakelandgateway.info).

Accommodation

Windermere doesn't have the waterside advantages of Bowness, but it does have a lot more accommodation. Good first places to look for **B&Bs** are on High Street and neighbouring Victoria Street, with other concentrations on College Road, Oak and Broad streets. At the bottom of town, halfway to Bowness, Lake

Road and its offshoots have a line of mid-range **guesthouses** and hotels, but these are a fair walk (or bus ride) from either Bowness or Windermere. Further out still is a selection of very grand **country–house hotels**, which make the most of their secluded locations, lake views and extensive grounds. At the other end of the scale there is a backpackers' hostel in Windermere itself – the nearest YHA **youth hostel** is at Troutbeck – while for **camping** you'll have to head down to Bowness.

In Windermere

Applegarth College Rd ☎015394/43206, ⓦwww .lakesapplegarth.co.uk. Detached hotel that retains its ornate Victorian interior (including stained-glass windows, a panelled lounge and bar, and conservatory restaurant) and terraced garden. The eighteen rooms are well proportioned – best (fell) views are at the back, at the top – including four singles and five four-poster rooms. Guests have free use of the pool and sauna at a local country club. No children under 12. Parking. ⑤, weekends ⑥

Archway 13 College Rd ☎015394/45613, ⓦwww.the-archway.com. Four trim rooms (two doubles, two twin) in a Victorian house, with the best light and views at the front. Known for its breakfasts (home-made granola, yoghurt, fresh and dried fruit with Scotch pancakes, kippers or traditional full English), served communally in a pine breakfast room; packed lunches (£5) also available. No smoking. Parking. No American Express. ③

Ashleigh 11 College Rd ☎015394/42292, ⓦwww.ashleighhouse.com. Choose from one of five tasteful rooms, which have been furnished in welcoming country pine. Breakfast includes home-made preserves. No smoking. Parking. No American Express. ③

Boston House The Terrace ☎015394/43654, ⓦwww.bostonhouse.co.uk. A beautifully restored Victorian Gothic house, located down a private drive just off the A591, a minute's walk from the tourist office. Five elegant rooms with four-posters and bright-as-a-button bathrooms, with burnished oak panelling, fresh flowers, scatter rugs and original art adding to the rather refined experience. Off-season discounts available. No smoking. Parking. No American Express. ⑤

Brendan Chase 1 College Rd ☎015394/45638, ⓦwww.placetostaywindermere.co.uk. Popular place with a warm, friendly welcome. The eight comfortable rooms here (some with en-suite facilities) are very reasonably priced, especially the spacious, bright family/group rooms which can sleep up to five. It's fully non-smoking, and there's parking and an enclosed yard for cycles. No credit cards. ②

Broadlands 19 Broad St ☎015394/46532, ⓦwww.broadlandsbedandbreakfast.co.uk. In a line of stone-terraced guesthouses, Broadlands stands out: a cheerily run family home with five rooms (the top one lovely and light), whose owners can provide local walk leaflets. ③

Coach House Lake Rd ☎015394/44494, ⓦwww.lakedistrictbandb.com. Comfort and contemporary design join hands in this stylish conversion of a Victorian coach house. Five classy rooms with wrought-iron beds, gleaming bathrooms and elegant touches are complemented by a relaxed breakfast with the morning papers, and use of a local leisure club. A good packed lunch (£6) is available for walkers, while off-season specials are a good deal. No smoking. Parking. ④

Haven 10 Birch St ☎015394/44017, ⓦwww .thehaven.windermere.btinternet.co.uk. Big windows let the light into three comfortably appointed rooms (one with a nice Victorian brass bedstead). Two have en-suite showers, the other a pretty private bathroom. Books, maps, drying facilities and packed lunches available. No smoking. Parking. ④

Meadfoot New Rd ☎015394/42610, ⓦwww .meadfoot-guesthouse.co.uk. One of the rooms at this friendly family villa opens directly onto the garden, while the others overlook it – as does the dining room and deck where you take breakfast. It makes for a comfortable touring base, with pine-furnished rooms, patio and summerhouse. Good off-season (Nov–Feb) discounts apply. Parking. ④

Around Windermere

Holbeck Ghyll Holbeck Lane, off A591, 3 miles north of town ☎015394/32375, ⓦwww .holbeck-ghyll.co.uk. See chapter map for location. A country house that once belonged to the Earl of Lonsdale, now with luxurious rooms either in the main house or in the lodge or suites in the grounds. It's a retreat in every sense – sherry decanter in each room, relaxing lounges, seven acres of gardens and woodland with trails, gym and spa, and Michelin-starred Anglo-French food of immense refinement. Meals are served on the terrace in summer, while the oak-panelled dining room retains its fine Arts and Crafts features and looks right across Windermere. Room rates start at around £230 (lake view and lodge rooms from £280), but include dinner as well as breakfast.

Two-night off-season breaks (Nov–May) offer significant savings. Parking. ⑨

Langdale Chase A591, 3 miles north of town ☎015394/32201, Ⓦ www.langdalechase.co.uk. See chapter map for location. Lounge on the magnificent lakeside terrace or swoon at the style in this lavish country-house hotel with its stupendous carved-oak interior (including a transplanted seventeenth-century fireplace), gardens, tennis courts and croquet lawn. The Boat House room is right on the water, or there's a secluded stone-built bungalow in the grounds whose six rooms open onto a wide terrace with Windermere views. Deluxe lake-view rooms are priced a category higher, while room rates including dinner in the well-regarded restaurant offer the best value if you intend to eat here – and at weekends (when there's a two-night minimum stay) you have to take dinner anyway. Parking. ⑦, with dinner ⑨

Miller Howe Rayrigg Rd (A592), half-mile west of town ☎015394/42536, Ⓦ www.millerhowe.com. See chapter map for location. Gorgeous Edwardian house occupying an elevated position above Windermere. The antique- and art-filled rooms are elegantly furnished, there's a conservatory for year-round use or in summer you can decamp to the terraces and landscaped gardens. Alternatively, sink into a plump armchair in one of the fire-warmed lounges and enjoy the stupendous lake views. Three self-contained suites in a cottage in the grounds provide an alternative to the main house. The price includes a supremely theatrical six-course dinner, plus early-morning tea and lavish breakfasts. Rates for rooms (up to £290) and cottage suites (up to £360) vary depending on their size and style or the season. Closed Jan. Parking. ⑨

Backpackers' accommodation

Lake District Backpackers' Lodge High St ☎015394/46374, Ⓦ www.lakedistrictbackpackers .co.uk. Twenty beds in small dorms (available as private rooms on request), a laid-back atmosphere and good facilities, including kitchen with washing machine, Internet access, satellite TV, bike storage and lockers. It's a bit of a squeeze when full, but the price includes a cereal, tea-and-toast breakfast, and there's information about local tours and work opportunities. No credit cards. Dorm beds from £11.50 (one-night stays £13.50), or £15.50 per person in a private room.

Eating and drinking

You don't need to make the trek down to Bowness as there are plenty of **cafés and restaurants** in Windermere. For the finest local dining, consider the gourmet experience that is *Holbeck Ghyll* (which has a Michelin star) or *Miller Howe* – both jacket-and-tie affairs open to non-residents (see "Accommodation" above). Dinner at either costs around £50 a head, plus drinks and service, though lunch is usually half that price, while the afternoon lakeland tea at *Miller Howe* is a widely celebrated affair. Good **pubs** are rather harder to come by in town, although a couple of locals will do for a drink after a day's sightseeing. The main **supermarket** is Booths, by the train station, which also has its own café.

Cafés and restaurants

Darryl's 14 Church St (the A591) ☎015394/42894. Cheap, filling café meals – specialities are the all-day breakfast and fish and chips – served from 8am (the earliest start in town). Daytime only; closed Tues & Wed. No credit cards. Inexpensive.

First Floor Lakeland Ltd, behind the train station ☎015394/88200. Occupying the impressive first-floor gallery of the kitchen/home-furnishings/design store, this superior café's snacks, lunches and high teas attract peak-period queues. There are always filled baguettes, tortilla wraps, soups, meat and cheese platters, salads, cakes and puddings, while a seasonally changing menu offers dishes such as salmon on a rocket and radicchio salad. Daytime only. Moderate.

Jericho's Birch St ☎015394/42522, Ⓦ www.jerichos.co.uk. The best in town offers seasonally changing Modern British menus for discerning diners – five choices, starters and mains, always including a vegetarian option, whipped up in the open kitchen. It's an informal, unpretentious night out, but reservations are advised. Dinner only; closed Mon (also closed Sun Jan–March). Expensive.

Lamplighter Bar Oakthorpe Hotel, High St ☎015394/43547. Very popular local choice for bistro meals, served in the hotel's bar-cum-dining room. English classics (steaks, gammon and egg, rack of lamb and fresh fish) plus a bit of sophistication (crab mornay, oysters or smoked salmon salad), all in big portions at value-for-money prices; the beer's good too and there's usually live music on Wednesday nights. Closed Sun & Mon lunch. Moderate.

Lighthouse Acme House, Main Rd
☎ 015394/88260. Contemporary café-bar that offers a street-side terrace with cane chairs, seats in the bar, or a first-floor dining room. Drop by either for drinks, cocktails and snacks, or lunch and dinner from the bistro menu (lamb shanks to sea bass). Moderate.

Renoir's Coffee Shop Main Rd ☎ 015394/44863. Amiable place for sandwiches, croissants, cakes, baked potatoes and frothy coffees – if the sun's

out, eat at the couple of tables outside. Daytime only. No credit cards. Inexpensive.

Pubs

Brookside Lake Rd ☎ 015394/43541. Nice little local, ten minutes' walk from the centre, which can be relied upon for a decent pint and a yarn at the bar.
Queen's Victoria St ☎ 015394/43713. The main pub in town, once the old coaching inn, but now with a fairly youthful clientele taking turns at the pool table and jukebox. Inexpensive meals are served and there's usually Castle Eden cask ale available.

Listings

Banks and exchange NatWest (High St), HSBC, Barclays and Abbey (all Crescent Rd) have ATMs, and there's an ATM outside Booths supermarket by the station. Travellers' cheques can also be exchanged at the post office.
Bike rental Country Lanes, The Railway Station (Easter–Oct daily 9am–5pm; Nov–Easter weekends and other times by arrangement; ☎ 015394/44544, ⓦ www.countrylanes.co.uk). Maps and routes provided.
Bookshop Fireside Bookshop, 21 Victoria St ☎ 015394/45855. Secondhand and antiquarian stockist; good for books on Cumbria and the Lakes.
Car rental Lakes Car Hire, rear of Windermere Social Club, New Rd ☎ 015394/44408, ⓦ www.lakeshire.co.uk.
Emergencies The nearest hospital is in Kendal; Westmorland General Hospital, Burton Rd; ☎ 01539/732288.
Internet access Windermere Library, Broad St (Mon 9am–7pm, Tues, Thurs & Fri 9am–5pm, Sat 9am–1pm, closed Wed & Sun; ☎ 015394/62400).

There's also access at the tourist information centre and (free) in Lakeland Ltd by the First Floor café.
Laundry Windermere Launderette, 19 Main Rd (Mon–Fri 8.30am–5.30pm, Sat 9am–5pm; ☎ 015394/42326).
Left luggage Available for £1 at Darryl's café, 14 Church St (the A591). Thurs–Mon 8am–6pm.
Pharmacy Boots, 10–12 Crescent Rd ☎ 015394/43093; David Carter, 16 Crescent Rd ☎ 015394/43417.
Police station Lake Rd, just after the war memorial ☎ 0845/330 0247.
Post office 21 Crescent Rd (Mon–Fri 9am–5.30pm, Sat 9am–12.30pm).
Swimming pool Troutbeck Bridge Swimming Pool, Troutbeck Bridge, 1 mile northwest of Windermere (daily 7.30am–9.30pm, though public admission hours and sessions vary; ☎ 015394/43243, ⓦ www.tbsp.org.uk).
Taxis Windermere Taxis ☎ 015934/42355. See also Bowness "Listings".

Bowness and the lake

BOWNESS-ON-WINDERMERE – to give it its full title – is undoubtedly the more attractive of the two Windermere settlements, spilling back from its lakeside piers in a series of terraces lined with guesthouses and hotels. Set back from the thumbprint indent of Bowness Bay, there's been a village here since at least the fifteenth century and a ferry service across the lake for almost as long. On a busy summer's day, crowds swirl around the trinket shops, cafés, ice-cream stalls and lakeside seats, but you can escape onto the lake or into the hills easily enough and there are several scattered attractions around town to fill a rainy day. And come the evening, when the human tide has subsided and the light fades over the wooden jetties and stone buildings, a promenade around Bowness Bay conjures visions of the Italian lakes.

▲ Waterhead (Ambleside)   Steamboat Museum & A592 (200yds) ▲   Windermere A5074 (¾ mile) ▲

BOWNESS-ON-WINDERMERE

Fallbarrow Park

Belle Isle

Cockshott Point

Braithwaite Fold

Windermere Canoe & Kayak

Marina

Cinema
Co-op Supermarket
World of Beatrix Potter & Old Laundry Theatre

St Martin's

Bus stop

Brantfell

ACCOMMODATION

Above the Bay	G
Belsfield	E
Blenheim Lodge	F
Burn How	H
Fayrer Garden House	K
Gilpin Lodge	J
Linthwaite House	I
Montclare House	B
New Hall Bank	C
Oakbank House	A
Old England	D

CAFÉS, PUBS & RESTAURANTS

2 Eggcups	4
Hole in't Wall	2
Jackson's Bistro	5
Porthole Eating House	3
Rastelli's	1
Ship Inn	7
Village Inn	6

0 ———— 200 yds

▼ Newby Bridge   ▼ Blackwell, Winster & Crosthwaite

The Town

What's left of the oldest part of Bowness survives in the few narrow lanes around **St Martin's Church**, consecrated in 1483. The church is notable for its stained glass, particularly that in the east window, now very difficult to make out but sporting the fifteenth-century arms of John Washington, a distant ancestor of first American president George Washington. Outside in the churchyard is the grave of one Rasselas Belfield (d. 1822), "a native of Abyssinia" who was born a slave – and found himself shipped to England – but as a free man became servant to the Windermere gentry.

Most tourists, though, bypass the church and everything else in Bowness bar the lake for the chance to visit **The World of Beatrix Potter**, in the Old

Laundry on Crag Brow (daily: Easter–Sept 10am–5.30pm; Oct–Easter 10am–4.30pm; £6, all-year family Freedom Pass £25; ⑦015394/88444, Ⓦwww.hop-skip-jump.com). It's unfair to be judgemental – you either like Beatrix Potter or you don't – but it is safe to say that the displays here find more favour with children than the more formal Potter attractions at Hill Top and Hawkshead. Heralded by a fifteen-foot high bronze outdoor sculpture symbolizing the Potter oeuvre, inside all 23 tales are featured in 3D form, and there are virtual walks to the places that inspired the author, plus interactive children's attractions, "emporium" gift shop and themed café.

The other main attraction is the **Windermere Steamboat Museum**, on Rayrigg Road (⑦015394/45565, Ⓦwww.steamboat.co.uk), a fifteen-minute walk north of Bowness centre. This is undergoing a major restoration during 2007 and possibly beyond, but parts may be open for public access during that time – call or check the website for details. The museum contains a wide variety of historic water craft, including the 1850 *Dolly*, claimed to be the world's oldest mechanically driven boat, and extremely well preserved after spending 67 years in the mud at the bottom of Ullswater. Other items relate to children's author Arthur Ransome and his *Swallows and Amazons* stories, notably Ransome's own boat, *Coch-y-Bondhu*, which became the boat *Scarab* in *The Picts and the Martyrs*.

Out on the lake

All the attractions in Bowness come second-best to a trip on **Windermere** itself – the heavyweight of Lake District lakes, at ten-and-a-half miles long, a mile wide in parts and a shade over two hundred feet deep. As so often in these parts, the name derives from the Norse ("Vinandr's Lake") and since "mere" means lake, references to "Lake Windermere" are tautologous. The only settlements are at Bowness and Ambleside, which means that the views from the water tend towards the magnificent: north to the central fells, or south along a wooded shoreline that

---

Windermere boat services and cruises

Windermere Lake Cruises (⑦015395/31188, Ⓦwww.windermere-lakecruises.co.uk) is the main operator on the lake, providing modern cruiser and vintage steamer services from Bowness to Lakeside at the southern tip (£7.95 return) or to Brockhole and Waterhead (for Ambleside) at the northern end (£7.50 return). There's also a direct service from Ambleside to the Lake District Visitor Centre at Brockhole (£5.75 return), and a shuttle service across the lake between Bowness pier and Ferry House, Sawrey (£2 one-way, £3.50 return). A 24-hour **Freedom-of-the-Lake ticket** (£13.95) is valid on all routes; it's discounted from November to March, when there's also a budget 48-hour version.

Services on all routes are very frequent between Easter and October (every 30min to 1hr at peak times and weekends), and reduced during the winter – but there are sailings every day except Christmas Day.

As well as these routes, from mid-May to mid-August the company operates an enjoyable 45-minute circular cruise **around the islands** (£5.75, departs from Bowness), plus summer **buffet-and-music cruises** once or twice a week (£25.95). There are also **combination boat tickets** available for the Lakeside and Haverthwaite Railway and the Aquarium of the Lakes – more information from the pier-side ticket office – and a **Bus-and-Boat Rider** (£7.50; buy on board #599 bus), which gives a day's travel by open-top bus and boat between Bowness, Waterhead and Ambleside. There's discounted **parking** available for customers at Bowness (Braithwaite Fold), Ambleside (Waterhead) and Lakeside.

△ The World of Beatrix Potter, Bowness

is mostly under the protection of the National Trust. The seasons are reflected in the changing colours and tree cover around the lake. Autumn can be a real treat, though global warming has put paid to the spectacular freezing winters of yesteryear – in the 1890s, excursion trains brought astonished sightseers to skate on the lake and marvel at the icicles hanging from the trees. Many of the private lakeside mansions built for Victorian Lancashire mill owners are now hotels, though **Belle Isle** – the largest of eighteen islets in the lake – is still privately owned. For over two hundred years (until the 1990s), its guardians were various members of the Curwen family who built the island's eye-catching Georgian round house, one of the first of its type in England. The current owners don't allow public access to the island, though the house is visible through the trees if you get close enough on a boat.

Rowboats and motorboats are available at **Bowness piers**, with more boating and water-sports outlets further around the bay by the Glebe Road marina. There's a 10mph **speed limit** on the lake (6mph in the more congested areas, where navigation can be hazardous, including Waterhead, and the Bowness Bay and Fell Foot Park areas).

Although it's freezing cold, people also jump in at various spots; indeed, every September there are a couple of **Windermere swims**. The first Thursday of the month sees a cross-lake swim between Wray Castle and Ambleside (which takes 30–45 minutes), while on the first Saturday is the ten-mile endurance route up the lake from Fell Foot Park to Ambleside, which has a nine-hour limit imposed upon it – the record is under four hours. Many people come here for the **fishing**, hooking perch, pike, roach and brown trout. You can also catch **char**, a reddish lake trout related to the Arctic char and landlocked in the Lakes after the last Ice Age. It thrives in the deep, cold waters of Windermere (and is usually on local menus between May and October). Daniel Defoe recommended potting this "curious fish" and sending it to your best friend.

The traditional **ferry service** is the chain-guided contraption which chugs across the water from Ferry Nab on the Bowness side to **Ferry House**, Sawrey (departures every 20min; Mon–Sat 7am–10pm, Sun 9am–10pm, final departure in winter 9pm; 50p, cars £3). It's a useful service, providing access to Beatrix Potter's former home at Hill Top and to Hawkshead beyond, but as it can take

While Bowness itself gets very busy in summer, there are plenty of other quieter lakeside spots in the vicinity. Even on the east shore, near the town, you can escape the crowds fairly quickly for an hour or two's stroll, while if you cross to Sawrey using the car-ferry or launch, the whole of the wooded west side as far as Wray Castle makes for an easy half- or full-day's circuit.

Rayrigg Meadow and Millerground

A mile north of Bowness (along the A592), past the Steamboat Museum, a path cuts west across **Rayrigg Meadow** to the lakeside and then traces the wooded shore for half a mile to the **Millerground** piers (there's parking here), where you can rejoin the main road. If you're not too muddy, then morning coffee or afternoon tea at nearby *Miller Howe* is a treat. The round-trip from Bowness, including walking along the road, is 2.5 miles, though from Millerground you can walk up through the woods to Windermere town, a mile away, if you want to make a circuit of it.

Brantfell

Best viewpoint is from **Brantfell** (626ft) – "steep hill" – about a mile southeast of Bowness, which takes an hour or so, there and back. Follow Brantfell Road up the hill from St Martin's Square and keep on the path (signposted as the "Dales Way") until you see the diversion up the hillside at Brantfell Farm. The views from the rocks at the top are all-embracing – Belle Isle to Morecambe Bay – and if you rejoin the Dales Way at the farm you could then follow the path east and north all the way into Windermere town (3.5 miles; 2hr, from Bowness) – though it's actually an easier, and nicer, route *from* Windermere to Bowness and the lake, diverting up Brantfell on the way.

Latterbarrow and Claife Heights

The Victorians liked to cross the lake to take tea on the shore below the woods on the west side, and if you're up for an afternoon's walk away from the crowds, this is still the best idea. Cross by car-ferry or launch to Ferry House at Sawrey, from where a gentle path runs two miles north along the shore to Belle Grange. From here you can climb up to **Latterbarrow** (800ft) for lake views before returning along the paths of **Claife Heights** and back to Sawrey. The steep descent through the woods from Far Sawrey to the ferry pier passes the ruins of **The Station**, a castellated viewing platform from which eighteenth-century tourists would view the lake and mountains through a "claude-glass" (named after Romantic landscapist Claude Lorraine), a convex mirror used to "frame" their view. These viewing-stations were very popular until well into the nineteenth century and formed part of any tour of picturesque Lakeland, but the views from this one have been lost to the overarching trees.

See Basics, p.35, for general walking advice in the Lakes; recommended maps are detailed on p.42.

only around eighteen cars at a time queues soon build up in summer. The Ferry Nab pier is a ten-minute walk south of the cruise piers, through the parkland of Cockshott Point (or follow the road signs from the promenade). There's also a useful **launch service** for pedestrians and hikers between Bowness piers and Ferry House, Sawrey (April–Oct daily 10am–5pm every 30min; £2 one-way, £3.50 return), saving you the walk down to the car ferry.

Practicalities

The A592 from the south runs into Bowness along the lake, past the piers, and then continues on, meeting the A591 northwest of Windermere town. There's free two-hour parking on Glebe Road, but otherwise you're going to have to put up with the **car park** charges, either at Glebe Park or Braithwaite Fold (both well signposted). **Bus** #599 (Easter–Oct daily every 20min; rest of year hourly) leaves Windermere train station for the fifteen-minute run down Lake Road to Bowness. The bus stops at the piers, which is also the terminus for the #517 (Troutbeck and Ullswater) and the #618 (Newby Bridge, Haverthwaite and Ulverston). For onward routes to Ambleside and Grasmere you have to return first to Windermere station, though the useful **Cross–Lakes Shuttle** provides a direct connecting boat-and-minibus service from Bowness pier 3 to Hill Top, Hawkshead, Grizedale Forest and Coniston Water (daily Easter–Sept plus Oct weekends). For local information, call in at the **Bowness Bay Information Centre**, near the piers on Glebe Road (daily: Easter–Oct 9.30am–5.30pm; Nov–Easter 10am–4pm; ☎015394/42895).

Accommodation

Budget accommodation in Bowness is in short supply, so if you want to spend a night by the lake you should book ahead. And be warned that a **lake view** itself doesn't come cheap – most places in town with even a glimpse of the water set their prices accordingly, while the local country-house hotels are in uniformly desirable locations. Apart from the places recommended below, Kendal Road has a line of other **B&B** possibilities. There's no youth hostel in Bowness (your best bet for a lakeside hostel is Ambleside), though there are two **campsites** (listed below), both within half a mile of Bowness centre and very popular – book at least a few days ahead in summer.

In Bowness

Above the Bay 5 Brackenfield ☎015394/88658, Ⓦwww.abovethebay.co.uk. An elevated house in a residential area, just off Kendal Rd, a 5min walk from the water. Three spacious rooms (with generously sized bathrooms) open out onto a private terrace with huge lake views. Free entry to local leisure club. Parking. No credit cards. ❹

Belsfield Kendal Rd ☎0870/609 6109, Ⓦwww.corushotels.com. Superbly sited old mansion (once the home of a Barrow steel magnate) in an elevated position above the ferry piers. Now a three-star hotel with an indoor pool and sauna, and sloping lawns where you can have lunch and tea. Rooms are modestly furnished and sized, but those at the front have magnificent lake panoramas (supplement payable), while some garden-view rooms have French windows opening on to the grounds. Two-night minimum stay, but D,B&B and off-season rates can provide big savings. Parking. ❼

Blenheim Lodge Brantfell Rd ☎015394/43440, Ⓦwww.blenheim-lodge.com. The steep climb from town is rewarded by great lake views (only one room doesn't overlook Windermere) and rooms which vary in size and style from country-pine to Victorian. Guests get use of a nearby leisure club, and there's a drying room and parking. Winter rates shave off a few pounds. No smoking. ❺

Burn How Back Belsfield Rd ☎015394/46226, Ⓦwww.burnhow.co.uk. Upscale chalet units – all family-sized – with sheltered private patios, or smart doubles (some with four-posters) in the main lodge. Breakfast is served in the restaurant, or you can have a continental service served in your room. Parking. ❻, weekends ❼

🏃 **Montclare House** Crag Brow ☎015394/42723, Ⓦwww.montclare guesthouse.co.uk. For simple B&B accommodation, these smart rooms (all with refurbished shower rooms) above a coffee shop are the best value in Bowness. Two family rooms with bunks also available, sleeping up to four people, and limited parking. Mention Rough Guides for a discount. No credit cards. ❸

New Hall Bank Fallbarrow Rd ☎015394/43558, Ⓦwww.newhallbank.com. Detached Victorian house with a lake view and a central location (a few yards from the Hole in't Wall pub). The en-suite facilities may be tiny, and the dozen rooms themselves not much bigger, but everything is pleasantly decorated, decked out in pine, with better views the higher you go. Parking. No American Express. ❺

Oakbank House Helm Rd ☎015394/43386, Ⓦwww.oakbankhousehotel.co.uk. Rugs and flowers, scatter cushions and coordinated furniture, and a welcoming sherry decanter single out the

Oakbank, some of whose rooms have lake views – all have TV and video, and there's free use of the pool and facilities at a local country club. Four superior rooms provide a bit more elegance, while parking, packed lunches (£6.95) and good winter discounts are available. No smoking. ⑤

Old England Church St ☎015394/42444, ⓦ www .macdonaldhotels.co.uk. This lakeside grande-dame with a Georgian kernel sports a small, heated outdoor pool, superb terrace and gardens, and snooker room. Lake-view rooms attract a small premium, though prices drop significantly between November and March. D,B&B rates are priced a category higher. Parking. ⑦

Around Bowness

Fayrer Garden House Lyth Valley Rd (A5074), 1 mile south of town ☎015394/88195, ⓦ www .fayrergarden.com. Quiet Victorian country house overlooking the lake, sporting a yesteryear elegance with heavy drapes, fresh flowers and plump cushions in its rooms and lounges. Standard rooms tend to be small and lacking in outlook, so it's best to go for a pricier garden or lake-view room – the latter all with king-sized beds, whirlpool baths, thick robes and CD players. Rates include a well-regarded four-course dinner. Closed two weeks Jan. Parking. ⑦, lake-view ⑨

Gilpin Lodge Crook Rd (B5284), 2 miles south-east of town ☎015394/88818, ⓦ www .gilpin-lodge.co.uk. A luxurious country-house retreat in twenty acres. Its small size ensures personal service and the fourteen elegant rooms in the main house are individually styled, some with four-posters, others with whirlpool baths or private patios – six more contemporary suites

have glass-fronted lounges leading to individual gardens with private hot tubs. It's renowned for its serious Michelin-starred Anglo-French cuisine, and the rates (rooms up to £270, garden suites £330) include an extraordinarily lavish breakfast and five-course, seasonally changing dinner. Or sample the food and fine china at more affordable rates with a lunchtime bowl of soup, a superior sandwich or a bistro-style dish. Minimum two-night stay at weekends. Parking. ⑨

Linthwaite House Crook Rd (B5284), 1 mile south of town ☎015394/88600, ⓦ www.linthwaite.com. Contemporary style has been grafted onto this ivy-covered country house, set high above Windermere. Rooms are superbly detailed – rich muted fabrics, Shaker-style furniture, king-sized beds with canopies, flat-screen TVs, modems and CD players. A conservatory and terrace offer grandstand lake and fell views, and you can work up an appetite for the Modern British dinner with a walk out in the extensive gardens to the hotel's private tarn. Room rates vary according to outlook and size, but run up to £290, suites £360, dinner included. Parking. ⑨

Campsites

Braithwaite Fold Glebe Rd ☎015394/42177. A site close to the lakeshore (near the ferry to Sawrey) for caravans and tents; a 10min walk from Bowness. Closed Nov–Easter.

Fallbarrow Park Rayrigg Rd ☎015394/44422, ⓦ www.fallbarrow.co.uk. Caravans and RVs only at this lakeside site with lawns, picnic areas and pub, a 5min walk from Bowness. Van and lodge rental (usual period is a week) for up to four people runs from around £130 to £790, depending on season. Closed mid-Nov to mid-March.

Eating, drinking and entertainment

There are lots of places in Bowness to get a pizza, a Chinese buffet or a budget **café** meal – a stroll along pedestrianized Ash Street and up Lake Road shows you most of the possibilities. Finer dining is available at a couple of local **restaurants**, as well as in the dining rooms of the major hotels – *Gilpin Lodge* and *Linthwaite House* (see "Accommodation" above), in particular, get rave reviews (dinner around £50 plus drinks and service, lunch around half that, reservations advised). The best **pub** by far is the *Hole in't Wall*, though others have their moments, while for morning coffee or sunset drinks you can't beat the terraces of the *Old England* or the *Belsfield* hotels, both open to non-residents.

The Royalty on Lake Road (☎015394/43364, ⓦ www.nm-cinemas.co.uk) boasts the Lake District's biggest **cinema** screen; and the Old Laundry Theatre on Crag Brow (☎015394/88444, ⓦ www.oldlaundrytheatre.com) hosts an annual autumn **Theatre and Film Festival** with two months of music, film, comedy and the performing arts.

Cafés and restaurants

2 Eggcups 6A Ash St ☎015394/45979. Serves the best sandwich in Bowness, plus other daily blackboard specials. A couple of outdoor tables catch the sun. Daytime only; closed Thurs. No credit cards. Inexpensive.

Jackson's Bistro St Martin's Sq ☎015394/46264. The local choice for a family dinner or romantic night out, with intimate dining on two floors and welcoming staff. Mussels, onion tart, poached salmon and grilled duck provide a classic bistro experience, or choose from the good-value three-course *table d'hote* menu (£13.95), available all night. Dinner only. Moderate.

Porthole Eating House 3 Ash St ☎015394/42793. The top restaurant in town serves quality Anglo-Italian cuisine in a converted seventeenth-century cottage. The signature dish is seared scallops with crispy black pudding on a bed of mash, but there's also home-made bread, antipasto, seasonal meat and fish, operatic warbling, open fires in winter, and a terrific wine list. Dinner only; closed Tues & 1st week Jan to mid-Feb. Very expensive.

Rastelli's Lake Rd ☎015394/44227. Budget-priced pizza and pasta in an amiable family-run restaurant – expect to have to wait for a table in summer. Dinner only. Closed Tues. Moderate.

Pubs

Hole in't Wall Fallbarrow Rd ☎015394/43488. The town's oldest hostelry, behind Bowness church (and officially the New Hall Inn), is named after the hole through which ostlers once had their beer passed to them. Inside are stone-flagged floors, open fires, real ales and bar meals; outside, a terrace-style beer garden that's a popular spot on summer evenings.

Ship Inn Glebe Rd ☎015394/45001. Located round by the marina, this has lakeside seats and views of the boats.

Village Inn Lake Rd ☎015394/43731. Known for its real ale selection (usually half a dozen on show), though many come for the well-priced bar meals and the chance to lounge on the patio opposite the church.

Listings

Banks and exchange NatWest (Lake Rd) has an ATM and there's a Barclays ATM (though no bank) on Crag Brow, Lake Rd. You can also change travellers' cheques at the post office (see below).

Bike rental There's great off-road biking across the lake around Claife Heights. Contact Windermere Canoe & Kayak, Ferry Nab Rd ☎015394/44451, ⓦwww.windermerecanoekayak.co.uk – you get a map of local trails and routes.

Emergencies The nearest hospital is in Kendal: Westmorland General Hospital, Burton Rd ☎01539/732288.

Internet access Intercontinental Café, 4 Windermere Bank, Lake Rd (Easter–Sept Mon–Fri 9am–6pm, Sat & Sun 9am–5pm; Oct–Easter Tues–Fri 10am–6pm, Sat 10am–5pm; ☎015394/45657, ⓦwww.teatoo.co.uk).

Pharmacy Lakeland Pharmacy, 5 Grosvenor Terrace, Lake Rd ☎015394/43139.

Post office 2 St Martin's Parade (Mon–Fri 9am–5.30pm, Sat 9am–12.30pm).

Taxis Bowness Taxis ☎015394/46664; Lakes Taxis ☎015394/46777 or 44055.

The Lake District Visitor Centre at Brockhole

The **Lake District National Park Authority** has its main visitor centre at **Brockhole** (Easter–Oct daily 10am–5pm; grounds and gardens open all year; free, though parking-fee charged; ☎015394/46601, ⓦwww.lake-district.gov.uk), a late-Victorian mansion set in lush grounds on the shores of Windermere, to the north of Bowness. Besides the permanent natural-history and geological displays, the centre hosts a full programme of guided walks, children's activities (including a popular adventure playground), garden tours, special exhibitions, lectures and film shows – the centre, and any local tourist office, can provide a schedule. On a warm day, the **gardens** are a treat, with their little arbours, lakeside paths, grassy lawns, wildflower meadow and picnic areas – the website tells you what's flowering month by month, while woodpeckers, deer, rabbits, foxes and badgers are all regular visitors. The landscaping is among the finest in the Lakes, the work of the celebrated Lancastrian garden architect Thomas Mawson (1861–1933), who also designed the grounds for other Victorian piles at Holehird, Langdale Chase, Holker Hall and Rydal Hall. Inside the former mansion (built originally for a Manchester silk merchant), there's a bookshop – one of the best in the region for local guides and maps – and a café whose outdoor terrace looks down to the lake.

The visitor centre is just off the A591, three miles northwest of Windermere. **Buses** #555/556 and #599 stop outside, though for a more enjoyable ride come by **Windermere Lake Cruises** launch, which docks at the foot of the gardens. There are services from either Waterhead, Ambleside (£5.75 return) or from Bowness (£7.50 return), and you can also take the launch from Brockhole jetty on a 45-minute circular cruise (£5.75) via Wray Castle, on Windermere's opposite shore.

Blackwell

A mile and a half south of Bowness, in an elevated position above the lake, stands the superbly restored mansion of **Blackwell** (April–Oct daily 10.30am–5pm; mid-Feb to March & Nov to Christmas daily 10.30am–4pm; £5; ⓣ015394/46139, ⓦwww.blackwell.org.uk). It's the masterpiece of **Mackay Hugh Baillie Scott** (1865–1945) – less celebrated an architect than his contemporaries, Sir Edwin Lutyens and Charles Voysey, but just as influential in the Arts and Crafts Movement that emerged from the ideas of John Ruskin and William Morris. The house is hugely significant as the only major Arts and Crafts house in such remarkable condition open to the public in Britain. Most are still in private hands, and Blackwell itself has had a variety of owners: from World War II until the 1970s the house was a girls' school, and was then leased by English Nature until it was bought and restored by the Lakeland Arts Trust.

Its origins – as with so many houses on the shores of Windermere – lie in the nineteenth-century explosion of wealth in the industrial cities. Given free rein by Mancunian brewer and Lord Mayor Sir Edward Holt, who wanted a holiday home in the Lakes, Baillie Scott grasped the opportunity to design an entire house, and Blackwell was completed to his specifications between 1898 and 1900. Taking his cue from Ruskin and Morris, who had championed the importance of traditional handicrafts allied with functionalism, Baillie Scott let Blackwell speak for his ideas and principles – from the almost organic nature of the free-flowing layout to the decorative emphasis on natural motifs and handcrafted designs. The use of natural light, in particular, is revealing, with the family rooms all south-facing, even though this orientates them away from the lake views for which, presumably, Sir Edward had paid a premium. Indeed, there's evidence that the Holts were never entirely comfortable in their designer holiday home. The family (of five children and six servants) soon cluttered Baillie Scott's harmonious interlinked rooms with the paraphernalia of the Victorian gentry – an old photograph shows the main hall encumbered with a heavy chandelier, potted ferns and a stuffed moose's head; and by the end of World War I, as the Arts and Crafts Movement lost its fashionable edge, the Holts visited Blackwell less and less.

The restored house grabs your attention from the very first, as you proceed from the entrance down an oak-panelled corridor, off which is the **main hall**.

Baillie Scott's idealized baronial design provides the sort of things you might expect to see in a showpiece country house – vast fireplace, oak panelling, minstrel's gallery and heraldic crests – but lightens the experience with huge dollops of inventive flair. An open-plan room with nooks and corners of varying proportions sports a peacock wallpaper frieze, a bluebell-and-daisy hessian wall-hanging, copper lightshades, Delft tiles and – above all – the recurring carved rowan leaves and berries from the family coat of arms. At the end of the corridor, sun streams into the **white drawing room** and here, and elsewhere in the house, you can sit in the cushioned bay windows and enjoy the garden and lake views. The **bedrooms** upstairs contain changing exhibitions of contemporary and historic applied arts and crafts, though the contents of the entire house are display pieces in their own right, from the early twentieth-century carved oak furniture by Simpson's of Kendal to the modern earthenware that is positioned throughout. But it's Baillie Scott's naturalistic touches that perhaps sum up the whole – such as the door handles shaped like leaves or the lakeland birds and flowers that are ever-present in the stained glass and stonework.

The best way to appreciate the overall design is to coincide with the informative introductory talk (usually daily at 2.30pm). There's also a pleasant **tearoom**, and a garden terrace where lunches, cream teas and lemonade are served on summer days. A **craft shop** sells works by leading designers, including jewellery, ceramics, scarves and handbags, as well as specialist books on architecture and the Arts and Crafts movement. If you're especially interested, you can head off from Blackwell on an **Arts and Crafts Trail** that links other period houses and sights in the southern Lakes – pick up a leaflet at the house or check the Blackwell website.

Blackwell is on the B5360, just off the A5074, one and a half miles south of Bowness. There's no public transport here, though it's only a 25-minute walk from Bowness.

Lakeside, Finsthwaite and Haverthwaite

From Bowness, boats head five miles down the lake to the piers at **LAKESIDE**, where gentle wooded hills frame Windermere's serene southern reaches. This is the quayside terminus of the **Lakeside and Haverthwaite Railway** (Easter–Oct 6–7 services daily; £5.20 return; ☎015395/31594, ⓦ www.lakesiderailway .co.uk), whose steam-powered engines puff along four miles of track through the woods of Backbarrow Gorge, the only surviving remnant of a line that used to stretch all the way to Ulverston and Barrow. There's parking and a station tearoom at Haverthwaite (closed Jan & Feb) and a chance to look around the engine shed, where (when it's not out on duty) Britain's oldest working standard-gauge loco, built in Manchester in 1863, is kept. Boat arrivals at Lakeside connect with train departures throughout the day and there's a joint boat-and-train ticket available from Bowness (£12.60 return) or Waterhead, near Ambleside (£17.30 return). The annual calendar also incorporates steam gala weekends, Victorian evenings and Santa specials – there's more information on the website. Haverthwaite station itself is on the A590, across the busy main road from the actual village of Haverthwaite – you can reach it on bus #X35 (from Kendal or Ulverston) or #618 (from Ambleside, Windermere, Bowness or Ulverston).

Also on the quay at Lakeside is the **Aquarium of the Lakes** (daily: April–Oct 9am–6pm; Nov–March 9am–5pm; last admission 1hr before closing; £7.50; ☎015395/30153, ⓦ www.aquariumofthelakes.co.uk), an entertaining natural-history attraction centred on the fish and animals found in and along a lakeland river and on the Cumbrian coast. There's a pair of frisky otters, plus rays from Morecambe Bay and a terrific walk-through tunnel aquarium (with huge carp and diving ducks), while educational exhibits, documentaries and daily presentations give the low down on everything from cockles to pike and leeches to lobsters. Enthusiastic staff are on hand to explain what's going on and afterwards you can grab a drink in the lake-view café and peruse the comings and goings of the boats. There's a joint ticket available with the boat ride from Bowness (£13.75 return) or Waterhead, near Ambleside (£20.50 return), which includes aquarium entry.

Half a mile up the hill from Lakeside, below Finsthwaite Heights, stands one of England's few working mills, **Stott Park Bobbin Mill** (Easter–Sept daily 10am–5pm; last tour 1hr before closing; £4.20; EH; ☎015395/31087). It was founded in 1835 to supply the British textile industry with bobbins – rollers or spools for holding thread – and, as elsewhere when the cotton industry declined, the mill later diversified, manufacturing pulleys, hammers, mallets, spade handles, yo-yos and even duffel-coat toggles. Commercial production finally ceased in 1971, at a time when plastic had replaced wood for most bobbins. Former workers guide visitors on a 45-minute tour through the processes of cutting, roughing, drying, finishing and polishing on machinery that hasn't changed since it was introduced in the mid-nineteenth century. Note that the steam engine driving the waterwheel operates only on Mondays, Tuesdays, Wednesdays and Thursdays.

From a car park above the mill (follow the road to Finsthwaite) there's a pleasant walk up through the woods to **High Dam**, the reservoir whose water used to drive the mill machinery – allow an hour or so to circle the water and return. Alternatively, if you head for **FINSTHWAITE** hamlet itself, half a mile above the mill, you can clamber up through the woods of **Finsthwaite Heights** to the naval commemorative tower. The only bus to the bobbin mill or Finsthwaite is a twice-a-week service from Lakeside, Newby Bridge or Ulverston, but the half-a-mile walk up from Lakeside is hardly off-putting.

Practicalities

Most people see the southern end of Windermere on a return boat trip from Bowness or Ambleside, but it can make a peaceful overnight stop if you plan ahead. There's limited **accommodation** at Lakeside itself, while just a mile

Bobbins and coppicing

For a time in the nineteenth century the south Lakes' **bobbin mills** formed an important part of the national economy, supplying up to half of all the bobbins required by the booming British textile mills. There were two reasons for the industry's strength in the Lakes: the fast running water from lakeland rivers to drive the mills and the seemingly inexhaustible supply of wood. To make bobbins and other items, **coppiced** wood was required, from trees cut to stumps to encourage the quick growth of long poles, which were then harvested for use. It's a technique that's been used for over five thousand years, and in more recent times in the southern Lakes, including the area around Stott Park, ash, beech, birch, chestnut, hazel and oak were all grown in this way. The bark was peeled off and used in the tanneries, while coppiced wood was also used widely in charcoal-making (another key local industry), thatching and the production of tent pegs, cask bindings, fencing, agricultural implements (such as rakes) and so-called "swill" baskets (cradle-shaped Cumbrian panniers).

south of the foot of the lake, down the River Leven, the *Swan Hotel* has a fine riverside location. From here, it's another couple of miles southwest along the A590 to the village of Haverthwaite, which also has a selection of B&Bs available. If you're going to stay, it's best not to be reliant upon **public transport**, though for accommodation at Lakeside you only need to step off the boat, while the #618 bus (from Ambleside, Windermere and Bowness) does call at Newby Bridge and Haverthwaite.

Accommodation and food

Boathouse Hotel Lakeside ☎015395/31381, ⓦwww.boathousehotel.co.uk. The nine rooms in this small hotel are very nicely turned out – Shaker-style in look, some with bare boards and rugs, and all with patchwork bedspreads and modern bathrooms with power showers. There's a restaurant and bar attached, and you're just 100 yards from the steamer jetty. Rates drop considerably in winter, when there's also a good-value two-night midweek D,B&B deal. No smoking in the hotel. Parking. ⑥

Coach House Hollow Oak, Haverthwaite ☎015395/31622, ⓦwww.coachho.com. Friendly B&B in a 200-year-old former coach house and stables, set in appealing gardens. There are only three rooms, two with en-suite facilities, one with its own bathroom down the corridor. The Haverthwaite village pub is just half a mile away and the knowledgeable owners can tell you anything else you need to know about the Lake District. No smoking. Parking. No credit cards. ②

Lakeside Lakeside ☎015395/30001, ⓦwww.lakesidehotel.co.uk. Across from the quayside and aquarium, this very hospitable four-star hotel makes the most of its lakeside location. Some rooms have private gardens or their own terrace, and most overlook the water – although individually furnished, they are all country-house in feel, with elegant fabrics and marble bathrooms. Six family rooms, with separate bunk-room for the

kids, are very spacious. There's a waterside conservatory and lakeside lawns and gardens, plus a large family-friendly indoor pool, as well as hot tub, sauna, gym and classy spa treatment facilities. Dining is either in the contemporary John Ruskin's Brasserie (table d'hote menu, £33) or the elegant but unstuffy fine-dining Lakeview Restaurant (£45). Rates start at £195 per night and vary considerably, depending on the room, though off-season and midweek deals offer good value. Parking. ⑨

Swan Newby Bridge ☎015395/31681, ⓦwww.swanhotel.com. This classic old inn, a winding mile or so to the south of Lakeside, has undergone extensive refurbishment to get it up to four-star standard. Stay and you get superior rooms (including king-sized beds, modem points and a sitting room in the executive suites) and comforts (indoor pool, hot tub and sauna). Meals are available in the restaurant or brasserie, or just come for a drink in the traditional bar, where you can take advantage of the riverside tables by the handsome five-arched bridge. Two-night minimum stay at weekends. Parking. ⑧

White Hart Bouth, off A590, 1.5 miles northeast of Haverthwaite ☎01229/861229, ⓦwww.whitehartbouth.co.uk. It's a short winding drive off the A590 to this seventeenth-century country inn, non-smoking throughout, with upgraded rooms in the eaves that retain their oak beams and idiosyncratic proportions. Locals know the pub for its food and real ales, both good. Parking. ④

Fell Foot Park and the Winster and Lyth valleys

Fell Foot Park, on Windermere's southeastern reach (daily 9am–5pm or dusk; free, though parking-fee charged; NT; ☎015395/31273), makes a relaxed picnic spot, where you can lounge on the Victorian landscaped lawns and explore the rhododendron gardens and oak and pine plantations. There was once a private mansion here, to go with the grounds, though that's long gone. But the mock-Gothic boathouse still stands and offers rowboat rental, while doubling as a rather superior **tearoom** (closed from Nov until Easter) – from the tables outside you can watch the Lakeside and Haverthwaite trains chuff into the station just across the lake. Windermere Lake Cruises run **launches** across to the park from Lakeside (Easter–Oct daily 11am–5pm; £1 each way), usually every twenty minutes depending on demand and the weather. By car, access is from the A592 (Bowness road), a mile north of Newby Bridge; bus #618, from Ulverston and Newby Bridge to Bowness, passes close by.

An ancient packhorse route from Newby Bridge to Kendal, now a steep and winding minor road, passes to the northeast behind Fell Foot. A mile up, there's free parking by the start of the footpath to **Gummer's How**, the gorse-topped fell which peers over the southern half of Windermere. It's an easy walk up to the little stone trig point on the summit – it'll take an hour there and back, including a rest at the top to gaze down at the Fell Foot marina and the snaking River Leven.

Two miles further along the road, at the brow of a hill at **Strawberry Bank**, the *Mason's Arms* (see below) is impeccably sited overlooking the low stony outcrops and tidy plantations of the **Winster Valley**. The pub's terrace is a great place for a beer – there are two hundred on offer, from all corners of the globe, including a damson beer made on the premises – and the food is especially good too. Arthur Ransome moved to the Winster Valley in 1925 and it was here that he wrote *Swallows and Amazons*. His house, known as **Low Ludderburn** (not open to the public), can be seen if you take the tortuous bracken- and bramble-lined road north from the pub for a couple of miles. To the south, exactly a mile from the *Mason's Arms* (follow the signposts), **St Anthony's Church** lies tucked into a hollow on the side of Cartmel Fell. The church dates from 1504 – it was built as an isolated, outlying chapel of Cartmel priory – and despite some brutal modern exterior cladding preserves a characterful seventeenth-century interior: exposed rafters, a triple-decker pulpit and twin "box" pews once reserved for the local gentry.

From Strawberry Bank, the road drops a mile to **Bowland Bridge**, where the *Hare & Hounds* – right by the bridge – is a nice old inn with a sheltered beer garden. Beyond Bowland Bridge, a minor road makes its way north along the upper Winster Valley, before joining the A5074 which runs to Bowness. Where the roads meet there's a sign pointing you northeast towards the tiny village of **Crosthwaite**, whose parish church and adjacent seventeenth-century *Punch Bowl Inn* (see below) nestle in the gentle **Lyth Valley**. Lyth Valley damsons are a staple of the local early summer fruit crop, used in these parts in desserts and preserves (and to flavour beer and gin) – they are a relic of Lakeland's former textile industry, when the fruit was used to make cloth dyes.

Accommodation and food

Mason's Arms Strawberry Bank, Cartmel Fell ☎015395/68486, ⊛www .masonsarmsstrawberrybank.co.uk. The renowned country inn has tables in the stone-flagged bar as well as a contemporary upstairs dining room – meals range from beef braised in local beer to seared tuna, and desserts include Cartmel's famous sticky toffee pudding and English Lakes ice cream. There's also accommodation in two decidedly chic cottages (which sleep 4/6) and three two-person suites, all available by the night – prices vary considerably, but all offer good discounts from November until February. Parking. Suites ❹–❻, cottages ❻–❼

Punch Bowl Inn Crosthwaite, next to St Mary's Church ☎015395/68237, ⊛www .the-punchbowl.co.uk. Owned by Hawkshead's Drunken Duck people, and given a similarly stylish makeover, the Punch Bowl's nine earth-toned rooms feature exposed beams, flat-screen TVs, clunky retro bedside radios, and superb bathrooms with stand-alone clawfoot bathtubs and quite possibly the largest bath towels in Britain. The excellent food is Modern British without being pretentious (meals around £30, plus drinks) and you can eat either in the bar (first come, first served) or book for the restaurant (it's the same menu). There's also a ploughman's and sandwich lunch menu served daily. Beer is courtesy of the Drunken Duck's Barngates Brewery and there's a well-judged wine list, with many available by the glass. Room rates vary (and weekends are more expensive), but all include a superb breakfast and afternoon tea. Parking. ❼–❽

Ambleside

AMBLESIDE, five miles northwest of Windermere, at the head of the lake, lies at the hub of the central and southern Lakes region. It's a popular, if commercial, base for walkers and tourers, but has lost most of its traditional market-town attributes. The original market square and associated buildings were swept away in a typically vigorous piece of Victorian redevelopment (though the market cross still stands) and today's thriving centre – more a retail experience than a lakeland town – consists of a cluster of grey-green stone houses, shops, pubs and

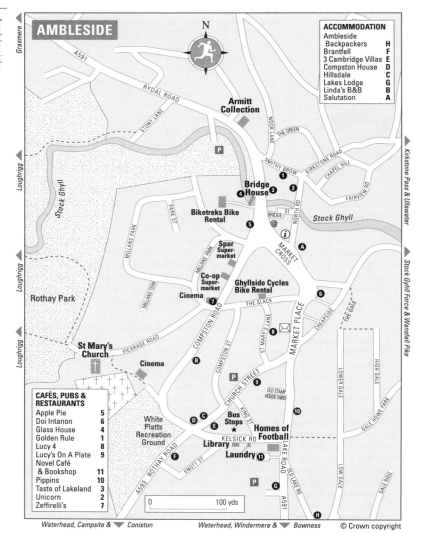

AMBLESIDE

N

Grasmere

Loughrigg

Loughrigg

Loughrigg

Kirkstone Pass & Ullswater

Stock Ghyll Force & Wansfell Pike

ACCOMMODATION

Ambleside	
Backpackers	H
Brantfell	F
3 Cambridge Villas	E
Compston House	D
Hillsdale	C
Lakes Lodge	G
Linda's B&B	B
Salutation	A

Armitt Collection

Bridge House

Biketreks Bike Rental

Spar Supermarket

Co-op Supermarket

Ghyllside Cycles Bike Rental

Cinema

St Mary's Church

Cinema

Rothay Park

Stock Ghyll

MARKET CROSS

MARKET PLACE

White Platts Recreation Ground

Bus Stops

Homes of Football

Library

Laundry

Old Stamp House Yard

CAFÉS, PUBS & RESTAURANTS

Apple Pie	5
Doi Intanon	6
Glass House	4
Golden Rule	1
Lucy 4	8
Lucy's On A Plate	9
Novel Café & Bookshop	11
Pippins	10
Taste of Lakeland	3
Unicorn	2
Zeffirelli's	7

0   100 yds

RYDAL ROAD
A591
STONY LANE
MILLANS PARK
PARK ST
MILLANS PARK
MILLANS TERR
VICARAGE ROAD
COMPSTON ROAD
THE SLACK
COMPSTON ST
ST MARY'S LANE
CHURCH STREET
KING ST
KELSICK RD
KNOTT ST
ROTHAY ROAD
A593
A591
LAKE ROAD
OLD LAKE RD
CHEAPSIDE
THE GALE
LOWER GALE
HIGH GALE
GALE HOW PARK
LOW GALE
GALE RIGG
THE GREEN
NOOK LANE
SMITHY BROW
KIRKSTONE ROAD
CHAPEL HILL
FAIRVIEW RD
NORTH RD
BRIDGE ST

Waterhead, Campsite & ▼ Coniston   Waterhead, Windermere & ▼ Bowness   © Crown copyright

B&Bs hugging a circular one-way system, which loops round just south of the narrow gully of Stock Ghyll.

The Town

Stock Ghyll once powered Ambleside's fulling and bobbin mills, whose buildings survive intact on either side of Bridge Street, as do a couple of restored

Harriet Martineau in the Lakes

Harriet Martineau, a delicate child and hard of hearing, was born into a Nonconformist East Anglian manufacturing family in 1802. Left penniless by the death of her father in 1826, Harriet began to earn a living by writing, contributing to the Unitarian periodical, *Monthly Repository*, and publishing a gospel history of Palestine, *Traditions of Palestine* (1829), which was well received.

Her forte, though, was the moral and devotional tale, which she called "Illustrations" of current political and economic theory. Martineau produced these on a monthly basis between 1832 and 1834 – and, much to the surprise of her publisher, who expected little from the unknown author, they made her famous overnight. The "Illustrations" were based on her own research and a close reading of the political economists of the day; through these tales, Martineau addressed such weighty matters as slavery, the Poor Laws, taxation, education and emigration. She travelled widely (with ear trumpet in tow), when it was not easy for a woman of her background to do so, and produced two successful books on America – *Society In America* (1837), lauded by Charles Dickens, and *A Retrospect of Western Travel* (1838). But, never fully well, she collapsed on a visit to Venice in 1839 and remained prone and weak for five years. Often dismissed as an "hysteric", like many Victorian women, Martineau had in fact suffered a prolapse of the uterus, which seriously curtailed her work and travel.

She ascribed an eventual improvement in her health to the powers of mesmerism, a popular "alternative medicine" of the 1840s. Convinced she had been cured – and even appointing a mesmerist, a Mrs Montagu Wynyard, to become part of her household – Martineau was later well enough to tour the Middle East and, on her return, visit the Lake District, where she decided to settle. She ordered the building of a house, The Knoll, in Ambleside, where she was to live for the rest of her life.

Literary England was welcome at The Knoll. Mrs Gaskell and Charlotte Brontë both visited; Matthew Arnold, the future poet, spent his school holidays up the road at his father's house, Fox How. Never an orthodox woman, Martineau cut a notable figure in lakeland society. Smoking a pipe or a cigar, she tramped around the fells in men's boots, picking plants for her garden, much to the amusement of the locals. It was said she bathed in the lake by moonlight; certainly she mixed with the lower orders (lecturing in Ambleside to a working-class audience in the Methodist Chapel) and harried local officials and churchmen. All this, of course, put her at odds with the conservative Wordsworths – with William, she would argue ferociously, while Mary Wordsworth couldn't stand being in Martineau's company and left Rydal Mount every time she came to call. Was there a subconscious prejudice, too? Martineau never married – an early engagement to a cleric was ended by his untimely death – and critics have suggested a latent homosexuality evident in her work and life. Martineau continued to write at The Knoll – her *Complete Guide to the English Lakes* (1855) followed the example of Wordsworth – with later works reflecting her loss of faith and turn to humanism. *Letters on the Nature and Development of Man* (1851) brought her harsh reviews by those who now thought her an atheist (including her own brother). Her health continued to worry her as she suffered from periodic bouts of illness, and after 1855 Martineau rarely left her house. By 1866, poor health had made work impossible and she was taking opium to relieve the pain of an ovarian cyst. She died at The Knoll in 1876 and was buried in Birmingham with members of her family.

waterwheels. Straddling Stock Ghyll is the town's favourite building, tiny **Bridge House**, originally built as a covered bridge-cum-summerhouse and used by a local family to access their orchards across the stream. It's had many other uses over the years, mainly for storage, though records show that in the nineteenth century it was briefly home to a family of eight.

For more on Ambleside's history, stroll for a couple of minutes along Rydal Road to the **Armitt Collection** (daily 10am–5pm; £2.50; ☎015394/31212, ⓦ www.armitt.com), the latest and most splendid incarnation of the town's literary museum and library. First founded in 1909 (by local society

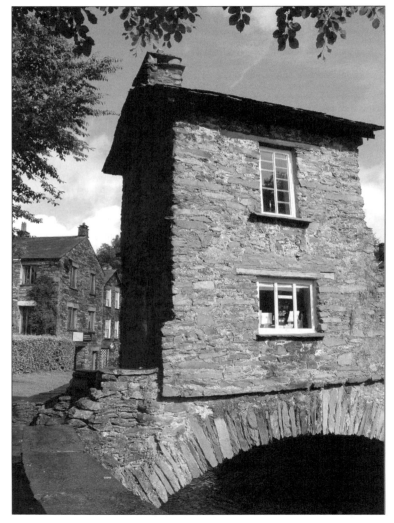

△ Bridge House, Ambleside

intellectual Mary Louisa Armitt), the collection catalogues the very distinct contribution to lakeland society made by writers and artists from John Ruskin to Beatrix Potter: others, like the writer Harriet Martineau (author of her own *Guide to the Lakes*; see box on p.71) and educationalist Charlotte Mason, made their home in the town, and the museum contains cases full of personal memorabilia – from a life-mask of Martineau to a lock of Ruskin's hair. There's plenty, too, on the remarkable Collingwood family (see p.121), plus displays related to the life and work of Herbert Bell (1856–1946), pharmacist of Ambleside turned pioneering lakeland photographer. And anyone driven to distraction by the bunny-and-hedgehog side of Beatrix Potter should be prepared to revise their opinion on viewing the changing selection of her early scientific watercolour studies of fungi and mosses – a beautifully painted sequence donated by Potter herself.

The old **market cross** still marks the centre of town, a reminder that – before the coming of the train and the growth of Windermere – Ambleside was the major commercial and business centre in this part of the Lakes. It was to here, for instance, that William Wordsworth had to travel from his house at Rydal Mount when on official duty as the **Distributor of Stamps for Westmorland** (a job he acquired in 1813). A plaque on a building at the top of **Church Street** marks the site of the office he once used. Further down, at the southern end of town, off Compston Road, you reach **St Mary's Church**, whose rocket-shaped spire is visible from all over town. Completed in 1854, it was designed by George Gilbert Scott – the architect responsible for London's Albert Memorial and St Pancras Station – and contains a mural of the town's annual rushbearing ceremony, its figures resplendent in their 1940s finery. The ceremony itself dates from medieval times and derives from the custom of replacing the worn rushes (or reeds) on unflagged church floors. In Ambleside, the event takes places on a Saturday in the first two weeks of July, with a procession through town of decorated rushes and the church congregation singing the specially commissioned Ambleside Rushbearers' Hymn. Behind the church, the green pastures of **Rothay Park** stretch down to the River Rothay, while above loom the heights of **Loughrigg Fell** (1101ft), with the climb to the summit signposted from near the humpbacked bridge at the foot of Rothay Park (and see also p.94).

Final port of call is soccer photographer Stuart Clarke's terrific gallery, **The Homes of Football**, 100 Lake Rd (Wed–Sun 10am–5pm; free, though charge for special exhibitions; ☎015394/34440, ⓦwww.homesoffootball.co.uk). What started as a peripatetic exhibition, recording games and grounds from the Premier League down to the smallest amateur teams, has blossomed into a huge permanent archive based on visits to over 3600 stadiums and matches – there's a massive selection of images on show here, all framed and available for sale, while changing exhibitions of football and non-football photography occupy the lower gallery. It's irresistible for fans, who just might be persuaded to part with £250–350 for a unique memento of their team – or rather less for a football-ground postcard.

Waterhead

The rest of town lies a mile south at **Waterhead**, a harbour on the shores of Windermere that's filled with ducks, swans and rowboats and overlooked by the grass banks and spreading trees of **Borrans Park**. Waterhead was the earliest settled part of Ambleside, known as Galava to the Romans, who built a turf-and-timber fort on the lake edge in 90 AD, later superseded by a larger stone

Walks from Ambleside

Ambleside is impressively framed – Loughrigg Fell to the west, the distinctive line of the Fairfield Horseshoe to the north and Wansfell to the east – and even inexperienced walkers have plenty of choice.

Stock Ghyll

The traditional stroll is up Stock Ghyll Lane (which starts behind the *Salutation Hotel*) and through the leafy woods of Stock Ghyll Park (with wonderful daffs in spring) to the tumbling waterfall of **Stock Ghyll Force**, which drops 60ft through a narrow defile. Allow an hour there and back if you linger on the viewing platform and rest on the benches.

Wansfell

Those with loftier ambitions can regain the lane by Stock Ghyll Park and, a little way further up, look for the signposted path (over a wall-ladder) up Wansfell to **Wansfell Pike** (1581ft) – an hour all told to the top, from where there are superb views of Windermere and the surrounding fells. Circular hikers either cut due south from the summit to Skelghyll and return via Jenkins Crag (2hr), or head east across a clearly defined path to Troutbeck and Townend before cutting back (4hr).

Jenkins Crag and Stagshaw Gardens

The viewpoint of **Jenkins Crag**, a mile from Waterhead, gives a glimpse of the lake as well as the central peaks of the Langdales and the Old Man of Coniston – *Country Life* magazine once reckoned this was Britain's most romantic picnic spot. From Ambleside, walk down Lake Road (though there's a handy car park near Hayes Garden World) and follow the signs up Skelghyll Lane, a thirty-minute walk. On the way back you can detour to the National Trust's woodland **Stagshaw Gardens** (Easter–June daily 10am–6.30pm; £2), at its best in spring for the shows of rhododendrons, camellias and azaleas.

Fairfield Horseshoe

The classic hiker's circuit from Ambleside is the **Fairfield Horseshoe** (11 miles; 6hr), which starts just out of town, off Kirkstone Road, and climbs up via High Sweden Bridge and **Dove Crag** (2603ft) to the flat top of **Fairfield** itself (2864ft), before dropping back along the opposing ridge to Nab Scar and Rydal, outside Grasmere. From Rydal, you can avoid most of the road back to Ambleside by following the footpath through the grounds of Rydal Hall. This really is a superb walk on a clear day, not too difficult yet encompassing eight different peaks.

See Basics, p.35, for general walking advice in the Lakes; recommended maps are detailed on p.42.

structure housing five hundred auxiliary soldiers, which was finally abandoned at the end of the fourth century. The Roman scholar Robin Collingwood first excavated the two forts in separate digs between 1913 and 1920 (the Armitt Collection holds many of the objects recovered), though there's little left to see *in situ* as the foundations of various buildings, including a large granary with hypocaust, are now largely grass-covered. But it's an emotive spot, backed by glowering fells and with views across the rippling Windermere waters – the perfect place for sunset-watching or star-gazing. Two or three little cafés by the piers have outdoor seats, while the lawns of the *Wateredge Inn* and *Waterhead* hotel also offer lovely views.

Practicalities

Buses (including National Express) all stop on Kelsick Road, opposite the library, with regular local services to and from Windermere, Grasmere and Keswick, plus services to Hawkshead and Coniston (#505), and Elterwater and Langdale (#516). Walking up to town from the **ferry piers** at Waterhead takes about fifteen minutes, though an electric **shuttle bus** service operates from the piers to the *White Lion* pub in the town centre (weather- and ferry-dependent, but usually daily Easter–Oct, weekends only Nov–Easter, 10.30am–5pm, roughly every 30min; £1.50). The A591 runs right through town and drivers are best advised to make straight for the signposted **car parks**, though be warned that these fill quickly in summer – you may not find a space on your first pass through. The main **tourist office** is in the centre of town in the Central Buildings on Market Cross (daily 9am–5pm; ☎015394/32582, ⊛ www.lakelandgate way.info). For **online information**, consult ⊛ www.amblesideonline.co.uk, a useful community website for the Ambleside area.

Accommodation

The town is busy year-round so advance reservations are recommended, wherever you plan to stay. Lake Road, running between Waterhead and Ambleside, is lined with **B&Bs**, and there are other concentrations on Church Street and Compston Road, as well as a **backpackers** just on the edge of town – all these are marked on the main Ambleside map. Fancier places tend to lie out of town, or a mile to the south at Waterhead by the lake (see Around Ambleside: Waterhead map), which is also where you'll find Ambleside's official **youth hostel**. This is one of the most popular in the country – advance reservations are essential during most of the year. The nearest **campsite** is three miles south, by the lake though too far out without your own transport to be used as a base for Ambleside itself.

AROUND AMBLESIDE:
WATERHEAD

Grasmere ▲   Rydal ▲   Grasmere ▲   Kirkstone Pass & Ullswater ▲

Rothay Park

Riverside

River Rothay

AMBLESIDE

LOUGHRIGG FELL

Elterwater & Coniston

A593

A591

Fishgarth's Wood

Rothay Bridge
Rothay Manor

A5075

N

River Brathay

Brathay Bridge

Galava Roman Fort

WATERHEAD

B5286

CLAPPERSGATE

Borrans Park

Wateredge Inn

Waterhead

Jetties

Ambleside YHA

0   500 yds

Windermere

© Crown copyright

Wray Castle, Campsite,
Dower House B & B, ▼ Hawkshead & Hill Top   Brockhole & Bowness ▼   ▼ Bowness

In Ambleside

Brantfell Rothay Rd ☎015394/32239, ⓦwww
.brantfell.co.uk. A Victorian house with a friendly
welcome, overlooking the recreation grounds and
encroaching fells on the edge of town. Seven
rooms are available, including a particularly large
one with a four-poster and views, and one single
room. There's a big choice at breakfast – traditional
or continental or things like smoked salmon, hash
browns, pancakes and kippers – while guests get
use of the lounge (with winter log fire) and free
entry to the pool at a local leisure club. Also
wireless Internet access. Parking. ❹

3 Cambridge Villas Church St ☎015394/32307,
ⓦwww.3cambridgevillas.co.uk. One of the best-
value places in town, with very reasonable prices
for its spick-and-span rooms. There are seven –
five of them en suite, two with private bathroom.
No American Express. ❸

Compston House Compston Rd
☎015394/32305, ⓦwww.compstonhouse
.co.uk. Inside this traditional lakeland house the
owners, Sue and Jerry from New York, have
cleverly created one of the Lakes' most individual
B&Bs – hung with iconic American prints, the lovely
light rooms are themed after various US states and
feature Egyptian cotton bed linen and snazzy small
bathrooms. There are also pancakes and maple
syrup for breakfast, alongside the traditional fry-up.
A free parking permit is provided. No smoking. No
American Express. ❹

Hillsdale Church St ☎015394/33174, ⓦwww
.hillsdaleambleside.co.uk. What a refreshing change
– instead of chintz, woodchip and UHT milk pots
you get modern colours, stylish light fittings, flat-
screen TVs and mini-fridges for fresh milk (room 7
has a thoroughly modern shower-room too). Guests
get passes for Low Wood leisure club, and there's a
sunny breakfast room and limited off-road parking.
No smoking. No American Express. ❹

Lakes Lodge Lake Rd ☎015394/33240, ⓦwww
.lakeslodge.co.uk. The lakeland slate exterior is no
preparation for the changes wrought inside, where
a bold lilac/lavender colour scheme announces
contemporary intent. A dozen spacious rooms have
been stylishly kitted out (room 10 has a glass sink,
and DVD players are standard) and bathrooms
upgraded, with those at the back sporting views
over Loughrigg. A good buffet breakfast (smoked
fish, local ham) is served in the informal café-style
breakfast room, wine and beer are available, and
you can have dinner or use the pool at Waterhead's
Regent Hotel. Two-night minimum stay at
weekends. Parking. No American Express. ❻

Linda's B&B Compston Rd ☎015394/32999. The
cheery spirit never flags and the bargain prices – the
lowest in Ambleside – go a long way to compensat-
ing for the simple facilities. Guests can use the
kitchen, while two of the four rooms (all of which
share a bathroom and a top-floor shower-room) can
sleep three or four. A room-only stay brings the price
down to as little as £13 a night. No credit cards. ❷

Salutation Lake Rd ☎015394/32244, ⓦwww
.hotelslakedistrict.com. There's not much of its
seventeenth-century origins left, but you couldn't
be much more central. Rooms are pretty compact,
though some "club rooms" (supplement payable)
have balconies and spa baths, and there's a sauna,
steam room and Jacuzzi on site and free use of the
pool in Grasmere's Red Lion. Rates drop a bit in
winter, while single Saturday-night stays attract a
surcharge. Parking. ❼

Around Ambleside

Dower House Wray Castle, off B5286 (Hawkshead
road), 3 miles south of Ambleside
☎015394/33211. It's very peaceful, the view at
breakfast could hardly be better – across the lake
to the fells – and the house (an estate house of
Wray Castle, which stands virtually next door) has
direct access to the Windermere shoreline. There
are four traditionally furnished rooms, including one
spacious single, all named after the fells they
overlook – aching hikers should ask for "Fairfield",
the only one with a bath (rather than shower).
Packed lunches (£4) and dinner (£16.50 – BYO
wine) are available, and you can get your walking
gear dried. Also a self-catering cottage available.
Parking. No credit cards. ❶

Riverside Under Loughrigg
☎015394/32395, ⓦwww.riverside
-at-ambleside.co.uk. Charming Victorian house on
a quiet lane facing the River Rothay, half a mile
(10min walk) from town – on foot, take any path
across the park, cross the bridge and turn left. Six
large, light country-pine-style rooms available (a
couple with whirlpool baths), including a river-
facing four-poster room and a family room
(minimum age 5) with bunks and a terrific
bathroom. Sit outside on the garden deck and plan
your day's walking with the library of guides, and
then build yourself up with the magnificent breakfast (including home-made preserves, bread, potato
cakes and fruit smoothies). Also a tasteful two-
bedroom apartment with kitchen-diner at the same
address (ⓦwww.gilbertscarfoot.co.uk; sleeps 4;
£390–680 per week). No smoking. Parking. No
American Express. ❺

Rothay Manor Rothay Bridge ☎015394/33605,
ⓦwww.rothaymanor.co.uk. This Regency-style
mansion, half a mile southwest of the centre, has
been run by the same family for four decades,

offering larger-than-average rooms (including decent-sized beds and spacious bathrooms, with baths), stylish decor, appealing grounds and good food served in a candlelit dining room. The most sought-after "superior" rooms at the front have their own private balcony, while three suites (up to £270) in the grounds provide more space for families. Guests have free use of a nearby leisure centre with pool. Parking. No single Saturday-night stays. ⑧, including dinner ⑨

Wateredge Inn Waterhead ☎015394/32332, ⓌwWww.wateredgeinn.co.uk. Lakeside inn with rooms either in the main hotel or garden-suites with balcony or patio. There's free use of the pool and sauna at a nearby leisure club, and a good-value brasserie-style menu in the waterside bar and restaurant – the terrace and grassy beer garden (open to non-residents) is a very popular place for lunch, dinner or just a drink, especially with families who can let children run free. Parking. ⑦

🏃 **Waterhead** Waterhead ☎015394/32566, ⓌWww.elh.co.uk. Designer town house-style accommodation provides the Lake District's classiest four-star lodgings. White high-ceilinged rooms feature sharp contemporary fabrics and furnishings, with no detail left unattended – king-sized beds with suede headboards, massive flatscreen TVs, monogrammed cups for morning tea and a champagne menu in the sparkling slate-and-marble bathrooms. It's very close to the lake, opposite the Waterhead piers, with a swanky garden-bar (open for lunch and drinks) and positively metropolitan restaurant (dinner from £30), both open to non-residents. Guests can use the pool at the nearby Low Wood leisure club. Parking. ⑧

Youth hostels

Ambleside Backpackers Old Lake Rd ☎015394/32340, ⓌwWww.englishlakesbackpackers .co.uk. This extended lakeland cottage, a 5min walk from town, has 72 beds in four- to twelve-bed single-sex dorms. There's not much space in the dorms themselves, though they do have lockers and washbasins and there's a fully equipped kitchen, dining room and lounge with video and Internet facilities – a cereal, tea and toast breakfast is included in the price, and there's parking outside. Dorm beds from £15, long-stay discounts available.

🏃 **Ambleside YHA** Waterhead, A591, 1 mile south of Ambleside ☎0870/770 5672, ⒺAmbleside@yha.org.uk. See "Around Ambleside: Waterhead" map for location. Impressive lakeside hostel with almost 250 beds divided amongst neatly furnished small dorms, twins, doubles and family rooms. A very good breakfast is included and facilities are first-rate – licensed bar and restaurant (with Fair Trade coffee), bike rental, Internet access, laundry, drying room and private jetty with adjacent water-sports centre. There's parking outside. Dorm beds from £20, double rooms ③

Campsite

Low Wray Campsite Low Wray, off B5286, 3 miles south of Ambleside ☎015394/32810. See chapter map for location. National Trust site on the western shore of the lake, where there's a small shop and canoe and bike rental; bus #505 (to Coniston) passes within a mile and from the stop it's a nice walk down a country lane. No advance reservations – it's first come, first served (so in summer, call ahead to check availability). Closed Nov–Easter.

Eating, drinking and entertainment

There's more choice in Ambleside for eating than just about anywhere else in the Lakes, from **cafés** and takeaways to gourmet **restaurants**, which is one of the reasons the town makes such a good base. Be warned, though, that prices in many are on the high side for what you get, while reservations for the better places are a good idea in the school holidays. **Pubs** are plentiful, too, a couple showing real character, though the nicest *al fresco* drinking is done down at Waterhead's *Wateredge Inn*. The two small local **supermarkets**, Spar and Co-op, are both on Compston Road. Zeffirelli's **cinema** (☎015394/33845, ⓌwWww .zeffirellis.com) has four screens at two locations in town, while for details of Ambleside's famous annual **festivals** – the Rushbearing and Ambleside Sports – see p.33 and p.34 respectively.

Cafés and restaurants

🏃 **Apple Pie** Rydal Rd ☎015394/33679. There's an internal patio-garden at the best café and bakery in town – breakfast is served until 11am (with free tea/coffee refills), or else choose

from things like BLTs, baked potatoes, soup or quiche. The trademark home-made pies come savoury (say, broccoli and stilton or sausage and cider) or sweet, with the Bramley apple variety laced with cinnamon and raisin. Daytime only. Inexpensive.

Doi Intanon Market Place ☎015394/32119. Ambleside's Thai restaurant makes a welcome change, with a standard stir-fry and curry menu bolstered by specials such as a fiery vegetable jungle curry or a grilled chicken appetizer wrapped in papyrus. And if you'll only eat where Hollywood royalty hang out, you'll be delighted to know that Renée Zellweger and co had their wrap party here after filming the Beatrix Potter movie, *Miss Potter*. Dinner only; closed Sun. Moderate.

Glass House Rydal Rd ☎015394/32137, �🌐www .theglasshouserestaurant.co.uk. After a ferocious TV wigging some years back from Gordon Ramsay, the Glass House has found its form again. It's a handsome place, housed in a renovated fulling mill with waterwheel and sunny courtyard, and the Modern British food (Caesar salad to braised Herdwick lamb) is nicely presented. Prices are fair, especially for the light lunch selection or early dinner menu (before 7.30pm, not Sat). Expensive.

Lucy 4 2 St Mary's Lane ☎015394/34666, �🌐www.lucy4.co.uk. Good-time wine bar and bistro offshoot of Lucy's On A Plate, with a pan-European mix-and-match menu (you're encouraged to share) and some very decent wines by the glass. There's no need to eat – in fact, there's a great chill-out bar upstairs playing smooth tunes as well as a heated outdoor deck. Dinner only (from 5pm). Moderate.

🏃 **Lucy's On A Plate** Church St ☎015394/31191, �🌐www .lucysofambleside.co.uk. Hugely enjoyable stripped-pine bistro offering a wide and inventive array of dishes – if they know you're coming, you'll probably find yourself namechecked in the chatty menu preamble. It's open from 10am as a café, with lunch largely Mediterranean in inspiration; dinner roams the globe, but sources lots of its materials locally (try the char when it's on, or the Cumbrian lamb or Grizedale venison). There's also a really good deli and specialist grocer's next door. Reservations pretty much essential. Expensive.

Pippins 10 Lake Rd ☎015394/31338, ⓦwww .pippinscafebar.co.uk. An easy-going, updated English café, serving everything from a full

breakfast to a steak dinner with a glass of fizz. Other day and night-time eats are pizzas, pastas, salads and burgers – and there's a full bar. It's open from 8.30am until late, with main meals served from noon. Moderate.

Taste of Lakeland 1 & 2 Rydal Rd ☎015394/32636. The shop sells all manner of lakeland produce – organic cheese, smoked meats from Brougham Hall, Penrith toffee, Hawkshead relishes, fell-bred lamb – while the tearoom dishes out home-made scones, sandwiches, coffee and cakes to hikers and passers-by. Daytime only. Inexpensive.

🏃 **Zeffirelli's** Compston Rd ☎015394/33845. Zeff's is a star – famous for its wholemeal-base pizzas, but also serving a full roster of Italian-with-a-twist starters, pastas and salads, all vegetarian. The funky downstairs dining room and conservatory is open from 10am for coffee, home-made cakes and light meals; dinner is from 6pm and evening reservations are advised. You'll also need to book in advance for the popular dinner-and-cinema special (£15.95), or just head upstairs to the bar (see below). Moderate.

Pubs and bars

Golden Rule Smithy Brow ☎015394/33363. The long-standing beer-lovers' and climbers' favourite – this is a cosy place for a post-hike pint (six real ales usually available) and a read of the Wainwright, with no jukebox, pool table, meals or other distractions. A bit of a patio catches the summer sun.

Unicorn North Rd ☎015394/33216. An enjoyable old backstreet inn with hearty bar meals, a selection of real ales and live music nights.

Zeffirelli's Café-Bar ☎015394/33845, ⓦwww .zeffirellis.com. The shiny black fashionable space above Zeffirelli's restaurant is a contemporary jazz bar, with live music at least a couple of nights a week (Saturday night is usually free). You'll catch anything from a local trio to an international act – see the website for advance schedules – and you can eat here too, from a shorter version of the restaurant menu.

Listings

Banks and exchange NatWest (Cheapside), Barclays and HSBC (both Market Place) have ATMs. You can also change travellers' cheques at the post office (see opposite).

Bike rental Biketreks, Rydal Rd (daily 9.30am–5pm; ☎015394/31245, ⓦwww.biketreks.net) – you get cycle maps for day rides included in the price. Also Ghyllside Cycles, The Slack (Easter–Oct

daily 9.30am–5.30pm; Nov–Easter closed Wed; ☎015394/33592, ⓦwww.ghyllside.co.uk).

Bookshop Don't miss Novel Café in the Artists' Courtyard, 101 Lake Rd (daily 11am–5pm; ☎015394/34096), which only stocks fiction. Browsing and lingering are positively encouraged, there's coffee, cakes and Internet access, and a couple more gallery/craft shops in the yard outside.

Emergencies Doctors at Ambleside Health Centre, Rydal Rd ☎015394/32693, ⓦwww .amblesidehealthcentre.co.uk. The nearest hospital is in Kendal (Westmorland General Hospital, Burton Rd; ☎01539/732288).

Internet access Ambleside Library, Kelsick Rd (Mon & Wed 10am–5pm, Tues & Fri 10am–7pm, Sat 10am–1pm; ☎015394/32507), has the most terminals, but there's also access at outdoor adventure company Adventure Peaks, Central Buildings, Market Cross (☎015394/33794), and at the Novel Café (see "Bookshop" opposite).

Laundry Ambleside Laundry Services, Kelsick Rd (varied hours; ☎015394/32231), does service washes.

Outdoors stores Ambleside is a good place to pick up walking and climbing gear and camping equipment at reasonable prices. For mountain boots there's F.W. Tyson (Market Place) as well as The Climber's Shop (Compston Corner; walking-boot rental available) and Stewart R. Cunningham (Rydal Rd), while large retailers include Black's (Compston Rd) and Gaynor Sports (Market Cross), the latter the country's biggest outdoors store.

Pharmacy Thomas Bell, Lake Rd ☎015394/33345; Boots, 8–9 Market Cross ☎015394/33355.

Post office Market Place (Mon–Fri 9am–5.30pm, Sat 9am–12.30pm).

Taxis Abacus ☎015394/88285; Brown's Taxis ☎015394/33263; John's Taxis ☎015394/32857; Kevin's Taxis ☎015394/32371.

Troutbeck

Troutbeck Bridge, three miles southeast of Ambleside along the A591 (and just a mile or so from Windermere town), heralds the start of the gentle **Troutbeck valley** below Wansfell, accessed by two roads, one either side of the valley's namesake beck. The main A592 to Patterdale runs north into the valley, passing the Lakeland Horticultural Society's splendid gardens at **Holehird** (daily dawn–dusk; free, though donation requested; ☎015394/46008), whose four acres encompass various different habitats, from rock and alpine gardens to rose gardens and shrubberies.

The better route, though, is up a minor road (Bridge Lane) running high above the west side of **Trout Beck** itself. A mile along here is the youth hostel (see p.80) and, under a mile further up the road, stands **Townend** (Easter–Oct Wed–Sun plus bank hols 1–5pm, last admission 4.30pm; £3.80; NT; ☎015394/32628), a seventeenth-century house, built in 1626 for George Browne, a wealthy yeoman farmer, one of that breed of independent farmers known in these parts as "statesmen", after the estates they tended. Remarkably, the house remained in the hands of eleven generations of the Browne family, for more than three hundred years, until 1943 when the National Trust took it over. It's an extraordinary relic of seventeenth-century vernacular architecture, with its round chimneys (of the sort admired by Wordsworth) surmounting a higgledy-piggledy collection of small rooms, some added as late as the nineteenth century. The house is well known for its woodcarvings and panelling, and lavishly embellished beds, fireplaces, chests, chairs and grandfather clocks are scattered around the various rooms. You'll also see the surviving laundry room (complete with mangle), dairy, library and parlour.

Townend is at the southern end of **TROUTBECK** village, really just a straggling hamlet with a post office (which sells cups of tea and ice cream). Several hikes pass through village and valley, with the peaks of Yoke (2309ft), Ill Bell (the highest at 2476ft) and Froswick (2359ft) on the east side forming the barrier between Troutbeck and Kentmere. The most direct route into Kentmere is the easy track over the **Garburn Pass**, while many use Trout-beck as the starting point for the five-hour walk along **High Street**, a nine-mile range running north to Brougham near Penrith. The course of a Roman road follows the ridge, probably once linking the forts at Brougham and Galava in Waterhead.

North of Troutbeck, the A592 makes a gradual ascent to **Kirkstone Pass**, four miles from the village, at the head of which there's a superbly sited pub, the *Kirkstone Pass Inn*, whose picnic tables (across the road) offer terrific views. A minor road from here cuts down directly to Ambleside – so precipitous that it's known as "The Struggle" – while the A592 continues over the pass and down the valley to Ullswater.

Practicalities

Public transport to Troutbeck is limited to bus #517 (Easter–Oct), which runs from Bowness piers and Windermere train station up the A592 and over Kirkstone Pass en route to Ullswater. It makes stops at the *Queen's Head* (see below) and the *Kirkstone Pass Inn*.

The most prominent places to stay in Troutbeck are the two traditional **inns**, the *Mortal Man* and the *Queen's Head*, at the north end of the village, both serving excellent food. As well as the superior B&B option listed below, there are also a couple of cheaper B&Bs in the village – local tourist offices should be able to check on space for you. Budget accommodation is at the valley's self-catering **youth hostel**, confusingly known as the *Windermere YHA* – a shuttle-bus service for hostellers operates from Windermere train station (meeting arriving trains) and from Ambleside youth hostel.

Inns and B&B

Fellside Studios Fellside ☎015394/34000, ⓦwww.fellsidestudios.co.uk. Two excellent studios available (one double, one twin), decorated in contemporary style, with oak floors, slate-tiled kitchens and shower-rooms, and attractive living/sleeping areas with TV/DVD players. A generous continental breakfast is brought to your door (cold meats, smoked-fish platter, cheese etc), and each studio has an outside dining terrace. The location is good too, only a 10–15min walk from either inn, with walks starting straight from the property. Two-night minimum stay at weekends, with a few pounds off for midweek, off-season or longer stays. No smoking. Parking. ❺

Mortal Man Bridge Lane ☎015394/33193, ⓦwww.themortalman.co.uk. A cosy spot with a dozen attractive rooms, lording it over the valley – wooden four-posters, hung with drapes, add a touch of romance to some rooms. For non-residents, coffee and biscuits or a meal is a great way to soak up the seventeenth-century surroundings, especially in the timeworn public bar. Or there's a more formal restaurant (D,B&B deals are available at a category higher than the B&B rate). The name, incidentally, derives from the doggerel written on the inn's sign: "O Mortal Man, that lives by bread, What is it makes thy nose so red? Thou silly fool, that look'st so pale, Tis drinking Sally Birkett's ale". Parking. Closed mid-Nov to mid-Feb. ❻

Queen's Head On the A592 ☎015394/32174, ⓦwww.queensheadhotel.com. An old coaching inn that oozes atmosphere, from the slate floors, oak beams and smoky fires to the carved bar fashioned from a four-poster bed. There are eleven rooms in the inn itself (the two largest, with great views, are nos. 10 and 11; the oldest, with an antique four-poster, no. 1) and four more, slightly smaller and cheaper, in the annexe. Dining is a treat, too, with everything from maple-cured pork to red-onion tarte tatin – it's £18.50 for three courses, or good-value inclusive D,B&B rates are available. Parking. Two-night minimum stay at weekends. ❼

Youth hostel

Windermere YHA High Cross, Bridge Lane ☎0870/770 6094, ⓔwindermere@yha.org.uk. Built originally as a private mansion, the house is now deprived of its turrets, ballroom and boating lake, though it still has magnificent lake views. Rooms are mostly four-bedded, though there is a twin and a triple room. Mountain bikes available for rent, and there's a kitchen and Internet access. An evening meal is served (note that the nearest pub is The Sun, three-quarters of a mile to the south on the A591 – the Troutbeck inns are a mile and a half away to the north). Dorm beds from £14, May–Sept £15, bank holiday weekends £16.50.

Staveley

Four miles east of Windermere, the little village of **STAVELEY** lies tucked away on the banks of the River Kent. The river has powered mills in Staveley for over seven hundred years, and in the eighteenth and nineteenth centuries there was prosperity of sorts as first cotton was produced and then wooden bobbins were manufactured here in sizeable quantities. These wood-turning skills have survived into modern times, with Staveley woodwork still a thing of beauty. **Peter Hall & Son** (Mon–Fri 9am–5pm, Sat 10am–1pm; ☎01539/821633, ⓦwww.peter-hall.co.uk), a mile out on the Windermere road, produces renowned handcrafted furniture and household goods, while other cottage industries occupy the old mill buildings themselves in **Mill Yard**, off Main Street. This is an ever-expanding collection of businesses, ranging from craft bakery to copper engravers, and with a cookery school (see p.39), plus café and bar (see listings p.82) it also makes a good stop for a meal or drink.

An easy half-hour stroll around the village starts by the restored tower of **St Margaret's** on Main Street, all that survives of Staveley's original fourteenth-century church. Follow the path at the side of the church tower down to the river, turn left and walk along the riverside path and road to the old bridge, from where you return through the village, passing the replacement nineteenth-century church of **St James** – inside which is a superb Burne-Jones-designed stained-glass window depicting a star-clustered heavenly choir surmounting the crucifixion.

Practicalities

Staveley is bypassed by the A591 – village visitors should follow the signs in to Mill Yard, where there's masses of free parking. You can also get here on the train line from Kendal or on the #555/556 bus, while walkers come past on the **Dales Way**, which follows the River Kent from Kendal, steers just south of the village and then cuts west across the low fells to Bowness. In fact, Staveley makes a good target for a day on the local fells. Free National Park-led **guided walks** start from *Wilf's Café* on spring and summer weekends. Otherwise, there's **bike rental** from Wheelbase in Mill Yard (☎01539/821443, ⓦwww.wheelbase .co.uk; open daily) – the bridleways and trails of Kentmere valley (see next section) are easily accessible from here, and the mountain bike centre has showers and changing rooms for cyclists.

Accommodation

Burrow Hall Plantation Bridge, A591, 1 mile south-east of Staveley ☎01539/821711, ⓦwww .burrowhall.co.uk. Seventeenth-century farmhouse on the main road (north side) that's been extended to provide four spacious country-style rooms with large bathrooms and rural views. It's very good value for the money, though you'll need a car to stay here. Parking. No American Express. ❸

Eagle & Child Kendal Rd ☎01539/821320, ⓦwww.eaglechildinn.co.uk. The village's nicest inn – right in the centre – has smallish, but tastefully decorated rooms, some overlooking the River Kent. There's a riverside garden, where you can sip a Cumbrian beer, and good, moderately priced food, including home-made soup, well-stuffed baguette

and ciabatta sandwiches, Kentmere lamb shanks or baked trout. Parking. ❹

Watermill Inn Ings (A591), 1.5 miles west of Staveley ☎01539/821309, ⓦwww.watermillinn .co.uk. A renowned real-ale pub with a huge choice of beers (there are sixteen on tap at any one time), a sun-trap garden and popular bar food. Eight non-smoking bedrooms are available, seven with showers, one with bath and balcony. The building was once an old bobbin mill, but has been imaginatively restored, with a bar fashioned from church pews and a beer-cellar viewing area – and there's now a craft brewery on-site, making ales for the pub. It's also the venue for tall tales once a month (first Tuesday) when the long-standing South Lakeland Storytelling Club meets. Parking. ❹

△ Wilf's Café, Staveley

Café

🏃 **Wilf's Café** Mill Yard ☎01539/822239, ⓦwww.wilfs-cafe.co.uk. Expansion has opened up the front of the building, but the heart of Wilf's was once the bobbin loft of an old wood mill – now there's dining on two floors and terraces out the back overlooking river and weir. The food is good value (nothing costs more than a fiver), hearty and mostly veggie – rarebits, chillis, filled baked potatoes, salads and home-made cakes and puddings are mainstays, though there's a black-board list of daily specials plus themed dinners held once a month. Daytime only. Inexpensive.

Bar

Hawkshead Brewery Beer Hall Mill Yard ☎01539/822644, ⓦwww.hawksheadbrewery.co.uk.

Handsome bar that's a showcase for the excellent beers of the independent Hawkshead Brewery. You can look down into the brew-house and taste before buying, or choose from other guest beers, organic juices, or wines by the glass – and as the bar connects with Wilf's (see above) you can take your drinks through to the café. Art exhibitions, DJ nights and live bands are all scheduled, and brewery tours are by appointment. Open daily from noon – call for closing times as they vary.

Campsite

Ashes Lane Ashes Lane, off the A591, 1 mile southeast of Staveley ☎01539/821119. Award-winning campsite between Kendal and Winder-mere; bus #555/556 can drop you off. Closed mid-Jan to mid-March.

Kentmere and Longsleddale

North of Staveley a narrow road runs its dappled way alongside the river, widening out after three miles into the splendid broad valley of **Kentmere**, with its isolated chapel perched on a bluff in the distance. Houses are few and far between, but the valley has been settled for over a thousand years – remains of a Viking-Age farmstead have been identified near the valley head. A later building, Kentmere Hall, a couple of hundred yards up the country lane from the chapel, retains a remarkably well-preserved fourteenth-century turreted pele tower, which you can see from the lane. The heather moorland further up the valley provides a habitat for ground-nesting birds like red grouse, curlew and merlin, while on the high fells, if you're lucky, you'll see wild ponies grazing.

Kentmere is at the junction of several strategic paths and bridleways and is a popular destination for walkers. On summer Sundays and bank holidays (end of May to mid-Sept) the #519 "Kentmere Rambler" **bus** from Staveley (with connections from Ambleside, Windermere and Kendal) is scheduled to allow an all-day hike. Otherwise, there's only extremely limited parking by the Kentmere Institute hall, behind the chapel, so on good days you'll need to get there early. Easy **routes** head west to Troutbeck and its pubs (via the relatively gentle Garburn Pass) or east to Sadgill and Longsleddale – you can make a six-mile circuit of the latter route by going one way via Green Quarter and Cocklaw Fell. A signposted route also runs up the valley bottom to **Kentmere Reservoir**, a little over two miles from the chapel, which is hemmed in by a ring of dramatic, steep-sided fells. These themselves are all incorporated into the excellent full-day hike known as the **Kentmere Horseshoe** (12 miles; 7hr), a fairly strenuous peak-bagging route along ridges and saddles high above Kentmere Reservoir that takes in Kentmere Pike, Harter Fell, Mardale Ill Bell, Froswick, Ill Bell and Yoke. At one point, crossing Nan Bield Pass, four bodies of water are in view (Haweswater, two tarns and the reservoir), and if you walk the circuit anticlockwise (most people don't) then you'll have magnificent views of Windermere and Morecambe Bay on the home stretch.

It's a fairly well-known fact that both Kentmere and **Longsleddale**, to the east, provide the rural environs that inspired the "Greendale" of John Cunliffe's *Postman Pat* stories. There's no lake in either valley, so Cunliffe used Grasmere as his model for "Berkmere". Longsleddale – pronounced "Longsleddle" incidentally – is less visited than Kentmere, due in part to its harsher upper reaches, and there's a similar parking shortage at graceful **Sadgill Bridge**, which is as far as you can go by car. Beyond here, hikers make their way up to the abandoned Wrengill Quarry and its waterfall and then along the old packhorse trail over Gatesgarth Pass to Haweswater.

Accommodation and food

Maggs Howe Lowfield Lane, Green Quarter, Kentmere ☎01539/821689. A half a mile or so east of the chapel (signposted from the bridge) there's either B&B in the house or a mattress on the floor in the bunkhouse next door (£9 per person), which has a couple of showers and a fully equipped kitchen; at weekends, the bunkhouse is for exclusive use by groups (£90 per night, sleeps up to 14). The nearest shop and pub is down in Staveley, but you can arrange to have a big cooked breakfast (£6) or an evening meal (from £12.50) at the B&B. No credit cards. ❸

Travel details

All timetables can be checked on Traveline ☎0870/608 2608; for Cross-Lakes Shuttle call ☎015394/45161.
Note: see "Windermere" for all stops on the main bus routes #555/556 and #559.

From Ambleside

Bus #505, "Coniston Rambler" to: Hawkshead (20min), Waterhead Hotel (Coniston Water) for Brantwood boat (30min) and Coniston (35min).

Service operates daily: Easter–Oct hourly; Nov–Easter every 1hr 30min–2hr.
Bus #516, "Langdale Rambler" (4–6 daily) to: Skelwith Bridge (10min), Elterwater (17min), Chapel Stile (20min) and Old Dungeon Ghyll (30min).

From Bowness

Bus #517, "Kirkstone Rambler" (3 daily) to: Windermere (8min), Troutbeck Queen's Head

(20min), Kirkstone Pass (30min), Brotherswater (45min), Patterdale (50min) and Glenridding (55min). Service operates daily from mid-July to early Sept, otherwise on Sat, Sun & bank hols from Easter to mid-July & Sept–Oct.

Bus #618 (4–5 daily) to: Newby Bridge (15min), Haverthwaite (18min) and Ulverston (30min); or to Windermere (7min), Troutbeck Bridge (11min), Brockhole (14min) and Ambleside (22min).

Cross-Lakes Shuttle (9 daily): launch from Bowness connects with #525 minibus from Ferry House, Sawrey, to Hill Top (5min) and Hawkshead (13min) – the first and last minibus of the day also runs to Grizedale Forest (25min), while for Coniston Water change in Hawkshead to the #505 bus, which connects with the Coniston Launch at the Waterhead Hotel, Coniston. Service operates daily Easter–Sept, and weekends in Oct.

From Windermere

Bus #555/556 (hourly) to: Troutbeck Bridge (5min), Brockhole (7min), Waterhead (12min), Ambleside (15min), Rydal (21min), Grasmere (30min) and Keswick (50min); also to Staveley (12min) and Kendal (25min).

Bus #599 to: Bowness (15min); also to Troutbeck Bridge (5min), Brockhole (7min), Waterhead (15min), Ambleside (20min), Rydal (26min), Dove Cottage (38min) and Grasmere (40min). Service operates Easter–Oct every 20–30min, Nov–Easter hourly and only to Bowness or Ambleside.

Bus #618 (4–5 daily) to: Bowness (6min), Newby Bridge (21min), Haverthwaite (24min) and Ulverston (35min); or to Troutbeck Bridge (4min), Brockhole (7min) and Ambleside (15min).

Train (hourly) to: Staveley (6min) and Kendal (14min), and onward services to Oxenholme, Lancaster and Manchester.

2

Grasmere and the central fells

CHAPTER 2 # Highlights

✳ **Visiting Wordsworth's grave, Grasmere** One of England's most famous literary pilgrimages is to the simple grave of the poet Wordsworth. See p.90

✳ **Dove Cottage, Grasmere** It's an obvious tourist attraction, but you shouldn't miss Wordsworth's first home in the Lake District. See p.98

✳ **The walk around Rydal Water** In a region of dramatic, energetic hikes, many visitors will be content with this gentle stroll. See p.102

✳ **Elterwater** Stay the night in one of the Lake District's most attractive hamlets. See p.104

✳ **Walking in Great Langdale** Routes up the famous Langdale Pikes, Crinkle Crags and Bowfell could keep serious hikers occupied for a week. See p.106

✳ **Old Dungeon Ghyll Hotel, Great Langdale** After a day on the fells, a drink in the stone-flagged hikers' bar of this atmospheric inn never disappoints. See p.108

△ Old Dungeon Ghyll Hotel, Great Langdale

Grasmere and the central fells

G rasmere – lake and village – is the traditional dividing line between the north and south Lakes, between the heavily touristy Windermere region and the more rugged fells on either side of Keswick. It lies on the only north–south road through the Lakes (the A591), which cuts through the pass of **Dunmail Raise** (782ft), three miles north of Grasmere – remembered (though with precious little evidence) as the site of the decisive battle in 945 between Dunmail, last independent king of Cumbria, and the Saxon king Edmund, who, in victory, handed Cumbria to Malcolm of Scotland.

Rather than for its own charms (which are considerable), Grasmere owes its wild popularity to its most famous former resident, William Wordsworth, who first moved here in 1799 and lived in a variety of houses in the vicinity until his death in 1850. Two are open to the public: Dove Cottage, where he first set up home in the Lakes with his sister Dorothy; and Rydal Mount, on Rydal Water, the comfortable family home to which he moved at the height of his fame. The influence of other literary lakeland names hangs heavily on Grasmere, too, notably those of Thomas De Quincey, who lived here for more than twenty years and married a local girl; and of the dissolute Coleridges – father Samuel Taylor and son Hartley, whose separate periods of residence often tried the Wordsworths' patience.

The region's other attraction is the proximity of the **central fells**, including some of the Lake District's most famous peaks and valleys. Routes from Grasmere and Ambleside forge west into the superb valleys of Great and Little **Langdale**, overlooked by the prominent rocky summits of hikers' favourites like the **Langdale Pikes**, **Bowfell** and **Crinkle Crags**. It's not all hard going though: there are easier walks to tarns and viewpoints in the bucolic surroundings of **Easedale** and Little Langdale, while hamlets such as **Skelwith Bridge** and **Elterwater** provide classic inns and country B&Bs for an isolated night's stay.

Grasmere

Four miles northwest of Ambleside, the village of **GRASMERE** consists of an intimate cluster of grey-stone houses on an old packhorse road which runs

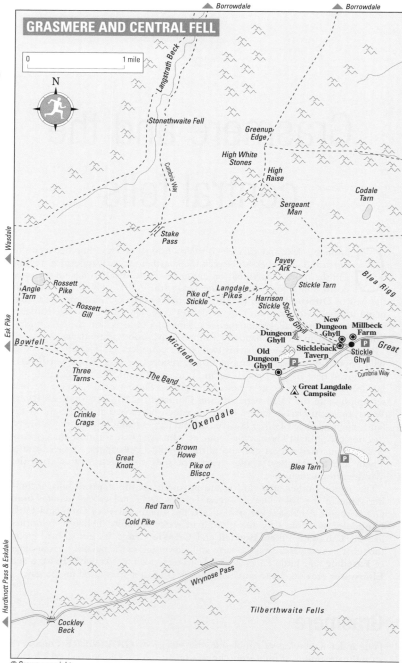

GRASMERE AND CENTRAL FELL

0   1 mile

N

Borrowdale

Borrowdale

Langstrath Beck

Stonethwaite Fell

Cumbria Way

Greenup Edge

High White Stones

High Raise

Codale Tarn

Sergeant Man

Stake Pass

Wasdale

Pavey Ark

Stickle Tarn

Blea Rigg

Angle Tarn

Rossett Pike

Langdale Pikes

Pike of Stickle

Harrison Stickle

Rossett Gill

Esk Pike

Mickleden

Stickle Ghyll

New Dungeon Ghyll

Millbeck Farm

Dungeon Ghyll

Bowfell

Stickleback Tavern

Stickle Ghyll

Great

Old Dungeon Ghyll

Three Tarns

The Band

Cumbria Way

Great Langdale Campsite

Crinkle Crags

Oxendale

Brown Howe

Great Knott

Pike of Blisco

Blea Tarn

Red Tarn

Cold Pike

Hardknott Pass & Eskdale

Wrynose Pass

Tilberthwaite Fells

Cockley Beck

▲ Thirlmere & Keswick   ▲ Grisedale

Grisedale
Tarn

Fairfield

Dunmail
Raise

Great Rigg

Rydal Beck

A591

Helm
Crag

Easedale
Tarn

Sourmilk Gill

Easedale

Rydal Fell

Greenhead Gill

Grasmere
Independent
Hostel

Traveller's
Rest

Heron
Pike

Allan Bank

Grasmere

B5287

Dove Cottage

White
Moss
House

Nab Scar

B5343

Langdale

Silver Howe

Grasmere

White Moss
Common

Banerigg
House

A591

Nab
Cottage

Coffin Trail

St.
Mary's

Rydal
Mount

Rydal
Hall

Rydal

Dow
Bank

Langdale
High Close
YHA

Loughrigg Terrace

Rydal Water

Rydal
Caves

Chapel
Stile

Langdale
Estate

Elterwater

B5343

Loughrigg Fell

River Rothay

Elterwater YHA

Eltermere
Country
House
Hotel

Loughrigg
Tarn

Lingmoor Fell

Elter
Water

Three Shires
Inn

Colwith
Force

Skelwith
Force

Skelwith
Bridge

A593

Clappersgate

Little Langdale

Little
Langdale
Tarn

Park Fell

River Brathay

Skelwith
Fold

B5286

A593

▼ Coniston   ▼ Hawkshead   ▼ Hawkshead

beside the babbling River Rothay. With a permanent population of under a thousand, and just a handful of roads which meet at a central green, it's an eminently pleasing ensemble, set in a shallow bowl of land which reaches down to an alluring lake. Thirty years before Wordsworth put down roots here, the "white village" on the water in this "unsuspected paradise" had also entranced the poet Thomas Gray (of "Elegy" fame) whose journal of his ground-breaking tour of the Lakes did much to bring the region to wider attention. Indeed, if you see Grasmere as being in the "very eye of the Romantic storm" (as does Melvyn Bragg in his novel *The Maid of Buttermere*) you have some idea of its enduring significance as a tourist magnet.

The village

For the most part, Grasmere's assorted gift shops, galleries, cafés and hotels occupy nineteenth-century buildings and houses, though the village is much older than that. St Oswald is reputed to have preached here in the seventh century, while the present church bearing his name dates from the thirteenth century – you can still follow the medieval "**Coffin Trail**" from Rydal over White Moss Common, along which coffin bearers struggled with their load on their way to the church.

The main point of pilgrimage is the **churchyard of St Oswald's**, around which the river makes a sinuous curl. Here, beneath the yews, Wordsworth is buried alongside his wife Mary and sister Dorothy, his beloved daughter Dora (buried in her married name Quillinan) and two of his much younger children, Catherine and Thomas, whose deaths marred the Wordsworths' early years in Grasmere. A worn Celtic cross behind the Wordsworth plots marks the grave of Hartley Coleridge, Samuel Taylor's son. Like his father, Hartley possessed an addictive personality, though – unlike his father – his lapses never produced a formal break with the Wordsworths, with whom Hartley remained a family favourite. Inside, the church's unique twin naves are split by an arched, white-washed wall. Wordsworth described its "naked rafters intricately crossed" in *The Excursion*, while Thomas De Quincey married a farmer's daughter, Margaret Simpson, here – a match disapproved of by the snobbish Wordsworths. Associations aside, it's a rather plain church, though there is a memorial plaque to Wordsworth ("a true philosopher and poet") on the wall to the left of the altar, as well as his prayer book on display in a small case in the nave. Also in the case is a medallion likeness of **Sir John Richardson**, surgeon, naturalist and Arctic explorer who accompanied John Franklin on the heroic, but futile, expedition of 1819 to discover the Northwest Passage. Richardson later came into the ownership of a Grasmere country house, Lancrigg in Easedale (now a hotel), where he supervised the laying out of the woods and gardens with specimens collected on his travels. He's buried in Grasmere churchyard (a few paces to the right from the rear entrance).

Right at the rear entrance to the churchyard stands **Sarah Nelson's Gingerbread Shop** (Mon–Sat 9.30am–5.30pm, Sun 12.30–5.30pm; ☎015394/35428, Ⓦ www.grasmeregingerbread.co.uk) – you'll smell the shop before you see it. Grasmere gingerbread has been made on the premises since the mid-nineteenth century and the recipe is a closely guarded secret (kept locked in an Ambleside bank vault). The shop was formerly the village schoolhouse, where Wordsworth taught for a time in 1812.

Wordsworth spent most of his Grasmere years living in houses outside the village – Dove Cottage and Rydal Mount – but the five years in-between these major residences (1808–13) saw the extended Wordsworth family and

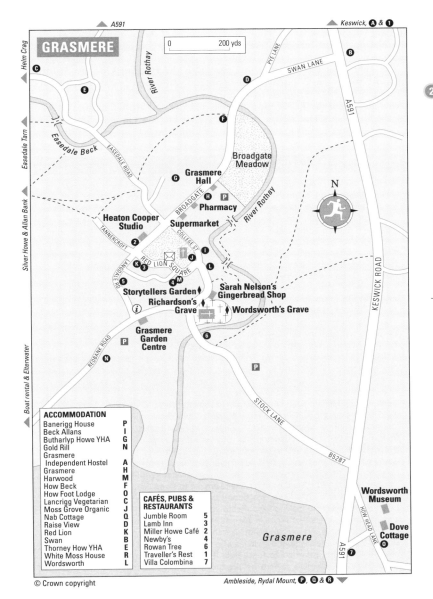

GRASMERE

0 ——— 200 yds

A591

Keswick, **A** & **1**

Helm Crag **C**

E

Easedale Tarn

Silver Howe & Allan Bank

Boat rental & Elterwater

River Rothay

Easedale Beck

EASEDALE ROAD

TANNERCROFT

LANGDALE RD

REDBANK ROAD

Pye Lane

SWAN LANE

D

B

A591

F

Broadgate Meadow

G Grasmere Hall

BROADGATE

H **P**

Pharmacy

Heaton Cooper Studio

Supermarket

COLLEGE ST

River Rothay

N

KESWICK ROAD

2

K **3** Red Lion Square

5

4 **M**

Storytellers Garden

Richardson's Grave

i

J

I

L

Sarah Nelson's Gingerbread Shop

Wordsworth's Grave

6

Grasmere Garden Centre

P

N

P

STOCK LANE

B5287

Wordsworth Museum

HOW HEAD LANE

Dove Cottage **O**

Grasmere

A591

7

ACCOMMODATION

Banerigg House	**P**
Beck Allans	**I**
Butharlyp Howe YHA	**G**
Gold Rill	**N**
Grasmere Independent Hostel	**A**
Grasmere	**H**
Harwood	**M**
How Beck	**F**
How Foot Lodge	**O**
Lancrigg Vegetarian	**C**
Moss Grove Organic	**J**
Nab Cottage	**Q**
Raise View	**D**
Red Lion	**K**
Swan	**B**
Thorney How YHA	**E**
White Moss House	**R**
Wordsworth	**L**

CAFÉS, PUBS & RESTAURANTS

Jumble Room	5
Lamb Inn	3
Miller Howe Café	2
Newby's	4
Rowan Tree	6
Traveller's Rest	1
Villa Colombina	7

© Crown copyright

Ambleside, Rydal Mount, **P**, **Q** & **R** ▼

visiting friends occupying two houses in the village itself. Both are closed to the public, though there's nothing to stop you walking past the **Old Rectory** (opposite St Oswald's) and the more imposing **Allan Bank** – the latter reached up a signposted path to Silver Howe (see box on p.94). **Samuel Taylor Coleridge** was a guest here for almost two years, producing his literary and political periodical, *The Friend*, from a room in the house while sinking ever further into drug-induced decline. Later, Canon Rawnsley of the National Trust (see p.152) owned the house; he left it to the Trust on his death.

The only other place to visit in Grasmere is the **Heaton Cooper Studio**, opposite the green (Mon–Sat 9am–6pm, Sun noon–6pm; Nov–March closes at 5pm; ⓣ015394/35280, ⓦwww.heatoncooper.co.uk). It's a showcase for the works of one of the Lakes' most durable and talented artistic families, headed by the landscapes and village scenes of Alfred Heaton Cooper (1864–1929). Cooper became a well-known illustrator of guidebooks, especially in the first

Coleridge in the Lakes

Samuel Taylor Coleridge (1772–1834) already knew both Robert Southey and William Wordsworth by the time he moved to the Lake District. With Southey, he shared an enthusiasm for the French Revolution and an unfulfilled plan to found a Utopian community in America; and in 1795 he'd married Sara Fricker, the sister of Southey's fiancée Edith. Later, while living in Somerset, Coleridge and Wordsworth wrote *Lyrical Ballads* together, which contained Coleridge's "The Rime of the Ancient Mariner". Coleridge sang Wordsworth's praises at every opportunity; a favour returned by the enamoured Dorothy, who thought Coleridge a "wonderful man . . . [whose] . . . conversation teems with soul, mind and spirit".

Thus, when Wordsworth moved to Grasmere in 1799, Coleridge needed little prompting to follow. Having toured the Lakes, he settled on the newly built Greta Hall in Keswick, leasing it for 25 guineas a year. The Coleridges – Samuel Taylor, his wife Sara, and four-year-old son Hartley – were installed by July 1800; a third son, Derwent, was born in the house that September (the Coleridges' second son, Berkeley, had died in 1798); and daughter Sara followed in 1802.

Coleridge spent much of his first two years at Keswick helping Wordsworth prepare a new edition of the *Lyrical Ballads*, but found plenty of time to explore. His notebooks detail the walks he took, and in the summer of 1802 he embarked on a nine-day walking tour of the Lakes; see p.274 for more.

But despite his first flush of excitement at lakeland living, Coleridge wasn't happy. He'd been taking opium for years – if *Kubla Khan* didn't spring from an opium-induced dream no poem ever did – and was in poor health, suffering from rheumatism. What's more, his relationship with his wife was deteriorating – spurred by the fact that Coleridge had fallen hopelessly in love with Wordsworth's sister-in-law, Sara Hutchinson (his "Asra"), by now living at Grasmere. Indeed, his last great poem, *Dejection: an Ode*, was originally sent to Sara as a letter in April 1802.

In September 1803, Southey and his wife arrived to share Greta Hall. As the Southeys had just lost a child Coleridge hoped that the two sisters might comfort each other, but he was also looking for a way to escape so that he might regain his health and inspiration. He left for Malta in June 1804 (where for two years he was secretary to the Governor) and never lived with his family again. Southey assumed full responsibility for Coleridge's wife and children who remained at Greta Hall.

When Coleridge returned to the Lakes it was to live with the Wordsworths at Allan Bank in Grasmere, where he produced a short-lived political and literary periodical, *The Friend*, helped by Sara Hutchinson. When she left, to go and live with her brother in Wales, a depressed Coleridge – once more dependent on drugs – departed for London. Wordsworth, sick of having him moping around the house, had described Coleridge to someone else as an "absolute nuisance", which Coleridge came to hear about: after this breach in 1810, Coleridge only ever made perfunctory visits to the Lakes, avoiding Wordsworth (though the two were later reconciled). He died in London on July 25, 1834, and is buried in Highgate cemetery.

two decades of the twentieth century, and was succeeded in this by his son, William Heaton Cooper (1903–95), who climbed with the pioneering lakeland mountaineers. William produced paintings and sketches for four topographical Lake District guidebooks and then virtually ensured a dynastic succession by marrying the sculptress Ophelia Gordon Bell. Examples of all their work are on show in the gallery, together with those of current family members – grandson Julian Cooper is the most notable, a climber-artist who produces huge oil paintings of the world's more remote locations.

If you're in the village in summer, you'll be able to see more art at **Grasmere Hall**, up Broadgate from the green, which hosts the annual exhibition of the **Lake Artists Society** (Ⓦwww.lakeartists.org.uk). The society was founded in 1904 by local writer and artist W.G. Collingwood and its summer exhibition – first held in Coniston, subsequently in Grasmere – has been a lakeland fixture every year since. The work displayed is varied, but the society's members are mostly resident in, and take their inspiration from, Cumbria and the Lake District.

The lake and surrounding fells

It's a ten-minute walk from the centre down Redbank Road to the western side of the fell-fringed **lake** itself. You can rent a rowboat at the *Faeryland Tea Garden* (March–Oct daily 10am–6pm, ☎015394/35060) by the landing stage – and take a picnic out to the wooded islet in the middle of the lake – or continue walking the mile to the southern reaches where **Loughrigg Terrace** sits under the crags of Loughrigg Fell (look for a track off the road through Redbank Woods, signposted "Loughrigg Terrace and YHA"). From the terrace there are tremendous views back up the lake and across the broad valley, culminating in the pass of Dunmail Raise.

Wordsworth composed most of his poetry during long rambles around the lake and up in the surrounding fells, and – clutching a volume of his collected verse – it's still possible to track down the sources of his inspiration. On the east side of the A591, for example, a path rises to the "tumultuous brook" of **Greenhead Gill**, whose surroundings formed the backdrop to the masterful early lyric poem "Michael" (1800), a moving tale of a shepherd abandoned by his wayward son. However, it's **Easedale** and its tarn (northwest of the village) that conjures the most resonant images. The first version of Wordsworth's autobiographical work, *The Prelude*, was partly composed after long hours tramping up and down the valley, while the tragic deaths of George and Sarah Green of Easedale – who died in a blizzard, leaving behind six children – prompted a memorial poem. ("Who weeps for strangers? / Many wept for George and Sarah Green; / Wept for that pair's unhappy fate, / Whose graves may here be seen.") The Wordsworths even took into care one of the orphans, a story exhaustively chronicled by De Quincey (in *Recollections of the Lakes and the Lake Poets*).

A brisk hike (follow Easedale Rd, past the youth hostel), up the tumbling, fern-clad, Sourmilk Gill to **Easedale Tarn** and back, takes around two hours – there's lakeland ice cream available from the *Oak Lodge* B&B teashop (closed mid-Sept to Easter), opposite the bridge across Easedale Beck at the start of the path, or wander up the drive to *Lancrigg Vegetarian Country House Hotel*, which offers light lunches and afternoon tea for walkers. You also come this way, up Easedale Road, to climb Grasmere's most celebrated peak, **Helm Crag** (1299ft), which takes about an hour from the village – see the box on p.94 for route details.

Grasmere makes a good base for a wide selection of walks, from lazy round-the-lake rambles to full-on day-hikes requiring a bit of experience. A decent cross section is detailed below, while note that you can also walk the Fairfield Horseshoe circuit (see p.74) clockwise from nearby Rydal.

Around Grasmere and Rydal Water

This is an easy circuit (4 miles; 2hr) that skirts the lake and Loughrigg Fell. From Loughrigg Terrace, the route heads east above **Rydal Water**, passing the dripping maw of Rydal Caves, a disused slate quarry (seen in Ken Russell's *The Lair of the White Worm*), before crossing the A591 to Rydal Mount. Above the house the **"Coffin Trail" bridleway** runs back high above the northern shore of Rydal Water, via **White Moss Tarn** (look out for butterflies), and emerges at Dove Cottage.

Loughrigg Fell

There are all sorts of possible ascents of **Loughrigg Fell** (1101ft) – and it's also easily climbed from Ambleside – but the simplest ascent is straight up the hillside from Loughrigg Terrace: the views are fantastic. A six-mile circuit from the terrace, over the undulating top to Ambleside and then back along the lower slopes via Rydal, takes three to four hours.

Silver Howe

The best direct climb from the village is up to the top of **Silver Howe** (1292ft), above the west side of the lake, from where the views take in the Langdale Pikes, Helvellyn and High Street. The easiest signposted route up from the village passes Allan Bank – it's a two-hour walk, climbing to the summit and then circling round via Dow Bank and down to the lakeside road, emerging just outside the village opposite the *Faeryland* tea garden and boat-rental place.

Helm Crag and High Raise

A reasonably tough high-level circuit to the west of Grasmere (10 miles; 6hr) starts with the stiff climb up to **Helm Crag** (1299ft) – follow the signs from the end of Easedale Road – whose distinctive summit crags are known as The Lion and The Lamb, and have thrilled visitors since Wordsworth's day. An undulating ridge walk then runs west to Greenup Edge, and up to **High Raise** (2500ft), popularly regarded as the Lake District's most centrally sited fell. Stay a while for the magnificent views from the summit (marked on maps as High White Stones), before turning back for Grasmere via **Sergeant Man** (2414ft) and then descending past Easedale Tarn.

See Basics, p.35, for general walking advice in the Lakes; recommended maps are detailed on p.42.

Practicalities

Grasmere lies west of the main A591 (Ambleside–Keswick road), with its centre just a few hundred yards down the B5287, which winds through the village. It is served by **buses** #555/556 (between Kendal and Keswick) and the #599 (from Bowness, Windermere and Ambleside), both of which stop on the village green. A **Central Lakes Day Rider ticket** (from £5.95) allows unlimited stops on the return journey between Bowness and Grasmere, allowing you to visit the Wordsworth houses as a day-trip. The main **car park** is on Redbank Road at the southern end of the village, by the garden centre. There's a second car park on Stock Lane, on the east side as you come in from Dove Cottage. There's no longer an official tourist office in Grasmere, though there is an informal **visitor information point** in the reception of the *Dale Lodge Hotel* (daily 10am–4pm), up the drive opposite the garden centre.

Accommodation

Accommodation can be hard to come by here in summer and you should book well in advance for accommodation in any budget, especially the popular **youth hostels** and **backpackers' accommodation**. You'll be able to walk into Grasmere village and to Wordsworth's Dove Cottage from any of the recommended choices in and around Grasmere. If you stay out at Rydal, you'll be handily placed for the other Wordsworth house, Rydal Mount, though you'll need to drive or catch the bus to the village for food and other services. If the Grasmere hostels are full, try *Langdale YHA* at High Close (see p.106), the nearest alternative – though it's a good two miles south of the village. Grasmere has no campsite.

In Grasmere

Beck Allans College St ☎015394/35563, ⊛www .beckallans.com. A quality B&B in a modern but traditionally built house in the centre – the more you pay, the larger the room, but all five are smartly furnished, well equipped and boast baths in the en-suite bathrooms. There are riverside gardens and private parking, while self-catering apartments (including a handsome 1930s caravan) are also available. No smoking. Parking. No credit cards. ❹

Gold Rill Red Bank Rd ☎015394/35486, ⊛www .gold-rill.com. Lakeside accommodation is at a premium in Grasmere, so the *Gold Rill* is a sought-after spot – rooms have lake or fell views, and there are pretty lakeside gardens with a small heated outdoor pool surrounded by deck chairs. A fire in the lounges keeps it nice and snug in winter. Special five-night breaks offer significant discounts. Dinner is included in the room rate. Parking. Closed two weeks in Jan. ❺

Grasmere Broadgate ☎015394/35277, ⊛www .grasmerehotel.co.uk. Elegant Victorian villa, all of whose rooms are named after lakeland literary figures. Warm colours predominate now that refurbishment has brightened all the rooms, some of which feature carved antique beds or four-posters, flatscreen TVs and baths as well as showers. A good four-course dinner (included in the price) is served in the ornate dining room, overlooking the gardens and River Rothay. No children under 10. Parking available. Closed Jan. ❼

Harwood Red Lion Sq ☎015394/35248, ⊛www.harwoodhotel.co.uk. Eight smallish rooms in a genial family-run hotel. A makeover has added contemporary colours, coordinated furniture and pine or brass bedsteads, while rooms (most with baths) have varied village outlooks. There's a two-night minimum stay at weekends; low-season

rates drop a category. No smoking. Limited private parking. No American Express. ❹

How Beck Broadgate ☎015394/35732, ⊛trevor .eastes@btinternet.com. Two rooms are available in this agreeable family house on the outskirts of the village with a sun lounge that overlooks the garden and fells. It's a great choice for vegetarians – there's a full veggie breakfast (with home-made bread and preserves) and fruit in the room. No smoking. ❸

How Foot Lodge Town End ☎015394/35366, ⊛www.howfoot.co.uk. The position – a few yards from Dove Cottage – couldn't be better for Wordsworth groupies. The light-filled Victorian villa has six spacious rooms (one with its own sun lounge), grand lounge and well-kept gardens. Guests get a discount on dinner at nearby *Villa Colombina*. No smoking. Parking. Closed Jan. No American Express. ❹

Moss Grove Organic ☎015394/35251, ⊛www.mossgrove.com. Rarely can a Victorian-era hotel have looked so stunning, from the luminous lighting that throws a blue glow upon the exterior slate to the luxurious high-concept rooms complete with high-speed Internet and Bose sound systems. Everything has been designed on organic, low-impact lines, so the extraordinary handmade beds are of reclaimed timber, the carpets are wool, the wallpaper coloured with natural inks, duvets made from duck down and the windows screened by natural wood blinds. The feel is less of a hotel and more a private house party – there are only eleven rooms and you're encouraged to forage in the kitchen for a superior buffet-style breakfast (produce largely local, the drinks Fair Trade) and take it back to your room. Two-night minimum stay at weekends. Parking. ❸

Raise View White Bridge ☎015394/35215, ⊛www.raiseviewhouse.co.uk. There are lovely fell views from every corner of this amiable guesthouse, plus a warm welcome and seven very comfortable rooms (including a single in the eaves). Breakfast is good too, and there's dinner by arrangement. No smoking. Parking. No credit cards. ⑤

Red Lion Red Lion Sq ☎015394/35456, ⓦwww .hotelslakedistrict.com. Sympathetically renovated eighteenth-century coaching inn, with views over the village and fells. Most of the attractively decorated rooms have Jacuzzi-baths, and wet days are no hardship since there's a very nice indoor pool, plus steam, sauna and spa room, as well as restaurant, conservatory, lounge, bar and next-door pub. Off-season discounts drop the price a category. Parking. ⑦

Swan Keswick Rd (A591), by Swan Lane ☎0870/400 8132, ⓦwww.macdonaldhotels.co.uk /swan. On the main road, on the edge of the village, this former coaching inn rated a mention in Wordsworth's "The Waggoner" ("Who does not know the famous Swan?") and remodelling hasn't robbed the public rooms at least of their essential eighteenth-century character. Bedrooms of course have been updated, while the traditional restaurant serves lakeland specialities and there's a cosy bar. Rates on weekdays are a category lower. Parking. ⑧

Wordsworth College St ☎015394/35592, ⓦwww .thewordsworthhotel.co.uk. Relaxed, attractive and comfortable four-star hotel, with a heated pool, Jacuzzi and spa, gorgeous conservatory and terrace. Rooms are traditional in decor and character, but they have all been upgraded (wireless Internet, plasma-screen TVs, power showers). There are light lunches and evening meals in the *Dove & Olive Branch* bistro and bar, and the food is also excellent in the *Prelude* restaurant, so D,B&B deals are worth considering. Otherwise, room prices vary according to the type of room, with some available at a category lower than the given rate. Parking. ⑧

Around Grasmere

Banerigg House 1 mile south on A591 ☎015394/35204, ⓦwww.baneriggguesthouse .co.uk. A detached lakeside property a 15min walk from the village, past Dove Cottage. It's a non-smoking house, with five doubles and one single – mostly en suite with lake views (though no TVs) – plus drying facilities, good breakfasts and the use of a boat. Parking. No credit cards. ④

Lancrigg Vegetarian Country House Easedale Rd ☎015394/35317, ⓦwww.lancrigg.co.uk. Half a mile northwest of Grasmere, the isolated country house has trimmed lawns and wildlife-filled woods, as well as connections with Wordsworth (he was a regular visitor and helped in its renovation). A

dozen variously sized rooms have been carved from the well-worn interior, including the former library (now with a lace-draped four-poster and private door into the garden), though the cheapest option is a room in the cottage annexe in the grounds. A four-course vegetarian dinner is included in the price (organic wines and beers available). Parking. ⑨

Nab Cottage 2 miles southeast on A591, Rydal ☎015394/35311, ⓦwww.rydalwater.com. Both De Quincey and Hartley Coleridge lived in this gorgeous seventeenth-century oak-beamed farmhouse facing Rydal Water. It's now a language school, but offers B&B in seven rooms (four en suite) when space is available – usually *not* between June and September, but call to check. Light suppers and evening meals available on request. Parking. No American Express. ③

White Moss House Rydal Water ☎015394/35295, ⓦwww.whitemoss.com. Look for the sign at the northern end of Rydal Water for the driveway to this secluded early eighteenth-century, ivy-clad house. Longtime owners, the Dixons, preside over five individually styled, antique-filled rooms in the main house (two share a lounge and terrace) and two more in a prettily sited cottage-suite with fine lake views. It's an extremely relaxed place to which people return year after year, as much for the food as the accommodation – a splendid five-course dinner (not always available) starts with drinks on the terrace in summer and the wine list is exemplary. Parking. Closed Dec & Jan. ⑥, cottage ⑦

Youth hostels and backpackers' accommodation

Butharlyp Howe YHA Easedale Rd ☎0870/770 5836, ⓔgrasmere@yha.org.uk. Closest of the hostels to the centre, this converted Victorian house is just five minutes north of the green. There are modern bedrooms, plentiful showers, carpeting and decent furniture throughout, and a dining room overlooking grassy gardens. There's also a children's play area and outdoor games available, and some of the rooms are available for families and couples. Evening meal served. Nov–Feb open Fri & Sat only. Dorm beds from £15.50.

Grasmere Independent Hostel Broadrayne Farm, A591, half a mile north of the village, past the *Traveller's Rest* pub ☎015394/35055, ⓦwww.grasmerehostel.co.uk. The best of its kind on the Lakes, Grasmere's stylishly presented backpackers' hostel has 24 beds, all in small, carpeted en-suite rooms – one available as a twin/family room with private bathroom when space allows. There's an impressively equipped kitchen, plus laundry and drying facilities, bike and luggage storage, even a sauna. You can get advice about local walks, or kick back in the comfortable common room, whose large circular window overlooks the valley. Three self-catering cottages also available (by the week) on the farm, each sleeping between two and five people. Dorm beds £16.50. **Thorney How** ⓣ 0870/770 5836, ⓔ grasmere @yha.org.uk. Grasmere's smaller, simpler YHA

hostel is further out of the village, a characterful (ie largely unmodernized) former farmhouse just under a mile along the road past *Butharlyp Howe*: look for the signposted right turn. It was the first hostel ever bought by the YHA, in 1931. The road's unlit so bring a torch. Evening meal served. Advance bookings required; family groups only Nov–Feb. No credit cards. Dorm beds from £13.

Eating, drinking and entertainment

There are plenty of **tearooms and cafés** in Grasmere catering for the mass of tourists that descends every day. Good independent **restaurants** are rather thinner on the ground, though there's enough choice to ring the changes over a few days' stay. The hotels soak up most of the bar trade as well – best is the *Wordsworth Hotel*'s "pub", the *Dove & Olive Branch*, a no-TV, no-music, real-ale bar with good bistro attached. Otherwise, the only real **pub** is that attached to the *Red Lion* in the centre, or you can walk out to the *Traveller's Rest* on the A591.

The two big annual summer **events** are the village's rushbearing ceremony and the traditional sports festival, both held in August. Also unique to Grasmere is the **Storytellers' Garden** (ⓦ www.taffythomas.co.uk) at the Northern Centre for Storytelling, which is located in the former National Trust shop opposite the church. Traditional tale-teller and raconteur Taffy Thomas presents open-air events throughout the year (story walks, firelight tales, music and juggling) – call in or check the website for details.

Cafés and restaurants

Jumble Room Langdale Rd ⓣ 015394/35188, ⓦ www .thejumbleroom.co.uk. Everyone likes this funky, relaxed dining spot, run with a light touch by an amiable Grasmere couple. With tables overlooked by sister-in-law Thuline's dramatic cow and animal oil paintings, the menu ranges the world – say, Tuscan crostini, Thai prawns, Herdwick lamb kofta or haddock in organic beer batter – and once ensconced, no one's in any hurry to leave. Dinner reservations advised. Closed Mon & Tues all year, and also Wed from Nov–March. Expensive.
Miller Howe Café Red Lion Sq ⓣ 015394/35234. When the sun shines, there's no better spot than the outdoor tables of this refined café near the green. On the menu – crusty breakfast rolls, inventive sandwiches, baked potatoes and a range of tempting mains (baked sausage with apple sauce, salmon with wine and prawn sauce). Daytime only. Moderate.
Newby's Deli and Bakery Red Lion Sq, under the *Harwood* ⓣ 015394/35248. Stuffed sandwiches, baguettes and ciabatta to take away, plus a reasonable choice of deli supplies (and Kendal Mintcake) – great for stocking up your picnic hamper. The coffee house at the rear of the deli goes in for toasted paninis, local cheese-and-chutney platters, and home-made pies and quiches. Daytime only. Inexpensive.

Rowan Tree Church Bridge, Stock Lane ⓣ 015394/35528. The main draw here is the outdoor terrace in a gorgeous position on a lazy bend in the river, opposite the church. A daytime tearoom menu gives way to Mediterranean-style dining at night, including fancy pizza and pasta choices, plus vegetarian and fish specials. Moderate.
Villa Colombina Town End ⓣ 015394/35268. The old *Dove Cottage Tearooms* is open during the day for snacks and light meals, and then sports an authentic Italian menu for dinner (6–9pm; reservations recommended) of pizzas, pastas, steak and chicken, as well as wild mushroom-and-red-pepper risotto and other specials. It's a cheery place to eat at any time, with hardwood floors and terracotta-coloured walls, and sofas on the upper gallery. Closed Jan, and possibly other days in winter; call for details. Moderate.

Pubs

Lamb Inn Red Lion Sq ⓣ 015394/35456. The public bar of the *Red Lion* is the best choice in Grasmere for a drink, and consequently is packed to the rafters at weekends. There are Theakston's and guest beers on tap, and a queue of local Fast Eddies waiting to drub you at pool.
Traveller's Rest Half a mile north on the A591 ⓣ 015394/35604. A popular place for real ales and bar meals (Cumberland sausage and mash to Thai curry), and there's a warming log fire in winter.

Banks and exchange There's no bank in Grasmere, though there is an ATM inside the post office (where you can also exchange travellers' cheques).

Bike rental The nearest bike-rental outlets are in Ambleside.

Emergencies The nearest doctors' surgery is at Ambleside Health Centre (Rydal Rd ☎015394/32693), the nearest hospital is in Keswick (Keswick Cottage Hospital, Crosthwaite Rd ☎017687/72012).

Laundry Apart from the facilities at the hostels and backpackers', the nearest laundry is in Ambleside.

Outdoors stores Outdoor equipment and walking gear from Edge of the World (Red Lion Sq), Stewart R Cunningham (Broadgate) and Summitreks (College St).

Pharmacy Grasmere Pharmacy, 1 Oak Bank, Broadgate ☎015394/35553.

Post office Red Lion Sq (April–Sept Mon–Fri 9am–5.30pm, Sat 9am–12.30pm; Oct–March Mon–Wed & Fri 9am–12.30pm & 1.30–5.30pm, Thurs & Sat 9am–12.30pm).

Taxis Grasmere Taxis ☎015394/35506.

Dove Cottage

On the southeastern outskirts of Grasmere village, in the former hamlet of Town End, stands **Dove Cottage** (daily 9.30am–5.30pm; closed early Jan to early Feb; £6.50, museum only £5.50; ☎015394/35544, ⓦwww.wordsworth .org.uk), home to William and Dorothy Wordsworth from 1799 to 1808 and where Wordsworth wrote some of his best poetry. The house stands just off the A591 and buses #555/556 and #599 stop close by on the main road.

Wordsworth first saw the house in November 1799 while on a walking tour with his friend Samuel Taylor Coleridge, with whom he had published *Lyrical Ballads* the previous year. Keen for a base in the Lakes, Wordsworth negotiated a rent of £8 a year for what had originally been an inn called the *Dove & Olive-Bough*; he and his sister moved in just before Christmas of that year. It was a simple stone house with a slate roof – Wordsworth at this time was far from financially secure – where the poet could live by his guiding principle of "plain living but high thinking". But its main recommendation as far as Wordsworth was concerned was one that is no longer obvious: the views he had enjoyed to the lake and fells were lost when new housing was erected in front of Dove Cottage in the 1860s. When the Wordsworths left in 1808, their friend Thomas De Quincey took over the lease and Dove Cottage is as much a monument to his happiest days in Grasmere (he married from here) as it is to Wordsworth's plain living; the house has been open to the public since 1917.

The **cottage** forms part of a complex administered by the Wordsworth Trust, whose guides, bursting with anecdotes, lead you around the rooms, little changed now but for the addition of electricity and internal plumbing. There's precious little space and – downstairs, at least – very little natural light: belching tallow candles would have provided the only illumination. William, not wanting to be bothered by questions of a domestic nature, kept to the lighter, upper rooms or disappeared off on long walks to compose his poetry. De Quincey later reckoned that Wordsworth had walked 175,000 to 180,000 miles in the course of his poetry writing – "a mode of exertion which, to him, stood in the stead of wine, spirits, and all other stimulants whatsoever to the animal spirits". Wordsworth married in 1802 and his new wife, Mary Hutchinson, came to live here, necessitating a change of bedrooms for everyone; three of their five children were later born in the cottage (John in 1803, Dora in 1804 and Thomas in 1806). Sister Dorothy kept a detailed journal of daily life and the endless comings and goings of visitors, notably Coleridge and his brother-in-law

Southey, but also Walter Scott, William Hazlitt and, once he'd plucked up the nerve to introduce himself, Thomas De Quincey (see box). The garden behind the cottage was tamed, while William chopped wood for the fire, planted runner beans, built a summerhouse and hid the disliked cottage whitewash behind a train of roses and honeysuckle. And with all this going on, Wordsworth produced a series of odes, lyric poems and sonnets that he would never better, relying on Dorothy and Mary to make copies in their painstaking handwriting. After eight years at Dove Cottage it became clear that the Wordsworths had

Thomas De Quincey in the Lakes

The direct object of my own residence at the lakes was the society of Mr Wordsworth.

Thomas De Quincey, *Recollections of the Lakes and the Lake Poets*.

The young **Thomas De Quincey** (1785–1859) was one of the first to fully appreciate the revolutionary nature of Wordsworth's and Coleridge's collaborative *Lyrical Ballads*, and as a student at Oxford in 1803 he had already written to Wordsworth praising his "genius" and hoping for his friendship. In reply, Wordsworth politely invited him to visit if he was ever in the area. It took De Quincey four years (and two abortive visits, abandoned out of shyness) to contrive a meeting, eventually through the auspices of Coleridge, a mutual friend.

De Quincey first came to Dove Cottage in November 1807 to meet his hero, trembling at the thought: the meeting is recorded in one of the more self-effacing chapters of his *Recollections*. When the Wordsworths moved to Allan Bank the following year, De Quincey – by now a favourite with the Wordsworth children – went too, staying several months. His small private income enabled him to take over Dove Cottage in February 1809, which he filled with books (in contrast to Wordsworth, who had very few). He also demolished the summerhouse and made other changes in the garden which annoyed the Wordsworths, while the relationship further cooled after 1812 following the deaths of young Catherine and Thomas Wordsworth. De Quincey was particularly badly affected by the loss of Catherine, his "sole companion", and for two months after her death passed each night stretched out on her grave in Grasmere churchyard.

The truth is, De Quincey wasn't a well man. Since his university days, he had been in the habit of taking opium in the form of laudanum (ie dissolved in alcohol), and at Dove Cottage he was taking huge, addictive doses – the amount of alcohol alone would have been debilitating enough. He closeted himself away in the cottage for days at a time, complaining that Wordsworth was spoiling the books he borrowed from him, and began an affair with Margaret (Peggy) Simpson of nearby Nab Cottage, a local farmer's daughter who bore him an illegitimate child. The drug-taking was bad enough for the upright, snobbish Wordsworths, but when De Quincey married Peggy in 1817 (at St Oswald's Church, Grasmere) any intimate relationship was at an end.

De Quincey was never suited to regular employment, and following a disastrous stint as editor of the *Westmorland Gazette* he became a freelance critic and essayist for various literary periodicals. His *Confessions of an English Opium-Eater* (1821) first appeared in the *London Magazine* and made his name, and he had sufficient resources to take on another house (Fox Ghyll, south of Rydal) for his growing family (he eventually had eight children), retaining Dove Cottage as a library. Growing success meant De Quincey spent less and less time in the Lakes, giving up Fox Ghyll in 1825 and finally abandoning Dove Cottage in 1830 to move to Edinburgh, where he lived for the rest of his life. It was only between 1834 and 1839 – long after he'd left the area – that De Quincey started writing his Lake "recollections", offending Wordsworth all over again.

outgrown their home and, reluctantly, the family moved to a larger, new house in Grasmere called Allan Bank – Wordsworth had watched it being built and referred to it as a "temple of abomination". They were never as happy there, or in the Old Rectory to which they later relocated, and it wasn't until 1813 and the move to Rydal Mount that the Wordsworths regained the sense of peace they had felt at Dove Cottage.

Most of the furniture in the cottage belonged to the Wordsworths, while in the **upper rooms** are displayed a battered suitcase, a pair of William's ice skates and Dorothy's sewing box, among other possessions. There are surprisingly few reminders of De Quincey's long tenancy, save a pair of opium scales, yet he lived here far longer than did the Wordsworths. In the nearby **museum** there's much to be learned about Wordsworth's life and times. It's full of paintings, portraits, original manuscripts (including that of "Daffodils"), pages from Dorothy's journals and more memorabilia, most poignantly Mary's wedding ring. The museum ticket allows entry to any special **exhibitions** currently running, while in good weather the **garden** is open for visits as well.

Wide-ranging as the museum is, it can only present a fraction of the complete collection held by the Wordsworth Trust, which amounts to some 70,000 manuscripts, first editions, books, letters, portraits and other items. These are stored in the adjacent **Jerwood Centre**, a £3-million facility opened in 2005 by Seamus Heaney, which is accessible to scholars and researchers. The centre hosts various related displays and events, while Dove Cottage is the headquarters of the **Centre for British Romanticism**, which together with the Wordsworth Trust sponsors special annual exhibitions, residential conferences and summer poetry readings, talks and workshops attracting some top names – call for details or check the website.

Rydal Mount

Following the deaths of their young children Catherine and Thomas in 1812, the Wordsworths couldn't bear to continue living in Grasmere's Old Rectory. In May 1813 they moved a couple of miles southeast of the village to the hamlet of Rydal, little more than a couple of isolated cottages and farms set back from the eastern end of Rydal Water. Here William rented Rydal Mount from the Flemings of nearby Rydal Hall, where he remained until his death in 1850. Buses #555/556 and #599 stop on the A591 at Rydal Church, 200 yards from the house.

Rydal Mount (March–Oct daily 9.30am–5pm; Nov–Feb Mon & Wed–Sun 10am–4pm; closed last 3 weeks in Jan; £5, garden only £2.50; ☎015394/33002, ⊛www.rydalmount.co.uk) is a fair-sized family home, a much-improved-upon Tudor cottage set in its own grounds, and reflects Wordsworth's change in circumstances. At Dove Cottage he'd been a largely unknown poet of straitened means, but by 1813 he'd written several of his greatest works (though not all had yet been published) and was already being visited by literary acolytes. More importantly, he'd been appointed Westmorland's Distributor of Stamps, a salaried position which allowed him to take up the rent of a comfortable family house. Wordsworth, Mary, the three surviving children (John, aged 10; Dora, 9; and William, 3) and Dorothy arrived, plus his wife's sister Sara Hutchinson, by now living with the family. Later the household also contained a clerk, a couple of maids and a gardener. Dances and dinners were held, the widowed Queen Adelaide visited, and carriage-loads of friends and sightseers came to call – a far cry from the "plain living" back at Dove Cottage.

Wordsworth only ever rented the property, but the house is now owned by descendants of the poet, who have opened it to visitors since 1970. It's a much less claustrophobic experience than visiting Dove Cottage and you're free to wander around what is still essentially a family home – summer concerts feature poetry readings by Wordsworth family members, and there are recent family pictures on the sideboard alongside more familiar portraits of the poet and his circle. In the light-filled **drawing room** and **library** (two rooms in Words-worth's day) you'll find the only known portrait of Dorothy, as an old lady of 62, and also Mary's favourite portrait of Wordsworth, completed in 1844 by the American portraitist Henry Inman. Memorabilia abounds: Wordsworth's black-leather sofa, his inkstand and despatch box, a brooch of Dorothy's and, upstairs in the attic, their beloved brother John's sword (recovered from the shipwreck

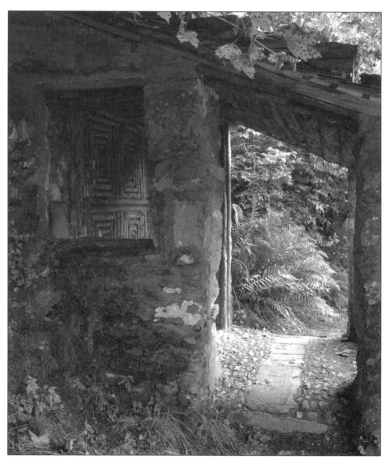

△ The summerhouse, Rydal Mount

in which he drowned) and the poet's own encyclopedia and prayer book. **William and Mary's bedroom** has a lovely view, with Windermere a splash in the distance; in daughter **Dora's room** hangs a portrait of Edward Quillinan, her Irish dragoon, whom she married in 1841, much against Wordsworth's will. The couple spent their honeymoon at Rydal Mount, while the delicate Dora – often ill and eventually a victim of tuberculosis – later came home to die in the house in 1847. The other bedroom was Dorothy's, to which she was virtually confined for the last two decades of her life, suffering greatly from what was thought to be a debilitating mental illness – an underactive thyroid is the current opinion. She died at Rydal Mount in 1855; Mary died there in 1859.

Many people's favourite part of Rydal Mount is the four-and-a-half-acre **garden**, largely shaped by Wordsworth who fancied himself a gardener. He planted the flowering shrubs, put in the terraces (where he used to declaim his poetry) and erected a little rustic summerhouse (for jotting down lyrics), from which there are fine views of Rydal Water. Lining the lawns and surrounding the rock pools are rhododendrons and azaleas, maples, beeches and pines. If you're looking for an unusual souvenir, head for the Rydal Mount **shop**, which sells fell-walking sticks fashioned from the wood found in the garden.

Rydal and Rydal Water

Rydal sits at the foot of its own valley, whose beck empties into the River Rothay. As a hamlet, it's hardly any bigger than it was in Wordsworth's day; though, having seen the poet's house of Rydal Mount, you may as well wander back down the road for the other local sights – namely Rydal's lake, church and hall and, under a mile west, Nab Cottage, the former home of Hartley Coleridge.

There was no local church in Rydal until **St Mary's** (at the foot of Rydal Mount on the main A591) was built in 1824 – Wordsworth was churchwarden here for a year in the 1830s. A swing gate by the church entrance leads into **Dora's Field** (always open; free; NT), a plot of land bought by Wordsworth when he thought he might have to leave Rydal Mount because the owners, the Flemings, wanted it back. Wordsworth planned to build a house here instead, but when the Flemings changed their minds, he gave the land to his daughter. On Dora's death in 1847, the heartbroken Wordsworths planted the hillsides with daffodils.

Across from the church, a driveway leads to **Rydal Hall**, erstwhile home of the Flemings. The hall has a sixteenth-century kernel but was considerably renovated during Victorian times; it's now a residential conference centre. The formal gardens to the front (open dawn to dusk; donation requested) were laid out by Thomas Mawson on classical lines in 1909 and there are captivating views of Rydal Water from the terrace. Around the back of the hall, a summer **tearoom** (daily 11am–5.30pm) has picnic tables from where you can watch Rydal Beck tumble under a moss-covered packhorse bridge. There's a series of small falls a few hundred yards up Rydal Beck, while a footpath runs south through the estate grounds to join the A591 road just outside Ambleside.

Few people bother much with **Rydal Water**, one of the region's smallest lakes at under three-quarters of a mile long and only fifty feet deep in parts. It's handsome enough – though it was considerably quieter before the A591 traced its northern shore – and there's a nice walk along the southern shore, back to Grasmere past Rydal Caves. For the best views of the water itself, follow the original route to Grasmere, along the "**Coffin Trail**", which starts directly behind Rydal

Mount and runs west under the craggy heights of Nab Scar (1450ft). Medieval coffin bearers en route to St Oswald's would haul their melancholy load along this trail, stopping to rest at intervals on the convenient flat stones.

Nab Cottage, less than a mile west of Rydal on the A591, overlooks Rydal Water. This was the family home of Margaret Simpson before she married Thomas De Quincey; and it was rented much later by the sometime journalist and poet Hartley Coleridge, a Wordsworth family favourite ("O blessed vision! happy child!") despite his trying ways. Abandoned by his father and effectively brought up in Robert Southey's Keswick household (see p.144), Hartley was a frail, precocious child who took to the demon drink and failed to live up to his early promise. But Wordsworth always retained a soft spot for him, and when Hartley died in Nab Cottage in 1849 Wordsworth picked out a plot for him in Grasmere churchyard. The cottage is now a language school, with B&B usually available outside the summer months (see p.96).

Skelwith Bridge and Little Langdale

Langdale ("long valley") is a byword for some of the region's most stunning peaks, views and hikes, and the route there starts at **SKELWITH BRIDGE**, around three miles south of Grasmere and the same distance west of Ambleside. Here, a cluster of buildings huddles by the bridge over the River Brathay, prime among them **Touchstone Interiors** (daily 10am–6pm; ☎015394/34711, ⓦwww.touchstoneinteriors.com), a contemporary design studio specializing in, among other things, items made from Westmorland green slate. There's terrace seating here outside ⅄ *Chesters Café By The River* (daily 10am–5.30pm; ☎015394/32553, ⓦwww.chesters–cafebytheriver.co.uk), which serves very superior lunches (crispy squid, mushroom-and-leek risotto and so on for £6.50–11.50; noon to 3pm) and also has excellent cakes and coffee. **Bus** #505 from Ambleside or Coniston stops at Skelwith Bridge, as does the #516 "Langdale Rambler" between Ambleside and the *Old Dungeon Ghyll* in Great Langdale.

From the bridge, there's a riverside stroll along a signposted footpath to Elterwater, a mile away, passing the fairly unimpressive gush that is **Skelwith Force**. For a finer waterfall altogether follow the hilly footpath west of Skelwith Bridge (it starts on the south side of the river) the mile or so to **Colwith Force**, hidden in the woods off the minor road to Elterwater. A circuit taking in both falls and Elterwater won't take more than a couple of hours. There's another local walk from Skelwith, north through Neaum Woods to pretty **Loughrigg Tarn**, where there's basic **camping** (toilets and a cold tap) at Tarn Foot Farm on the south side.

Heading west, a very narrow minor road off the A593 twists into **Little Langdale**, a bucolic counterweight to the dramatics of Great Langdale to the north. The bedrooms at the *Three Shires Inn* (☎015394/37215, ⓦwww.threeshiresinn.co.uk; ⑥), about a mile west of Colwith Force, make the most of the valley views, and the inn is the traditional starting point for local walks, notably the stroll down to the old packhorse crossing of Slater Bridge and to Little Langdale Tarn. A longer route – shadowed by a very minor road – runs north over **Lingmoor Fell** (1530ft) via **Blea Tarn** (where there's parking) into Great Langdale – the eight-mile circuit, returning to the *Three Shires Inn* via Elterwater, takes around four hours. The name of the inn, incidentally, is a reference to the fact that it stands near the meeting point of the old counties of Cumberland, Westmorland and Lancashire. West from Little Langdale, the ever-narrower, ever-hairier road climbs to the dramatic **Wrynose Pass** (1270ft), before dropping down to Cockley Beck for the Duddon Valley or on to the Hardknott Pass.

Elterwater and Chapel Stile

ELTERWATER village lies half a mile northwest of its water, named by the Norse for the swans that still glide upon its surface. It's one of the more idyllic lakeland beauty spots, with its riverside setting, aged inn, spreading maple tree

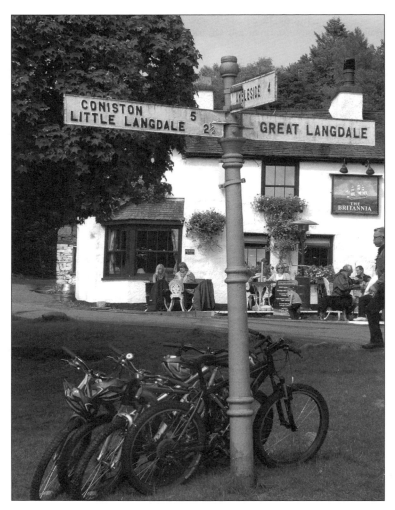

△ Village green, Elterwater

and aimless sheep getting among the sunbathers on the pocket-sized green. Historically, the village made its living from farming, quarrying and lace-making, though these days it's almost entirely devoted to the passing tourist trade: only around a quarter of the houses here are lived in, the rest are used as holiday cottages. There are no sights here, as such, just the quiet comings and goings of a country hamlet, albeit one inundated on fine summer days and bank holidays with vehicles disgorging hikers. Before you head off, you might spare some time first for **Judy Boyes' Studio** (Easter–Oct Wed–Sat 10am–5pm; Nov & Dec Thurs–Sat 10am–4pm; ℡07071/780533, ⓦwww.judyboyes.co.uk; free), near the inn, which displays a changing exhibition of the artist's locally inspired watercolours.

Elterwater sees its fair share of Langdale-bound hikers – not least because of the two local youth hostels – and numerous fell or riverside walks start straight from the village. Everyone should make the easy half-mile stroll northwest up the river – through the slate-quarry workings, still in use after over 150 years – to **CHAPEL STILE**, where a simple quarrymen's chapel sits beneath the crags. There's a pub and café for those that need a target and, suitably refreshed, you can push on from Chapel Stile, either on the level walk alongside the beck into the lower reaches of Langdale or up through the crags to the north and across Silver Howe to Grasmere.

Practicalities

The #516 "Langdale Rambler" **bus** stops by Elterwater village green. There's **parking** on the common outside the village and more limited space close to the bridge in the centre. Overnight **accommodation** is relatively thin on the ground, though there are plenty of **self-catering cottages** available by the week (sometimes less during winter); contact the Langdale Estate (see below) or Wheelwright's (℡015394/37635, ⓦwww.wheelwrights.com), who should be able to fix you up with something in the vicinity. The **village shop** and **post office**, Maple Tree Corner (open daily), opposite the inn, has basic grocery supplies and can sell you a newspaper or a map. In nearby Chapel Stile, the **Langdale Co-operative** (open daily), in business since 1884, has everything else – from cornflakes to hiking boots.

Hotels

Britannia Inn Elterwater ℡015394/37210, ⓦwww.britinn.co.uk. The hugely popular pub on Elterwater's green has nine rooms available, and while not overly spacious (the inn is over 500 years old) they are comfortable following a full refurbishment. It's known for its wide range of beers and good-value food – from home-made pies, lamb shanks and Cumberland sausage to seared scallops and vegetarian specials – served either in the dining room (booking advised) or cosy front bar. The simple stone-flagged back-room bar is where the hikers congregate, while the merest hint of good weather fills the outdoor tables on the slate-covered terrace. Two-night minimum stay at weekends. Limited parking available outside the inn. ⑥

Eltermere Country House Elterwater ℡015394/37207, ⓦwww.eltermere.co.uk. An imposing country house just a little way past the *Elterwater YHA* with grounds stretching down to the lake. Its seventeenth-century origins are well hidden, though some of the seventeen rooms still sport exposed oak beams. Many also have uninterrupted lake views. If you're going to eat in the restaurant D,B&B rates (a category higher than those given) offer the best deal. Special deals are often available, even in summer. Parking. ⑥

Langdale Estate Elterwater ℡015394/37302, ⓦwww.langdale.co.uk. Spreading up the valley, north of the village, this luxurious complex blends in well with its surroundings. Set in the grounds of a former woollen mill and gunpowder works, it contains a variety of very comfortable hotel rooms, well-equipped self-catering Scandinavian-style lodges, a superb pool, gym, games room, squash court, two restaurants and a café-bar – plus an estate pub (*Wainwrights Inn*, see p.106) within walking distance. It's never anything less than pricey, though there are good off-season discounts and other special offers. Parking. ⑧

Youth hostels

Elterwater YHA ☎ 0870/770 5816, ✉ elterwater@yha.org.uk. A converted farmhouse and barn, just across the bridge from the pub, provides simple hostel facilities in two- to eight-bedded rooms. It's not at all fancy, but it's beautifully sited in great hiking country – walking and activity weekends are held year-round – and there's mountain-bike rental available, too. Hostel parking is extremely limited and, while you can unload here, you'll probably have to park overnight in the village car park. Evening meals are served. Open daily March–Oct, and most weekends in winter – call to check availability. Dorm beds from £13.50.

Langdale YHA High Close, Loughrigg, 1 mile northeast of Elterwater ☎ 0870/770 5908, ✉ langdale@yha.org.uk. This large Victorian mansion set in its own grounds sits high on the road over Red Bank to Grasmere. It's popular with schools and groups. Open fires in winter and evening meal available. Closed Nov–Feb. Dorm beds from £12.

Café

Brambles Langdale Co-operative, Chapel Stile ☎ 015394/37500. The store's upstairs café serves large breakfasts as well as filled rolls and picnic lunches for hikers (who can get their flasks filled with tea or coffee). Daytime only. Inexpensive.

Pub

Wainwrights Inn Chapel Stile ☎ 015394/38088. Welcoming slate-floored pub with local beers on tap and popular bar meals – the terrace outside is a good spot to rest weary feet.

Great Langdale

Beyond Chapel Stile you emerge into the wide curve of **Great Langdale**, flanked by some of the Lake District's most famous peaks – Crinkle Crags, Bowfell and the Langdale Pikes. It's a dramatic, yet sobering, valley, one of the few in the Lakes where you get a real sense of scale from the lie of the land. It's also one of the oldest occupied parts of the region, the evidence in the shape of Stone Age axes found in "factory" sites in the upper valley. A footpath from Elterwater (signposted as the Cumbria Way) runs up the valley to its head – eight miles from Ambleside – from where there are popular onward hiking routes over the passes to Wasdale and Borrowdale. Parking by the side of the B5343 road is discouraged, and drivers should make for either of the valley's main (signposted) car parks, depending on their target for the day.

From the car park at **Stickle Ghyll**, where the Langdale Pikes and Pavey Ark form a dramatic backdrop, Stickle Ghyll itself provides a stiff hour's climb up to **Stickle Tarn**, following a wide stone-stepped path that's been put in place to prevent further erosion of the hillside. Another obvious target is the dramatic sixty-foot waterfall of **Dungeon Ghyll**, around half an hour's climb from the car park – the "dungeon" in question is a natural cave, and after rain the thundering fall itself is an impressive sight. The other car park, a mile further west up the road by the **Old Dungeon Ghyll Hotel**, is the starting point for a series of more hardcore hikes (see box), though there's the option of an easier walk south over Lingmoor Fell (see p.103).

Practicalities

The #516 "Langdale Rambler" **bus** from Ambleside runs via Skelwith Bridge, Elterwater and Chapel Stile to the road end at the head of the valley. It passes all the **accommodation** reviewed below en route and turns around by the *Old Dungeon Ghyll*. The local **campsite** is immensely popular with climbers and hikers, and is first come, first served, so it's wise to call to check on space at busy times. **Eating and drinking** in Langdale isn't a problem – all the hotels and pubs serve food – though for groceries and supplies of any kind you'll have to head back down to Elterwater or Ambleside. For local **information** consult ⓦ www.langdaleweb.co.uk.

Walking in Great Langdale isn't necessarily an expeditionary undertaking, but you do need to be more aware than usual of time, weather conditions and your own ability before setting off on a hike. Once you leave the valley bottom there's nothing much that's simply a stroll – then again, of the classic routes picked out below, all save Jack's Rake are within the average walker's ability.

Pavey Ark

Behind Stickle Tarn stands the fearsome cliff face of **Pavey Ark** (2297ft), which can actually be climbed relatively easily if you approach it up the grassy path to its rear (north). Gung-ho walkers make the more dramatic climb up the cleft that is **Jack's Rake**, which ascends the face right to left and is the hardest commonly used route in the Lake District – in parts it's effectively rock-climbing and requires a head for heights and steady nerves. An alternative climb, up Easy Gully (it isn't), starts from near the base. However you get up, count on it taking an hour from Stickle Tarn.

The Langdale Pikes

From the top of Pavey Ark it's a straightforward walk on to the renowned "pikes" (from the Viking word for a summit): first, **Harrison Stickle** (2414ft), then down to the stream forming the headwaters of Dungeon Ghyll and then slowly up to **Pike of Stickle** (2326ft). To make a long walk of it, aim then for **Stake Pass** to the northwest and return down the old Langdale packhorse route. Or you could walk the Pikes the other way round, starting with the approach up Dungeon Ghyll and finishing with a descent from Stickle Tarn. Either way, the walking is around seven miles and takes about five hours.

Pike o'Blisco

For a short(ish), sharp climb out of Langdale, **Pike o'Blisco** (2304ft) is a tempting target – you can see its summit cairn from the valley floor, and you'll be on the top in ninety minutes glorying in the views. The easiest route follows the path from the *Old Dungeon Ghyll* road-end, through Stool End farm, and then crosses Oxendale Beck to climb up via Brown Howe to Red Tarn (1hr) for the final push to the pike. Total walk is five miles, a three-hour round trip, but experienced hikers won't find it any problem to incorporate Pike o'Blisco in a full-day Crinkle Crags and Bowfell circuit (see below).

Crinkle Crags, Bowfell and Esk Pike

The orthodox route up to the distinctive **Crinkle Crags** (2816ft) – the name, as you'll see, is deserved – is via Oxendale and Red Tarn. From the summit, an exciting ridge walk north along the "crinkles" drops down to Three Tarns (from where there's a possible descent down The Band to Langdale) or you continue north instead up to the rocky, conical summit of **Bowfell** (2960ft) – one of Wainwright's half-dozen favourite fells. From Bowfell, descend via Ore Gap to **Angle Tarn**, and then back to the *Old Dungeon Ghyll* down Rossett Gill and Mickleden Beck. This is a nine-mile (6hr) circuit, though determined peak-baggers will also want to add **Esk Pike** (2903ft) to the route, after Bowfell (total 11–12 miles, 7–8hr), before swinging back round and down to Angle Tarn.

See Basics, p.35, for general walking advice in the Lakes; recommended maps are detailed on p.42.

Hotels and B&B

Millbeck Farm ☎ 015394/37364, ⓦ www.millbeck farm.co.uk. "What you see is what you get", says the owner – basically, three small, country-style rooms in the farmhouse (all sharing a bathroom and toilet),

a big breakfast and glorious valley views. The farm is up the narrow lane by the bridge, just before the *New Dungeon Ghyll.* Parking. No credit cards. ❷
New Dungeon Ghyll ☎ 015394/37213, ⓦ www .dungeon-ghyll.com. Victorian-era hotel near

Stickle Ghyll, beneath the Langdale Pikes. It's a more modern experience than the "Old DG", a mile up the road, and though rooms are a few pounds pricier they've all got nice bathrooms, up-to-date furnishings and expansive views. There's a restaurant and bar, open to non-guests (good bar meals available on the outdoor terrace), while off-season and multi-night deals offer real savings. Parking. ⑥, with dinner ⑦

🚶 **Old Dungeon Ghyll** ☎015394/37272, ⓦ www.odg.co.uk. Langdale's most famous inn is decidedly old-school in character and appearance – well-worn oak, floral decor and assorted dubious watercolours – but walkers have long appreciated its unrivalled location, while plump armchairs and an open fire in the lounge do much to soothe the day's aches and strains. The en-suite rooms (not all are) offer the best value. Dinner (around £25, reservations essential) is served in the dining room at 7.30pm, but all the action is outside on the terrace or in the barebones, stone-flagged *Hikers' Bar*, which has a range of

real ales and filling chips-with-everything meals. Minimum two-night stay at weekends. Parking. ⑥

Campsite
Great Langdale ☎015394/37668. The National Trust's very popular campsite lies about a quarter of a mile south of the *Old Dungeon Ghyll* (which is where everyone goes at night). It has a laundry and drying room, a well-stocked shop and a children's playground.

Bunkhouse and pub
Sticklebarn Tavern ☎015394/37356. Langdale's budget choice is next to the *New Dungeon Ghyll*, with a sunny terrace outside the bar for drinks with views. There are sixteen beds available in the bunkhouse, which is centrally heated and carpeted, big breakfasts are served every day (from 9am) and bar meals available all year round, plus *glühwein* and hot chocolate for those chilly days. Parking. Dorm beds from £11.

Travel details

All timetables can be checked on Traveline ☎0870/608 2608.

From Grasmere

Bus #555/556 (hourly) to: Dove Cottage (2min), Rydal (5min), Ambleside (20min), Brockhole (30min), Windermere train station (35min), Kendal (1hr); or to Keswick (20min).
Bus #599 to: Dove Cottage (2min), Rydal (5min),

Ambleside (20min), Brockhole (30min), Windermere train station (35min), Bowness piers (45min). Service operates Easter–Oct every 20–30min.

To Langdale

Bus #516, "Langdale Rambler" from Ambleside (4–6 daily) to: Skelwith Bridge (10min), Elterwater (17min), Chapel Stile (20min), *Old Dungeon Ghyll* (30min).

Coniston Water, Hawkshead and the south

CHAPTER 3 # Highlights

✳ **Climbing the Old Man of Coniston** The finest single climb in the area for anyone who wants to say they've been up a classic Lake District mountain. See p.115

✳ **Ruskin Museum, Coniston** The best of Coniston – its history, trades, pastimes and personalities – all under one roof. See p.116

✳ **Steam Yacht Gondola** The sumptuous way to cruise Coniston Water and reach Ruskin's Brantwood home is on the elegant nineteenth-century steam yacht. See p.118

✳ **Swallows and Amazons cruise** See the locations that inspired Arthur Ransome to write his famous children's books. See p.118

✳ **Hill Top, Near Sawrey** No serious Beatrix Potter fan should miss touring the house she bought with the proceeds of her first book, The Tale of Peter Rabbit. See p.128

✳ **Go Ape in Grizedale Forest** The high-wire adventure course in the trees of Grizedale Forest brings out the Tarzan in visitors young and old. See p.130

✳ **The Duddon Valley** Drive – or better still, walk – the Duddon Valley, celebrated in sonnet form by Wordsworth, but often overlooked today. See p.133

△ Beatrix Potter's house, Near Sawrey

3

Coniston Water, Hawkshead and the south

Coniston Water – five miles west of Windermere as the crow flies – is not one of the most immediately imposing of the lakes, yet it's one of the oldest settled parts of Lakeland. For as long as there has been human habitation, there has been industry of sorts around Coniston, whether fishing in the lake by the monks of Furness Abbey, copper-mining and slate-quarrying in the northwestern valleys and fells, or coppicing and charcoal-making in the forests to the south and east. The lake's understated beauty – and very possibly its association with these traditional lakeland trades – attracted the Victorian art critic, essayist and moralist John Ruskin, who moved here in 1872. **Brantwood**, his isolated house on the lake's northeastern shore, provides the most obvious target for a trip, though boat rides on the National Trust's elegant steam yacht, *Gondola*, or on the lake's wooden motor-launches, also provide a powerful reason for a visit.

Those wanting to stay in the area usually look no further than the cute cottages and cobbled streets of **Hawkshead**, three miles east of Coniston Water, with its connections to the big two literary lakeland names of William Wordsworth (who went to school here) and Beatrix Potter (whose husband's former office has been turned into an art gallery). Certainly, the former mining village of **Coniston** itself has to work hard to keep visitors in the face of such stiff competition, but it grows on some after a while and is the usual base for an ascent of the **Old Man of Coniston**, the distinctive peak that backs the village. Wherever you stay, there are easy side trips: to the renowned local beauty spot of **Tarn Hows**, the woodland paths and sculptures of **Grizedale Forest**, or Beatrix Potter's former house of **Hill Top** – the latter one of the most visited attractions in the Lake District. Routes south towards the Furness peninsula take you through the pretty **Duddon Valley** – immortalized by Wordsworth in a series of sonnets – and to the quiet market town of **Broughton-in-Furness**, on the southern edge of the National Park.

CONISTON WATER, HAWKSHEAD AND THE SOUTH

N

Hardknott Roman Fort

Hardknott & Wrynose Pass

Dale Head

Eskdale

Harter Fell

Seathwaite Tarn

P

Birks Bridge

Troutal

Devoke Water

Muncaster

Wallowbarrow Crag

River Duddon

Dow Crag

Goat's Water

Wallowbarrow

Seathwaite

Ulpha Fell

Torver High Common

Dunnerdale Fells

Ulpha

Duddon Valley

Ulpha Bridge

P

Dunnerdale Fells

River Duddon

A593

Thwaites Fell

Woodland Fell

Broughton Mills

Duddon Bridge

Broughton-in-Furness

A595

A595

Millom & Ravenglass

Foxfield

Grizebeck

A5092

A595

A5093

A595

Duddon Sands

CONISTON WATER, HAWKSHEAD AND THE SOUTH

Millom

Barrow-in-Furness

Ambleside ▲   **Ambleside** ▲

Swirl How

Tilberthwaite Gill

Yew Tree Tarn

Drunken Duck Inn ⊙

Levers Water

Yew Tree Farm
Yewdale Fells

Tarn Hows

⊙ **Yewfield**

Outgate

Latterbarrow

Coniston Fells

Hawkshead Hill

Coniston Coppermines YHA ⊙

Coniston Holly How YHA ⊙

Hawkshead

Colthouse

Claife Heights

Old Man of Coniston

Coniston

Monk Coniston

Thwaite Cottage

Waterhead

Esthwaite Water

Bluebird Lodge

⊙ **Bank Ground Farm**

Hawkshead YHA ⊙

Coniston Hall

Moor Top

Hawkshead Trout Farm

Near Sawrey

Far Sawrey

Torver Beck

Brantwood

Hill Top

Crag Head

Torver Common Wood

Torver

G R I Z E D A L E

ⓘ

F O R E S T

Coniston Water

Dodgson Wood

Peel Island

Rigg Wood

Satterthwaite

Windermere ▶

Blawith Fells

Lake Bank

Beacon Tarn

Force Mills

High Nibthwaite

Cumbria Way

Water Yeat

Rusland ✝

Blawith

Lowick Bridge

Lowick

River Crake

Spark Bridge

| 0 | | 2 miles |

113

© Crown copyright

Coniston

Its dimensions are nothing out of the ordinary – five miles long, half a mile across at its widest point – and its only village is the plainest in the Lakes, but the glassy surface of **Coniston Water** weaves a gentle spell on summer days. Wooded on its eastern shores (and traced by a minor road from the south), with much of the western side accessed only by the Cumbria Way footpath, it's easy to lose the worst of southern Lakeland's crowds around the lake. At the end of the nineteenth century, **Arthur Ransome** spent his childhood summer holidays at the still serene southern end, near Nibthwaite, and was always "half-drowned in tears" when it was time to leave. His vivid memories of messing about on the water, camping on the islets, making friends with the local charcoal-burners and playing make-believe in the hills surfaced later in his children's classic, *Swallows and Amazons*, when Peel Island became the "Wild Cat Island" of the book (for more on Ransome, see p.131). The sheltered waters also attracted speed-adventurers **Sir Malcolm and Donald Campbell**, father and son, who between them set a series of records on Coniston Water, starting with

CONISTON

ACCOMMODATION

Bank Ground Farm	I
Beech Tree	C
Black Bull Inn	G
Bluebird Inn	K
Coniston Lodge	L
Coppermines YHA	D
Crown	F
Holly How YHA	B
Lakeland House	H
Meadowdore	E
Thwaite Cottage	J
Yew Tree Farm	A

Ambleside & **A**

Hawkshead

Ruskin Museum

Summitreks

Co-op Supermarket

Campbell's Grave

HAWKSHEAD OLD ROAD

TILBERTHWAITE AVE

Campbell Memorial

Coppermines Cottages Office

St Andrew's

Ruskin's Grave

Petrol Station

STATION RD

LAKE ROAD

0   250 yds

© Crown copyright   Campsite, Torver & Broughton-in-Furness   Coniston Water

Sir Malcolm's world water-speed record of 141mph in 1939. After raising the record in successive years, Donald reached 260mph here in 1959 (and 276mph in Australia five years later), but on January 4, 1967, having set out once again to better his own mark, his jet-powered *Bluebird* hit a patch of turbulence at an estimated 320mph, which sent the craft into a somersault. Campbell was killed immediately, and his body and boat lay undisturbed on the lake bed until both were retrieved in 2001.

Walks from Coniston

The classic walk from Coniston village is to the top of the Old Man of Coniston, which is tiring but not overly difficult – Wainwright's flippant reference to ascending crowds of "courting couples, troops of earnest Boy Scouts, babies and grandmothers" isn't that far wide of the mark. Other Coniston walks are similarly accessible to most abilities, ranging from lakeside strolls to ghyll scrambles.

Old Man of Coniston

Most walkers can reach the summit of the **Old Man of Coniston** (2635ft) in under two hours from the village, following the signposted path from Church Beck. It's a steep and twisting route, passing though abandoned quarry works and their detritus, but there's a pause on the way up at Low Water tarn while the views from the top are tremendous – to the Cumbrian coast and Morecambe Bay, and across to Langdale and Windermere.

Old Man circular routes

Hardier hikers combine the Old Man in a ridge-walk loop with **Swirl How** (2630ft) and **Wetherlam** (2502ft) to the north – a seven- or eight-mile walk (5–7hr). Wetherlam, too, is pitted with caves, mines and tunnels, requiring caution on the various descents to Coppermines Valley. Or instead of heading north you can loop around to the south, descending via **Goat's Hause** and Goat's Water tarn, under the fearsome **Dow Crag** (a famed lure for rock climbers). This eventually deposits you in Torver (see below), with the full circuit back to Coniston being something like eight miles (5hr).

Lakeside walks

From Coniston village the Cumbria Way footpath provides access to Coniston Water's west side. The route runs past sixteenth-century Coniston Old Hall (note its traditional circular chimneys) and through Torver Common Wood to **Torver**, where there are a couple of pubs and the possibility of climbing up Torver Beck to see its waterfalls. There are also several park-and-walk spots on the lake's **east side** – nearest to the village is the northern pier of Monk Coniston – with trails and picnic tables in the National Trust woodland.

Tilberthwaite Gill and Yewdale

North of Coniston the crags, beck and tarn of **Yewdale** offer a multitude of short walks. **Tilberthwaite Gill** is a quiet, narrow glen set among dramatic old quarry workings – there's free parking up a signposted lane off the Ambleside road (one-and-a-half miles from Coniston), or you can walk here from Coppermines Valley via Hole Rake. **Yew Tree Tarn**, right on the Ambleside road (two miles from Coniston), is another pretty spot – there's parking back down the road, and a footpath to Tarn Hows, as well as a useful tearoom at *Yew Tree Farm* (11am–4pm: daily July, Aug & school hols, weekends rest of the year).

See Basics, p.35, for general walking advice in the Lakes; recommended maps are detailed on p.42.

Coniston village

Copper has been taken from the Coniston fells since the Bronze Age, though the Romans were the first to mine it systematically. The industry again flourished in the seventeenth century, and by the nineteenth century hundreds of workers were employed in the local copper mines – producing ore used for the "copper-bottoming" of the wooden hulls of ships. Together with slate-quarriers – first recorded here in the seventeenth century – Coniston's industrious miners established themselves in the village of **CONISTON** (a derivation of "King's Town").

That it was originally a mining village, pure and simple, is clear from the rather drab, utilitarian, rows of cottages and later Victorian shopfronts which make up the slate-grey-green settlement. By the late nineteenth century the copper-mining business was in terminal decline and the railway, built in 1859 to remove the mined copper and quarried slate, began to bring the first tourists, who then, as now, nearly all made time to ascend the craggy, mine-riddled bulk of **The Old Man of Coniston**, which looms to the northwest. It may sound an odd name, but "Man" is a common fell term hereabouts, signifying a peak or summit, while "Old" is merely a corruption of the Norse "alt", or high. Even if you're not game for the climb, it's worth the initial stroll from the village up Church Beck and over the old Miner's Bridge – along what's known as **Coppermines Valley** – to get a glimpse of the scars and gouges from the industrial past.

The village itself is a functional kind of place, with a population of around 800 and just enough shops, pubs and cafés to kill an hour or two. It keeps to itself to such an extent that some first-time visitors are surprised to find it has a lake – the water is hidden out of sight, half a mile southeast of the village. Before you leave, though, don't miss the few sights that Coniston village does muster: Ruskin's and Campbell's graves and the excellent local museum.

The church and cemetery

St Andrew's church, by river and bridge, sits right in the centre of the village. The **grave of John Ruskin** lies in the churchyard beneath a beautifully worked Celtic cross, and most people spare a minute or two here before proceeding to the lake or museum. The other person inextricably linked with the village is, of course, Donald Campbell, and a memorial plaque set in a slate wall and dedicated to Campbell (and his chief mechanic, Leo Villa) dominates the small green in the centre. When his body was eventually retrieved from the lake in 2001, Campbell's funeral was held at the church, before the blue coffin (the colour of his boat) was carried through the village by horse and carriage to the small church cemetery behind the *Crown Hotel*. Here you can view the **grave of Donald Campbell** (1921–67).

Ruskin Museum

Coniston's **Ruskin Museum**, on Yewdale Road (Easter to mid-Nov daily 10am–5.30pm; mid-Nov to Easter Wed–Sun 10.30am–3.30pm; £4.25; ☎015394/41164, ⓦwww.ruskinmuseum.com) – named after its most famous resident but devoted to all aspects of local life and work – is the most thought-provoking in the Lakes. The village's first museum had its genesis in the memorial exhibition held following John Ruskin's death in 1900. Organized by his long-time secretary and literary assistant W.G. Collingwood (for more on whom, see p.121), the exhibition appropriated manuscripts and mementoes from Ruskin's house at Brantwood and raised sufficient funds for a permanent

△ Donald Campbell exhibit, Ruskin Museum, Coniston

museum, largely devoted to Ruskin himself. This was housed in Coniston's Mechanics Institute, a local cultural society supported by Ruskin during his life. The latest building stands at the back of this, and is still first port of call for anyone interested in tracing Ruskin's life and work. In relating his ideas and theories to local trades and pastimes the museum also doubles as a highly effective record of Coniston's history through the ages.

The museum begins with a walk-through timeline, placing the village and Ruskin within the wider historical context. Stone and Bronze Age artefacts give way to an exposition of the local geology, essential for an understanding of why Coniston became an important mining and quarrying district. The slate quarried locally has been used for centuries to roof buildings and build bridges and walls – here in the museum, it flags the floors. You'll learn about dry-stone walling (there's a fine example outside the museum) and sheep farming, as well as about the traditional trades that Ruskin himself promoted as a means of sustaining local employment, notably woodcarving and the making

Ruskin linen and lace

Encouraged by Ruskin, who had his own theories about the sanctity of traditional labour (see "Brantwood", p.121), a local woman, Marion Twelves, revived the trade of flax hand-spinning in Elterwater in 1884. It had almost died out in the Lake District, and the flax itself had to be imported from Ireland. The **linen trade** flourished, assisted financially by Ruskin's own Guild of St George, though contemporary tastes dictated that the finished article would be more attractive to purchasers if it was embroidered. Ruskin provided a series of designs inspired by those of Renaissance ruffs, and hand-cut **lace** was attached to the plain linen to make cushion and sideboard covers and bedspreads. Ruskin's own name was used to promote the work after 1894; his funeral pall (displayed in the museum) was a particularly fine example. The industry continued until the 1930s, though by then few were relying upon it as a principal means of income.

of **Langdale linen** and the famous **Ruskin lace** – examples of these are contained in slide-out panels and drawers. In the museum's separate **Ruskin Gallery** are found artefacts from the original memorial exhibition (including a pair of his socks and his matriculation certificate from Oxford), alongside a mixed bag of letters, manuscripts, sketchbooks and a series of Ruskin's own watercolours. Most enterprisingly of all, an interactive side-gallery lets you view pages of Ruskin's sketchbooks at the click of a mouse.

The museum is also the place to track the latest developments in the reconstruction of Donald Campbell's powerboat **Bluebird**, whose wreckage was lifted from the bottom of Coniston Water. The boat will eventually be displayed here in a purpose-built gallery, though for now the Bluebird tailfin, plus photographs of Campbell, his funeral and the recovery of the craft are on display, along with related mementoes. For the full story you can see the Campbell section on the museum website or visit Ⓦ www.bluebirdproject.com.

Coniston Water

It's a ten-minute walk down Lake Road from the village to **Coniston Water** and its piers, where a second Campbell memorial plaque is sited. The pebble shoreline and grassy verges are very popular on sunny summer days, while the National Park's **Coniston Boating Centre** (Ⓣ015394/41366; free parking available) can provide the wherewithal for fooling around on the water, either in rowboats or electric motorboats, or sit-on kayaks or Canadian canoes. Coniston's sheltered waters also lend themselves to learning to sail, and the centre hires out dinghies or offers lessons and weekend courses. Also right by the lake here is the *Bluebird Café*, a nice place with outdoor tables, serving meals, snacks, ices and drinks.

Boat speeds are limited to 10mph, a graceful pace for the sumptuously upholstered and quilted **Steam Yacht Gondola** (Easter–Oct hourly departures 11am–4pm, weather permitting; £6 round trip; Ⓣ015394/35599, Ⓦwww .nationaltrust.org.uk/gondola), first launched in 1859 but fully restored by the National Trust. This leaves Coniston Pier for hour-long circuits of the lake, though you can stop off at Ruskin's Brantwood if you prefer. Evening cruises are also sometimes available – call for current details.

The other lake service is the **Coniston Launch** (Easter–Oct hourly departures 10.30am–4.30pm; Nov–Easter up to 4 daily depending on demand and weather; Ⓣ015394/36216 or 0797/108 0370, Ⓦwww.conistonlaunch.co.uk), whose two solar-powered wooden vessels operate on two routes around the lake – north to the *Waterhead Hotel* pier, Torver and Brantwood (£5.25 return) and south to Torver, Lake Bank and Brantwood (£7.80 return). You can stop off at any pier on either route, and there are walk leaflets available onboard showing routes from the various piers. Special **cruises** once or twice a week (Easter–Oct; around £7–9; call for details) concentrate on the various sites associated with *Swallows and Amazons* and the speed-racing Campbells, or show you the lake at sundowner time – you can bring your own wine on the latter and soak up the scenery with a drink.

Practicalities

Most **buses** – principally the #505 "Coniston Rambler" (from Kendal, Windermere, Ambleside or Hawkshead) and the #X12 (Ulverston) – stop by the *Crown Hotel*, on the main road (B5285) through the village. A **Ruskin Explorer ticket** (from £12) gets you return bus travel on the #505, plus use of the Coniston Launch and free entrance to Brantwood – buy the ticket on the bus. The **Cross-Lakes Shuttle** minibus service from Bowness runs as far as the Coniston Launch pier (for Brantwood and lake services) at the *Waterhead Hotel*, at the head of Coniston Water, half a mile out of the village. Drivers will come in on either the A593 (Ambleside road) or the B5285 (from Hawkshead) – the latter runs through the village as Tilberthwaite Avenue. The main **car park** is signposted; it's right in the centre (off Tilberthwaite Avenue), next to the excellent community-run **Coniston Information Centre** on Ruskin Avenue (daily: Easter–Oct 9.30am–5pm; Nov–March 9.30am–4pm, though hours may vary; ☎015394/41533, ⓦwww.conistontic.org). There's also useful online information on ⓦwww.coniston-net.com.

Accommodation

Accommodation is plentiful and, for the most part, reasonably priced. Holiday **cottages** are fairly thick on the ground, too, though none so intricately linked with the area's heritage as *The Coppermines* (☎015394/41765, ⓦwww.coppermines.co.uk), a series of converted dwellings in the old saw mill in Coppermines Valley, behind the Coppermines **youth hostel**; note that the road up here is steep and largely unsurfaced.

In Coniston

Beech Tree Guesthouse Yewdale Rd ☎ 015394/41717. Coniston's former vicarage, 150 yards north of the village, makes a charming vegetarian base. Decorated with zest, half of the eight rooms have their own showers, the others (priced a pound or two less) share a bright bathroom; and there's a garden, with fell views, where you can have tea. No smoking. Parking. No credit cards. ❸

Black Bull Inn Coppermines Rd, by the bridge ☎015394/41335, ⓦwww.conistonbrewery.com/blackbull.htm. The village's best pub has a variety of reasonably spacious B&B rooms available, either in the main building (where refurbishment is adding smarter bathrooms, new furnishings and carpets) or in the renovated Old Man and Bluebird cottages. Those two names are a familiar sight in the pub itself (they're two of the beers brewed on the premises), while the hearty bar meals are very popular – there's always homemade soup and a veggie dish, while local lamb, sausage and trout are menu mainstays. Two-night minimum stay at weekends. ❺

Coniston Lodge Sunny Brow, Station Rd ☎015394/41201, ⓦwww.coniston-lodge.com. Six immaculate cottage-style rooms (with bath as well as shower) occupy the extension of the Robinsons' comfortable family home, just a minute or two from the village centre. There's a very cosy feel inside – the lounge is stuffed full of antiques and mementoes – while a verandah overlooks the garden. No smoking. Parking. ❻

Crown Tilberthwaite Ave ☎015394/41243, ⓦwww.crown-hotel-coniston.com. The nicely refurbished rooms at the *Crown* offer a fair amount of space for your money, and many have both baths and showers, a boon for aching walkers. There's a traditional bar downstairs (with meals) and an outdoor terrace. Two- and four-day breaks (including dinner and a packed lunch for your day on the fells) are a steal. Parking. ❺

Lakeland House Tilberthwaite Ave ☎015394/41303, ⓦwww.lakelandhouse.com. A centrally located budget option accustomed to travellers, walkers and cyclists – broadband Internet, bike storage, drying facilities and packed lunches are all available. The ten rooms have all been upgraded, each has a shower room and many have decent views, while downstairs there's a café. Charge made for payment by credit card. ❸

Meadowdore Café Hawkshead Old Rd ☎015394/41638, ⓦwww.meadowdore-cafe.co.uk. The B&B available at the café is of a high quality and excellent value – there are two en-suite rooms and one with a lovely private bathroom, all three are tastefully furnished, and two have great views. Breakfast is taken in the café, which has a conservatory extension and slate patio – walkers can have sandwiches made up to take away, and the café's open until late in summer. Parking. No American Express. ❸

Around Coniston

Bank Ground Farm Coniston Water, east side, north of Brantwood ☎015394/41264, ⓦwww.bankground.com. The model for Holly Howe Farm in *Swallows and Amazons* (and used in the 1970s film), sixteenth-century *Bank Ground Farm* is beautifully set on its own part of the shoreline, 2 miles by road from Coniston. There are seven traditionally furnished rooms in the main house (oak beams, carved beds, heavy furniture), five of them en-suite, many with sweeping views, especially room 8 which has three windows overlooking lake and fells. Also on the working farm are several self-catering holiday cottages and a classily converted barn, retaining original features and log fires. No American Express. ❹

Bluebird Lodge Waterhead, B5285
☎015394/41442, ⊚www.bluebirdlodge.co.uk. Less than ten minutes' walk from the village, just 200 yards from the north end of the lake and with views to the Old Man of Coniston, it's easy to see why this small guesthouse fills quickly. There are currently five rooms, though new owners plan to add more, and a pretty garden and parking. It's dog-friendly too. No credit cards. ❹

Thwaite Cottage Waterhead, B5285
☎015394/41367, ⊚www.thwaitcot.freeserve .co.uk. Half a mile (10min walk) east, set back from the Hawkshead road up a little lane. There are three well-appointed rooms available in this peacefully located slate-flagged house, with plenty of atmosphere supplied by the oak beams and panelled walls, plus a log fire in the guests' lounge and a couple of acres of gardens. Parking. No credit cards. ❸

🏃 **Yew Tree Farm** A593, 2 miles north of Coniston ☎015394/41433, ⊚www .yewtree-farm.com. Peaceful, rural accommodation in a historic seventeenth-century farmhouse with munching sheep and a tearoom – Beatrix Potter bought the house in 1930 and furnished it for the tenants (so it's fitting that the house doubled as Potter's home, Hill Top, in the Renée Zellweger film *Miss Potter*). Three atmospheric rooms with valley views (one en suite) are tucked away amid the oak beams and panelling. Tea and coffee are provided

on arrival, there's an excellent breakfast, and walks straight from the farm gates (Tarn Hows is only half a mile away). No smoking. Parking. No credit cards. ❷, en suite ❸

Youth hostels

Coniston Coppermines YHA Coppermines Valley ☎0870/770 5772, ⓔcoppermines@yha.org.uk. The hikers' favourite (perfectly placed for ascents of the Old Man and Wetherlam) has a dramatic mountain setting a steep mile-and-a-quarter from the village – follow the "Old Man" signs past the *Sun Hotel* or take the small road between the *Black Bull* and the Co-op; both routes lead to the hostel. It's simpler than *Holly How*, with 26 bunks in four-, six-and eight-bedded rooms. Easter–Oct, may be closed some nights; also closed all Nov–March. Dorm beds from £13.

Coniston Holly How YHA Far End, A593 ☎0870/770 5770, ⓔconistonhh@yha.org.uk. The closest hostel to the village is in a slate house (with some four-bedded family rooms) set in its own gardens just a few minutes' walk north of Coniston on the Ambleside road. It's popular with schools and families (it's open every school and bank holiday) but only has limited weekend opening outside the main summer-holiday period. Evening meal and bike rental available. Dorm beds from £15.

Campsite

Coniston Hall Campsite Haws Bank, off A593 ☎015394/41223. The most convenient campsite for the village is a mile south of town, set in spacious grounds by the lake, with showers, toilets, laundry facilities and a small shop. Booking is essential. Closed Nov–Easter.

Eating, drinking and entertainment

All-day **breakfasts** are served at the *Meadowdore* and *Lakeland House* cafés, while the *Jumping Jenny* tearoom at nearby Brantwood (see opposite) is worth a special trip. Otherwise, a couple of other **cafés** and bakeries take care of lunch and snacks, while the best **pub** food is at the *Black Bull*, whose outdoor tables are perfect for a pint after a day on the fells. The Co-op **supermarket** on Yewdale Road has basic supplies, but for anything more exotic you'll have to go to Ambleside. Annual festivals include the week-long **Coniston Water Festival** (beginning of July), a celebration of arts, sports, leisure, food and drink, and the **Coniston Country Fair** (end of July), when all manner of traditional country trades, crafts, contests and entertainment take place in the grounds of Coniston Hall.

Listings

Banks and exchange There are ATMs in the petrol station and post office (fee charged at both), but not one at the bank (Barclays, Bridge End; open Mon, Wed & Fri only). Otherwise, the nearest facilities are in Ambleside.

Bike rental Ask at Summitreks, Yewdale Rd (daily 9am–5pm; by arrangement only in winter; ☎015394/41212, ⊚www.summitreks.co.uk) – though the bikes themselves (for adults only) are available from the unit down Lake Rd.

Emergencies The nearest hospital is in Kendal (Westmorland General Hospital, Burton Rd; ☎01539/732288).

Internet access There's one terminal at the *Village Pantry*, 16 Yewdale Rd (daily in summer, closed Sun Nov–March) and high-speed broadband access at *Lakeland House* (see "Accommodation").

Outdoor stores Two or three places in the village sell all the walking gear you might need; the best is Summitreks, which also rents out boots, rucksacks and waterproofs.

Pharmacy The nearest pharmacy is in Hawkshead (Collins & Butterworth, Main St ☎015394/36201).

Post office Yewdale Rd (Mon–Fri 9am–5.30pm, Sat 9am–12.30pm).

Taxis Sarah's Taxis ☎015394/41171.

Brantwood

Nestling among trees on a hillside above the eastern shore of the lake is **Brantwood** (mid-March to mid-Nov daily 11am–5.30pm; mid-Nov to mid-March Wed–Sun 11am–4.30pm; £5.95, garden only £4; ☎015394/41396, ⓦwww .brantwood.org.uk), the magnificently sited home of **John Ruskin** (1819–1900). It's only two and a half miles by road from Coniston, off the B5285, though the approach is greatly enhanced if you arrive by either the Steam Yacht *Gondola* or Coniston Launch. The Ruskin Explorer ticket (see Coniston's "Practicalities" combines bus and launch travel and Brantwood entry, and there's also a combination Coniston Launch and Brantwood ticket available which you can buy on board the boat.

Ruskin lived here from 1872 until his death: at first sight he was captivated though by the stunning mountain and lake views and not by the house itself which he complained was "a mere shed". Indeed, the house today bears little resemblance to the eighteenth-century cottage bought for £1500 in 1871 from Radical engraver William James Linton. Ruskin spent the next twenty years expanding it, adding another twelve rooms and laying out its gardens. Thus adapted, Brantwood – "brant" is a Cumbrian dialect word meaning steep – became Ruskin's lair, where the grand old *éminence grise* of Victorian art and letters gardened, wrote, painted and pontificated.

The Collingwoods

Few families have had as sure a feel for the Lake District as the **Collingwoods**, whose home was at **Lanehead** at the northern end of Coniston Water. Local scholar, historian and artist William Gershorn **(W.G.) Collingwood** (1854–1932) was born in Liverpool, but visited the Lake District on holiday as a child and moved here as soon as was practicable. He became an expert on lakeland archeology, the Vikings and early Northumbrian crosses (his *Northumbrian Crosses of the Pre-Norman Age*, published in 1927, is a classic), writing his own guide to *The Lake Counties* (1902) and even a lakeland saga, *Thorstein of the Mere*, largely set around Coniston. While at Oxford University, Collingwood had studied under John Ruskin (who was Professor of Fine Art) and was immediately impressed by his mind and ideas; later, Collingwood became Ruskin's trusted secretary and literary assistant. It was W.G. who designed Ruskin's memorial cross and established the first Ruskin Museum in Coniston. The family befriended the young Arthur Ransome, who was of a similar age to W.G.'s son **Robin Collingwood** (1889–1943). Robin was later to become an Oxford professor of philosophy, influential historiographer and an authority on Roman Britain – he excavated the Galava site and fortifications at Waterhead near Ambleside. W.G.'s wife **Edith** and two daughters, **Barbara** and **Dora**, were also highly talented: Edith and Dora as painters, Barbara as a sculptor. Barbara's bust of the elderly Ruskin is on display in the Ambleside Museum. The family graves all lie, with Ruskin's, in Coniston's churchyard.

The precocious only child of a wine merchant, Ruskin was from a wealthy background and could afford to indulge his passion for art from an early age, travelling in Europe with his parents and maintaining diaries and sketchbooks. He went up to Oxford in 1836, publishing his first book, *The Poetry of Architecture*, a year later when he was just 18. He made his name as an art critic with the publication of the first part of his celebrated *Modern Painters* (1843), conceived as a defence of J.M.W. Turner, whose work he had admired (and collected) since his student days. Later a champion of the Pre-Raphaelites and, after his wide European travels, a proponent of the supremacy of Gothic architecture, Ruskin came to insist upon the indivisibility of ethics and aesthetics. He was appalled by the conditions in which the captains of industry made their labourers work and live, while expecting him to applaud their patronage of the arts. "There is no wealth but life," he wrote in his study of capitalist economics, *Unto the Last* (1862), elaborating with the observation: "That country is richest which nourishes the greatest number of noble and happy human beings."

Drawing a distinction between mere labour and craftsmanship, he intervened in the lakeland economy by promoting a revival of woodcarving, linen and lace-making, and ventures like this as well as his architectural theories did much to influence such disparate figures as Proust, Tolstoy, Frank Lloyd Wright and Gandhi. Nonetheless, not all Ruskin's projects were a success, partly because of his refusal to compromise his principles. A London teashop, established to provide employment for a former servant, failed since Ruskin refused to advertise; meanwhile, his street-cleaning and road-building schemes, designed to instil into his students (including Arnold Toynbee and Oscar Wilde) a respect for the dignity of manual labour, simply accrued ridicule. Perhaps more relevant today is the very Ruskinian notion of ecological conservation – some see him as the first "Green" – espoused in his opposition to the expansion of the railways and the creation of Thirlmere reservoir.

House and gardens

Once you've paid to go in the **house**, you're free to wander around the various rooms. Ruskin's study (hung with handmade paper to his own design) and dining room boast superlative lake views; they are bettered only by those from the Turret Room where Ruskin used to sit in later life in his bathchair – itself on display downstairs, along with a mahogany desk and Blue John wine goblet, amongst other memorabilia. A twenty-minute video expands on the man's philosophy and whets the appetite for rooms full of his watercolours, as well as for the surviving Turners from Ruskin's collection that weren't sold off after his death. Other exhibition rooms and the Coach House Gallery display Ruskin-related arts and crafts, while there's also a well-stocked **bookshop** for those who want to bone up on the Pre-Raphaelites or the Arts and Crafts Movement. There's a summer **theatre** season here, too, held in the grounds, and various other lectures, recitals, craft fairs and **activities** scheduled throughout the year (including Ruskin lace-making demonstrations every Thursday from April–Oct) – the website has all the latest details.

The 250-acre estate surrounding the house boasts a nature trail, while paths wind through the lakeside meadows and into eight distinct **gardens**, some based on Ruskin's own plans. You can potter about, as did Ruskin, among the native flowers, fruit, herbs, moorland shrubs and ferns – his slate seat is sited in the Professor's Garden – or climb the heights behind the house to Crag Head for some splendid views. Free guided garden walks take place several times a week (April–Oct).

John Ruskin was certainly looking for something other than mere bricks and mortar when he acquired **Brantwood** in 1871. Following his father's death in 1864 he was independently wealthy, lauded for his works, and regarded as the country's foremost authority on art and architecture – indeed, he had just been appointed Slade Professor of Fine Art at Oxford University. But Ruskin's personal life was complicated by two singular relationships, which perhaps led him to seek simplicity and harmony in the lakeland fells.

His **marriage** to Euphemia (Effie) Gray in 1848 – they honeymooned in the Lakes – had been annulled in 1854, with the divorce a cause célèbre of the day, sensationally alleging Ruskin's impotence. Euphemia eventually married the artist John Everett Millais, which – given Ruskin's unflinching support of the Pre-Raphaelites – was a hard blow. Ruskin later formed a long attachment with the young **Rose La Touche**, who was almost thirty years his junior. Her parents disapproved (a proposal in 1866 came to nothing) and when Rose died in 1875, Ruskin was affected badly. Retreating to his lakeland house, he suffered the first of a series of mental breakdowns in 1878.

At Brantwood he was looked after by his married cousin Joan Severn and her husband Arthur, whose family moved into the house in the early 1880s, supervising Ruskin's visits from the Victorian great and good. **W.G. Collingwood**, for one, was always suspicious of the Severns' influence and it's clear that they eventually restricted the number of Ruskin's visitors. The Severns would argue it was to protect Ruskin's health and they had a point, since the last years of his life were punctuated by bouts of depressive illness and mental breakdown. From 1885, he began to produce sections of his **autobiography**, *Praeterita*, and, eventually, it was the only thing Ruskin would work on. Tellingly selective in content, there was no mention of his former wife, Effie. Ruskin broke down again in 1889 and fell into silence, writing nothing after this time, rarely receiving visitors or even speaking. He caught influenza and died at Brantwood on January 20, 1900. **The Severns** inherited Brantwood, ignored Ruskin's wishes that the house be open to the public for a set number of days each year and sold off many of his paintings. Joan died in 1924, Arthur in 1931, following which the house and its remaining contents were sold to **J.H. Whitehouse**, founder of the Birmingham Ruskin Society, who began the task of restoration.

The *Jumping Jenny* **tearoom** (☎015394/41715; open same days as the house) – named after Ruskin's boat – serves very nice (mostly veggie) food, especially its soups, cakes and flans, and there are more fine views from the outdoor terrace. You can eat here without paying to go inside either house or gardens.

Hawkshead

HAWKSHEAD, midway between Coniston and Ambleside, wears its beauty well, its patchwork of whitewashed cottages, cobbles, alleys and archways backed by woods and fells and barely affected by modern intrusions. This is partly due to the enlightened policy of banning traffic in the centre. Large car parks at the village edge take the strain, and when the crowds of day-trippers leave, Hawkshead regains its natural tranquillity. The village sits at the head of **Esthwaite Water**, a skinny lake less than two miles long that empties into Windermere. This isn't troubled by too many visitors, though it's renowned for its trout-fishing and Wordsworth rambled and splashed around its perimeter as a boy. Best view of the water is from the car-park access point on the far southwestern shore, two miles from Hawkshead.

The Village

The Vikings were the first to settle the land here, Hawkshead probably founded by and named after one Haukr, a Norse warrior. In medieval times it became an important wool market, the trade controlled by the monks of Furness Abbey, whose last remaining manorial building – **Hawkshead Courthouse** (key available from National Trust shop, Main St) – is sited half a mile north of the village, where the Ambleside and Coniston roads meet.

This early wealth explains the otherwise puzzling presence in such a small community of **Hawkshead Grammar School** (Easter–Sept Mon–Sat 10am–12.30pm & 1.30–5pm, Sun 1–5pm; Oct same days, but closes 4.30pm; £1), whose entrance lies opposite the tourist office. This was founded in 1585 and – even by Wordsworth's day, when the wool trade had much declined – was considered to be among the finest schools in the country. Wordsworth and his brother Richard were sent here following the death of their mother in 1778 to acquire an expensively bought education; "grammar" of course being Latin grammar, knowledge of which was the mark of every gentleman. In the simple yet rather forbidding school room the Wordsworth boys were taught geometry, algebra and the classics at timeworn wooden benches and desks (some date back to the school's foundation); you'll be shown the desk on which the rapscallion William carved his signature – a foolhardy stunt given the anecdote that miscreants were suspended from a pulley in the centre of the room to be birched. He also wrote his first surviving piece of poetry, a paean to the bicentenary of the school's foundation, before leaving in 1787 to go up to Cambridge. The only other things to see are the headmaster's study upstairs, a small exhibition on the history of English grammar schools and a few quills and nibs. The school closed in 1909.

During his schooldays Wordsworth attended the fifteenth-century church of **St Michael's** sited above the school, which harks back to Norman and

△ Hawkshead Grammar School

Romanesque designs in its rounded pillars and patterned arches. It's chiefly of interest for the 26 pithy psalms and biblical extracts illuminated with cherubs and flowers, painted on the walls during the seventeenth and eighteenth centuries. Wordsworth's other connection with the village is that during term-times he lodged with a local woman, **Ann Tyson** – someone he remembered kindly as "my old Dame" in *The Prelude*. Her Hawkshead cottage is now a guesthouse (see p.126), though the Tyson family, and Wordsworth, actually lived for longer in another (unknown) house after 1783 when they moved half a mile east to Colthouse.

From its knoll the churchyard gives a good view over the village's twin central squares, anchored by a couple of pubs and several cafés. Past the *Queen's Head* on Main Street, the **Beatrix Potter Gallery** (Easter–Oct daily except Fri 10.30am–4.30pm, plus weekends in March; last admission 4pm; £3.80, discount available for Hill Top visitors; NT; ☎015394/36355) hoovers up all Hawkshead's remaining visitors; in summer, its popularity is such that timed-entry tickets are issued. The gallery occupies rooms once used by Potter's solicitor husband, William Heelis, whom she met while purchasing land in the Hawkshead area. There had been a Heelis law firm in the village since 1861 and William was a partner in the family firm from 1900 until he died in 1945, when the building passed to the National Trust (Heelis's prewar office is maintained downstairs). If you were ever going to crack the enduring mystery of his wife's popularity you'd think this would be the place, since the upstairs rooms contain an annually changing selection of Potter's original sketchbooks, drawings, watercolours, letters and manuscripts. Although never formally schooled, she had drawn fossils, fungi and pet animals since childhood and her work is certainly closely observed. Her animals aren't caricatures, but neither are they "art" in any meaningful sense (Potter herself thought it "bosh" to think so), and to a non-Potterite, the paintings and drawings are pleasant without ever being more than mere fluff: the less devoted will find displays on her life as a keen naturalist, conservationist and early supporter of the National Trust more

© Crown copyright

diverting. Potter bought eighteen fell farms and large parcels of Lake District land, which she bequeathed to the Trust on her death.

Practicalities

The main **bus service** to Hawkshead is the #505 "Coniston Rambler" between Windermere, Ambleside and Coniston. This is complemented by the seasonal **Cross-Lakes Shuttle**, whose minibuses run from Hawkshead down to the Beatrix Potter house at Hill Top and on to Ferry House, Sawrey, for boat connections back to Bowness. The B5285 between Coniston and Sawrey skirts the eastern side of Hawkshead; no traffic is allowed in the village itself, but everything lies within five minutes' walk of the **car parks**. There's no longer a tourist office in Hawkshead, though Summitreks, the outdoor activity and equipment store on The Square (daily 9am–5/5.30pm; ☎015394/36284), has a touch-screen **information point** and accommodation phone-booking service.

Accommodation

Reserve a long way ahead if you want to stay in Hawkshead during the peak summer season. For **cottages**, barn and farm conversions in Hawkshead and the surrounding area, contact Lakeland Hideaways Cottages next to the National Trust office on The Square (☎015394/42435, ⓦwww.lakeland -hideaways.co.uk).

In Hawkshead

Ann Tyson's Cottage Wordsworth St ☎015394/36405, ⓦwww.anntysons.co.uk. Wordsworth briefly boarded here and the old street has changed little since, though the house has been upgraded over the years. There are now three rooms in the main house and two superior conversions in what was formerly an adjoining chapel – these have slate floors, underfloor heating and nice bathrooms. Also one self-catering cottage available at the same address. Parking permit available. No American Express. ❹, superior rooms ❺

Ivy House Main St ☎015394/36204, ⓦwww .ivyhousehotel.com. Elegant Georgian house whose rotunda lights up the country-house-style interior. There are six rooms in the main house (some with four-poster beds, supplement charged), five more in the lodge behind. The restaurant (dinner, £20) is open to non-guests. Parking. No American Express. ❺

🏃 **King's Arms** Market Sq ☎015394/36372, ⓦwww.kingsarmshawkshead.co.uk. This venerable inn has bags of character, with the nine rooms retaining their oak beams and idiosyncratic proportions; bathrooms and furnishings, though, are reassuringly up to date. A snug little bar with a fire and a fine beer selection does the honours when you're thirsty, while good-value meals include sarnies, salads and hot lunches as well as a wider-ranging dinner menu featuring the likes of fell-bred lamb, steak-and-ale pie or mushroom risotto. Free parking provided in the village. ❺

Queen's Head Main St ☎015394/36271, ⓦwww .queensheadhotel.co.uk. Guest rooms in the old inn have been thoroughly modernized, with good beds and repro antique furnishings. Though not huge, the family rooms can sleep three or four. Downstairs, the sixteenth century reasserts itself in the oak-and-panel interior – there's a wide-ranging menu, available in the lounge or dining room, or you can just have a pint and a sandwich at an outdoor table. ❺

Around Hawkshead

🏃 **Drunken Duck Inn** Barngates crossroad, 2 miles north of Hawkshead off B5285 ☎015394/36347, ⓦwww.drunkenduckinn.co.uk. This 400-year-old inn – more a restaurant-with-rooms these days – is many people's favourite in the Lakes, and it's easy to see why. The sixteen bedrooms mix antiques and cool colours with bold contemporary design; standard rooms in the inn itself are on the small side, but there's more spacious superior and deluxe accommodation across the courtyard, including an open-beamed Garden Room with sensational views and a balcony. Food is the main event, with a locally sourced Modern British menu of great refinement – and to the whole experience you can add sharp but unstuffy service, a great selection of wines by the glass, home-brewed ales, a suntrap garden with private tarn, and glorious valley views. While rates vary per room, most fall within the categories given, though midweek standard rooms are priced a cate-gory lower. Parking. ❼, superior/deluxe rooms ❽

Yewfield Hawkshead Hill, 2 miles west of Hawkshead off B5285 ☏015394/36765, ⊛www.yewfield.co.uk. An off-the-beaten-track gem, the panoramically sited vegetarian guest-house sits amidst organic vegetable gardens, orchards and wildflower meadows. The house is a Victorian Gothic beauty, whose owners have filled it with Eastern artefacts, contemporary art and photography from their travels, while breakfast is a real treat – either a full cooked veggie or a wholefood continental buffet. Best views are from the two "luxury" rooms at the front of the house, while the old coach house and stables are rented out as self-catering apartments. There are also plans to add designer woodland cabins to the grounds. No smoking. Parking. Closed mid-Nov to Jan. ❺

Youth hostel

Hawkshead YHA Newby Bridge Rd ☏0870/770 5856, ⊜hawkshead@yha.org.uk. The local hostel is a mile to the south, on Esthwaite Water's west side, housed in a Regency mansion which retains many of its original architectural features. There are over 100 beds and, with 14 three- or four-bedded rooms, and a separate family annexe, it's very popular with families and small groups. Evening meals and bike rental available. The Cross-Lakes Shuttle bus passes by. Dorm beds from £15.

Campsites

The Croft North Lonsdale Rd, beyond the car parks on the edge of the village ☏015394/36374, ⊛www.hawkshead-croft.com. The closest camp-site to the centre – and billed as family- and couple-friendly – is this relatively expensive spot with full facilities, including coin-op laundry and games/TV room. Also caravans (sleep 6) and holiday flats (sleep 2–6) available to rent on site (by the week, from around £225). Closed Nov to mid-March.

Hawkshead Hall Farm half a mile north of Hawk-shead on the Ambleside road ☏015394/36221. Escape some of the crowds at this basic, tap-and-toilet campsite; bus #505 passes the farm on the way into Hawkshead. Closed Dec–Feb.

Eating, drinking and entertainment

Hawkshead's **pubs** provide the main eating options, the top choice being the *King's Arms* followed by the *Queen's Head* (see "Accommodation" opposite), both of which have bar meals and outdoor tables as well as more formal dining rooms. The best local dining, however, is at the *Drunken Duck Inn* (see "Accommoda-tion", opposite), where wonderfully inventive meals run to around £35 a head, excluding drinks and service (reservations essential). There are also a couple of **cafés** in and around the village square and a small **supermarket**, while a couple of places offer picnic supplies and local produce, namely the Honey Pot deli (for bread, sandwiches, preserves, biscuits, smoked meats and cheese) and the Hawk-shead Relish Company (⊛www.hawksheadrelish.com), where there are free tastings of their chutneys, relishes, mustards, pickles, preserves and dressings.

Rural activities and entertainment are offered each August during the **Hawk-shead Agricultural Show**, while up at *Yewfield* guesthouse at Hawkshead Hill there are free monthly classical **concerts** and recitals (see website for details).

Listings

Banks and exchange There's no bank in Hawks-head, though there is an ATM inside the Co-op and the post office will exchange travellers' cheques. Otherwise, the nearest banking facilities are in Ambleside.

Bike rental Bikes are available at the YHA, at Grizedale Forest and in Coniston.

Emergencies The nearest hospital is in Kendal (Westmorland General Hospital, Burton Rd; ☏01539/732288).

Fishing Hawkshead Trout Farm (☏015394/36541, ⊛www.hawksheadtrout.com) offers loch-style day-fishing from boats (including for beginners) on Esthwaite Water (southwest side), catching wild rainbow and brown trout. Tuition, barbecue and picnic facilities available.

Outdoor stores The village is the home of the country-and-outdoor-wear store Hawkshead (⊛www.hawkshead.com). There are now around thirty branches nationwide, but the first is still trad-ing here on Main Street.

Pharmacy Collins & Butterworth, Main St ☏015394/36201.

Post office At Hawkshead Newsagents, Main St (Easter–Oct Mon–Sat 9am–5.30pm, Sun 10am–3pm; Nov–Easter Mon–Fri 9am–5.30pm, Sat 9am–12.30pm).

Tarn Hows

A minor road off the Hawkshead–Coniston road (B5285) winds the couple of miles northwest to **Tarn Hows**, a beautiful body of water surrounded by spruce and pine, circled by paths and studded with grassy picnic spots. The land was donated to the National Trust by Beatrix Potter in 1930 – one of several such grants – since when the Trust has carefully maintained it. It takes an hour to walk around the tarn on its well-kept paths, during which you can ponder on the fact that this miniature idyll is in fact almost entirely artificial – the original owners enlarged two small tarns to make the one you see today, planted and landscaped the surroundings and dug the footpaths. It's now a Site of Special Scientific Interest – keep an eye out for some of the Lakes' (and England's) few surviving native **red squirrels**.

Tarn Hows is one of the Lake District's most popular beauty spots, and the best way to appreciate it is to walk there, so that its charms are gently unveiled as you approach. It's about two miles on paths and country lanes from either Hawkshead or Coniston, with a half-mile or so detour possible from the tarn to the tearoom at *Yew Tree Farm* (see p.120). By bus (Cross-Lakes Shuttle or #505) you can ask to be dropped at High Cross, halfway between Hawkshead and Coniston Water, which saves you about a mile of the walk. Drivers will have to pay to use the designated National Trust car park.

Hill Top

It's two miles down the eastern side of Esthwaite Water from Hawkshead to the twin hamlets of Near and Far Sawrey, overlooked by the woods and tarns of Claife Heights. Near Sawrey in particular – a cluster of flower-draped white-washed cottages in a shallow vale – receives an inordinate number of visitors since it's the site of Beatrix Potter's house, **Hill Top** (Easter–Oct Mon–Wed, Sat & Sun 10.30am–4.30pm, last admission at 4pm; £5.40; garden entry free on Thurs & Fri when house is closed; NT; ☏015394/36269). The seasonal Cross-Lakes Shuttle service runs directly here from Bowness or, on its way back, from Hawkshead.

Hill Top is an almost mandatory stop on many tours of England (London, Stratford, Hill Top) and the house furnishings and contents have been kept as they were during Potter's occupancy – a condition of her will. The small house is always thronged with visitors, so much so that numbers are often limited. In summer, expect to have to pick up a timed ticket and wait in line. The carved oak bedstead and sideboards, the small library of bound sets of Gibbons and Shakespeare, and the cottage garden are all typical of well-to-do, if unexceptional, Edwardian taste – though the few mementoes and curios do nothing to throw light on Potter's character. But if you love the books then Hill Top and the Sawrey neighbourhood will be familiar (the *Tower Bank Arms*, next door, for instance, is the inn in *The Tale of Jemima Puddle-Duck*). And where better to buy a Mrs Tiggy-Winkle salt-and-pepper shaker or a Peter Rabbit calendar?

A Londoner by birth, **Beatrix Potter** (1866–1943) spent childhood holidays in the Lakes, first at Wray Castle on Windermere and later in houses with grand gardens, at Holehird (Troutbeck) and Lingholm (Derwent Water). Her landscape and animal sketching was encouraged by Canon Rawnsley, a family friend, who inspired her to produce her first book, *The Tale of Peter Rabbit*, which she had privately printed in 1901 before it was taken up by Frederick Warne publishers. It was an instant success, and with the proceeds, Potter – remembering her happy holidays – bought the lakeland farmhouse at Hill Top in 1905. There were to be 23 tales in all, with half a dozen of the later books set in and around Hill Top, though Potter still lived for much of the year in London. Following her marriage to a local solicitor in 1913, when she was 47, Potter retained the house as her study but installed a manager at Hill Top to oversee the farm. Only known locally as Mrs Heelis the farmer (rather than Beatrix Potter the author), she lived down the road in another house, Castle Cottage (not open to the public), but visited Hill Top most days, usually to work on business associated with her increasing portfolio of farms, which took up more and more of her time. She actually wrote very few books after her marriage, preferring to develop her interest in breeding the local Herdwick sheep, for which she won many prizes at local shows. When she died, her ashes were scattered locally by the Hill Top farm manager: the place has never been identified and there's no other memorial to her, save the house.

Near and Far Sawrey

The little hamlet of **NEAR SAWREY** regains its equilibrium once the Beatrix Potter house of Hill Top has closed for the day. It makes a lovely overnight stop if you can find a room, and if you can't you can console yourself with a drink in the pub, the *Tower Bank Arms*, the very model of an English country inn. A mile or so away, across the hay fields, lies **FAR SAWREY**, an equally miniature hamlet, though this time with a church, shop and post office, and also with a pub, the *Sawrey Hotel*, which has a beer garden. From here, tracks fan out across **Claife Heights**, past its little tarns and down through the woods to the western shore of Windermere – the most direct route runs steeply downhill to Sawrey ferry pier, where you can catch the car-ferry or passenger launch across to Bowness. It must be the only route in England signposted in Japanese (the Japanese have a special fondness for Beatrix Potter). Coming from the lake, it takes about an hour to walk from the ferry pier to Near Sawrey and Hill Top; going back downhill, slightly less.

Accommodation

Buckle Yeat Near Sawrey ☎015394/36446, ⓦwww.buckle-yeat.co.uk. Gorgeous seventeenth-century cottage close to the Potter house (and illustrated in Potter's *The Tale of Tom Kitten*), offering six double/twin rooms and one single (this one doesn't have private facilities). There's always a colourful display of flowers and baskets outside the cottage; inside, the cosy guest lounge has a slate-flagged floor, big armchairs and a log fire. Packed lunches available. No smoking. ❹

Ees Wyke Near Sawrey ☎015394/36393, ⓦwww.eeswyke.co.uk. Georgian country house – Beatrix Potter stayed here on childhood holidays – most of whose eight elegant rooms have matchless views across the fields to Esthwaite Water. Dinner (included in the price) is the high point, with more lovely views accompanied by five courses

served from a refined daily-changing menu. Parking. No American Express. ❽

Sawrey House Near Sawrey, overlooking Esthwaite Water ☎015394/36387, ⓦwww.sawrey-house.com. Victorian grace and comfort in this country house, with panoramic views of Esthwaite Water and three acres of grounds. The dozen traditionally decorated rooms are variously sized and priced (the best have king- or queen-size beds). Breakfast specials include wild mushrooms and smoked haddock, while D,B&B rates are also available for another £30 or so a head. Parking. ❼

Tower Bank Arms Near Sawrey, next to Hill Top ☎015394/36334, ⓦwww.towerbankarms.co.uk. The cosy non-smoking pub – a National Trust property – retains its oak beams and slate floors and has three refurbished rooms available (two doubles, one twin); totter downstairs for good

Grizedale Forest

Historically, much of the land between Coniston and Windermere was thickly forested, as indeed it is today, though by the eighteenth century successive generations of charcoal-making, coppicing and iron-smelting had taken their toll and stripped the fells and dales virtually bare. Regeneration by the Forestry Commission has restored thick oak, spruce, larch and pine woodland to **Grizedale Forest**, whose picnic spots, open-air sculptures, cycle trails and high-wire adventure course make a great day out in good weather. Red deer are seen here occasionally and the forest also provides a habitat for badgers and squirrels, grouse, woodcock and woodpeckers.

The best starting point is the visitor centre (see "Practicalities"), which is the hub of the waymarked trails that spread across both sides of the Grizedale Valley. These extend for between two and fourteen miles on undulating tracks, with the longest, the **Silurian Way**, linking the majority of the ninety-odd remarkable stone and wood **sculptures** scattered amongst the trees. Since 1977 artists have been invited to create a sculptural response to their surroundings using natural materials. Some of the resulting works are startling, as you round a bend to find pinnacles rising from a tarn, sculpted wooden ferns, a hundred-foot-long wave of bent logs or a dry-stone wall slaloming through the conifers.

On a bike (available for rent at the forest centre, see p.132), you can see much of Grizedale in a day, and while there are climbs involved on every route you'll be rewarded on occasion by some excellent fell views. There are five general waymarked cycle trails and the rather more challenging ten-mile **North Face Trail** on the west side of the forest, which gets rave reviews from serious mountain-bikers.

Off the trails, two miles south down the road from the visitor centre, the forestry hamlet of **Satterthwaite** has a pub, the *Eagle's Child*, while some clever route-finding in the narrow lanes the same distance beyond brings you to rustic **Rusland church**. Surrounded by undulating grazing land, it's a serene setting for the simple graves of children's writer **Arthur Ransome** and his wife Eugenia.

Go Ape

Perhaps the most exhilarating forest activity is the excellent **Go Ape** (Feb–Oct daily; Nov weekends only; closed Dec & Jan; £20, though price may rise; advance booking essential ℡0870/458 9189, Ⓦwww.goape.co.uk), an aerial assault course through the Grizedale trees, starting near the visitor centre. After a full safety briefing participants are let loose to follow the inter-linked rope bridges, Tarzan swings, aerial ladders, tree platforms, scramble nets and zip slides, and as you're attached to a safety line at all times the experience turns even the most vertiginous visitor into Spiderman without too much effort. The high point on the Grizedale course is at an adrenaline-inducing 59ft above floor level. It takes a good two hours to complete the course, while friends and family can follow on foot – there's a minimum age of 10 and a minimum height of 4ft 7in, but apart from that anyone can undertake the course.

Arthur Ransome (1884–1967) was born in Leeds and spent early childhood holidays with his brother and sisters at Nibthwaite by Coniston Water. His boyhood holiday pursuits were all put to use in his books, though it was the friendship he made with the outgoing Collingwood family as a young man of 20 which cemented his love affair with the Lakes – sailing with them on Coniston Water, picnicking on Peel Island, and visiting the local copper mines.

Ransome's first job was with a London publisher, though he was soon published in his own right, producing critical literary studies of Edgar Allan Poe and Oscar Wilde, and an account of London's bohemia. He met and **married** Ivy Constance Walker and they had one daughter, Tabitha, in 1910, but the marriage was never happy. In part this prompted a bold solo move to Russia in 1913, after which his marriage was effectively at an end. Ransome was keen to learn the language and had a special interest in Russian folklore – a well-received translation and adaptation of various fairy tales (*Old Peter's Russian Tales*) appeared in 1916.

During World War I, ill health prevented him joining up and he was hired as a **war correspondent** by the *Daily News*. Consequently, when the Russian Revolution broke out, he was well placed to report on events. Ransome clearly knew his Russian politics and was a sympathetic but critical observer of the Bolshevik Revolution, producing two books of on-the-spot reportage. He interviewed Lenin and other leading figures, and was introduced to Trotsky's secretary, Eugenia, who – on the final break-up of his first marriage – became his second wife.

Ransome spent much of the following ten years in Russia and the Baltic States, latterly as special correspondent for the *Manchester Guardian*, for whom he travelled widely. In 1925 he bought his first lakeland house at **Low Ludderburn**, in the Winster Valley, and, having eventually abandoned journalism, it was here he wrote **Swallows and Amazons** (published in 1930). This was the first of twelve books he produced in the series (the last in 1947), most, but not all, set in the Lake District – spells in Norfolk and Suffolk provided the background for *We Didn't Mean To Go To Sea* and *Coot Club*.

Ransome was inspired to write for and about the five children of the **Altounyan family**, whose father, Ernest, brought them to the Lake District on holiday in 1928. Ernest Altounyan, married to Dora Collingwood, a long-time Ransome family friend, bought two boats (one called *Swallow*) and he and Ransome first taught the children to sail. That the Altounyan children were models for the "Swallows" is now accepted – the first edition of the book was dedicated to them – though when the relationship cooled in later years, Ransome denied this and withdrew the dedication. Other friends and local characters appeared in the books, while Coniston locations figured heavily – Peel Island as "Wild Cat Island", the Coniston fells and mines in *Pigeon Post* and the Old Man of Coniston as "Kanchenjunga". Ransome and Eugenia lived in Coniston itself between 1940 and 1945, but settled in retirement at a house called **Hill Top** in Haverthwaite. He died on June 3, 1967.

Eugenia donated various effects and mementoes of her husband's to Abbot Hall in Kendal, which maintains an Arthur Ransome exhibition and doubles as the HQ of The Arthur Ransome Society (TARS), whose zealous members keep his flame alive by means of literary events, publications and activities. For more information, contact the museum or visit the expansive Arthur Ransome website: ⊛ www.arthur-ransome.org/ar.

Practicalities

Access to the forest is easiest from Hawkshead, which is just two-and-a-half miles northeast of the visitor centre, while you can walk through the forest from the east side of Coniston Water, from Monk Coniston and from Brantwood. With the seasonal **Cross–Lakes Shuttle** service, the first and last minibus of the day (from Bowness, via Hill Top and Hawkshead) runs to Grizedale, allowing you several hours at the forest. Otherwise, the only public transport is on the weekday postbus or schoolbus from Ulverston to the south, though the timings on either aren't much use for day-trips.

Buses stop by the **Grizedale Visitor Centre** (daily: March–Nov 10am–5pm; Dec–Feb 10am–4pm; free; ☎01229/860010, ⓦ www.forestry.gov.uk/grizedale forestpark), where there's also plenty of parking (fee charged). Opposite the centre is a **tearoom** with very nice food at reasonable prices, while occupying another nearby building is **Grizedale Mountain Bikes** (March–Oct daily 9am–5.30pm; Nov–Feb weekends only 9am–4.30pm, though hours/days may vary; ☎01229/860369, ⓦ www.grizedalemountainbikes.co.uk), which provides a wide variety of rental bikes, plus trail maps and cycling gear.

Broughton-in-Furness

Southwest of Coniston Water, a quiet triangle at the southern edge of the National Park is anchored by the small market town of **BROUGHTON-IN-FURNESS**. It dates back to medieval times, though its aspect is pure Georgian. Tall houses surround an attractive square, complete with spreading chestnut tree, commemorative obelisk, stone fish slabs and stocks. In the eighteenth century the market was a staging post for wool, wood and cattle, shipped out of the area from the nearby Duddon estuary. Follow Church Street to the edge of town and you'll reach the **church of St Mary Magdalene**, originally twelfth century though now much restored. The town's only literary connection is a slight one: the scapegrace Brontë brother, Branwell, taught here briefly before terminally pickling himself in Haworth.

Just ten miles from Coniston, Broughton makes a handy local walking base. It's also well-sited for touring the **Furness peninsulas**, which lie just south of the National Park: it's only ten miles south to Dalton-in-Furness (burial place of the artist George Romney) and the South Lakes Animal Park, and another four to Furness Abbey, the medieval powerhouse of the lakeland economy. The most direct route here is along the A593 from Coniston, via Torver, through the gentle charms of the **Woodland Valley** – the way the branch railway line (now dismantled) used to run. **Cumbria Way** hikers cut through an even less-frequented sector of the park, as their route takes them above the **Crake Valley**, through the bracken and heather of Blawith Fells, past Beacon Tarn. The A5084 parallels the path, sticking closer to the River Crake as it falls away from Coniston Water; turn west at Lowick for the main road to Broughton.

Practicalities

The most frequent **bus services** to Broughton are from the south on the #511 (not Sun), from Ulverston, every hour and a half, or twice a day from Millom. The **tourist office** is in the old town hall on The Square (April–Oct daily 10am–12.30pm & 1.30–4pm; Nov–March Mon–Sat 10am–12.30pm; ☎01229/716115, ⓦ www.broughton-in-furness.co.uk). Other facilities are scarce (the nearest ATM is in Millom), but there's a post office/store, bakery and grocer's shop among others.

Accommodation is available in a couple of the local pubs – most notably, the *Manor Arms* on The Square (☎01229/716286; ❸), a pleasant old local with a large real-ale selection, and breakfast (and drinks) served in your room, though no other meals are available. Broughton's best **tearoom**, the *Square Café*, at

Annan House on The Square (☎01229/716388, ⓦwww.thesquarecafe.biz; ❸), also has three cosy B&B rooms available (one en suite, two sharing a bathroom), furnished with old oak furniture and original fireplaces. For **bar meals**, the *Black Cock Inn* (☎01229/716529), around the corner from the square on Princes Street, is the town favourite – you'll need to book ahead for dinner at weekends. The best country-pub choice is the venerable *Blacksmiths Arms* (☎01229/716824) at **Broughton Mills**, just over two miles to the north off the A593, with a good beer selection and fine, moderately priced food.

The Duddon Valley

A mile west of Broughton, from Duddon Bridge, the minor road up the stunning **Duddon Valley** – marked Dunnerdale on some maps – twists and turns its increasingly dramatic way northeast to the foot of the Wrynose and Hardknott passes. Wordsworth wrote a sequence of 34 sonnets about the valley (published as *The River Duddon* in 1820), his conclusion "Still glides the Stream, and shall for ever glide" – a comment on the ephemeral nature of man. Lofty thoughts indeed as you navigate around the rocky outcrops and through the wandering sheep crowding the road.

On warm days cars line the verges at **Ulpha Bridge**, five miles north of Broughton, as picnics are spread on the riverbanks and kids plummet from the bridge into the water. A small post office/shop a little way up from the bridge sells ice cream. At **Seathwaite**, another three miles along the road, there's a pub and a church, and a popular short walk to **Wallowbarrow Crag**, below which the river tumbles through a gorge. The pub, the highly attractive 🏃 *Newfield Inn* (☎01229/716208, ⓦwww.newfieldinn.co.uk), was visited by Wordsworth on his ramblings, and today features Coniston's Bluebird bitter on tap and a beer garden which looks up onto the fells. Good food (organic trout, home-roast chicken, free-range eggs from the inn's hens, etc) is served daily between noon and 9pm. Two self-catering flats are also available by the night, or there's **farmhouse B&B** at nearby *Troutal Farm* (☎01229/716235, ⓦwww.troutalfarm .co.uk; no credit cards; ❷), up the road towards Birks Bridge, on the left-hand side. It's a working Herdwick sheep farm and the owners offer occasional day courses in sheep-dog handling or dry-stone walling.

Beyond Seathwaite the road is ever more tortuous, though there's parking a couple of miles further north close to **Birks Bridge**, an ancient crossing which spans a twenty-foot-deep chasm. People picnic here, too, or climb through the forestry land to the west to ascend **Harter Fell** (2140ft), whose summit is a jumble of rocky outcrops with excellent views. A good circular walk from Birks Bridge (7 miles; 4hr) climbs first to Hardknott Pass and then down to the Roman fort there, before climbing again to Harter Fell for a final descent through the plantation land to the River Duddon.

Shortly after Birks Bridge the head of the valley widens dramatically at Dale Head, whose "Big Sky" perspective is quite out of keeping with the confined Lakes – more New Zealand than Cumbria. The river is at its widest here, and at the bridge and junction of **Cockley Beck** you can debate the dubious pleasures of attempting your onward route: west over Hardknott Pass into Eskdale or east over Wrynose Pass to Little Langdale; both passes require careful driving or, in the case of out-of-condition cyclists, an oxygen tent. *Cockley Beck Farm* (☎01229/716480) by the bridge has a farmhouse tearoom. Writer John Pepper spent several winters in a simple farm cottage here, recounted in his classic "back to nature" book, *Cockley Beck* (see p.259), marvelling at a place where "peaks rose into the stars like psalms" but enduring temperatures that "plummeted so dramatically, even dreams froze".

There's a very slow early-morning **postbus** once a day (not Sun) from Broughton-in-Furness to Cockley Beck, via Ulpha and Seathwaite; a quicker afternoon service (Mon–Fri) only goes as far as Seathwaite. Realistically, though, you need your own transport to see much of the Duddon Valley – or be prepared to walk or cycle.

Travel details

All timetables can be checked on Traveline ☏0870/608 2608; for Cross-Lakes Shuttle call ☏015394/45161.

From Coniston

Bus #505 "Coniston Rambler" to: Hawkshead (16min), Ambleside (35min), Brockhole (41min), Windermere (47min). Service operates Easter–Oct roughly hourly; Nov–Easter frequency is much reduced.
Bus #X12 (Mon–Sat 7–8 daily) to: Torver (7min), Ulverston (40min).

From Hawkshead

Cross-Lakes Shuttle (9 daily): minibus #525 to Hill Top (8min) and Ferry House, Sawrey (13min, for launch connection to Bowness). There's also a first and last service of the day to Grizedale Forest (12min), while for Coniston Water change in Hawkshead to the #505 bus, which connects with the Coniston Launch at *Waterhead Hotel*, Coniston (14min). Service operates daily Easter–Sept, and weekends in Oct.

Keswick, Derwent Water and the north

CHAPTER 4 # Highlights

✳ **Castlerigg Stone Circle** The mysterious standing stones above Keswick are a brooding presence. See p.143

✳ **Evening cruise on Derwent Water** Sit back and enjoy the sunset as the shadows fall across the lake. See p.150

✳ **Climbing Cat Bells** This celebrated climb and viewpoint above Derwent Water is a real family favourite. See p.153

✳ **The #79 bus route** The "Borrowdale Rambler" runs through some of England's most spectacular valley scenery. See p.155

✳ **Honister Slate Mine** A thrilling tour explores the tunnels and caverns dug deep into the mountains above Honister Pass. See p.159

✳ **St John's in the Vale** This hidden valley has some splendid walking and you can stop for ice cream at Low Bridge End Farm. See p.160

✳ **View the ospreys, Bassenthwaite** Between April and August, you can usually see wild ospreys on Bassenthwaite Lake. See p.164

✳ **Caldbeck** Most come to see the grave of huntsman John Peel, but this attractive old village also boasts a restored riverside mill housing a café-restaurant. See p.167

△ View from Cat Bells

Keswick, Derwent Water and the north

K eswick – main town in the lakeland north – has one of the region's most advantageous settings: standing on the northern shores of beautiful Derwent Water, backed by the imposing heights of Skiddaw and Blencathra, and lying at the junction of the main north–south (A591) and east–west (A66) routes through the Lake District. Despite its long history as a market and mining town, it's now almost entirely devoted to the tourist trade, though most of Keswick's visitors are the type who like to rock-hop in the dramatic surroundings rather than clamber from tour-bus to gift shop. Consequently, there's slightly less of the themed lakeland packaging that afflicts the southern towns, and rather more of an outdoors air, with walkers steadily coming and going from their peregrinations. The town also has solid literary connections – not with Wordsworth for a change, but with the other members of the poetical triumvirate, Samuel Taylor Coleridge and Robert Southey, who both settled in Keswick in the early years of the nineteenth century.

Derwent Water lies just a few minutes' walk from the town centre, its launch service providing easy access to long-famed beauty spots such as Ashness Bridge, Watendlath and the Lodore Falls. And even with just a day in town you should make the effort to take in the charms of **Borrowdale**, the glorious meandering valley to the south of Derwent Water that's been a source of inspiration to artists and writers over the centuries. There are fellside scrambles, isolated tarns and waterfalls, riverside walks and tranquil farming hamlets, while the lonely settlements of Rosthwaite, Seatoller, Stonethwaite and Seathwaite are the jumping-off points for the many walking routes to the peaks around **Scafell Pike**, the Lake District's (and England's) highest mountain.

Keswick also makes a good base for climbing either of its shadowing northern bulks, **Skiddaw** or **Blencathra** – the first, one of the four Lakes' mountains that clocks in at over the magic 3000-feet mark, but easy to conquer; the second, a couple of hundred feet lower but with several rather more challenging approaches. Also north of town lies **Bassenthwaite Lake**, from where minor roads and footpaths head northeast into the region known locally as **Back o' Skiddaw**, a little-visited neck of the lakes hidden behind Skiddaw itself. This is as off the beaten track as it gets in the National Park, though handsome villages such as **Caldbeck** and the unsung heights of **Carrock Fell** make a trip worthwhile. East of Keswick, the old railway line footpath makes a fine

Penrith & Ullswater ▲

2 miles

N

0

A66

Hutton
Roof

Haltcliff
Bridge

Bowscale

Stone
Ends

Mosedale

P

Carrock Fell

Bowscale
Tarn

Bowscale Fell

Mungrisdale

Bannerdale

Scales

Caldbeck

▲ Carlisle

Hesket
Newmarket

Hudscales

Nether Row

Fellside

High Pike

Cumbria Way

Foule
Crag

Sharp
Edge

Blencathra

Knowe
Crags

Blease
Fell

Back o' Skiddaw

Aughertree
Fell

Uldale

Uldale Fells

Orthwaite

Great
Cockup

Cumbria Way

Cumbria Way

St James'

Over Water

Skiddaw

Carl Side

Little Man

Lyzzick
Hall

Ireby

Ruthwaite

Bassenthwaite

Bassenthwaite
S Common

Southerndale

Longside Edge

The Edge

Old
Sawmill
Tearooms

P

Dodd Wood

Dodd

A591

Ravenstone
Hotel

St Bega's

Mirehouse

Bothel

A591

Castle
Inn

Trotter's
World
of Animals

Armathwaite
Hall Hotel

Dubwath

Bassenthwaite Lake

Barf

The Bishop

Pheasant
Inn

A66

Spout
Force

▲ Carlisle

Cockermouth ▲

Cockermouth ▲

Cockermouth & Buttermere ▲

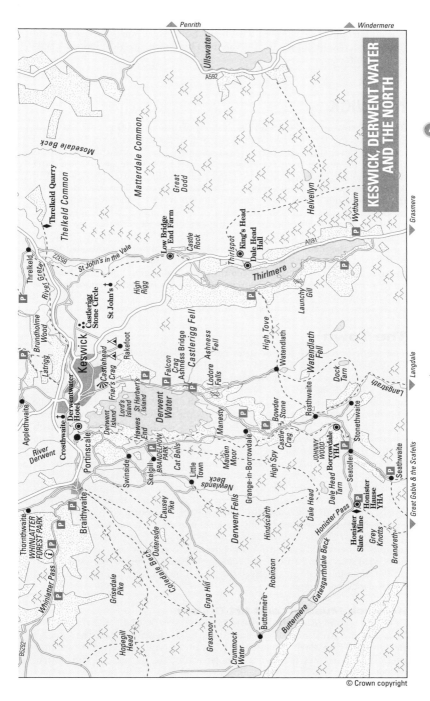

KESWICK, DERWENT WATER
AND THE NORTH

4

Penrith

Windermere

Ullswater

A592

Grasmere

Langdale

Great Gable & the Scafells

Mosedale Beck

Threlkeld Quarry

Threlkeld Common

Matterdale Common

Great Dodd

Helvellyn

Wythburn

Low Bridge
End Farm

Castle Rock

Thirlspot

King's Head

Dale Head
Hall

A591

Threlkeld

River Greta

St John's in the Vale

BS322

Thirlmere

Launchy
Gill

Castlerigg
Stone Circle

St John's

High
Rigg

Keswick

Brundholme
Wood

Latrigg

Castlehead

Rakefoot

Friar's Crag

Falcon
Crag

Ashness Bridge

Castlerigg Fell

Ashness
Fell

High Tove

Watendlath

Watendlath
Fell

Dock
Tarn

Langstrath

Lodore
Falls

Derwentwater
Hotel

Applethwaite

Crosthwaite

River
Derwent

Portinscale

Derwent
Island

Lord's
Island

Hawes
End

St Herbert's
Island

Derwent
Water

Manesty

Bowder
Stone

Castle Crag

Rosthwaite

JOHNNY
WOOD

Borrowdale
YHA

Stonethwaite

Seathwaite

Swinside

Skelgill

BRANDELHOW
PARK

Cat Bells

Little
Town

Newlands
Beck

Maiden
Moor

Grange-in-Borrowdale

High Spy

Dale Head

Dale Head
Tarn

Seatoller

Thornthwaite

WHINLATTER
FOREST
PARK

Braithwaite

Coledale Beck

Outerside

Causey Pike

Derwent Fells

Hindscarth

Honister
Slate Mine

Honister Hause
YHA

Honister Pass

Grey
Knotts

Whinlatter Pass

Grisedale
Pike

Grag Hill

Hopegill
Head

Grasmoor

Robinson

Buttermere

Buttermere

Gatesgarthdale Beck

Brandreth

B5292

Crummock
Water

Crummock
Water

139

approach to the little village of **Threlkeld**, from where some are drawn south through bucolic **St John's in the Vale** to **Thirlmere**, the Lake District's largest reservoir.

Keswick

The modern centre of **KESWICK**, a town of around 5000 people, sits south and east of the River Greta, though its origins lie around an early medieval church just over the river in Crosthwaite. Scattered farms probably provided its first local industry, if the town's name (*kes*, meaning cheese, and *wic*, meaning dairy farm) – is anything to go by. Granted its market charter by Edward I in 1276 – **market day** is still Saturday – Keswick became an important centre for trading wool and leather until around 1500, when these trades were supplanted by ore-mining and, later, the discovery of local graphite, which formed the mainstay of the local economy until the late eighteenth century. The railway (long defunct) arrived in the 1860s, since when Keswick has turned its attention fully to the requirements of tourists. There's plenty of accommodation and some good cafés aimed at walkers, while several bus routes radiate from the town, getting you to the start of even the most challenging hikes. For those not up to a day on the fells, the town remains a popular place throughout the year, with its handsome park, three interesting museums and several old pubs – and you're only ever a short stroll away from the shores of Derwent Water.

The Town

The centre of Keswick fills the space between Main Street and the wide River Greta, which makes a lazy curve through town and park. Most of the main sights – including the Pencil Museum, Crosthwaite church and Castlerigg stone circle – lie outside this area, but don't abandon the largely Victorian centre without a quick walk around. The **Moot Hall** (1813), marooned in the middle of pedestrianized Market Place, was formerly the town hall and prison, but now houses the tourist office. Down St John's Street, sandstone **St John's Church** dates from the same year, notable only for its handsome spire (a landmark from all over town) and for the fact that the novelist Sir Hugh Walpole – who set his Herries novels in Borrowdale and the Back o' Skiddaw – is buried in the churchyard: follow the sign to where the "Man of Letters, Lover of Cumberland, Friend of his fellowmen" lies beneath a Celtic cross, looking towards the west side of Derwent Water, where his house still stands. By way of quite extraordinary contrast, the **Cars of the Stars Motor Museum**, on Standish Street (Easter–Nov daily, weekends only in Dec, plus Feb school hols, 10am–5pm; £4; ☎017687/73757, ⊛www.carsofthestars.com), does no less than its name suggests. James Bond's Aston Martin DB5, the Batmobile, Emma Peel's Lotus Elan, Mad Max's Ford Falcon, the *Back to the Future* Delorean, Mr Bean's Mini – all of these and more are displayed in glorious incongruity in a restored garage in a Keswick back street.

Keswick Museum and Art Gallery

Keswick's terrific **Museum and Art Gallery** is on Station Road (Easter–Oct Tues–Sat and bank hols 10am–4pm; free; ☎017687/73263), at the edge of the riverside **Fitz Park**. Founded in 1780, the museum is a classic of its kind, its elderly glass cases preserving singular archeological, mineral and butterfly collections, as well as stuffed birds, a set of lions' teeth, antique climbing

KESWICK

Latrigg & Skiddaw

Castlerigg & Threlkeld

A66, Crosthwaite & Hospital

Campsite

Campsite

Cumberland Pencil Museum

Keswick Mountain Bikes

Keswick Leisure Pool

HIGH HILL

SOUTHEY LANE

STATION AVE

BRUNDHOLME RD

Greta Bridge

Fitz Park

Keswick Museum & Art Gallery

Launderette

Co-op Supermarket

STANGER ST

OTLEY RD

GRETA SIDE

River Greta

STATION RD

Fitz Park

Booths Supermarket

Bookends

Police Station

MAIN ST

BANK ST

VICTORIA ST

Cars Are The Stars

Bus Station

Library

HEADS LANE

MARKET PLACE

BELL CL

STANDISH ST

NEW ST

PENRITH RD

CROW PARK RD

THE HEADLANDS

THE CRESCENT

DERWENT CL

PACKHORSE CT

Moot Hall

STATION ST

BLENCATHRA ST

GRETA STREET

WORDSWORTH ST

SKIDDAW ST

THE HEADS

Alhambra Cinema

SOUTHEY ST

HELVELLYN ST

LEONARD ST

ESKIN ST

ST HERBERT ST

CROSS ST

George Fisher's

LAKE RD

DERWENT ST

ST JOHN'S ST

HIGH ST

CHURCH ST

ACORN ST

RATCLIFFE PLACE

MANOR PARK

Hope Park

BORROWDALE RD

St John's

AMBLESIDE ROAD

CASTLEHEAD

CAFÉS, PUBS & RESTAURANTS

Abraham's Tearooms	8
Bank Tavern	2
Café-Bar 26	M
Dog and Gun	5
Four in Hand	6
Lakeland Pedlar	1
Lemon and Lime	9
Mayson's	10
Morrel's	7
Number XVII	4
Salsa	3

ACCOMMODATION

Acorn House	N
Bluestones	H
Bridgedale	A
Café-Bar 26	M
Cranford House	K
Denton House	B
George	G
Highfield	L
Howe Keld	I
Keswick Lodge	F
Keswick YHA	C
Queen's	D
Ravensworth	E
Sweeney's	J

Crow Park

LAKE ROAD

HEADS ROAD

B5289

Theatre by the Lake

0 — 200 yds

Derwent Water

Keswick Launch

© Crown copyright

Friar's Crag & Walla Crag

Borrowdale

4

KESWICK, DERWENT WATER AND THE NORTH

Keswick

B ▸ A66 & Penrith

A591, Grasmere & Campsites

equipment and cock-fighting spurs. The most famous exhibit is the massive set of xylophone-like "musical stones" – cordierite-impregnated slate known as hornfels – which sound in tune when you strike them. They were collected from the Skiddaw hillsides by musical stonemason Joseph Richardson in the 1830s, who painstakingly fashioned them into instruments, added percussion and bells and then toured Victorian England with his sons as the "Rock, Bell and Steel Band". The stones came to the museum in 1917, and sometimes now go out on tour (but you can hear tunes played on them at Ⓦ www.myspace .com/musicalstones). Meanwhile, under protective covers in the literary room sits a huge array of letters, manuscripts and poems by Southey, Wordsworth, De Quincey, (Hartley) Coleridge, Walpole and Ruskin. There's interesting memorabilia too, including a cheque for thirty pounds drawn on Ruskin's account, and Southey's gloves, leather chair and desk.

Cumberland Pencil Museum

For the town's industrial history, you need to pop along to the **Cumberland Pencil Museum** (daily 9.30am–4pm, July & Aug until 5pm; £3; ☎017687/73626, ⓦ www.pencils.co.uk), west along Main Street by Greta Bridge. For centuries Borrowdale shepherds marked their sheep with a locally occurring substance they knew as wadd and, later, as plumbago or black lead. It was, of course, graphite (a pure carbon) from the Borrowdale fells, and after about 1500, when it was discovered that it could also be carved and cut to shape, graphite mining became commercially viable. In the early days, graphite was used in several ways – rubbed on firearms to prevent rusting, to make cannon-ball moulds and as a medicinal cure for stomach disorders. With the idea of putting graphite into wooden holders (prototype pencils were used by Florentine artists), Keswick became an important pencil-making town – the mines and shipments were so valuable that they were put under armed guard to thwart smugglers. The town prospered until the late eighteenth century, when the French discovered how to make pencil graphite cheaply by binding the common amorphous graphite with clay. Keswick's monopoly was quickly broken, though its major pencil mills by the River Greta – first established in 1832 – continued to thrive. Today, however, the graphite is imported from the Far East and the wood used is American cedar.

All this, and more than you'll ever need to know about the pencil-producing business, is explained inside, where a mock-up of the long-defunct Borrowdale mine heralds multifarious examples of the finished product, including the world's longest (almost 26-foot) pencil, duly acknowledged as such by the *Guinness Book of Records*. There are free **demonstration days** held throughout the year (check the website for forthcoming dates), when local artists lead hands-on sessions showcasing various drawing techniques; there's also a coffee shop at the museum, and you don't need to pay for entry to use this.

△ Cumberland Pencil Museum

Crosthwaite

Over Greta Bridge, it's a fifteen-minute walk down High Hill and Church Lane to the edge of town and **Crosthwaite Church**, dedicated to St Kentigern (or Mungo), the Celtic missionary who founded several churches in Cumbria. Evidence suggests that Kentigern passed through in 553 AD and planted his cross in the clearing ("thwaite") here, though it's unlikely a permanent church was built on this site until the twelfth century, while the present structure dates from 1523. The poet **Robert Southey** is buried in the churchyard, alongside his wife and children; his quasi-imperial marble effigy (inscribed by Wordsworth, who attended the funeral) stands inside the church, as does a plaque honouring Canon Hardwicke Drummond Rawnsley, one of the co-founders of the National Trust. Both men had strong links with Keswick. Rawnsley was the vicar at Crosthwaite between 1883 and 1917, while Southey moved into his brother-in-law Samuel Taylor Coleridge's house in the town in 1803 and, after Coleridge moved out, continued to live there for the next forty years. Southey was Poet Laureate from 1813 until his death in 1843 and his house, a Georgian pile known as **Greta Hall**, played its part in the Lakes' literary scene: it had a library stuffed with 14,000 books, which Southey delighted in showing to his visitors – Wordsworth (who tended not to hold with libraries) laments in his memorial inscription, "Loved books, no more shall Southey feed upon your precious lore." Greta Hall is now part of Keswick School (closed to the public) whose playing fields lie across from the church.

Castlerigg Stone Circle

Keswick's most mysterious landmark, **Castlerigg Stone Circle** (always open; free), can be reached by path along the disused railway line to Threlkeld (signposted by the *Keswick Country House Hotel*, at the end of Station Road) – after half a mile, look for the signposted turning to the right. The site is a mile further on atop a sweeping plateau, dwarfed by the encroaching fells. Thirty-eight hunks of Borrowdale volcanic stone, the largest almost eight feet tall, form a circle a hundred feet in diameter; another ten blocks delineating a rectangular enclosure within. The array probably had an astronomical or timekeeping function when it was erected four or five thousand years ago, but no one really knows. Whatever its origins, it's a magical spot – and particularly stunning in winter when frost and snow blanket the surrounding fells.

The Stone Circle is signposted off both the A66 and A591 on the way into Keswick. The "Caldbeck Rambler" bus #73/73A runs here twice a day in summer school holidays and on Saturdays all year, or town bus #86 comes this way twice a day (not Sun).

Practicalities

Buses (including National Express services) use the terminal at The Headlands, behind Booths supermarket, off Main Street. The town is a major transport hub, with regular services to and from Grasmere, Ambleside, Windermere and Kendal (#555/556), Borrowdale (#79), Caldbeck (#73/73A), Buttermere (#77/77A), and Bassenthwaite, Cockermouth and Penrith (#X4/X5), among others – see "Travel details" at the end of the chapter for full routes. Parking is easier than in many places: disc zones in town allow one or two hours' free parking, while large **car parks** down Lake Road near the lake, and on either side of Market Place, soak up most of the visiting and shopping traffic. There are no restrictions in the streets off Southey Street (where most of the B&Bs are) or on Brundholme Road behind the park.

Few better or more blameless men have ever lived, than he; but he seems to lack colour, passion, warmth.

Nathaniel Hawthorne, *English Notebooks*, 1855

Robert Southey (1774–1843) – his surname, incidentally, pronounced "Sow-thee" and not "Suh-thee" – first visited the Lake District in 1801 at the request of his brother-in-law, Samuel Taylor Coleridge. The two poets already had a spiky relationship – a failed plan to form a Utopian society abroad dwindled into recriminations later as, having married Edith Fricker in 1795, Southey was accused of pushing Coleridge into an unhappy marriage with her sister, Sara. Moreover, Southey was already a published poet when Coleridge and Wordsworth produced their *Lyrical Ballads* (1798), which Southey reviewed, infamously, for the *Critical Review*. He was harsh about Wordsworth's efforts and dismissive of Coleridge's "Rime of the Ancient Mariner" ("a poem of little merit").

Reconciliation came with the deaths of Coleridge and Sara's second son Berkeley, and Southey and Edith's first child, Margaret Edith. Coleridge, unhappy with his life at Greta Hall, repeated the invitation to Southey, who accepted, thinking the visit might alleviate Edith's grief. The Southeys arrived in September 1803 and Edith soon became pregnant again. Southey enjoyed the landscape and when Coleridge suggested leaving for Malta for his health, Southey agreed to stay on and pay the rent. With Sara Coleridge now effectively a lodger in her own home, Edith's other sister (and widow), Mary Lovell, also arrived to stay – soon the family joke was that Greta Hall was the "Aunt Hill".

Coleridge himself never returned to live there, but Sara Coleridge now had three children at Greta Hall; Mary Lovell, one son; plus the Southeys' eventual brood – Edith May, Herbert, Emma, Bertha, Kate, Isabel and Cuthbert. Emma, Isabel and Herbert died before adulthood, but there were still up to ten children in the house at any one time, who Southey entertained with stories and poems, including his *Tale of Three Bears*. All the children were taught languages, music and drawing at home, though the boys were eventually sent to Ambleside school.

The **National Park Information Centre** is in the Moot Hall on Market Place (daily: April–Oct 9.30am–5.30pm; Nov–March 9.30am–4.30pm; ☏017687/72645). **Guided walks** – from lakeside rambles to mountain climbs – depart from the Moot Hall (Easter–Oct daily 10.15am; £8, some longer walks £10; ⓦwww.hillwalker.ic24.net); just turn up with a packed lunch. There's **online information** for the Keswick area at ⓦwww.dokeswick.com and ⓦwww.keswick.org.

Accommodation

B&Bs and guesthouses cluster around Southey, Blencathra, Church and Eskin streets, in the grid off the A591 (Penrith road). Smarter guesthouses and hotels line The Heads, overlooking Hope Park, a couple of minutes south of the centre on the way to the lake, and there's also a clutch of guesthouses and hotels out at **Portinscale**, a small village a couple of miles west of town around the lake. Nearly all the town **pubs** offer accommodation too – the best are picked out below – while if you're in the mood for an upmarket country house-hotel experience, Keswick's rugged environs have plenty of choice. The town's riverside **youth hostel** and out-of-town **backpackers** are open all year and usually have space; hostels at nearby Derwent Water and in Borrowdale really require advance reservations in summer. The same applies to the main **campsites**, which are all very popular. For self-catering **cottages** in the area, call local

Southey's poetry sold slowly and most of his income was derived from journalism and other works. Early visits to an uncle in Portugal sparked an interest in the Portuguese empire and a *History of Portugal* was planned on a huge scale, though only the volumes on Brazil (1810–19) were completed. This was the work Southey considered his best, though it was his *Life of Nelson* (1813) – only moderately successful during his life – that later became the work most associated with him.

Although never in financial difficulty, Southey was not well off, certainly given the size of his household, and he was compelled to accept the Poet Laureateship in 1813 (the best of the sinecures offered to him over the years). This opened him up to attack from the likes of a young Shelley, who came to stay at Keswick and rather ungratefully belittled Southey as the "paid champion of every abuse and absurdity". It's true Southey had long outgrown the radicalism of his youth, but perhaps the greater irony is that, with the assumption of the laureateship, he gave up on large-scale poetry altogether. *Roderick*, the last of his epic poems, appeared in 1814.

At home, Edith was suffering bouts of depression, brought on by the steady loss of her children. After Isabel died in 1826 (the fourth of the Southeys' eight children to die), Edith was sent to a progressive retreat in 1834 in York, but never really regained full mental health. She died in November 1837 and within a year Southey had married an author, Caroline Bowles, twelve years his junior, with whom he had corresponded for almost twenty years.

Southey, ill by now, never consummated the marriage and suffered a stroke. Caroline's arrival at Greta Hall had upset everyone, especially the Southey girls, and when their father died on March 21, 1843 – a silent invalid for the last two years – the family was divided. Son Cuthbert was left in charge of the literary estate, which Wordsworth and others felt he wasn't up to – a point on which they felt vindicated following the poorly received publication of Southey's *Life and Correspondence*. And Southey's vast library – his pride and joy, catalogued by Sara Coleridge and his daughters – was broken up and sold.

specialists Keswick Cottages (℡017687/78555, 🌐www.keswickcottages.co.uk) or Lakeland Cottages (℡017687/76065, 🌐www.lakelandcottages.co.uk).

In Keswick

Acorn House Ambleside Rd ℡017687/72553, 🌐www.acornhousehotel.co.uk. The handsome eighteenth-century house offers nine generously sized rooms with period furniture, including a couple of antique four-posters. Nice touches proliferate – bedside choccies, and corkscrew and wine glasses provided – and it's a quiet, friendly base, just 5min from the centre. Breakfasts are good too. Parking. No smoking. ❹

Bluestones 7 Southey St ℡017687/74237, 🌐www.bluestonesguesthouse.co.uk. A welcoming guesthouse that's used to families (check out the classic Dinky car collection) and groups of walkers – three en-suite rooms available, with extra bed or bunks as required. And there's fresh fruit and yoghurt at breakfast. No American Express. ❸

Bridgedale 101 Main St ℡017687/73914, 🌐www.insiteswd.co.uk/bridgedalecottage.

Keswick's most amenable landlady, Mrs Taylor, makes her half-dozen rooms suit all requirements. The Shirley Bassey-style lamé shower curtain aside, there are few frills, but whether you're looking for an early breakfast before a day on the fells (weather forecast and packed lunch provided), a room-only deal, en-suite room or cycle storage, you'll find it here. There's a summer tea garden out back, left-luggage facilities and parking. No credit cards. ❸

Café-Bar 26 26 Lake Rd ℡017687/80863, 🌐www.cafebar26.co.uk. Three stylishly decorated rooms on the first floor above the café offer a chintz-free base right in the town centre. They're all nice and light, with pretty tiled shower rooms. No smoking. ❸, weekends ❹

Cranford House 18 Eskin St ℡017687/71017, 🌐www.cranfordhouse.co.uk. Classy town-house B&B, whose appealing rooms feature large comfortable beds and decent linen and furnishings

Keswick walks fall into three categories: strolls down by the lake or up to scenic viewpoints, and the considerably more energetic peak-bagging of Skiddaw and Blencathra. If you've got time to make only one local hike, there's a case for making it up Cat Bells (see Derwent Water, p.153), which forms the distinctive backdrop to many a Keswick view.

Latrigg

Latrigg (1203ft), north of town, gets the vote for a quick climb (45min) to a fine viewpoint – up Bassenthwaite Lake and across Derwent Water to Borrowdale and the high fells. Driving first to the Underscar car park gets you even closer, within twenty minutes of the summit. For a circular walk (4–6 miles; 2–3hr), follow the eastern ridge to Brundholme, returning through Brundholme wood or along the railway line path.

Walla Crag

South of town, the best half-day walk is to **Walla Crag** (1234ft) and back (5 miles; 4hr), approaching via Friar's Crag and Derwent Water. At Calf Close Bay you cross the Borrowdale road (B5329) and climb through Great Wood to the summit, which provides terrific views of the lake, St Herbert's Island and the fells beyond. The descent back to town is via Rakefoot, with a possible diversion to Castlehead (530ft) for lesser, but still attractive, lake views.

Skiddaw

Easiest of the true mountain walks is the hike up the smooth mound of splintery slate that is **Skiddaw** (3053ft). From the Underscar car park it's a steady (and, it has to be said, boring) walk up a wide, eroded track, with a possible diversion up Skiddaw **Little Man** (2837ft), before reaching the High Man summit. Straight up and down is around five miles and takes about five hours, but there's a much better route back, descending to the southwest, along the ridge above Bassenthwaite formed by Longside Edge, **Ullock Pike** (2230ft) and The Edge, before dropping down into Dodd Wood (8 miles; 7hr). Either catch the bus along the A591 back to Keswick, or keep off the road on the signposted Keswick path from Dodd Wood.

Blencathra

Blencathra (2847ft) – also known as Saddleback – could keep hikers occupied for a fortnight. Wainwright details twelve possible ascents of its summit, and, though made of the same slate as Skiddaw, it's a far more aggressive proposition. Many use Threlkeld as the starting point: easiest route is via Blease Fell and Knowe Crags (an ascent that Wainwright pooh-poohs as too dull); the path starts from the car park by the Blencathra Centre. The more adventurous steer a course up any of the narrow ridges, whose names (Sharp Edge, Foule Crag) don't pull any punches – for most of these, the best starting point is the *White Horse* pub at Scales, another mile-and-a-half up the A66 (towards Penrith) from Threlkeld.

See Basics, p.35, for general walking advice in the Lakes; recommended maps are detailed on p.42.

– you're guaranteed "absolutely no ornaments, doilies, nylon sheets or flowery wallpaper"! The six rooms include two singles (these share a bathroom), while the two rooms at the top have rooftop views and exposed beams. Breakfast (English, vegetarian or continental) is taken in front of the open fire. No smoking. ❸

George St John St ☎017687/72076, ⓦwww .georgehotelkeswick.co.uk. Keswick's oldest inn has bags of character. The rooms themselves have been modernized (ask if you want a bath instead of a shower), and are comfortable enough, though you'll be easily tempted downstairs where the snug bars are lined with portraits, pictures and curios, and feature wooden settles in front of the fire. Jennings' beers accompany classic bar meals, or there's a fancier menu available in the restaurant, where dinner ranges from venison casserole to local trout. Limited parking. ⑤

Highfield The Heads ☎017687/72508, Ⓦwww .highfieldkeswick.co.uk. Beautifully restored Victorian stone hotel whose eye-catching feature rooms include two perky turrets and even a converted chapel, the latter with lots of space and a four-poster bed. Some front rooms have balconies and lake views, all have comfortable beds, and there's free internet access for guests, garden seating, a bar and an inventive restaurant with a daily-changing menu (dinner included in the price). Parking. No smoking. ⑦

🏃 **Howe Keld** 5–7 The Heads ☎017687/72417, Ⓦwww.howekeld.co.uk. The Fishers' guesthouse has a reputation for great breakfasts, including organic bread, pancakes and syrup, fishcakes, veggie rissoles and other home-made specialities. Rooms have fell views and pretty fabrics, plus compact bathrooms with power showers and toiletries. There's also a view-laden lounge supplied with walking books. Private parking. No smoking. ④

Keswick Lodge Main St ☎017687/74584, Ⓦwww.keswick-lodge.co.uk. Old coaching inn with decently priced rooms, and good beer downstairs in one of Keswick's jollier hostelries, warmed in winter by an open fire. Ask about the three-for-two-night offers (not available over weekends or throughout Aug). ④

Queen's Main St ☎017687/73333, Ⓦwww .queenshotel.co.uk. The traditional central hotel has a very cosy bar and a huge variety of rooms, all reasonably sized, many with good views. Some have been upgraded more recently than others, so ask to see first – the cheapest are priced a category lower. Parking available (fee charged) and free pass provided to Keswick pool. ⑥

Ravensworth 29 Station St ☎017687/72476, Ⓦwww.ravensworth-hotel.co.uk. Small, friendly town-centre hotel that makes a real effort to please. The nine rooms are smartly turned out (and many have fell views), organically grown lakeland lilies adorn the lounge, while breakfast presents a choice of organic tomatoes, locally sourced meats, free-range eggs and the like. There's also wi-fi access throughout, maps and printed walks available, and a free parking permit provided. No smoking. Two-night minimum stay at weekends. No American Express. ④

Sweeney's 18–20 Lake Rd ☎0500/600725, Ⓦwww.sweeneysbar.co.uk. Four bright en-suite rooms (including two large twin/family rooms)

located above a contemporary bar-brasserie. It makes a comfortable base, with fell views from some windows, a good breakfast and the town's most spacious beer garden out back. Free parking permit provided. ④, weekends ⑤

Around Keswick

Derwentwater Portinscale, 2 miles west of town, off the A66 ☎017687/72538, Ⓦwww .derwentwater-hotel.co.uk. See chapter map for location. Three-star lakeside retreat with very comfortable rooms – nice enough in the "classic" (ie standard) range and rather splendid at the "deluxe" level (at about £200 a night), where you also get repro-Victorian furniture, lounge areas, sherry decanter, CD and video players. The public lounges, conservatory and restaurant all rate highly too, while guests get free use of a nearby health spa and pool. Two-night D,B&B rates are a good deal, while self-catering one- and two-bedroomed apartments and cottages are available at adjacent Derwent Manor. Parking. ⑧

Lyzzick Hall Under Skiddaw, A591 ☎017687/72277, Ⓦwww.lyzzickhall.co.uk. See chapter map for location. A couple of miles northwest of town, this relaxed country-house hotel is a bit heavy on the floral decor but is set in its own lovely grounds with sweeping views, plus an indoor pool, lounges warmed by log fires and a very good restaurant. In fact, D,B&B rates offer the best deal. Parking. ⑦

Youth hostels and back-packer accommodation

Denton House Penrith Rd ☎017687/75351, Ⓦwww.vividevents.co.uk. Keswick's cheapest bed is at the independent backpackers housed in a former stationmaster's house and cadet barracks, a 10min walk from the centre (by the railway bridge, just after the ambulance/fire station). A rolling refurbishment is in hand, but all the basics are in place (kitchen, washing machine, lockers, bike storage, free tea and coffee), while single-sex/mixed dorms range in size from four to twelve beds (56 in total). Breakfast is £3 (when available, usually at weekends when groups are in residence). Sign up for outdoor activities and tours at reception; office open at least Mon–Fri 9am–1pm. Parking. No credit cards. Dorm beds £12.50.

Derwentwater YHA Barrow House, 2 miles south of Keswick on the B5289 (Borrowdale) road ☎0870/770 5792, ℮derwentwater@yha.org .uk. See Derwent Water map for location. Based in a 200-year-old mansion with fifteen acres of grounds sloping down to the lake. It's a bit far to walk in and out for the shops and pubs, but bus

#79 runs past and the Keswick Launch stops at a nearby pier. There are 88 beds, mostly in four- to eight-bedded rooms (the family rooms book up fast), a drying room and laundry, and bike rental and evening meals available. Parking. Dorm beds from £13.95.

🚶 **Keswick YHA**, Station Rd ☎ 0870/770 5894, ✉ keswick@yha.org.uk. Once a riverside woollen mill, Keswick's town YHA has a new, contemporary look after a major overhaul. Dorms and public areas have been completely revamped, and families, walkers and travellers all seem to approve – it's big (over 90 beds) but you're still advised to book at any time of year. Facilities are up-to-date (allergy rooms available, plus Internet access, drying room, laundry, lounge with pool table and bike rental), there's free tea and coffee on arrival, while a restaurant and bar offer good-value meals at lunch and dinner. Dorm beds from £17.50 (May–Sept from £19), breakfast included.

Campsites

Castlerigg Farm Rakefoot Lane, off A591, Castlerigg ☎ 017687/72479. Mainly for tents (with showers and a small shop), just over a mile southeast of the centre. Closed Nov–Easter.

Castlerigg Hall Rakefoot Lane, off A591, Castlerigg ☎ 017687/74499, ⊕ www.castlerigg .co.uk. Large tent-and-caravan site; it's the first one you reach up this road, just over a mile southeast of the centre. There are no advance bookings for tents, but van rental is available by the week (£200–420), and there's a shop, campers' kitchen, laundry, lounge and games room, plus a breakfast room (open mornings only) supplying cooked breakfasts. Closed Nov–Easter.

Derwentwater Camping and Caravan Club Site Derwent Water ☎ 017687/72392. Less than a 10min walk from the centre, down by the lake (which means it's always busy); turn off Main Street and head past the bus terminal. Closed Dec & Jan.

Eating, drinking and entertainment

Keswick is a real metropolis compared to anywhere else in the National Park, which means for once that there's no shortage of places to eat and drink, especially down Lake Road, which is fast becoming Keswick's "food street". Daytime **cafés** are firmly aimed at the walking and shopping crowd – you won't want for a big bowl of soup or a cream tea – and there are some decent **restaurants** and lots of **pubs**. The two **supermarkets**, Booths and the Co-op, are near the bus station, off Main Street.

If you're planning to be around for any length of time, it's worth a call to see what's on at the **Theatre by the Lake**, whose full repertoire of performances, concerts and events makes Keswick something of a cultural centre for the Lake District. Otherwise, the biggest events in town are the annual **jazz festival** and **mountain festival**, both in May, the June **beer festival**, and the traditional **Keswick Agricultural Show** (August bank holiday), which is the place to learn more about sheep-shearing and other rural pursuits.

Cafés and café-bars

Abraham's Tearooms George Fisher, 2 Borrowdale Rd ☎ 017687/72178. The top-floor tearoom of the outdoors store (housed in the former quarters of the Abraham's lakeland photography studio, hence the name) comes to your aid with warming mugs of *glühwein*, home-made soups, big breakfasts with free-range eggs and daily specials. Daytime only. No credit cards. Inexpensive.

Café-Bar 26 26 Lake Rd ☎ 017687/80863, ⊕ www.cafebar26.co.uk. By far the finest of the town's contemporary café-bars, this is a relaxed place with squishy leather sofas, wi-fi access, good coffee and a decent range of wines and beers. Lunch here is a reliable bet (Tues–Sun noon–2.30pm) – the likes of steak-frites, haddock fishcakes or lamb-and-mint burger

– while a patio out the back catches the sun. Moderate.

🚶 **Lakeland Pedlar** Henderson's Yard, Bell Close Car Park ☎ 017687/74492, ⊕ www.lakelandpedlar.co.uk. Keswick's best café serves a tasty and inventive range of Mediterranean/Tex-Mex wholefood veggie dishes, from breakfast burritos to vegetable crumble or chilli. The coffee is great too, while a few outdoor tables soak up the sun and look up to the fells. Daytime only, but until 9pm in school holidays. Moderate.

Number XVII Coffee Shop 17 Station St ☎ 017687/71171. A few small tables at the back of the deli provide intimate seating for "light bites" (spicy beanburgers, mozzarella melts), stuffed bagels and wraps, grilled sandwiches and all-day brunches. Daytime only. Inexpensive.

Restaurants

Lemon and Lime 31 Lake Rd
☏ 017687/73088. A good choice if you can't decide on a cuisine, *Lemon and Lime* offers a list of round-the-world tapas-style starters followed by an equally broad-ranging menu of mains, from burgers and steaks to noodles and Thai curries. There's an easy-going café-like feel, with chatty staff and big picture windows on to the street. Moderate.

Mayson's 33 Lake Rd ☏ 017687/74104. Under the tumbling houseplants this licensed, self-service restaurant serves lasagne, moussaka, pies, curries and stir-fries, accompanied by rice, baked potatoes and salad. May–Oct open until 9pm; daytime only rest of the year. No credit cards. Inexpensive.

Morrel's 34 Lake Rd ☏ 017687/72666, ⊛ www .morrels.co.uk. You'll eat well in this handsome-looking restaurant – modern British and Mediterranean styles prevail – and while it's at the top end of Keswick dining, there's a bargain Sunday *table d'hote* menu and a decent selection of wines by the glass. It's also the closest restaurant to the Theatre by the Lake and opens at 5.30pm for pre-theatre meals. Dinner only, closed Mon. Expensive.

Salsa 1 New St ☏ 017687/75222. Billed as a "Mexican bistro", on the right night *Salsa* can be a real buzz (it's best to book at weekends in summer) – have a drink in the downstairs bar and then move upstairs for hearty portions of fajitas, tacos, ribs, wraps, grilled fish or steak. Dinner only. Moderate.

Pubs

Bank Tavern 47 Main St ☏ 017687/72663. Currently has a local reputation for its bar meals, which means that every table is often filled. The beer's good too (Jennings and guest ales), while a terrace at the back looks up Market Square.

Dog and Gun 2 Lake Rd
☏ 017687/73463. The top pub in town retains its old slate floor and oak beams, and shows off a series of classic Abraham brothers' climbing pictures. A changing selection of local guest ales is available, while many come for the food – the house special is Hungarian goulash with dumplings, made every day to a recipe handed down over the years.

Four in Hand Lake Rd ☏ 017687/72069. A popular old coaching inn where the bar meals get a lot of takers.

Theatre and cinema

Alhambra St John's St ☏ 017687/72195, ⊛ www .keswick-alhambra.co.uk. The cinema shows mainstream releases, but there are foreign-language and indie screenings most Thursdays, while Keswick Film Club (⊛ www.keswickfilmclub.org) puts on arthouse movies on Sundays (Oct–March) and hosts an annual Film Festival (in Feb) featuring the best of world cinema.

Theatre by the Lake Lake Rd ☏ 017687/74411, ⊛ www.theatrebythelake.com. England's newest repertory theatre company hosts a full programme of drama, concerts, exhibitions, readings and talks. "Words By The Water", a literature festival, takes place here in the spring, while on selected mornings there's a guided backstage tour of the theatre (advance booking required; £3).

Listings

Banks and exchange There are ATMs at Barclays and HSBC (both on Market Sq); Lloyds-TSB (4 Main St); and NatWest (28 Main St). You can exchange travellers' cheques at the post office.

Bike rental Keswick Mountain Bikes, Southey Hill, Greta Bridge (daily 9am–5pm; ☏ 017687/75202, ⊛ www.keswickmountainbikes.co.uk).

Bookshop Bookends, 66 Main St
☏ 017687/75277, ⊛ www.bookscumbria.com, has a good selection of local-interest books and hiking guides, plus discounted books and novels.

Car rental Keswick Motor Company, Lake Rd
☏ 017687/72064.

Hospital Keswick Cottage Hospital, Crosthwaite Rd, Keswick ☏ 017687/72012.

Internet access U-Compute, 48 Main St, upstairs at the post office (Mon–Sat 9am–5.30pm, Sun 9.30am–4.30pm; ☏ 017687/75127), and at various other places around town – including wi-fi access at *Café-Bar 26* on Lake Rd.

Laundry Keswick Launderette, Main St, next to the Co-op (daily 7.30am–7pm; ☏ 017687/75448).

Left luggage There's no official place to leave luggage, but you can try *Bridgedale* guesthouse, 101 Main St, which sometimes obliges for non-residents (£2–3 a day).

Outdoor stores George Fisher, 2 Borrowdale Rd (☏ 017687/72178, ⊛ www.georgefisher.co.uk), is perhaps the most celebrated outdoors store in the Lakes, with a full range of equipment and maps, boot rental, a daily weather information service and café. Needle Sports, 56 Main St (☏ 017687/72227, ⊛ www.needlesports.com), is the local climbing and mountaineering specialist. But Keswick also has a dozen other outdoors stores, most found along the western half of Main Street, between the post office and the bus station.

Pharmacies Boots, 31 Main St ℡017687/72383; Lightfoot's, 25 Main St ℡017687/72108; J.N. Murray, 15–17 Station St ℡017687/72049.
Police station 8 Bank St ℡0845/330 0247.
Post office 48 Main St (Mon–Fri 8.30am–5.30pm, Sat 8.30am–1pm).
Swimming pool Keswick Leisure Pool, Station Rd
(Easter–Sept daily 9am–5pm; winter limited hours, call for details; ℡017687/72760, ⓦwww .carlisleleisure.com/keswick). It has a wave machine, waterslide, fitness centre and poolside café.
Taxis Davies Taxis ℡017687/72676; KLM ℡017687/75337.

④

KESWICK, DERWENT WATER AND THE NORTH | Derwent Water

Derwent Water

Derwent Water may not be that big – three miles long and, at most, a mile wide – but it's among the most attractive of the lakes. What's more, it's only five minutes' walk south of the centre of Keswick, down Lake Road and through the pedestrian underpass, and is fully served by a launch service that circles the lake at regular intervals. Standing on the northern shore, headed by the grassy banks of **Crow Park** and ringed by glowering crags, you look down the lake to its islets. One of these, Derwent Island, was settled by sixteenth-century German miners brought to Keswick to mine its ores. Another, **St Herbert's Island**, in the middle of the lake, is thought to be the site of the seventh-century hermitage's cell of St Herbert, disciple and friend of St Cuthbert of Lindisfarne. Derwent Water is also a relatively shallow lake, eighty feet at its deepest point but averaging more like twenty feet deep; so shallow in fact that roe deer from the surrounding woods sometimes swim across to **Lord's Island**. There's a mysterious floating island, too, which appears only after sustained periods of dry weather.

Derwent Water marks a geological divide, where the slate of Skiddaw gives way to the volcanic rock of Borrowdale, something you'll notice at jutting Falcon Crag, halfway down the east side. Falcons still nest and breed here; indeed, Derwent Water supports several **wildlife** habitats, including those of the sandpiper and yellow wagtail, as well as Britain's rarest fish, the plankton-eating vendace (like the char, an Ice Age survivor). But the otters and wild cats remembered in place names around the lake are long gone.

Human interaction has shaped the lakeside: you can still see the scars from the old mines on the west side, though further damage has been prevented by the intervention of the National Trust, whose first purchased parcel of land in the Lake District was that of **Brandlehow woods and park** in 1902. During the eighteenth and early nineteenth centuries, the lake saw regular regattas,

Keswick Launch

Keswick Launch (℡017687/72263, ⓦwww.keswick-launch.co.uk) runs services right around the lake calling at six points en route (£1.40 per stage; £7.50 round trip, family ticket £18). Between Easter and the end of November, services run hourly from 10am until 6pm, both clockwise and anticlockwise around the lake (ie a service leaves every 30min in one direction or another). Services are extended into the early evening from the Spring bank holiday until mid-September, with the last departure at 7pm (8pm in summer school holidays). From December until Easter services depart on Saturdays and Sundays only, three times daily in each direction. There's also an enjoyable one-hour **evening cruise** (£8.50, family ticket £20) from May Day bank holiday until mid-September, with anecdotal commentary and a glass of wine or soft drink included; it's best to pop down earlier in the day to buy a ticket and ensure a place.

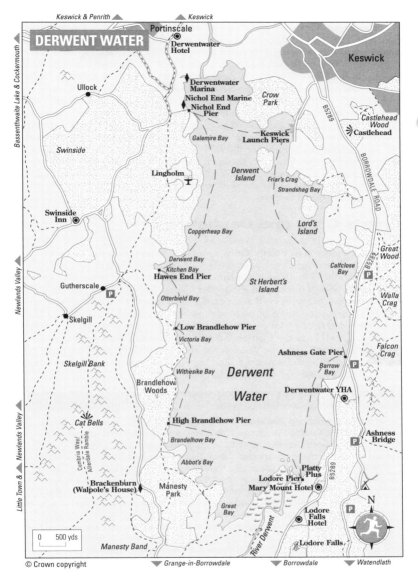

orchestrated initially by Joseph Pocklington, a wealthy banker, for whom the word eccentric seems woefully inadequate. He built himself a house, church and fortress on **Derwent Island** (the house is still there, owned by the National Trust; tours on certain days from June–Aug, ☎015394/35599) and appointed himself "Governor and Commander-in-Chief", blasting off brass cannons at the boats. The house that's now Derwentwater YHA was also his; he had the rocks behind it dynamited to fashion an artificial waterfall.

The ferry service around the lake is provided by the **Keswick Launch** (see box on p.150), whose piers are just a few minutes' walk from Keswick town centre on the northeastern edge of Derwent Water. The launch departures during the day are frequent enough to combine a cruise with a walk and picnic, though you can also walk around the entire lake from Keswick (9–10 miles; 3–4hr); the path around the western side forms part of the Cumbria Way and Allerdale Ramble long-distance routes. You can rent **rowboats** and self-drive motorboats at the Keswick Launch piers, though for kayaking, canoeing, sailing and windsurfing you'll need to contact one of the other **water-sports outlets** on the lake, at Portinscale or Lodore. **Bus services** to points around the lake involve catching either the #79 "Borrowdale Rambler" (operates all year; day rider ticket from £4.80) down the B5289 from Keswick to Seatoller, or the seasonal (Easter–Oct) #77A "Honister Rambler" (day rider ticket from £6), which runs along the western shore via Portinscale, Cat Bells (for Newlands Valley) and Grange.

Friar's Crag and Castlehead

The most popular short walk on the lake – no more than ten minutes from the launch piers – is to **Friar's Crag**, a wooded peninsula on the northeastern shore from where medieval pilgrims left for St Herbert's Island to seek the hermit's blessing. The Friar's Crag land was acquired by the National Trust in 1922, and is held in memory of its founder Canon Rawnsley (see box), though it's long been a beauty spot. Ruskin's childhood visit to Friar's Crag famously inspired "intense joy, mingled with awe", which is a bit over the top, but the grass banks and little rocky coves nearby are very attractive. For a longer walk, return to Keswick via the **Castlehead** (530ft) viewpoint, from where you can look straight down Derwent Water to Castle Crag, with Scafell Pike rising in the distance. Castlehead is reached from the lake by cutting up to and crossing the B5289 – a round trip of three miles or one and a half hours from town.

Canon Rawnsley and the National Trust

Hardwicke Drummond Rawnsley (1851–1920) was ordained in 1875, gained his first living in the Lakes (at Wray, near Ambleside) two years later, and was appointed vicar at Crosthwaite, Keswick, in 1883. It was a period of rapid industrial development and the conservation-minded Canon Rawnsley found himself opposing the proposed Braithewaite and Buttermere Railway, fighting footpath disputes and lining up with Ruskin (an old Oxford college friend) against the creation of Thirlmere reservoir – though Rawnsley later accepted the needs of the northern cities for water and even attended Thirlmere's official opening. His time served on the County Council and the newly formed Lake District Defence Society convinced him of the need for a preservation society with money and teeth. In 1893, together with Octavia Hill and Sir Robert Hunter, and the backing of the Duke of Westminster, he established the **National Trust**. This received its first piece of donated land (in Wales) the following year and encouraged subscriptions to buy endangered property elsewhere: between 1902 and 1908 the Trust acquired much of Derwent Water and Borrowdale and is now easily the largest landowner in the Lake District.

Rawnsley remained an active part of the Trust while continuing to preach and write – he produced many collections of lakeland sonnets, poems, histories and guides, including an entertaining book of "reminiscences" of Wordsworth by the local peasantry (none of whom thought the Poet Laureate's poetry was any good). After Rawnsley's wife died in 1916 he retired to Wordsworth's old house at Allan Bank in Grasmere. He married again in 1918, but died only two years later on May 28, 1920.

Ashness Bridge and Watendlath

The pier at **Ashness Gate** (or bus #79) provides access to a narrow road branching south off the B5289 that climbs a steep half-mile to the photogenic **Ashness Bridge**, an old dry-stone packhorse bridge providing marvellous Derwent Water views. The minor road past Ashness Bridge (and a well-used footpath) ends two miles further south at **Watendlath**, an isolated farmstead, tearoom and tarn which can be hopelessly overrun at times in summer. Watendlath – the Norse "end of the lake" – provided the setting for Hugh Walpole's most famous episode of his Herries Chronicles, *Judith Paris* (1931). You can buy a copy in the tearoom and lounge about for an hour or two on the grass, or rent boat and rod from the farm for a trout-fishing trip on the tarn.

From Watendlath tarn, walkers have a few options, all pleasant, all easy: south via smaller Dock Tarn to Stonethwaite in Borrowdale; southwest over the tops to Rosthwaite; or east, up and over High Tove, to the western shore of Thirlmere.

Lodore and Lodore Falls

At **Lodore** landing stage there are rowboats for rent and other water sports available at Platty Plus, and a couple of rather elegant places to stay. The #79 bus stops on the road nearby, from where a path heads to the **Lodore Falls**, much visited in Victorian times by the romantically inclined though only really worth the diversion after sustained wet weather. Then, you'll be able to appreciate Robert Southey's magnificent, alliterative evocation of the falls in "The Cataract of Lodore": "Collecting, projecting, receding and speeding, and shocking and rocking, and darting and parting", and so on, for line after memorable line. However, even in dry weather there's some lovely woodland clambering to be done around here, and with a keen sense of direction (or a map) you'll be able to find the Watendlath path and road, east of the falls.

Accommodation and food

Lodore Falls ☎017687/77285, ⓦwww .lakedistricthotels.net/lodorefalls. The most prominent accommodation at this end of Derwent Water, the three-star *Lodore Falls* has lakeshore and woodland gardens, a bar and restaurant, and all manner of other facilities including a leisure centre, tennis court and two pools (one indoor, one outdoor). There are lake or fell views from all rooms, most of which have been attractively refurbished in a contemporary style. At weekends, it's two nights D,B&B only. ❽, D,B&B ❾

Mary Mount ☎017687/77223, ⓦwww .marymounthotel.co.uk. Even closer to the lake – just a few yards from the Lodore piers – is this more intimate, modest family-run affair, nestling under the crags in four acres of lake-side and woodland gardens. The twenty rooms are either in the main house or the lodge-style bungalow in the grounds, with half-a-dozen rated "superior" (room 25, for example, has bay windows and big lake views). There's a nice oak-panelled bar serving lunch (available outside on the terrace), a moderately priced restaurant with picture windows, and they'll pack you a picnic lunch and fill a flask if you ask. ❺, superior rooms ❻

Cat Bells, Lingholm and Portinscale

Asked to pick a favourite Lake District walk and climb, many would plump for **Cat Bells** (1481ft), a renowned vantage point above the lake's western shore. It's not difficult (possible for all the family), the views from the top are stupendous, and it's easy to combine with the launch to or from Keswick. The name derives from the age-old belief that the fell once harboured a wild cat's den (*bield*, the Norse word for den, was later corrupted to "bells"). Most people climb up and down the path from Hawes End (launch pier), near where there's also a small car park (Gutherscale), though the longer haul up from Manesty to the south (High Brandlehow launch) has its merits. Return to either launch pier along the lakeside path through Manesty Park and Brandlehow woods and park, allowing, say, two-and-a-half hours for the entire walk. Walpole fans should note that Sir Hugh lived and worked for many years in the lee of Cat Bells, at the house he called **Brackenburn**, by Manesty Park.

The *Swinside Inn* (see "Newlands Valley" below) is only a mile from Hawes End, a welcome stop for a post Cat Bells pint, while a signposted path from Hawes End pier runs all the way back to Keswick, which is only a couple of miles away through the woods and round the top of the lake. Under a mile north of Hawes End you'll pass the entrance to **Lingholm Gardens** – now sadly closed to the public, but featuring fabulous rhododendron displays. Beatrix Potter spent many childhood holidays at the grand house at Lingholm and, hardly surprisingly, the surroundings here and in the lovely Newlands Valley to the southwest (see below) appeared in several of her later stories. Just beyond, there are refreshments at hand at the lakeside café (☎017687/73082 daily until 5pm, 8pm July & Aug) at **Nichol End**, a marine store and boat rental place. The name is a corruption of "St Nicholas' Ending", as the site was once an embarkation point for medieval pilgrims crossing to St Herbert's Island (Saint Nicholas being the patron saint of sailors). After Nichol End, the path joins the main road as it snakes through the village of **Portinscale**, a satellite of Keswick, where you can relax with a drink in the conservatory-bar and lakeside gardens of the *Derwentwater* hotel (see "Keswick: Accommodation"), before striking off over the River Derwent and through the fields to emerge by Greta Bridge in town.

Newlands Valley

A valley for connoisseurs unfolds along Newlands Beck, to the west of Cat Bells and Derwent Water. Save for the very minor road over Newlands Hause to Buttermere, there's little in the isolated farms and sparse hamlets of the **Newlands Valley** to lure touring drivers. But hikers have the choice of two fine circuits, one following the pastoral valley lowlands, the other tracing the encircling ridges and peaks. The **valley walk** (5 miles; 3hr) follows a path from the Cat Bells (Gutherscale) car park to Little Town – the main valley hamlet, with an isolated chapel – beyond which can be made out the old Goldscope lead mines. These have been long abandoned, but were a hive of activity as far back as the sixteenth century when German miners were brought here to work the seams. Better, if you (and the weather) are up to it, is the exhilarating **Newlands Horseshoe** (11 miles; 6–7hr), which begins with the ascent of Cat Bells (see above) and then links Maiden Moor (1887ft), High Spy (2143ft), Dale Head (2473ft) and Hindscarth (2385ft) in a terrific circular walk above and around the valley. The views, needless to say, are magnificent.

Either walk can be done from Keswick, via the launch to Hawes End, and should culminate in a visit to the valley's only **pub**, the excellent *Swinside Inn* (☎017687/78253, ⓦ www.theswinsideinn.com; ❹), three miles from Keswick, whose beer garden gazes up to the encroaching fells.

Borrowdale

Beautiful **Borrowdale** stretches beyond the foot of Derwent Water, south of Keswick, and it's difficult to overstate the attraction of its river flats, forested crags, oak woods and yew trees. Early visiting writers and poets, including

Thomas Gray who marvelled at the prospect in 1769, saw it as an embodiment of their Romantic fancy; Turner and Constable came to paint it; and Wordsworth praised its yews, "those fraternal Four of Borrowdale, joined in one solemn and capacious grove". But the dale's sonorous place names suggest a more prosaic heritage. The numerous "thwaites" were the site of Norse clearings, while by the thirteenth century the monks of Furness Abbey were farming the valley from their "grainge" (an outlying farmhouse), grazing sheep and smelting iron-ore along the becks. The valley's higher reaches were later extensively mined and quarried, activities that impinged upon the indigenous wood cover. Borrowdale's oak woods once effectively formed part of a temperate rainforest – the surviving fragments are still known for their mosses, ferns, liverworts and lichens, and provide cover for a wide range of berries and birds, including warblers and flycatchers.

In summer there's a fairly steady stream of traffic taking hikers to the head of the valley, overshadowed by the peaks of Scafell and Scafell Pike (the two highest in the Lakes) and Great Gable, the latter one of the finest-looking mountains in England. Public transport access is by **bus** #77A (along the minor road on the west side of Derwent Water) and the highly scenic #79 "Borrowdale Rambler" (along the B5289), which runs south to Grange and Seatoller, dropping day-trippers and hikers at points of interest and walk-access points all the way down. A **Borrowdale Day Rider** (from £4.80) gives a day's unlimited travel between Keswick and Seatoller on the #79 service; buy it from the driver.

BORROWDALE

Portinscale & Keswick
Derwent Water
R. Derwent
Keswick
B5289
Cumbria Way
Borrowdale Gates
Leathes Head
Grange-in-Borrowdale
Grange Bridge Cottage
Hollows Farm
King's How
Bowder Stone
Castle Crag
Honister Pass & Buttermere
Cumbria Way
Rosthwaite
Hazel Bank
Royal Oak Hotel
Scafell Hotel
Yew Tree Farm
Johnny Wood
Borrowdale-YHA
Stonethwaite Beck
Seatoller
Yew Tree Inn/ Seatoller House
Stonethwaite
Langstrath Inn
B5289
Great Gable
Langdale
N
Allerdale Ramble
Seathwaite
Seathwaite Farm
Borrowdale Fells
Scafell Pike
Glaramara
© Crown copyright
0   500 yds

Grange and around

The riverside hamlet of **GRANGE-IN-BORROWDALE**, four miles south of Keswick, sits back from an old twin-arched packhorse bridge, under which the River Derwent tumbles from the narrower confines of Borrowdale and runs across the flood plain to the lake. And flood it does on occasion, which is why the raised wooden walkways snake across the flats between here, Lodore and Manesty. It's always nice to stop for a drink at the **tearoom** at *Grange Bridge*

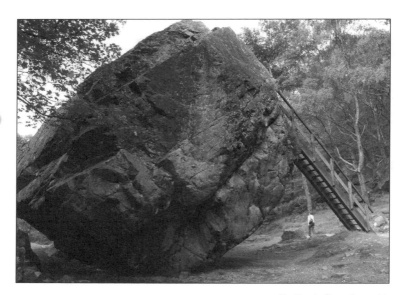

△ The Bowder Stone, Borrowdale

Cottage (☎017687/77201; closed Nov–Feb, though open in school holidays), which is in a great spot, right by the bridge.

South of Grange, the valley narrows at a crag-lined gorge known as the **Jaws of Borrowdale**. Until the eighteenth century, the route beyond was considered wild and uncertain, and there was no permanent road through until the mid-nineteenth century, when travellers other than locals first began to venture into the valley. The views are famed from **Castle Crag** (985ft), possibly the site of an ancient fort and one of the western "teeth" of the Jaws, which you can reach on paths from Grange or Rosthwaite. Across the valley from the crag, also around a mile from Grange, stands the 1870-ton **Bowder Stone** (there's a car park on the B5289), a house-sized lump of rock scaled by wooden ladder and worn to a shine on top by thousands of pairs of feet. Controversy surrounds the origin of this rock, pitched precariously on its edge. Some say it came from the fells above, others contend it was brought by glacier movement during the last Ice Age. The crag behind the Bowder Stone, **King's How**, is named in memory of Edward VII. It's a fair climb to the top, but the views are worth it.

Accommodation

Borrowdale Gates Grange ☎017687/77204, ⓦwww.borrowdale-gates.com. The traditional choice hereabouts is this superbly sited country-house hotel in two acres of wooded gardens, 200 yards up the western shore road, past the church. It has a deserved reputation for its food, and dinner (included in the price) is accompanied by fine views from the restaurant. Closed Jan. ❽
Hollows Farm ☎017687/77298, ⓦwww .hollowsfarm.co.uk. Three B&B rooms set on a

working National Trust hill farm, half a mile from Grange – breakfast from the kitchen Aga. You can camp here too next to the river, and there are showers and toilet facilities. Closed mid-Dec to end Jan. No credit cards. ❷, en suite ❸
Leathes Head B5289, 1 mile north of Grange ☎017687/77247, ⓦwww.leatheshead.co.uk. Welcoming family-run, non-smoking hotel with a dozen spacious rooms, all with fell views – two in particular (supplement payable) have windows on two sides, making them lovely and light. The

elegant, polished Edwardian house has three interlinked lounges, including a conservatory with telescope, while dinner (included in the price) is the main event every night – there's plenty of choice from a changing *table d'hote* menu that always has a fish and vegetarian selection. ➐

Rosthwaite

The riverside path and the B5289 lead on to the straggling hamlet of **ROSTHWAITE**, two miles south of Grange. Its whitewashed stone buildings, backed by the encroaching fells, sustain the most concentrated batch of accommodation in the valley, while at the Rosthwaite **village shop** (open daily) – the only one in the valley – you'll be able to put together a basic picnic and buy a map or a postcard. Both hotels on the road, the *Royal Oak* and the *Scafell*, offer drinks and teas to non-guests, while the *Scafell* is also the starting point of the annual **Borrowdale Fell Race** (first Sat in Aug), an eighteen-mile gut-buster that takes in the peaks of Scafell Pike and Great Gable. The winners clock in at well under three hours, their names immortalized on an honours board displayed in the hotel's *Riverside Bar*. Tortoises can reflect on these hare-like exploits while seated on the memorial bench in the hotel grounds dedicated to Walter ("W.A.") Poucher (1891–1988), author, fellwalker and photographer, whose classic *Lakeland Peaks*, first published in 1960, is the only serious rival in scope and breadth to the Wainwright guides.

Hotels and B&B

Hazel Bank 200 yards from the road, over the bridge ☎017687/77248, ⒲www.hazelbankhotel.co.uk. Victorian-era country house set in its own serene gardens, with magnificent fell views to all sides. There are eight elegant rooms, often full, since guests return year after year, drawn by the seclusion, the intimate atmosphere and the well-regarded food – a daily-changing four-course candlelit dinner is included in the price, with coffee and chocolates served afterwards in the cosy lounge. Parking. No smoking. ➑

Royal Oak On the main road ☎017687/ 77214, ⒲www.royaloakhotel.co.uk. The hikers' favourite – an expanded eighteenth-century farmhouse with barn annexe, where a hearty lakeland dinner (no choice, but vegetarian alternative available) is served promptly at 7pm, a bacon-and-eggs breakfast at 8.30am. Weather conditions are posted daily, packed lunches and filled flasks supplied, but if the rain comes down you may prefer to repair to the firelit sitting room for tea and scones, or to the stone-flagged bar. Parking. Rates include dinner. ➏

Scafell On the main road ☎017687/77208, ⒲www.scafell.co.uk. Set back from a trimmed lawn, with period furnished rooms in the main building and more modern, slightly less spacious ones in the annexe, all with baths and showers. Food is traditional country-house "fayre" (prawn cocktail, silver service, meet-and-greet owner), but despite the formalities it's a friendly, relaxed place to stay. The four-course *table d'hote* dinner is £24, though the attached *Riverside Bar* – the only local pub – serves cheaper bar meals, including smoked trout and grilled salmon. Special hotel breaks and last-minute rates are good value. Parking. ➏

Yew Tree Farm 200 yards up the narrow road opposite the shop ☎017687/77675, ⒲www.borrowdaleherdwick.co.uk. Traditional farmhouse B&B with three rather florally decorated rooms. It has the unofficial royal seal of approval, since Prince Charles stays here occasionally on incognito walking trips. The farm also has a tearoom, the *Flock-In* (closed Wed), where you can sit in the garden with a tea or coffee (available in pints for thirsty walkers) and gaze across the valley fields – some of the farm Herdwicks end up in the tearoom's sausages and burgers. Parking. No smoking. Closed Dec & Jan. No credit cards. ➌

Youth hostel

Borrowdale YHA Longthwaite, 1 mile south of Rosthwaite ☎0870/770 5706, ⒺBorrowdale @yha.org.uk. Located right on the riverside footpath to Seatoller, this has some rooms available for couples and families, as well as dorms. It's a peaceful place to stay, with riverside picnic tables in the grounds. Dorm beds from £16.50.

Campsite

Chapel House Farm B5289, half-mile south of Rosthwaite ☎017687/77602. A simple farm field site, with toilets and showers available. Closed Nov–Feb.

Stonethwaite, Seatoller and Seathwaite

STONETHWAITE, a place of some antiquity just to the southeast of Rosthwaite and half a mile up a side road, is the trailhead for those aiming to walk into Langdale via Langstrath and the watershed of Stake Pass. There's more foot traffic than you might expect, since it's on the route of both the Cumbria Way and the Coast-to-Coast walk. Pretty whitewashed stone cottages huddle around the sixteenth-century *Langstrath Country Inn* (see opposite), which features in the Lake District section of Ian McEwan's Booker prize-winning novel *Amsterdam* (1998). The bleak Langstrath valley beyond – "one long frown set in stone", according to McEwan – makes for a tough day's outing.

Another mile or so up the valley from Rosthwaite, and eight miles from Keswick, lies the old farming and quarrying settlement of **SEATOLLER**, where there's a National Trust car park. There's a path from here into **Johnny Wood**, with its moss-covered boulders and lichen-draped trees, while thirty yards up the road a few slate-roofed houses cluster around the *Yew Tree* café-restaurant, which was fashioned from seventeenth-century stone-flagged quarrymen's cottages. **Seatoller House**, next door, is owned by the family of the historian G.M. Trevelyan, who first visited a century ago as a Cambridge undergraduate and later organized "hare and hound" hunts on the fells above – stalking people rather than animals – which are still held here each year. A community-run visitor centre opposite the restaurant can help out with any other local questions.

A minor road south runs to **SEATHWAITE**, twenty minutes' walk away, where there's limited parking, a farmhouse campsite and camping barn (see opposite) and a basic café at Borrowdale Trout Farm (Easter–Sept daily 10am–6.30pm; ☎017687/77293), serving all-day breakfasts, sandwiches, and fresh and

Scafell Pike and Great Gable

In good weather the minor road to Seathwaite is lined with cars by 9am as hikers take to the paths for the rugged climbs up some of the Lake District's major peaks, including Scafell Pike, England's highest mountain. Technically, they're not too difficult; as always, though, you should be well prepared and reasonably fit.

Scafell Pike

For England's highest peak, **Scafell Pike** (3205ft), the approach from Seathwaite is through the farmyard and up to **Styhead Tarn** via Stockley Bridge. This is as far as many get, and on those all-too-rare glorious summer days the tarn is a fine place for a picnic. From the tarn the classic ascent is up the thrilling **Corridor Route**, then descending via Esk Hause – a fairly arduous eight-mile (6hr) loop walk in all from Seathwaite.

Great and Green Gable

A direct but very steep approach to **Great Gable** (2949ft) is possible from Styhead Tarn, though most people start out from Seathwaite campsite, climb up Sourmilk Ghyll and approach the peak via **Green Gable** (2628ft), also an eight-mile (6hr) return walk. However, the easiest Great Gable climb is actually from Honister Pass (see opposite), following a six-mile (4hr) route past Grey Knotts and Brandreth to Green Gable, before rounding Great Gable and returning along an almost parallel path to the west.

See Basics, p.35, for general walking advice in the Lakes; recommended maps are detailed on p.42.

smoked salmon and trout. This is a major departure point for walks up the likes of Great Gable and Scafell Pike (see box). Prospective campers might like to know that Seathwaite is always accused of being the wettest inhabited place in England, since it once recorded over 120 inches of rain in a single year.

Accommodation and food

Langstrath Country Inn Stonethwaite ☎017687/77239, ⓦwww.thelangstrath.com. An upmarket pub with nine traditionally furnished rooms, a cosy bar and pretty little beer garden. The food is mostly locally sourced – trout, sausages, lamb, beef – but non-guests will need to reserve in advance if they want to eat, which doesn't make it the most convenient stop for hikers. ❹

Seathwaite Farm Seathwaite ☎017687/77394. The hardcore hikers' favourite, at the end of the Seathwaite road and last stop before the high fells. It has a very popular campsite (open all year; shower block, toilets, and hot and cold water) as well as a refurbished camping barn that sleeps up to ten, with bunk beds, kitchen and lounge with pot-bellied stove. No credit cards. Bunk beds, £10 per person – individuals welcome, though may be full at weekends with groups.

Seatoller House Seatoller ☎017687/77218, ⓦwww.seatollerhouse.co.uk. Stay the night in a beautifully preserved seventeenth-century Borrowdale farmhouse, which boasts plenty of original panelling, a library, parlour and fire. There's an honesty bar, while communal dinners (7pm, not Tues) using local produce are served at two oak tables in the former kitchen. Closed Dec–Feb. Price includes dinner. ❺

Yew Tree Seatoller ☎017687/77634. The best stop this side of the mountains is Seatoller's amiable café-restaurant that offers "English by day, African by night". Basically what this means is a daytime café and bar serving sandwiches, pies, omelettes and the like, while at night the steak-house menu introduces tasty South African specialities, including *bobotie*, grilled ostrich, beef *espadatos* (skewers of beef) or lamb on butternut mash (mains £9–16). Closed Mon & Jan to mid-Feb. Moderate.

Honister Pass and Slate Mine

Overlooked by the steep Borrowdale Fells, the B5289 cuts west at Seatoller, up and over the dramatic **Honister Pass**, dominated by the dread thousand-foot heights of Honister Crag. From the top of the pass the road down to Buttermere is an absolute beauty, following tumbling Gatesgarthdale Beck. Bus #77A comes this way, making the initial, steep mile-and-a-quarter grind from Seatoller to the car park at the top of Honister Pass. Nearby is the supremely isolated **youth hostel**, *Honister Hause YHA* (☎0870/770 5870, ⓔhonister@yha.org.uk; flexible opening Nov–March; dorm beds from £14), with all accommodation in two- to four-bedded rooms. It's superbly sited for mountain walking and there's an evening meal served, which is just as well if you're on foot since it's a fair slog down into Borrowdale to the nearest pub.

Slate has been quarried on the pass since Elizabethan times, and by the eighteenth century the local green roofing slate was much sought-after. Miners – living in wooden huts on the mountainside and working by candlelight – hand-dug eleven miles of tunnels and caverns within the bulk of Fleetwith Pike, leaving vicious scars, slate waste piles and old workings that are visible even today. Until well into the nineteenth century, the finished slate was either carried down the severe inclines in baskets on men's backs, or guided on heavy hand-pulled wooden sledges, since pit ponies couldn't get a foothold on the scree. Needless to say, this was ridiculously dangerous work. Full commercial quarrying ceased in 1986, but **Honister Slate Mine** (☎017687/77230, ⓦwww.honister-slate-mine.co.uk) is now in operation again as a working and heritage enterprise, with ornamental and roofing slate for sale, and a visitor centre (daily 10.30am–5pm), where you can buy souvenirs and browse the slate stone garden. Best of all, you can get an idea of what working life was like by donning a hard hat and lamp and joining one of the hugely informative **guided**

tours (daily at 10.30am, 12.30pm & 3.30pm; £9.75; booking recommended), which start by showing you the "riving" (hand-shaping) process and then lead you through narrow tunnels into illuminated, echoing, dripping caverns. A more extreme version of the tour takes you around "The Edge", a high-level shortcut into one of the most extensive mine workings.

❹ Threlkeld to Thirlmere

The A591 between Keswick and Grasmere runs directly past **Thirlmere**, and this is the way the buses go. But if you're in no particular hurry, it's more pleasant to detour east to **Threlkeld** first and then turn south along the minor road through **St John's in the Vale**. You can come this way entirely on foot too – it's an extremely attractive route (7 miles; 4hr) – and pick up the #555/556 bus back up the A591 to complete the circuit back to Keswick.

Threlkeld

Keswick's disused railway path (signposted by the *Keswick Country House* hotel on Station Road) runs straight to **THRELKELD** ("Thrall's Spring"), three miles east of Keswick; or it's a quick ride on bus #X4/X5 or the #73/73A. The riverside walk's a delight, enhanced by the promise of a drink in one of Threlkeld's charming old pubs at the end, either the *Horse & Farrier* or the *Salutation*. Threlkeld is the starting point for many of the strenuous hikes up Blencathra and there's parking at a couple of places up the signposted road to the Blencathra Centre.

A century ago Threlkeld was a busy, dirty industrial centre, with lead and copper mined in the valley and granite quarried from the hillsides for road- and railway-making. At **Threlkeld Quarry** (March–Oct daily 10am–5pm; Nov–Feb usually weekends only, call for times; museum and site £3, plus £5 for mine tour; ☎017687/79747, ⓦwww.threlkeldminingmuseum.co.uk), volunteers help run a fascinating open-air industrial history museum which covers all facets of the local mining industry. There's a comprehensive indoor collection of mining artefacts and minerals, but you're also welcome to roam around the site and have a look inside the locomotive shed and machine shop, where restoration work is being carried out on the impressive vintage excavators and quarry machinery. There are 45-minute guided tours down a recreated lead and copper mine – children will enjoy the underground experience and gritty anecdotes – while the relaid narrow-gauge mineral railway provides rides up into the inner quarry and back. The quarry lies across the A66 from Threlkeld; take the B5322 (St John's in the Vale road) and follow the brown signs off the road and a mile up the track, through the old quarry works.

St John's in the Vale

A bucolic walk from Threlkeld cuts south from the railway path, across Threlkeld Bridge and through the fields into **St John's in the Vale**; the B5322 shadows the same route. The old chapel of St John's and views of the Blencathra ridges behind are the draws, with the southward path hugging the base of **High Rigg** (1163ft) and eventually following the river to 🏕 *Low Bridge End Farm* (☎017687/79242, ⓦwww.campingbarn.com). This is a little hive of activity in a very peaceful spot, with a rustic tea garden (serving home-made lemonade and local ice cream), a woodland trail, pottery and craft workshops.

Writers and artists in the Lake District

The Lake District stands out on the literary and artistic map of England, as prominent as Shakespeare's Stratford-upon-Avon, the Brontë's Haworth and Constable's Stour Valley. But it's not just "Wordsworth's Grasmere" that's the draw, though the poet, his homes and his extended circle form the undoubted focus of most visits. Since the eighteenth century, a wide variety of artists and writers have been drawn to every corner of the region, all looking for inspiration in its unrivalled combination of light, lakes and mountains.

The Lake Poets

Wordsworth, Coleridge and Southey dominate the Cumbrian literary landscape to an almost overbearing degree. They are the "Lake Poets" of popular description, a clique of fluctuating friendships with a shared passion for the Lake District at its core. Only William Wordsworth (1770–1850) – born in Cockermouth, schooled in Hawkshead, longtime resident of Grasmere – could be considered a true local, but it was actually as a young man in England's west country that he first forged his relationship with Samuel Taylor Coleridge (1772–1834), with whom he published the landmark *Lyrical Ballads* in 1798. When Wordsworth moved to Grasmere the following year, Coleridge soon followed as, later, did Coleridge's brother-in-law Robert Southey (1774–1843), who settled in nearby Keswick. The interconnections between the three played out across the years – when Coleridge descended into opium-fuelled depression and fell out with Wordsworth it was Southey who was left to bring up Coleridge's children; while on Southey's death, it was Wordsworth who succeeded him as Poet Laureate. There's an argument, too, for extending the bounds of the renowned triumvirate to include Dorothy Wordsworth (1771–1855), the poet's sister. She devoted her life to her brother and his work, and William placed great reliance on the observations recorded in her journal.

An alternative Wordsworth Trail

1. **Wordsworth House**, Cockermouth. Where it all began – the birthplace of William and Dorothy, lovingly restored by the National Trust. See p.237.
2. **Ann Tyson's Cottage**, Hawkshead. William boarded here as a schoolboy and you can still stay the night today. See p.125.
3. **Dora's Field**, Rydal. When the Wordsworths' beloved daughter Dora died, they planted daffodils across the hillside below their house, Rydal Mount. See p.102.
4. **The Duddon Valley**. The southern valley is well off most tourist routes, but Wordsworth wrote an entire book of sonnets about it. See p.133.
5. **Church Street**, Ambleside. Wordsworth had a day job for many years as a "Distributor of Stamps" – a plaque marks the site of his office. See p.73.

Not just Wordsworth...

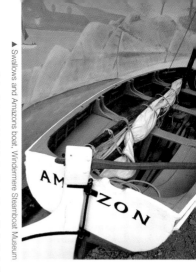

Grasmere's towering presence isn't the only literary name in the Lakes. Journalist, critic, essayist and "opium-eater" **Thomas De Quincey** moved to the Lakes specifically to meet the famous poet and even lived in the Wordsworths' former home, Dove Cottage (see p.98). Victorian social philosopher and art critic **John Ruskin** settled at Brantwood (see p.121), outside Coniston, in 1872, and much of his feeling for the countryside permeated through to two later literary immigrants – **Arthur Ransome** (p.131), writer of the children's classic *Swallows and Amazons*, and **Beatrix Potter**, whose favourite lakeland spots feature in her timeless stories. Potter, in fact, is the only serious rival to Wordsworthian dominance, with her home at Hill Top (p.128), a gallery in Hawkshead (p.125) and a museum in Bowness (p.58) all packed with international visitors throughout the year. Children's authors seem to take particular inspiration from the surroundings

– **John Cunliffe**'s *Postman Pat* stories, for example, are largely set in the quiet valleys between Kendal and Windermere. Other well-known writers include self-appointed champion of the region **Hunter Davies** (born in Scotland but raised in Carlisle; diverse biographer of – among others – The Beatles, Wainwright, Wordsworth and Wayne Rooney) and his Carlisle-born wife, the biographer and novelist **Margaret Forster**, both long-time residents of Loweswater. Finally, there's broadcaster and writer **Melvyn Bragg**, born in Wigton, whose series of historical and autobiographical novels (p.262) captures the very essence of Cumbria through the ages.

Art and the Romantics

The move away from classicism to the so-called Picturesque Movement of the mid-eighteenth century made the grandeur of the Lakes an acceptable subject for artists of the Romantic period. Engraved views by the likes of **William Bellers** had been popular since the 1750s, but the sheer sweep of the fells and lakes moved to the fore only with the work of landscapist **Joseph Farington**, who spent several years in the Lake District in the 1770s and was later an influential figure in the London art world. There was a visit by **Thomas Gainsborough** towards the end of his life in 1783 – a pencil sketch of the Langdale Pikes is usually on display at the Dove Cottage museum – while **J.M.W. Turner** toured the Lakes in 1797, and later exhibited

▲ John Constable's *Saddleback and Part of Skiddaw*, 1806

Dust to dust

➤ **St Oswald's Church**, Grasmere. One of Britain's most visited literary shrines – the graves of William Wordsworth and his family. See p.90.

➤ **Haystacks**, Buttermere. Where else would you expect the ashes of fellwalker extraordinaire Alfred Wainwright to have been scattered, but up a 1900-foot mountain? See p.194.

➤ **Rusland Church**, near Grizedale Forest. Burial place of Arthur Ransome, creator of *Swallows and Amazons*. See p.130.

➤ **Crosthwaite Church**, Keswick. Poet Laureate Robert Southey lived in Keswick for forty years and is buried there alongside his wife and children. See p.143.

➤ **Claife Heights**, Far Sawrey. Somewhere up here – and no one knows exactly where – were scattered the ashes of Beatrix Potter, at her request. See p.129.

➤ **St Andrew's Church**, Coniston. A magnificent Celtic cross marks the grave of Victorian writer, art critic and social philosopher John Ruskin. See p.116.

oils of Buttermere and Coniston at the Royal Academy. Also an Academy regular in this period was the gloriously named landscapist **Julius Caesar Ibbetson** (named, apparently, after his Caesarian birth), Yorkshire-born but resident in Ambleside for three years from 1801. Although a young **John Constable** had yet to make his reputation when he visited in the autumn of 1806, he produced almost a hundred lakeland sketches and watercolours in which art historians can see the first strivings towards his mature style.

An Ambleside exile

His challenging, subversive collages considered "degenerate" by the Nazis, German abstract and performance artist **Kurt Schwitters** (1877–1948) was forced to flee Hitler's Germany in 1937, moving first to Norway and then to Britain in 1940 where, initially, he was interned as an enemy

alien. He spent the later war years scratching a living in London before arriving in the Lake District in 1945 – impoverished, ill and largely unknown. Schwitters became a familiar figure in Ambleside, painting local portraits and landscapes, though it is his "**Merzbarn**" for which he's remembered. Schwitters had already produced two earlier versions of this pioneering form of installation art, in Germany and Norway, and the third was begun in 1947 in an old stone barn in Elterwater. Constructed from discarded, salvaged and organic materials, it was an embodiment of Schwitters' longstanding "Merz" concept that art could spring from cast-off, found or otherwise useless objects. Schwitters died of pneumonia in 1948 – there's a memorial stone in Ambleside churchyard – and the unfinished Merzbarn is now at Newcastle University, though both the Armitt Collection in Ambleside and Abbot Hall in Kendal hold examples of his portraits, sketches and collages.

◀ Kurt Schwitters' *Railway, 2nd Class*, 1923

The range of overnight **accommodation** options includes a small campsite, and self-catering available in the old stable and hayloft, either by the week in the flat (sleeps 2–4; £175–330, call the farm) or overnight in the camping barn (£6 per person; breakfast and packed lunches available; reservations on ☎01946/758198). From the farm the A591 is under a mile away – on the way, keep an eye out for climbers scaling **Castle Rock** across the river, Walter Scott's model for the fairy castle in his poem "Bridal of Triermain".

Thirlmere

Thirlmere, a five-mile-long reservoir at the southern end of St John's in the Vale, was created from two smaller lakes at the end of the nineteenth century when Manchester's booming population and industry required water. Over a hundred miles of gravity-drawn tunnels and pipes still supply the city with water from here. In an ultimately unsuccessful campaign – but one that fore-shadowed the founding of the National Trust – the fight against the creation of Thirlmere was led by Ruskin and other proto-environmentalists, outraged at a high-handed raising of the water level, which drowned the hamlet of Armboth and various small farms. No one was best pleased either by the subsequent regimental planting of thousands of conifers around the edge (to help prevent erosion), which dramatically changed the local landscape. The century since the creation of the reservoir has softened the scene – these are among the oldest planted trees in the park – and you'd be hard pushed now to tell that Thirlmere was man-made.

The only side served by public transport (take any bus along the A591 between Grasmere and Keswick) is the eastern one, from which some visitors choose to make the climb up Helvellyn and back – in which case, you'll be pleased at the thought of a pint in the roadside *King's Head* at **Thirlspot** (☎0500/600725, Ⓦwww.lakedistrictinns.co.uk/kingshead.html; ❺, weekends ❻). Nearby *Dale Head Hall* (☎017687/72478, Ⓦwww.daleheadhall.co.uk; ❼) – an Elizabethan building with a Victorian adjunct – has a lakeside location, with gardens that run right down to the shores of Thirlmere.

To enjoy fully the waterside paths, forest trails (through planted conifers and mixed woodland) and viewpoints, you need to be on the minor road that hugs the western shore. There are several small car parks, with trails leading off from each, like at **Launchy Gill**, an oak and birch woodland Site of Special Scientific Interest. Alternatively, the #555/556 bus can drop you at the foot of the reservoir for the six-mile walk up the western side and around to Thirlspot.

Braithwaite, Thornthwaite and Whinlatter Pass

Just under three miles west of Keswick, the cottage gardens of **BRAITHWAITE** (bus #X5 from Keswick) line the banks of Coledale Beck, with the distinctive Grisedale Pike towering above. As an alternative walking base to Keswick, the village provides immediate access to the fells between Derwent and Crummock waters, notably on the stupendous Coledale Horseshoe circuit (see p.163). There's a village shop and B&B **accommodation** in and around Braithwaite (particularly along the minor Thornthwaite road), but the most atmospheric lodgings are at the *Coledale Inn* (☎017687/78272, Ⓦwww.coledale-inn.co.uk; ❺) on the hillside above the village. Once a mill, this is now a cosy lakeland inn

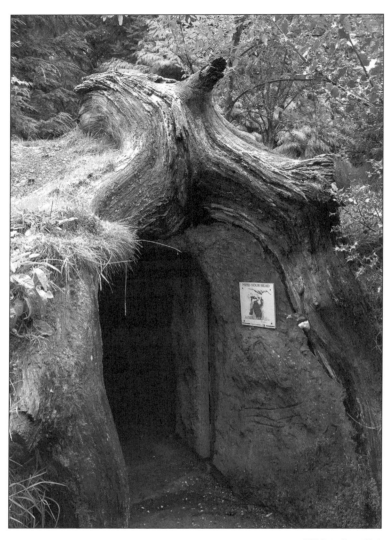

△ Whinlatter Forest Park

with a dozen (mostly upgraded, reasonably spacious) rooms, a sheltered garden and good-value bar meals. They'll make you up a packed lunch for your day's walking. The other pub choice is the *Royal Oak* (☏017687/78533, ⓦwww .tp-inns.co.uk; ❺), down in the village itself, with modernized rooms, Jennings beers and a wide bar-meal menu. Or you can splash out a bit on the Modern British food at nearby *Ivy House* (☏017687/78338; dinner only; advance reservations required; closed Sun), a private members' hotel and **restaurant** whose dining room is open to non-residents.

The great advantage of basing yourself in Braithwaite is that you can walk straight out of the door and on to the fells. Grisedale Pike is the traditional climb, which can be incorporated into a much longer circular, or "horseshoe", walk. It's one of the Lakes' best one-day hikes, and dedicated Wainwright peak-baggers can knock off up to ten summits on the one circuit. The start of the route up Cat Bells (see p.153) is only two miles to the south of the village, as well, which means you could also walk the Newlands Valley (p.154) from Braithwaite.

Grisedale Pike

From the small quarry car park on the Whinlatter road, just above the village, it's 90min to the top of **Grisedale Pike** (2593ft), along a very well-worn route. Moving on to **Hopegill Head** (2525ft) – from where the Isle of Man can be seen on the best days – you then drop to the head of the valley at Coledale Hause for the straightforward valley return to the village (total trip 5 miles; 3hr).

Coledale Horseshoe

Unless you're pushed for time, on a clear day you'd be mad not to complete the circuit since, having gained the height at Grisedale Pike and Hopegill Head, there's a relatively small amount of extra climbing involved to return to Braithwaite via **Sail** (2530ft), **Outerside** (1863ft) and **Barrow** (1494ft) – with a possible diversion to **Grasmoor** (2791ft, superb Crummock Water views) en route, and an alternative return via **Scar Crags** (2205ft) and **Causey Pike** (2035ft, Newlands Valley views). It's a hugely satisfying circuit, with changing panoramas all the way round. Depending on your peak choices, it's nine to twelve miles, six to eight hours, on clearly defined paths and ridges, with just the odd bit of scrambling.

See Basics, p.35, for general walking advice in the Lakes; recommended maps are detailed on p.42.

A mile north up the minor road shadowing the A66, pretty **THORNTHWAITE** looks across the Derwent basin to the Skiddaw range. There's parking a mile or so further up the road, from where you can climb **Barf** (1536ft), whose distinctive craggy protuberance – usually painted white – is known as "The Bishop". Back in the village, the refined **Thornthwaite Galleries** (March–Oct Mon & Wed–Sun 10.30am–5pm; Nov to mid-Dec Fri–Sun 10.30am–5pm; free; ☎017687/78248, ⊛www.thornthwaitegalleries .co.uk) exhibits a good range of lakeland arts and crafts – from paintings and sculpture to jewellery and fabrics – and some of the artists demonstrate their work during special sessions in the summer. The tearoom is open until 4.30pm, though muddy boots and their owners will have to give it a miss.

The B5292 climbs west past Braithwaite to the **Whinlatter Pass** (1043ft), on the way to Buttermere or Cockermouth. A couple of miles up are the extensive woodland plantations of **Whinlatter Forest Park**, England's only true mountain forest, whose excellent visitor centre (daily: April–Oct 10am–5pm; Nov–March 10am–4pm; free; parking fee; ☎017687/78469, ⊛www.forestry .gov.uk) can put you on track for a day's exploration. Bus #77 runs here directly from Keswick. Seasonal exhibitions concentrate on the area's wildlife, most notably Bassenthwaite's wild **ospreys** (see p.164), which can usually be seen on the visitor centre's live video nest-cam link (April–Aug only). In addition, there are walks (up to Spout Force falls, for example) and viewpoints, plus waymarked trails for hikers and cyclists, a permanent orienteering course and adventure playground. The centre's *Siskins Café* (☎017687/78410) is worth a stop in any case, with really good food, proper coffee and a terrace that looks over the plantations and down the valley.

Bassenthwaite Lake

Pub-quiz bores love **Bassenthwaite Lake** as it's the only lake in the Lake District (all the others are known as waters or meres). It's also the northernmost of the major patches of water, but it doesn't receive much attention otherwise, partly because of the difficulty in actually reaching its shores. Although just three miles from Keswick, and linked by the River Derwent which flows across the broad agricultural plain between the two, most of the shoreline is privately owned. Powerboats are banned and there are no-boating zones, restrictions that are intended to preserve the lake's rich variety of plants and animals. The shoreline habitat is the best-preserved example in the National Park, where over seventy species of birds and wildfowl (including ospreys) winter and breed, while Bassenthwaite is one of the only two places in Britain (with Derwent Water) where the vendace, a nine-inch fish related to other Arctic species, is found. However, the habitats are currently under threat from increased silting and pollution and invasion by alien plants and other species, all factors that have prompted a long-term lake restoration programme to improve the water quality at Bassenthwaite.

There's a three-mile path up the west shore as far as **Dubwath**, but as this is paralleled by the busy A66 the noise of traffic is ever present. There are plans to create a wetland nature reserve at Dubwath, but until it's complete the main interest is really on the **east shore** of the lake, though again access is restricted to certain sections, all clearly marked on maps; buses #X4, #73/73A and #555 run this way from Keswick.

Dodd Wood and the ospreys

The only permitted parking places close to the east shore are at the heavily planted Forestry Commission land of **Dodd Wood**. Starting from the *Old Sawmill Tearooms* (Easter–Oct daily 10am–5.30pm; ☎017687/74317) there are four marked trails of varying length. Some of the crowded pines, planted in the 1920s, are now 120ft high, which makes the climb (3 miles; 3hr return) to the heights of **Dodd** (1612ft) itself a rather disorienting experience. But native trees – including oak, ash, hawthorn and hazel – are being replanted in the wood to prevent hillside soil erosion, and you should also keep an eye out for wildlife: roe deer and some of the Lakes' few surviving red squirrels are occasionally seen around here.

However, the main interest in recent years has been the arrival of **wild ospreys** to nest and breed on the shores of Bassenthwaite, below the woods. A quarter-mile path (15min uphill climb) from the tearooms leads to an open-air **viewing platform** (telescopes provided, staffed April–Aug daily 10am–5pm; free; Ⓦwww.ospreywatch.co.uk) from where, on most days, you'll be able to see the ospreys fishing and feeding, hovering over the lake, then plunging feet first to catch roach, perch, pike and trout. The birds recolonized Bassenthwaite in 2001 and, although there's no guarantee, they have returned every year since – in 2006, three chicks were reared here for the first time. The ospreys usually arrive at the beginning of April; the eggs hatch in June, and the ospreys leave for Africa in August or September. For an even closer look, don't miss the live video feed from the nests shown over at Whinlatter Forest Park.

Mirehouse

The bus stop and parking by the *Old Sawmill Tearooms* also provides access to **Mirehouse** across the road (house Easter–Oct Wed & Sun 2–5pm, plus Fri in Aug 2–5pm; gardens Easter–Oct daily 10am–5.30pm; house & gardens £4.80; gardens only £2.60; ☎017687/72287, ✆www.mirehouse.com), a manor house and woodland gardens that are among the region's finest treasures. The house (built 1666) has been the home of the Spedding family since 1802 and is still lived in today, which explains the restricted opening days but also lends it a welcoming, informal air that's quite delightful. A pianist plays in the Music Room as you wind through the other rooms and corridors, while the claim that "little has been thrown away over the years" is demonstrably true – gentlemen's clay pipes, a Victorian knife-cleaner and an unexploded World War I grenade-turned-paperweight are just a few of the items displayed. Mirehouse has notable literary connections – Sir James Spedding (1808–81) was a respected biographer of Francis Bacon, and friend of Tennyson (who is supposed to have sought inspiration for his *Morte d'Arthur* here) and Thomas Carlyle among others, and the varied portraits, drawings, manuscripts, letters and books on show reveal the close relationships that many had with Carlyle's "dear hospitable Spedding". Outside are gardens, lawns, mixed woodland (with children's adventure playgrounds) and wildflower meadows, all connected by a circular signposted lakeside walk that takes around an hour to complete.

A short diversion from the Mirehouse grounds runs down through the fields and past two-hundred-year-old oak trees to the **church of St Bega** on the shores of Bassenthwaite. Originally Norman, and heavily restored, it's completely serene and protected by the looming flanks of Skiddaw. There's a public right of way from the road as well, so you don't need to pay for Mirehouse to visit the church.

Trotters World of Animals

Signs from the head of Bassenthwaite Lake direct you to **Trotters World of Animals** at Coalbeck Farm (daily 10am–5.30pm or dusk; £6.50; ☎017687/76239, ✆www.trottersworld.com), around the back of *Armathwaite Hall*. This is an excellent attraction, well worth an extended visit, since what started life as a simple animal farm is now a highly individual wildlife conservation project, presenting domestic, endangered and exotic animals within an educational framework. It's nothing if not all-encompassing: in spring you can help feed a newborn Cumbrian lamb, while as home to the only Canadian lynx in the UK, for example, the park highlights the plight of the related (and severely threatened) Iberian lynx. A recreated early medieval roundhouse is used to demonstrate sustainable crafts, while in the surrounding enclosures you'll come across a lively troop of gibbons, plus lemurs, meerkats, marmosets, tapirs and Asian fishing cats. Handling the animals is encouraged (even the snakes) during feeding programmes, demonstrations and other activities. There are flying displays every day with the hawks, vultures and owls, plus children's play areas, tractor and pony rides, a tearoom and picnic sites. There's always something going on, though school holidays tend to offer the pick of the child-oriented events, like the popular candlelit tours during December.

Practicalities

There's a renowned inn on the west side of Bassenthwaite Lake (the *Pheasant*) and another pub in the small village of **Bassenthwaite** (bus #73/73A), a couple of miles east of the top end of the lake. Other than that, though, the *Old Sawmill Tearooms* opposite Mirehouse is the best place for a snack or a meal.

Accommodation

Armathwaite Hall B5291, northern end of Bassenthwaite Lake ℡017687/76551, ⊛www.armathwaite-hall.com. Live the noble life at one of the Lake District's most glamorous country-house hotels, a restored sixteenth-century hall set in 400 acres of deer park and woodland and with terraces overlooking lawns that sweep down to the lakeside. It's of four-star standard and rooms (up to £270) are every bit as gracious as you might imagine; there's wood panelling and log fires throughout, plus pool and spa, steam room and gym, tennis court and other leisure activities. Two-night breaks include dinner, which softens the considerable bill a little. ⑨

Pheasant Inn Off the A66, just before Dubwath ℡017687/76234, ⊛www.the-pheasant.co.uk. This handsome old coaching inn features a carefully preserved period bar and comfortable lounges filled with flowers where superior bar lunches and

afternoon tea are served. Dinner is a more formal affair in the restaurant, after which you can repair to one of the thirteen characterful rooms, all tastefully decorated – two rooms are in the Garden Lodge while three suites offer a bit more space. ⑥

Ravenstone A591, 5 miles northwest of Keswick ℡0800/163983, ⊛www.ravenstone-hotel.co.uk. A Victorian hotel in two acres of grounds, with terrific views over Bassenthwaite Lake and enough decorative oak to denude a small forest. There's a handsome firelit lounge, full-sized snooker table, restaurant and bar – a lakeland dinner is included in the price. ⑦

Pub

Sun Bassenthwaite village ℡017687/76439. Retains its seventeenth-century air – oak beams, open fires – and serves good bar meals from noon to 2pm and 6 to 9pm. You can sit outside on a warm day too.

Back o' Skiddaw

People often complain that the Lake District is too crowded, that tourists (including themselves) have overwhelmed the infrastructure and transformed the villages – none of which, happily, is true of the **Back o' Skiddaw**, the local name for the arc of fells and valleys that stretches around the back of Skiddaw mountain, tucked into the northernmost section of the National Park. For the most part it's countryside that really does deserve the epithet "rolling", with farmland tumbling down from Skiddaw's gentle humps to encircle small hamlets and villages that see little tourist traffic. The only **public transport** is the #73/73A "Caldbeck Rambler" bus, which runs daily in the school summer holidays, on Saturdays throughout the year, and on selected Sundays and bank holiday Mondays (see "Travel details" at the end of the chapter).

Uldale and Ireby

From the *Castle Inn* junction, half a mile from the northern edge of Bassenthwaite Lake, the sweeping road into Uldale ends three miles further on at **ULDALE** village where the cow dung on the road announces its farming credentials. Farming in the Lakes is a precarious business at the best of times: what it must have been like in the past in "wolf's dale" doesn't bear thinking about. Walpole used the quiet village and moorland surroundings as the backdrop in the middle two Herries novels, *Judith Paris* and *The Fortress*, with the fictional Fell House as the Herries family lair. There's a pub – the *Snooty Fox* (℡016973/71479, ⊛www.snootyfox-uldale.co.uk) – and a tearoom in the old Victorian school, now the Uldale Gallery (Tues–Sun 10am–5pm; closed Jan & Feb; ℡016793/71778), which displays local arts and crafts. A mile and a half south of the village lies tiny **Over Water**, the northernmost splash of water in the Lake District, with the farms of Orthwaite beyond. Only bad things await, surely, on the heights of **Great Cockup** (1720ft), an easy two-mile walk east from Orthwaite.

In the other direction, Uldale's **St James church** lies a full mile from the village on the Ireby road, a pretty building with some interesting old grave-stones and uninterrupted fell views. Another mile beyond is sleepy **IREBY**, with its lion's-head drinking trough. You can eat well in the venerable beamed-and-nooked *Sun Inn* (☎016973/71346), whose small beer garden is a restful spot on a sunny day.

Caldbeck

Prosperity came easily to **CALDBECK**, six miles east of Ireby and just twelve from Carlisle, and it remains one of the Lakes' most appealing villages. The fast-flowing "cold stream" from which it takes its name provided the power for the rapid expansion in the number of mills here in the seventeenth and eighteenth centuries. Corn, wool and wooden bobbins flowed out, lead and copper from the fells was carted in; and the many surviving contemporary buildings (look for the dates carved on the lintels above the doors) attest to its wealth. A signposted quarter-mile walk from the car park up to the limestone gorge known as **The Howk** shows you the river in all its rushing glory, as well as the restored ruins of one of the old bobbin mills.

The village is anchored by its **church of St Kentigern**, dedicated to the sixth-century saint better known as Mungo, who journeyed from Scotland through Cumberland to Wales to preach the gospel to the heathen Saxons and Celts. The well he is supposed to have used for baptism lies by the pack-horse bridge, next to the churchyard. The first stone church here was built in the twelfth century, and although a medieval tombstone survives in the chancel, today's church bears the brunt of heavy nineteenth-century resto-ration. No matter, since all the interest is outside in the churchyard, where you'll easily find the ornate tombstone of **John Peel** of Ruthwaite (d. 1854), emblazoned with reliefs of hunting horns and his faithful hound. Peel's is a name synonymous with fox-hunting, yet he was just one of several hardened and hard-drinking nineteenth-century hunting men of local repute; his fame

© Crown copyright

today derives squarely from the song ("D'ye ken John Peel") written about him by one of his friends. Eighteen paces from his grave, walking away from the church, is the tombstone of the Harrisons of Todcrofts: Richard was a simple farmer; it's his wife Mary (d. 1837) who is better known – as Mary, the Maid of Buttermere, the most celebrated beauty of her day (see p.193). These days, Caldbeck's most famous resident is mountaineer and writer Chris Bonington. **Priest's Mill** (mid-Feb to Oct Tues–Sun 11am–5pm, Nov & Dec Tues–Sun noon–4pm), near the church, was a corn mill for over 200 years, but was restored in 1986 and has been turned into a little arts and business centre, with a café (see below), jeweller and cooperative woolshop among the outlets.

For a stretch of the legs, Caldbeck's most favoured local walk is the climb up **High Pike** (2157ft), the fell to the south, mined for its minerals in the nineteenth century. The most obvious route is from Nether Row, a mile south of Caldbeck – count on five miles, three hours, there and back. Views from the cairn and bench at the summit sweep from the Solway Firth to the Yorkshire hills, with Blencathra and Bowscale Fell in the foreground.

Practicalities

Caldbeck makes a peaceful night's stop and, although there's no tourist office, you can check local **information** online at ⓦ www.caldbeckvillage.co.uk. The **bus** drops you by the churchyard, there's free **parking** near the river, and a choice of local accommodation (including several farmhouse B&Bs, which are listed on the website). A very well-kept village **B&B**, *The Briars* (☎016974/78633; no credit cards; ❸), near the car park and next to the doctor's surgery, has one single and a twin sharing a nice large bathroom, while

△ John Peel's gravestone

an en-suite double at the back looks on to the local hillside. The **pub**, the *Oddfellows Arms* (☎016974/78227, ⓦ www .oddfellows-caldbeck.co.uk; ❸), boasts good-value trim rooms in a converted mill at the back. The bar meals here are very popular (restaurant bookings advised at weekends), or you can eat at the riverside ✻ *Watermill Café* at Priest's Mill (☎016974/78267, ⓦ www.watermillcafe.co.uk; closed Jan to mid-Feb), open throughout the day for snacks, meals, organic hot chocolate and herbal teas, and serving dinner by arrangement (usually once a month on Friday). The *Old Smithy* (☎016974/78246) on the river, behind the pub, also serves tearoom favourites, while for a drive out to a country pub, there's the attractive *Royal Oak* at **Welton**, about four miles to the north.

Hesket Newmarket

There's a path from Caldbeck a mile-and-a-half southeast through the fields to the small eighteenth-century village of **HESKET NEWMARKET**, which straddles a long village green. Markets were long held here, though the last was a century ago, and the prosperous village once supported half a dozen inns, yet the ⚔ *Old Crown* (☎016974/78288, ⓦwww.theoldcrownpub.co.uk) by the green is the only survivor. It's a cosy local of great charm, owned by a local cooperative (the first such in Britain), and brewing a variety of excellent ales out the back in the Hesket Newmarket Brewery. The food is very popular, too, with many coming for the speciality curries. There's a tearoom at *Fellside Stores*, the local grocer's and post office, while the other way, past the pub, friendly *Denton House* (☎016974/78415, ⓦwww.dentonhouseguest house.co.uk; no credit cards; ❸) has eight B&B rooms available. A mile or so southwest of the village, on the flank of the fells, Hudscales Farm **camping barn** (☎01946/758198; £6) offers simpler overnight accommodation for hikers and cyclists.

Incidentally, if Caldbeck can boast John Peel and Chris Bonington as local famous names, Hesket Newmarket is not to be outdone – road-haulage king and spotter's cult hero Eddie Stobart started out here in the family firm.

Carrock Fell, Mosedale and Mungrisdale

The road south from Caldbeck and Hesket Newmarket winds the eight miles back to the A66, effectively down the eastern boundary of the Lake District. Away to the east lie fields not fells, and beyond is the Eden Valley and Yorkshire. The bulk looming to the west, behind Blencathra and Bannerdale, is **Carrock Fell** (2174ft), best climbed from Stone Ends Farm – you can park by the road – three miles from Hesket Newmarket. The fell is riddled with abandoned mines (keep back – exploration is dangerous), while a huge tangle of fallen rocks litters the hillside: Charles Dickens and Wilkie Collins had a particularly disastrous time climbing Carrock Fell in mist, described in Dickens' *The Lazy Tours of Two Idle Apprentices* (1857).

The broad valley of **Mosedale**, another mile or so down the road, has a minor road running up to meet the Cumbria Way at the valley's head. Day walkers usually head instead for **Bowscale Tarn**, 1600ft up, scooped dramatically out of Bowscale Fell and ringed by crags. It's an easy walk (1hr) from the roadside parking at nearby Bowscale, following a clear bridleway for much of the route. The summit of **Bowscale Fell** (2306ft) itself is reached from the tarn by a further, gut-busting, 45-minute climb, and to make a circular walk of it (5 miles; 4hr) you can then drop down into **Mungrisdale**, a narrower valley whose foot embraces a few stone houses, a small church and the *Mill Inn* (☎017687/79632, ⓦwww.the-millinn.co.uk; ❹), where a stone mill wheel props up the bar. The rooms have been nicely refurbished and there's good, moderately priced food in the bar or restaurant – home-made pies are a speciality, celebrated at the pub's Pie Festival held every November. Almost next door – and not to be confused with it – the *Mill Hotel* (☎017687/79659, ⓦwww.themillhotel.com; no credit cards; ❼, including dinner ❾; closed Nov–Feb) is a more intimate, highly personalized country-house experience with a reputation for excellent food.

Travel details

All timetables can be checked on Traveline ☎ 0870/608 2608.

From Keswick

Bus #73/73A "Caldbeck Rambler" circular route to: Castlerigg Stone Circle (6min), Threlkeld (13min), Mungrisdale (25min), Mosedale (30min), Hesket Newmarket (45min), Caldbeck (50min), and around to Mirehouse (1hr 20min) and back to Keswick; or to Mirehouse (14min), Uldale (30min), Ireby (35min), Caldbeck (50min), and around to Mungrisdale (1hr 10min) and back to Keswick. Service operates mid-July to end-Aug 2–3 daily; plus Sat all year, and Sun & bank hols from end-May to mid-July.

Bus #77/77A "Honister Rambler" circular route to: Cat Bells (11min), Grange (20min), Seatoller (30min), Honister Pass/YHA (40min), Buttermere (50min), Lorton (1hr 10min) and Whinlatter Pass (1hr 20min); or to Whinlatter Pass (15min), Lorton (25min), Buttermere (45min), Honister Pass (1hr),

Seatoller (1hr 5min) and Grange (1hr 15min). Service operates Easter–Oct 4 daily.

Bus #79 "Borrowdale Rambler" (every 30min–1hr) to: Lodore (15min), Grange (20min), Rosthwaite (25min) and Seatoller (30min).

Bus #86 Keswick Town Service: to Portinscale (Mon–Sat 5 daily; 8min); and to Castlerigg Stone Circle (Mon–Sat 2 daily; 11min).

Bus #208 "Ullswater Connection" to: Aira Force (25min), Glenridding (35min) and Patterdale (40min). Service operates mid-July to end-Aug 5 daily, plus Sat, Sun & bank hols end-May to mid-July.

Bus #555/556 (hourly service) to: Thirlspot (10min), Grasmere (25min), Ambleside (45min), Windermere (1hr) and Kendal (1hr 30min); and also (3 daily) to Carlisle (1hr 10min).

Bus #X4/X5 (Mon–Sat every 30–60min, Sun every 2hr) to: Threlkeld (11min), Rheged (30min) and Penrith (35min); and also to Braithwaite (6min), Bassenthwaite (15min) and Cockermouth (30min).

5

The western fells and valleys

CHAPTER 5   # Highlights

✱ **Silecroft beach** The only stretch of beach within the National Park extends for miles, providing a habitat for wildlife. See p.176

✱ **Ravenglass & Eskdale Railway** The finest approach to quiet Eskdale is in the toy-town carriages of the Ravenglass & Eskdale Railway. See p.178

✱ **Muncaster** A great family day out – gardens, ghosts and owls. See p.178

✱ **Viking cross, Gosforth** This intricately carved stone cross is the finest reminder of the Norse influence on the Lakes. See p.185

✱ **Wasdale Head Inn** Relive the old days in the atmospheric rural inn, where walkers and climbers congregate over drinks and dinner. See p.187

✱ **Haystacks** The favourite peak of avid fellwalker Alfred Wainwright, whose ashes are scattered here. See p.194

△ Wast Water

The western fells and valleys

reat Gable and the Scafells stand as a formidable last-gasp boundary between the mountains of the central lakes and the mostly gentler land to the west, which smooths out its wrinkles as it descends to the Cumbrian coast. Here, in the **western fells and valleys**, lies some of the National Park's most diverse scenery – the stunning lakeland vistas you'd expect around Wast Water and Buttermere, tempered by the forested swathes of Ennerdale, the deeply rural hamlets of Wasdale and Eskdale, and a little-known coastline. Indeed, it's the west Cumbrian coast that impinges most upon this part of the region. The old industrial ports of Whitehaven, Workington and Maryport all lie outside the National Park but their influence is felt in subtle ways: for one hundred and fifty years water has been drained from Ennerdale to supply the towns, and only a spirited defence in the late 1970s by environmental protesters prevented a scheme to build a higher weir at Ennerdale Water and raise the water level. The driving force behind the proposed increase in water extraction was the Sellafield nuclear reprocessing plant, a major local employer that lurks on the coast just north of Ravenglass. It's changed its name twice, from Calder Hall to Windscale and then to Sellafield, in what might seem, to a cynic, an attempt to hide its manifest dangers.

The main road, the **A595** between Broughton-in-Furness and Workington, is the principal means of approach for the western fells and valleys. It runs along the coastal plain, with minor roads striking off north and east into the valleys, and it's this limited access that preserves the region's relative isolation – only Eskdale and Buttermere can be reached by road from the central fells. **Eskdale**, for that reason, is among the most popular targets, though the narrow-gauge **Ravenglass & Eskdale Railway** has as much to do with it. **Wast Water**, which points its slender finger towards Great Gable, remains one of the most isolated of the lakes, and a night at the inn at **Wasdale Head** is unlikely to be forgotten. "No part of the country is more distinguished by sublimity", claimed Wordsworth, who – no mean walker himself – thought Wasdale "well worth the notice of the traveller who is not afraid of fatigue". It's actually a toss-up whether Wast Water or **Ennerdale Water** is the better-looking lake, though Ennerdale is, if anything, even more remote. En route north to Cockermouth, a few interested visitors are drawn to tiny **Loweswater** and its excellent inn, though the biggest attractions are the twin lakes of **Crummock Water** and **Buttermere**. These are situated on a

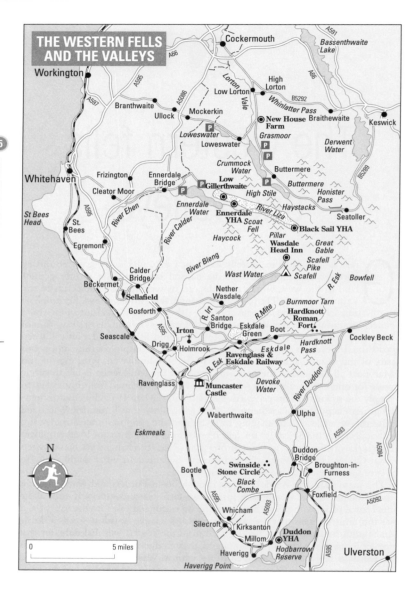

THE WESTERN FELLS AND THE VALLEYS

well-defined circuit from Keswick but there's enough grandeur in the surrounding fells to make the summer crowds bearable.

Public transport is limited. You can reach Ennerdale Water and Loweswater by public bus, but only on summer Sundays and public holidays, while the daily Buttermere service from Keswick is also seasonal (Easter–Oct). At all other times, you're going to find yourself walking between the lakes and villages, over mountain passes and across fells whose names (Pillar, Great Gable, the Scafells) are among the most resonant in the region.

Millom, Black Combe and the coast

The short section of the **west Cumbrian coast** that falls within the National Park – the twenty miles between Silecroft and Ravenglass – is neither particularly dramatic nor appealing. Its one unique feature is the bulky **Black Combe**, which dominates the southern part of the coast, the only Lake District fell to fall straight to the sea. This gives climbing it a certain appeal, since the views are tremendous and, unusually for the Lakes, only run out with the horizon. To the southeast, just outside the National Park boundary, the former iron-ore mining town of **Millom** tries hard to capture some of the passing traffic, though more are drawn to the fine duned beaches out of town at **Haverigg** or to the long sandy stretches from **Silecroft** northwards.

Millom and around

Road and rail shadow the coast from **MILLOM** (which lies just outside the National Park), the small, plain town split by the railway line and flanked to the south and east by the shifting sands of the Duddon Channel. A late-medieval settlement here – to the north of the current town – focused on the castle and church of the local lords, the Hudlestones, whose seat is now largely in ruins (there's no regular public access to the castle ruin or church). It wasn't until the mid-nineteenth century – and the local discovery of high-grade iron ore – that Millom itself was established around the mining and ore-processing operations on the neighbouring Hodbarrow peninsula. In its day, it was a massive operation, with millions of tons of iron ore extracted by thousands of workers housed in drab, company-built streets. Their employment came to an end in 1968 when the mine finally closed, but working and living conditions are graphically recalled in Millom's excellent **Folk Museum** (Easter–Oct Tues–Sat 10.30am–4.30pm; £2; Ⓦwww.millomfolkmuseum.co.uk), sited with the tourist office at the town's train station. There's a re-creation of one of the old mines, using original items from the last pit to close, as well as other reassembled shop and domestic interiors, and any number of local finds, photographs, relics and memorabilia.

The museum is also the place to discover something about Millom's famous son, the poet **Norman Nicholson** (1914–87). An only child, he contracted TB at 16 and spent two years in a Hampshire sanatorium before returning to Millom, where it was another twelve years before he was considered cured. His wide reading in convalescent isolation was one of the main factors, he considered, that made him a reflective poet; that, and his deep attachment to his Cumberland roots, whose industry, landscape, people and history informed all his work. Nicholson spent his life in Millom. His house, at 14 St George's Terrace, just off the small market square, two minutes from the train station, is marked by a blue plaque – it's now a health-food store and tearoom. In **St George's Church**, up the drive opposite the square, a beautiful contemporary stained-glass window celebrates Nicholson's life and work – ask about access at the tourist office – while he is buried with his wife in the new part of St George's churchyard. The grave lies beyond the church and down to the right, in front of a wooden bench by a wooden fence, and is inscribed with a moving line from his last published work, *Sea to the West*: "Let our eyes at the last be blinded/Not by the dark/But by dazzle."

Black Combe and Swinside Stone Circle

The A595 makes a V-shape around the **Black Combe** massif, with the angle at the hamlet of **Whicham**, near Silecroft, where there's a path up to the **summit** (1857ft) that starts from the minor Kirkbank road, behind the church. It's not a particularly demanding climb (around 3 miles there and back; 2hr 30min), and the views from the top are hugely rewarding, stretching out to sea to the Isle of Man, up the coast to St Bees Head and south to Morecambe Bay. It's traditionally claimed that you can see up to fourteen English and Scottish counties from here, plus Snowdon and the Irish coast, but that would require one of those all-too-rare crystal-clear days and Clark Kent-like vision.

The fell's northeastern side shelters the **Swinside Stone Circle**, though this is best reached from back up the A595 towards Broughton-in-Furness: look for the minor Broadgate turn-off, park by the farm buildings and walk the mile up the rough fell track to the ancient standing stones. They stand in a natural amphitheatre, with the local name for the stones, Sunkenkirk, reflecting the belief that the devil struck (or sunk) the stones of an ancient church (kirk) into the ground. A pagan winter solstice ceremony is held here each year.

Respects paid, the local beach at **Haverigg** beckons. A mile to the south, it's typical of what's to come – a lengthy, duned stretch that leads a quiet existence, even in summer. There's a children's playground and a beach café. The nearby **Hodbarrow RSPB Reserve**, two miles from Millom (always open; free; Ⓦ www.rspb.org.uk) – sited around a freshwater lagoon formed from flooded mine workings – is a good place for a stroll. The lagoon is of national importance for wintering waterfowl such as wigeon, goldeneye, red-breasted merganser and pintail, while in summer three species of tern nest on the reserve and can be viewed from the hide on the sea wall. The number and variety of orchids at Hodbarrow also catch the eye in summer – not just the plentiful marsh, spotted and pyramidal orchids but the largest colony of bee orchids in Cumbria.

Practicalities

The **train station** is on Station Road, while the **tourist office** next door (Easter–Oct Mon–Fri 10am–1pm & 2–4.30pm; ☏01229/774819, Ⓦ www .western-lakedistrict.co.uk) has local **accommodation** details. There are a few town B&Bs, but if you are going to stay you might as well immerse yourself in Millom's estuarine surroundings. From the station, follow St George's Road then Devonshire Road to find the friendly, no-smoking *Duddon Pilot Hotel* (☏01229/774116, Ⓦ www.duddonpilot.co.uk; ⑤), under a mile out of town by the estuary and old iron works. There's a nautical theme throughout – family members were once ships' pilots on the River Duddon, hence the name. Three hundred yards further on, closer to the river and sands, the *Duddon Estuary YHA* (☏0870/770 6107, Ⓔduddon@yha.org.uk; advance bookings essential; beds from £12) is a small, eighteen-bed cottage **youth hostel** perched on the edge of the peninsula, with terrific views and plenty of local walks on the doorstep. It's self-catering only, with the nearest shops and supermarket back in Millom, though the *Duddon Pilot* has a restaurant and bar meals. Or there's *Surees* (☏01229/775662; open Wed–Sun dinner, call for lunch times), a Thai restaurant based in the train station buildings.

The coast: Silecroft to Eskmeals

Next decent sweep of beach is at **Silecroft**, four miles northwest of Millom. The coastal scrub here is a habitat for the natterjack toad; and, as elsewhere along the Cumbrian coast, terns, oystercatchers and ringed plovers nest and breed, scraping the shingle over their camouflaged eggs. There's a pub at Silecroft (near the station, not the beach), where you can get a lunchtime sandwich, though some prefer the *King William IV* at **Kirksanton**, a mile back down the A5093 towards Millom. At **Bootle**, five miles up the A595, the sandstone-faced church is split from its cemetery by the road. Bootle's nearest beach is three miles to the northwest, at **Eskmeals**, which has a stony foreshore, though when the tide is out a large expanse of sand is exposed, from which you can admire the views as far north as St Bees Head. North of here, as far as Ravenglass, the coastline itself is off limits – red flags fly over an experimental firing range – while beyond lie the hard-to-miss towers and buildings of Sellafield. Whether you'd choose to swim anywhere in the vicinity of a nuclear-reprocessing plant is, of course, entirely a matter for you.

Ravenglass and around

The principal coastal stop before the headland of St Bees is **RAVENGLASS**, a sleepy village at the estuary of three syllabically challenged rivers, the Esk, Mite and Irt. The village is the starting point for the narrow-gauge Ravenglass & Eskdale Railway, but it merits a closer look before you take the train or visit nearby Muncaster Castle. Its single main street preserves a row of plain nineteenth-century cottages. These back on to estuarine mud flats and dunes, which are accessible when the tide's out – the northern section, across the Esk, is a nature reserve where black-headed gulls and terns are often seen. The Romans, who used the estuary as a harbour, established a supply post at Ravenglass in the first century AD for the northern legions manning Hadrian's Wall. Nothing remains of what the Romans knew as Glannaventa save the remarkably complete buildings of their **bathhouse**, part of a fort that survived in Ravenglass until the fourth century. It's on the road out of the village, just past the station, 500 yards up a (signposted) single-track lane.

△ Ravenglass

Ravenglass & Eskdale Railway

The **Ravenglass & Eskdale Railway** (known locally as La'al Ratty) opened in 1875 to carry iron ore from the Eskdale mines to the coast at Ravenglass. Long converted to tourist use and running on a 15-inch-gauge track, the little train takes forty minutes to wind for seven miles through two of the Lake District's prettiest valleys, first along Miterdale under Muncaster Fell and then into the valley of the River Esk, where it terminates at Dalegarth station, near Boot. You can break your journey with an "Explorer" ticket (see below), allowing you to get off and walk from one of the half-dozen stations en route; the full return journey, without a break, takes an hour and forty minutes. At **Dalegarth**, there's a visitor centre, shop and café, and bike rental (from £9.50 a day) whenever the trains are running – printed Eskdale cycle routes are available at the station. Or you can take your own bike up on the train and cycle back from Dalegarth down the traffic-free **Eskdale T-Rail** (8.5 miles; one-way ticket plus bike carriage £8.80); it takes around two hours, and a route guide (£2) is available from stations at either end (you'll need to call the station a day in advance to book your cycle on the train).

Between March and November there are at least seven daily **departures** from Ravenglass; there are also trains most winter weekends, plus at Christmas, New Year and February half-term holidays. An **Explorer Ticket** (£9.60, family ticket £24.90) gives one day's unlimited travel on the line, while special days out, involving Thomas the Tank Engine and the like, are held throughout the year.

For more **information**, contact the Ravenglass & Eskdale station (℡01229/717171, ⓦwww.ravenglass-railway.co.uk), adjacent to the Furness coastal line station. There's parking at Ravenglass station, a small **railway museum** (same days and times as rail service), a short video showing you the route, a café on the platform and a shop, where budding engine drivers can buy an all-important driver's cap. The station **café** serves drinks and light meals while, over by the main station, the *Ratty Arms* (℡01229/717676) has real ales, daily specials and sandwiches, served on a sunny terrace.

Muncaster Castle

A mile east of Ravenglass, on the A595, spreads the estate of **Muncaster Castle** (Feb half-term hols to first week Nov: castle Mon–Fri & Sun noon–5pm; gardens, owl centre and maze daily 10.30am–5pm or dusk; £9.50, £7 without castle entrance; ℡01229/717614, ⓦwww.muncaster.co.uk) whose house, grounds and attractions are one of the region's best days out. There's parking at the castle, or bus #6/X6 runs daily from Whitehaven via Ravenglass (and on Sundays from Millom). Or you can walk here (30min) on the path from Ravenglass, up past the Roman bathhouse and across the fields.

The **castle** itself was built around a medieval pele tower, and has been home to the Pennington family since the thirteenth century; family members still live here today, as photographs throughout and contemporary portraits in the Drawing Room attest. An audio tour points out the family treasures (a Gainsborough here, a Reynolds there), and leads you through various rooms, notably the impressive octagonal library and the Tapestry Room, with its Flemish wall hangings and mighty Elizabethan fireplace. An electromagnetic "spectre-detector" provides evidence to back up Muncaster's claim to be one of the most haunted houses in Britain – sceptics and others can test their nerve with an all-night vigil in the Tapestry Room (Ghost Sit, from around £450 for up to six people, breakfast included). The seventy-acre **grounds and gardens** win plaudits too (best in spring and autumn), with a stupendous view straight up Eskdale from the Terrace Walk, and half a dozen other marked trails, including one winding through a hilly Sino-Himalayan Garden. The plants here, all grown from seeds from Bhutan, Vietnam, and Yunnan and Sichuan provinces in China, thrive in conditions apparently similar to those 11,000 feet up a Far Eastern mountain – which doesn't say a lot for Cumbrian weather patterns.

The castle is also the headquarters of the World Owl Trust, whose excellent **Owl Centre** (☎01229/717393, ⓦwww.owls.org) in the grounds acts as a breeding centre for endangered species (including England's own barn owl). The aviaries contain birds from fifty different owl species, some of which are put through their paces on the castle lawns at the informative daily "Meet the Birds" display (2.30pm); the wild herons feed at 4.30pm (3.30pm in winter). Finally, the **meadowvole maze** is a light-hearted look at mole-sized life in the wildflower meadows, where escaping being eaten by an owl is the challenge for younger visitors.

The castle is closed in winter, though the grounds, owl centre and maze remain open in November and December (daily 11am–4pm; £5), when you can also experience **Darkest Muncaster** (call for details), an illuminated walk through the grounds, packed with interactive surprises.

Refreshments are provided by the **café**, *Creeping Kate's Kitchen*, in the stable yard, while smart B&B **rooms** in the former coachman's quarters (see opposite for contact details; ❺, family rooms ❻) offer a comfortable night's stay. No meals are served other than breakfast, though guests have the use of a lounge and kitchen, and it's only a mile's walk down the path to Ravenglass and the *Ratty Arms* – or stick a bottle of bubbly in the fridge and toast yourself on the Muncaster lawns. Guests also get free access to the gardens and owl centre, and a discount on the Ravenglass & Eskdale Railway.

Eskdale

Eskdale, accessed most easily from the Cumbrian coast, is just twelve miles long from start to finish, but what a finish it provides – in the dramatic high-fell surroundings of Hardknott Pass. It's a fairly gentle valley in its early stages, with various approach roads (from Ulpha in the Duddon Valley, from Wasdale

© Crown copyright

or along the River Esk itself) meeting at the elongated hamlet of **Eskdale Green** (a stop on the Ravenglass & Eskdale Railway), on a rise above the valley. From Eskdale Green, the valley road continues east, passing **Dalegarth station** (terminus of the Ravenglass & Eskdale Railway), which lies just a short walk from the valley's isolated church and from Eskdale's other hamlet, **Boot**. Here there's an old mill to explore, an excellent inn and several more local hikes, not to mention the walk or drive up and out of the valley to the superbly sited **Hardknott Roman Fort**.

Eskdale Green

First village stop on the Ravenglass & Eskdale Railway is **ESKDALE GREEN**, where you can access short walks into nearby Miterdale Forest and up to the valley head, or even plan on hiking back along the spine of Muncaster Fell to Ravenglass. This is around four miles and shouldn't take more than a couple of hours. Up the road (left out of the station and past the Outward Bound centre), the simple village **church of St Bega** doubles as an unstaffed visitor centre, with some display boards in the entrance covering the local sights and history. There's a nearby car park, by the Miterdale bridleway, and an inconspicuous sign

Walks from Eskdale

Eskdale is a great choice for a walk at any time of year: you'll rarely come across many other people on the routes outlined below, even on the shorter strolls. There's parking at Dalegarth station and in Boot, and as the train runs year-round the valley makes a fine off-season day out.

Dalegarth Force and the River Esk

Footpaths along both sides of the **River Esk** between Eskdale's St Catherine's church and Doctor Bridge (near the *Woolpack Inn*) allow an easy two-mile (1hr) riverside walk – in low water you can cross the river below the church by stepping stones, or there's a bridge further up. You can combine this with the steep climb up the wooded ravine that holds the impressive sixty-foot falls of **Dalegarth Force** (also known as Stanley Ghyll Force), in full spate for much of the year.

Hardknott and the Esk Falls

It's harder going east of Doctor Bridge, where a path to the foot of the **Hardknott Pass** keeps to the south side of the River Esk beneath Birker Fell, before cutting up, via the farm at Brotherikeld, to the Roman fort. Keeping to the Esk, you can hike on up the narrow valley between overhanging crags to **Lingcove Bridge**, beyond which tumble the **Esk Falls** – an eight-mile (5hr) round-trip that requires fine weather and good visibility, otherwise you risk getting bogged down and lost.

The Woolpack Walk

The most strenuous hike from Eskdale – and one of the most extreme in the Lakes – is the **Woolpack Walk** (18 miles; 10–12hr), a tough high-level circuit topping the two highest mountains in England (the Scafells) and several others (Bowfell, Crinkle Crags, Harter Fell) that aren't much lower. It is not easy going and a certain amount of scrambling is required, but the views and the varied terrain make this one of the finest lakeland walks. Traditional start- and finishing-point is the *Woolpack Inn*, where full route details and advice are available.

See Basics, p.35, for general walking advice in the Lakes; recommended maps are detailed on p.42.

on the bridleway, just a few yards from the road, which leads up through Giggle Alley Wood to Eskdale Green's curious **Japanese Garden**. The series of pools, surrounded by bamboo, magnolia and maples, was originally laid out in 1913, and is now being restored by the Forestry Commission. The pools fill after rain, and the encompassing shrub- and woodland is a good place for a family stroll.

Nearest **pub** to the station (200 yards away to the right, by the turn-off to Boot) is the ivy-strewn *King George IV* (☎019467/23262, ⓦwww.kinggeorge -eskdale.co.uk; ❹), a traditional hostelry with an impressive collection of real ales and malt whiskies. The local **campsite** is 400 yards further up the Boot road, at *Fisherground Farm* (☎019467/23349, ⓦwww.fishergroundcampsite .co.uk; closed Nov–Feb) – it's a family-friendly place with its own station on the Ravenglass & Eskdale Railway.

Heading the other way, west, through Eskdale Green, you'll pass the Outward Bound Centre, the church and a small general store, and, further on, a narrow country lane leading to **Irton Road station** and *Forest How Guest House* (☎019467/23201, ⓦwww.foresthow.co.uk; no credit cards; ❸, en suite ❹). This has a lovely patio with rural views and six country-style bedrooms (four en suite, with sparkling bathrooms) in the main house, plus an annexe with two rooms and a private bathroom, suitable for families. Back on the road, at the Santon Bridge turn-off, there's the *Bower House Inn* (☎019467/23244, ⓦwww .bowerhouseinn.co.uk; ❺), with a selection of real ales (some local), bar meals and a restaurant serving a *table d'hôte* dinner for £25.

Dalegarth station and Boot

By the time the valley road and train line reach **Dalegarth station**, two miles east of Eskdale Green, the fells beyond can be seen more clearly and eyes are drawn ever upwards to the singular skyline. Passengers pile off the train for the

△ Boot

walk to Dalegarth Force, heading down a track opposite the station, which leads in a couple of hundred yards to Eskdale's **St Catherine's church**. Its riverside location is handsome in the extreme, and in the small cemetery you can't miss the distinctive gravestone of Thomas Dobson (d. 1910), former hunt Master of the Eskdale and Ennerdale Hounds whose likeness grins from the top of the stone, above a carved fox and hound. Dobson actually died in the *Three Shires Inn* in Little Langdale, which involved his coffin being carted to Eskdale over the gruelling Wrynose and Hardknott passes. If he hadn't already been dead the bearers would probably have killed him for his thoughtlessness.

It's another 350 yards up the valley road from Dalegarth station to the turning for the dead-end hamlet of **BOOT**. The few stone cottages and pub, cowering beneath the fells, mark the last remnant of civilization before the road turns serious. The mines near Boot that supplied ore for the railway to Ravenglass never really paid their way and closed in 1913. But there's been industry of sorts here for centuries, since the Furness Abbey monks first introduced a corn mill into Eskdale. Over the packhorse bridge at the back of the hamlet, the sixteenth-century **Eskdale Mill** (April–Sept open at least 5 days a week for visits, 11.30am–5.30pm, call to check ℡019467/23335; £1.50) preserves its wooden machinery and you can picnic near the waterfalls that power the wheels. For a stretch of the legs, follow the signposted path up the heights to **Eel Tarn**, a mile away.

Dry-stone walls

A dry-stone wall
Is a wall and a wall,
Leaning together
(Cumberland and Westmorland
champion wrestlers),
Greening and weathering,
Flank by flank,
With filling of rubble
Between the two.

From "Wall", by Norman Nicholson

The hundreds of miles of **dry-stone walls** that crisscross the Lake District are one of the region's most characteristic sights. Although the earliest farmers had identified boundaries and enclosed fields, these tasks assumed greater significance with the medieval expansion of sheep farming. As early as the thirteenth century the monks of Furness Abbey were enclosing extensive tracts of moorland within stone-built walls, traces of which can still be seen in upper Eskdale. Walls provided the means of converting unproductive high land into enclosed sheep farms: separating grazing areas, providing flocks with shelter (and preventing them straying), and facilitating sheep-driving and collection (by means of stone-built "pounds"). At first built on an ad hoc basis, walls tended to follow irregular patterns to suit local needs – often they were no more than dumping grounds for stones cleared from new pastures.

Irregularly walled enclosures gave way to systematic patterns during the eighteenth and nineteenth centuries as the Enclosure Acts (1801) prevailed – basically, statutes sanctioning the grabbing of once common or wild land by the bigger, richer landowners. Not only was common land seized, but small farmers were deprived of traditional grazing, cropping and wood-gathering rights, forcing them either to become tenants or to move. Behind this larceny was a rapidly increasing demand for food and wool, driven by the mushrooming population of the newly industrialized cities and the effect of the blockades during the Napoleonic War which kept food prices high. For many, the resulting walls – now an integral part of the landscape, but then a novelty

Boot has a fair smattering of **accommodation and services**, which makes it the obvious base for extended walks in the valley. All the overnight options are covered here, from rooms in old inns to youth-hostel accommodation. A small **general store–post office** in Boot sells lakeland ice cream and rents out hiking boots. Local **information** is available online at ⓦ www.eskdale.info and ⓦ www.eskdaleweb.co.uk. The **Boot Beer Festival** each June (ⓦ www .bootbeer.co.uk) splits its festivities between the valley's three inns, while the **Eskdale Show** (last Sat in Sept) is the annual valley celebration of traditional ways and sports.

Inns and B&B

Brook House Inn 350 yards east of Dalegarth station, at the Boot road junction ☏ 019467/23288, ⓦ www.brookhouseinn.co.uk. Cheery, family-run hotel with seven rooms, which serves morning coffee and meals in its bar (real ales always available) and also has a separate, moderately priced restaurant where the food's a cut above ordinary pub fare – including some varied veggie options and home-made puddings. ⑤

Boot Inn Boot ☏ 019467/23224, ⓦ www.bootinn .co.uk. The traditional hikers' choice is a genial place, right in the centre of the hamlet, with nine upgraded en-suite rooms, plus a boot room and drying facilities, and a peaceful beer garden for examining maps and blisters. The good restaurant and bar meals are for hearty appetites and use local produce where possible, some of it homegrown. At weekends, when D,B&B rates apply, there's a 2-night minimum stay. Parking. ⑤, D,B&B ⑥

– symbolized the growing hardship of the small farmer. Nineteenth-century English "peasant poet" John Clare wrote bitterly that: "Enclosure came, and trampled on the grave of labour's rights, and left the poor a slave."

The increased demand for walls outstripped the capabilities of most farmers and inspired a new trade, undertaken by bands of itinerant craftsmen (not strictly masons, but skilled nonetheless). Sleeping on the fells and using the stone they found *in situ* – which explains the homogeneous, almost organic quality of lakeland walls – these "wallers" would set about erecting what are known locally as "dykes". A good waller could build seven yards of wall a day, though often less as many walls in the Lakes are unnecessarily thick – surplus stone had to be used up to maximize the grazing land. Tools and methods varied: shovel or spade, pick and stone hammer were common utensils; many wallers preferred to rely on sight rather than use builders' "lines"; others used a "walling frame" (two boards fastened with cross-pieces) to establish the height of the wall and the slope of its sides.

As its name makes clear, a dry-stone wall has no mortar to hold it together. Instead, it's built on the cavity-wall principle – that is, as a double wall with the space between packed with small stones (guts). Ideally a two-person job (someone working alone has to keep changing sides), the wall starts off at anything up to 3ft wide, narrowing to around a foot wide at the top. Long stones (throughs) are placed at intervals through the width for stability, while the walls are topped by slanted stones (cams) so that the rain drains off. To allow sheep access from one pasture to another, a space (hogg hole) might be left in the base of a wall. A waller requires a good eye, both for the line of the wall and the selection of stones, which must either have a smooth side or be suitable for corners. The finished product is remarkably hardy: dry-stone walls might last fifty or a hundred years without shifting or collapsing, often longer.

While not exactly a growth industry these days, new dry-stone walls are still needed on modern sheep farms and existing walls require maintenance. The old skills have been kept alive by a dedicated band of wallers: you'll see them in action at annual agricultural shows, while there are also dry-stone wall-building demonstrations every summer, coordinated by the Lake District Visitor Centre at Brockhole.

Dale View The Post Office, Boot ☎019467/23236, ⓦ www.booteskdale.co.uk. The post office has two doubles, a twin and a single, all sharing a bathroom, and can pack you a lunch (£4) for a day's walking – the *Boot Inn* is right over the road for meals. Advance reservations recommended in winter, when B&B is not always available. No credit cards. ❸

🏃 **Woolpack Inn** Eskdale, Hardknott Pass road, 1 mile east of Boot ☎019467/23230, ⓦ www.woolpack.co.uk. The friendly inn provides all the essentials – eight cosy rooms (five currently en suite, more in the pipeline), a fell-view garden and mountainous portions of good, inexpensive home-cooked food. It's also a real-ale place, with beers from the pub's own brewery, plus ales from other Cumbrian microbreweries, Solway cider and Belgian beers. You'll get good hiking advice, wherever you're heading, and if residents complete the infamous Woolpack Walk in less than nine hours, they get a free pint. Dinner reservations required. Parking. No American Express. ❺

Youth hostel

Eskdale YHA Eskdale, Hardknott Pass road, 200 yards east of Woolpack Inn ☎0870/770 5824, ⓔ eskdale@yha.org.uk. A secluded, detached house nestling under Eskdale Fell, with some rooms available to couples and families. Bike rental, laundry facilities and drying room available. Evening meals available. Closed Nov–March; also closed occasional nights in season. Dorm beds from £13.

Campsite

Hollins Farm Eskdale, Hardknott Pass road, 200 yards east of Boot ☎019467/23253. Small campsite, beautifully sited in the Esk valley.

Hardknott Fort and Pass

Three miles beyond Boot and 800ft up the twisting road, the remains of **Hardknott Roman Fort** (always open; free access) – known as Mediobocdum to the Romans – command a strategic and panoramic position just below Hardknott Pass. If ever proof were needed of how serious the Romans were about keeping what they had conquered, then Hardknott proves the point. This full-scale fortification was built during the reign of Hadrian by a cohort of Dalmatian (Croatian) troops, who gave it walls twelve feet thick and a double-towered gateway, and endowed it with granaries, bathhouses and a plush, stone-built *praetorium* or commandant's quarters. The troops had to endure the discomforts of timber barracks, though since the *praetorium* was built along Roman lines – rooms ranged around an open courtyard – the commandant probably cursed his luck at his assignment every time the wind blew (about every ten seconds up here). Much of the lower part of the defensive wall is original Roman work; elsewhere, the foundations of the granaries and various other buildings have been re-erected to indicate their scale. Needless to say, the views back down into Eskdale and up to the Scafells are stunning.

Past the fort, after negotiating the narrow switchbacks of **Hardknott Pass**, the road drops to Cockley Beck (for the Duddon Valley), before making the equally alarming ascent of Wrynose Pass, gateway to Little Langdale.

Wast Water and around

Nothing prepares you for the first sight of **Wast Water**, England's deepest lake, and certainly not the gentle approach from the southwest through the forestry plantations and farmland between the Wasdale hamlets of **Santon Bridge** and **Nether Wasdale**. Bracken-covered walls hide the fields from view, while the roads cross little stone bridges and pass farm shops selling jars of bramble jelly or bags of new potatoes. A mile and a half east of Nether Wasdale the lake comes into view and the initial glimpse of the water brings gasps – not for the lake itself (just three miles long), but for the crowding fells that surround it and the awesome screes that plunge to its eastern shore. These tumble 1700ft from Illgill Head, separating Wast Water from Eskdale to the south, while the highest peaks in England – Great Gable and the Scafells – frame **Wasdale Head**, the tiny settlement at the head of the lake. You'll have seen the view up the lake to Great Gable, unwittingly, countless times already since the National Park Authority uses the outline as its logo on every publication, signpost and notice board. For a true measure of your own insignificance, take a walk along the eastern lakeshore path, approaching the impassable, implacable screes and look up. Thomas Wilkinson, an overawed eighteenth-century Quaker, fancied that he was gazing upon "the Pyramids of the world, built by the Architect of the Universe".

Isolated Wasdale Head and its famous *Wasdale Head Inn* are very much the main events in Wasdale, though on the way you should also make time to see the ancient cross in **Gosforth**, a village just off the A595. There's currently no **public transport** to Wasdale Head, save a limited-service, pre-booked taxi from Gosforth via Nether Wasdale and *Wasdale Hall YHA* (call Traveline ☏0870/608 2608 or Wasdale Taxis ☏019467/25308). Drivers should note that the road beyond Nether Wasdale is single-track for the most part and hugs Wast Water's western shore, with occasional parking spots by bosky groves, stony coves and little promontories.

Gosforth and around

At the Wasdale turn-off from the A595, **GOSFORTH** ("ford of geese") – a large if unremarkable village, with a couple of pubs, a bank and petrol station – has one extraordinary attraction: the tall, carved **stone cross** in the churchyard of **St Mary's** on the eastern edge of town. Signposted as the

"Viking" cross, it's a rare example in Cumbria of the clash between pagan and Christian cultures, with the four faces of the slender shaft carved with Norse figures from the Sagas, which are surmounted by a Christian cross. There's been a church on this site since at least the tenth century, though it's been rebuilt many times since: nineteenth-century restoration revealed the church's other treasures, the two Viking "hogback" **tombstones**, found buried in the foundations. If your imagination is captured by the Gosforth cross, you should really drive the three miles south back down the A595, through Holmrook, and take the left turn signposted to Santon Bridge. A mile up the ruler-straight road, a signposted track – accessible with care for cars – leads to isolated **St Paul's**, Irton, which has a worn tenth-century stone cross in its churchyard.

The *Lion & Lamb* **pub** in the centre can provide a bite to eat, as can the *Lakeland Habit Café* (☎019467/25232) above the village shop and post office. Gosforth also has a bakery (locally famed for its meat pies), farm grocery shop and an ATM, which makes it the most reliable place for services and supplies in this neck of the woods.

Nether Wasdale and Santon Bridge

East of Gosforth, the hamlet of **NETHER WASDALE**, a mile and a half before the lake, has some useful accommodation, including two hotels right by the green: five rooms and a nice public bar serving meals at the *Screes Inn* (☎019467/26262, ⓦwww.thescreesinnwasdale.com; ➍), and more rooms plus a fancier restaurant over at *Strands Hotel* (☎019467/26237, ⓦwww.strandshotel .com; ➎), where you can dine well on locally sourced produce, including organic lakeland trout, fell-bred lamb, Wasdale goat's cheese and Windermere char. Or there's nearby *Low Wood Hall* (☎019467/26100, ⓦwww.lowwoodhall .co.uk; ➎, superior rooms ➏, restaurant closed Sun dinner), a restored Victorian country house whose gardens look toward the fells. Budget accommodation is either at *Murt Barn* (☎01946/758198; £6), a basic farmhouse **camping barn** 250 yards from the village on the Wast Water road, or at the **youth hostel**, *Wasdale Hall YHA* (☎0870/770 6082, ✉wastwater@yha.org.uk; advance

---

Don't believe a word of it

The *Bridge Inn* at Santon Bridge is best known for hosting the annual **Biggest Liar in the World** competition every November, a tradition started in the late nineteenth century by publican **Will Ritson** (1808–90) of nearby Wasdale Head, who told famously tall tales of country life to his gullible guests. The Victorian gentlemen fell-walkers and pioneer mountaineers – mostly professional men and academics from the cities – were, for example, given to believe that Wasdale turnips grew so large that farmers quarried them for food and then used the hollowed-out husks for sheep sheds. The annual contest is open to all-comers (though, for obvious reasons, lawyers and politicians are barred from entering), who have five minutes to tell the biggest lie they can. The winner gets a cup and £25, and entrants have to convince a sceptical local crowd that their tall tales of lakeland life just might have something in them, whether it's Cumbrian mermaid farms, dogs with false teeth being pursued by foxes, or (the 2006 winner) flatulent sheep causing the hole in the ozone layer. Practised local fibbers have a head start – and some have won the title several times – but in 2003 the Biggest Liar award went to South African Abrie Kruger, while 2006 saw another break with tradition, when TV and radio comedienne Sue Perkins (of Mel and Sue fame) became the first woman to win.

△ St Olaf's church, Wasdale Head

reservations essential; from £13), another mile and a half to the east, at the foot of the lake. It's an impressive converted country house set in a wooded hollow – nearby **Low Wood** has one of the Lakes' finest displays of spring bluebells. There are dramatic lake views from some of the dorm rooms, and the hostel offers an evening meal, or a choice of pubs at either Nether Wasdale or Wasdale Head (three miles away).

In the other direction, two miles to the southwest of Nether Wasdale, **SANTON BRIDGE** has the *Bridge Inn* (℡019467/26221, Ⓦwww.santonbridgeinn.com; 2-night minimum at weekends July & Aug; ❺), a modest country pub by the River Irt, providing bistro meals, weekend walkers' breakfasts and packed lunches. A few hundred yards away (on the Irton road, to the A595), there are teas, meals and cakes at the *Woodlands Tea Rooms* (℡01946/726281), attached to a country crafts and gift shop.

Wasdale Head

The Wast Water road ends a mile beyond the lake at **WASDALE HEAD**, a Shangri-La-like clearing between the mountain ranges, where you'll find the **Wasdale Head Inn**, one of the most celebrated of all lakeland inns. British

Walks from Wasdale Head

Wasdale Head is at the heart of some serious walking and climbing country, offering popular climbs up to Scoat Fell, Pillar, the Scafells and Great Gable, among others, and classic routes over the passes into Ennerdale or Borrowdale. It's not really beginners' country, though walks down to the lake, a scramble along its eastern shore or the hike over moorland to Burnmoor Tarn and Eskdale should be within most capabilities.

A Mosedale horseshoe

Mosedale – the valley to the northwest of Wasdale Head – is crowned by an impressive ring of high peaks and crags. A terrific horseshoe circuit starts from the **Overbeck Bridge** car park (2 miles from Wasdale Head, down the lake road) and then climbs up via Yewbarrow (2060ft), Red Pike (1710ft) and Scoat Fell (2760ft) to **Pillar** (2927ft). The walk then continues along the ridge via Looking Stead to the top of **Black Sail Pass**, from where you descend down the old Mosedale packhorse trail right to the door of the *Wasdale Head Inn* for a welcome drink. The whole route is around 12 miles, or six to seven hours' fairly tough walking.

Scafell

Scafell (3163ft) is England's second-highest mountain, though it's actually more prominent seen from many directions than the superior Scafell Pike. The two peaks are connected by the col known as **Mickledore**, though the Broad Stand rock face – the most direct approach – presents an impassable obstacle to walkers. Meanwhile, the classic ascent of Scafell from Wasdale via **Lord's Rake** is now off-limits because of dangerous rock falls. Instead, walkers from Wasdale will need to make the long-winded ascent via **Foxes Tarn**. The easier route from Wasdale to the summit of Scafell (3hr) is the circuitous one taken since Victorian times, from Burnmoor Tarn and the old corpse road – either route starts at Brackenclose car park, at the head of Wast Water.

mountain-climbing was born here in the days when the inn's landlord – and champion liar – was the famous Will Ritson: black-and-white photographs pinned to the panelled rooms inside show Victorian gents in hobnailed boots and flat caps scaling dreadful precipices with nonchalant ease (for more on the birthplace of British mountain-climbing, see p.274). The inn's gone a bit upmarket since those days, but still attracts a genuine walking and climbing crowd, not bothered in the slightest by the lack of TV or mobile phone reception in the valley.

What's reputed to be England's smallest church, **St Olaf's**, lies a couple of hundred yards from the inn, encircled by evergreens and dwarfed by the surrounding fells. The small cemetery contains graves and memorials to several of those killed while climbing them. There's been a church at Wasdale since medieval times and though no one knows quite how old this plain chapel is, its current appearance – moss-grown slate roof and all – dates from a complete overhaul in 1892. The path over Eskdale Moor, via **Burnmoor Tarn**, was the former "corpse road" along which the dead were carried for burying in Eskdale church, since St Olaf's had no consecrated churchyard until 1901.

The Wasdale Web (🌐 www.wasdaleweb.co.uk) is the best source of local **information**, including **accommodation** listings – the farm and B&B listed below are each only a short walk from the inn, while other farmhouse B&Bs lie scattered down the valley. The **Barn Door Shop** (☎019467/26384, info@barndoorshop.co.uk) next to the inn has basic foodstuffs, Kendal Mintcake, and outdoor clothes, equipment and walking advice; check in here before pitching a tent at the adjacent field, tap-and-toilet **campsite** (no reservations; open all year). The other local campsite is the **National Trust campsite** (⏀019467/26220; open all year), a mile to the south at the head of the lake, which provides tent space, showers and a laundry room beneath the trees.

Accommodation and food

Burnthwaite Farm ⏀019467/26242, Ⓦwww .burnthwaitefarm.co.uk. A handsome old working sheep farm with six traditional B&B rooms available, with and without en-suite facilities. There is also a self-catering apartment (sleeps four, from £300/week, or £50 a night when available). Packed lunches available. Parking. Closed mid-Nov to Jan. No credit cards. ❸

Lingmell House ⏀019467/26261, Ⓦwww .lingmellhouse.co.uk. This guesthouse was once the vicarage and now has three agreeable rooms sharing a couple of bathrooms, all glorying in fine fell views. Tim, the owner, can point you in the right direction for a hike and pack you a lunch. Parking. Closed Jan. No credit cards. ❹

Wasdale Head Inn ⏀019467/26229, Ⓦwww.wasdale.com. There's no finer sight at the end of a day's hiking than the famous inn at the head of the valley. The compact rooms all have supremely comfortable beds, though for more space ask for one of the "superior rooms" in the adjacent cottage conversion, which have a kitchenette, lounge area and full bathroom (though breakfast is not included with these). There are also six self-catering apartments in a converted barn (sleeps two to four). Local hiking information and a daily weather forecast are on hand. The inn brews its own beer, the breakfasts are legendary and, though there are good bistro meals in the bar, four-course dinner (£25) in the oak-panelled dining room is one of the Lake District's best buys. No smoking. Parking. ❼

Ennerdale

Ennerdale (Ⓦwww.wildennerdale.co.uk), the next major valley north of Wasdale, is about as far off the beaten track as you can get in the western fells and valleys. There's only one very small village, limited public transport and no road at all around Ennerdale Water, which makes it one of the most inaccessible of the lakes – or one of the best for walkers, depending on how you look at it. Having made the effort, you'll find that Ennerdale Water is among the most alluring of the lakes, its quiet two-and-a-half-mile length (fiddle-shaped according to Coleridge) ringed by crags and dominated at the head by the dramatic heights of **Pillar**. If you haven't seen this peak before, you'll not recognize it from the name alone – the bulky fell takes its name instead from one of its northern crags, the devilish Pillar Rock, the proving ground of British mountaineers for over a century.

The village, **ENNERDALE BRIDGE**, straddles the River Ehen, a mile and a half west of the lake, encircled by a bowl of rounded fells and tucked just inside the National Park boundary. It's only ten miles from Cockermouth (from where there's a regular bus service) and seven from the coast, but seems much further from anywhere, especially in the peaceful shaded churchyard; still "girt round with a bare ring of mossy wall", as Wordsworth described it at the beginning of *The Brothers*. A small post office-shop and a couple of pubs provide what few facilities there are, though the village sees a fair amount of foot traffic as it's the first overnight stop on the Coast-to-Coast walk from St Bees.

Car parks on **Ennerdale Water** provide access for walkers, with two at the western end of the lake, near the village, and a third at **Bowness Knott**, midway along the northern shore, this also the terminus of the summer-Sunday

Afforestation

There's nothing new about **conifer plantations** in the Lake District. Wordsworth was already complaining about the spread of larch and fir plantations in his *Guide to the Lakes*; a "vegetable manufactory" he called it, which thrust every other tree out of the way. In the early days afforestation was carried out as much for aesthetic reasons as for profit, though once the battle for Thirlmere was lost (see p.161) another was joined as the water authorities planted the shores of the new reservoir with regimented conifers to prevent erosion. With the formation of the Forestry Commission in 1919, the planting of soft woods for profit picked up pace, with Ennerdale, Bassenthwaite and the Duddon Valley heavily forested by the 1930s. Only local resistance prevented Eskdale, Wast Water and Buttermere going the same way.

The problem is the very nature of the forests. In England's mild climate, larch, spruce and pine plantations grow quickly, blocking out the light and carpeting the valley floors with slow-decomposing acidic needles. As a consequence, wild plants (and therefore animals) are forced out of their natural habitat. However, almost a century of commercial planting has taught the Forestry Commission several lessons and its planting policy has changed accordingly over the years. Its information centres are keen to explain matters and to point out that plantations imposed upon previously bare fellsides help soil conservation and encourage animal and bird shelter. Managed forests, moreover, help preserve the surviving indigenous broad-leaved woods, which were increasingly threatened by the local practice of wintering sheep among the trees (the animals ate the seedlings). Behind the mission to explain is the undeniable economic sense of afforestation: Britain currently imports eight percent of the timber it uses and, in a bid to even out the figures, over £1 billion has been invested in timber-processing over the last decade. Currently, 75,000 tonnes of timber is produced annually from Lake District forests.

"Ennerdale Rambler" bus #263 from Cockermouth, Buttermere and Loweswater. Cars aren't allowed any further than Bowness Knott – though there is a track for vehicle access to Low Gillerthwaite and Ennerdale YHA (see opposite) and a couple of nearby lakeside picnic areas.

A series of forest trails at Bowness Knott announces the start of Ennerdale's thick blanket of **Forestry Commission** land, either side of the River Liza. It may now be an accepted part of the landscape but before 1930 the upper part of Ennerdale was a desolate, rocky wilderness, devoid of trees. The mass imposition of uniform conifer plantations irrevocably changed the landscape, and though time and more enlightened planting policies (mixing in broad-leaved trees and following the contours instead of straight lines) have softened the scenery, many still wish Ennerdale had been left untouched.

Ennerdale walks soon escape the tree cover in any case. The **circuit of the lake** (8 miles; 4hr) is an enjoyable low-level walk, with the option of a scramble up **Angler's Crag** on the southwestern promontory. Sterner tests are provided by any of the peaks on the valley's southern side, though unless you're staying at either of the Ennerdale youth hostels you've got to add the valley walk-in and return to Bowness Knott car park to your day's hike. For that reason, you won't see too many others en route (most choose to climb Pillar, say, from Wasdale), which is a recommendation in itself: an **Ennerdale peaks circuit** (12 miles; 7hr) from Bowness Knott, taking in Haycock (2618ft), Scoat Fell (2760ft), Steeple (2687ft) and Pillar (2927ft), is one of the most exhilarating fell walks in the region.

Accommodation and food

Black Sail YHA 6 miles east of Bowness Knott ☎07711 108450. The Lakes' most isolated and basic hostel (no road access – only foot visitors) is a former shepherd's bothy with just sixteen beds, but it's stunningly set at the head of Ennerdale and the walking is marvellous, either up the local peaks, or over the passes into Buttermere or Wasdale. It's not a complete *Cold Comfort Farm* experience – there's gas-powered central heating, and electricity from solar panels and a gas-powered generator, plus a full meals service and an alcohol licence. You're advised to call in advance to check vacancies – main season is April–Sept, when it's open daily, otherwise closed 2 days a week in Oct, and closed for individuals from Nov to March. Dorm beds from £10.95, school hols from £14.95.

Ennerdale YHA 2.5 miles east of Bowness Knott ☎0870/770 5820, ✉ennerdale@yha.org.uk. Ennerdale's main YHA hostel is converted from two old forestry cottages, providing 24 beds for hostellers. The bathroom and kitchen facilities have been refurbished, but everything is in keeping with the old character (though the gas-lights have given way to hydroelectric power). Family rooms are available, plus two-hostel deals that allow multi-night stays here and up the valley at Black Sail. Also a full meal service and drinks licence. Open daily April to Aug, closed 2 days a week Sept & Oct, and closed for individuals from Nov to March.

Parking for up to 6 cars. Dorm beds from £10.95, school hols from £14.95.

Low Cockhow 1.25 miles south of Ennerdale Bridge ☎01946/861354, ⊚www.walk-rest-ride .co.uk. The farm is right on the Coast-to-Coast walk, and has three B&B rooms, as well as a twelve-bed bunkhouse (£17 with breakfast) with cooking and shower facilities. Evening meals, packed lunches and horse-riding available. Parking. ❸

Low Gillerthwaite Field Centre 2.5 miles east of Bowness Knott ☎01946/861229, ⊚www.lgfc .org.uk. Before the Forestry Commission changed the face of Ennerdale this had long been prime sheep-farming country. Fifteenth-century Low Gillerthwaite farmhouse has been refitted as an outdoor activity centre, used by small groups but available for individual overnight stays for hikers – call in advance to check. It's bunkhouse style (bring your own sleeping bag), and there's a decent self-catering kitchen, lounge with open fire and drying room. Even if the house is full, you can probably camp outside. Parking. Dorm beds from £10.75.

Shepherd's Arms Ennerdale Bridge ☎01946/861249, ⊚www.shepherdsarmshotel .co.uk. Cosy old inn that is a popular Coast-to-Coast stopover. The comfortable bar has a winter fire and serves hearty bar meals and a good choice of beers. There's a daily weather forecast posted, plenty of hiking advice to hand, and bikes available to rent. Parking. ❻

Lorton Vale and Loweswater

Southeast of Cockermouth the B5292 rolls into the pastoral **Lorton Vale**, turning east to tackle the Whinlatter Pass on the way to Keswick. The scattered settlement of **LORTON** – divided into Low and High – has a twelfth-century church, St Cuthbert's, of minor interest, but there's also a pub and post office-general store, and some gentle walking in the fields near the River Cocker. The Quaker George Fox preached to a seventeenth-century Lorton crowd under a spreading yew tree, which Wordsworth later commemorated ("pride of Lorton Vale") in his poem "Yew-trees" (1803).

Keeping south on the B5289, the fells – and Buttermere – are beckoning, but a diversion to **Loweswater**, six miles from Cockermouth, provides an opportunity to see one of the region's smallest, shallowest and least-known lakes. The water only averages a depth of sixty feet, and the reeds and lily pads that cling to the shores are a habitat for many species of insects and birds. You'll never be bothered by crowds here. There's no village to speak of, rather a collection of houses, a church and a telephone box, with a couple of signs pointing you towards the *Kirkstile Inn* (see p.192). Loweswater itself is a mile beyond the inn and really the only thing to do is to walk around it, on a gentle low-level route (4 miles; 1hr 30min) that stays under a woodland canopy for much of the duration. A detour in Holme Wood up to **Holme Force** adds a bit of interest after sustained rain; while the best views of the water are from Waterend, at the northern end of the lake. The distinctive volcano-shaped peak that towers above the southern end of Loweswater is **Mellbreak** (1676ft), fairly easily climbed from the *Kirkstile Inn* in around an hour or so.

There are a couple of small **parking** places at Waterend, and a National Trust car park (unmarked on most maps) near Watergate Farm at the southern end. The #263 "Ennerdale Rambler" **bus** from Buttermere also passes Loweswater, running along the northern shore road past Waterend. For Lorton and the Whinlatter Pass, the service is the #77A from Buttermere, which runs up the B5289 before turning east along the B5292 towards Keswick.

Accommodation and food

🏃 **Kirkstile Inn** Loweswater ☎01900/85219, 🌐www.kirkstile.com. The welcoming sixteenth-century riverside inn has given its rooms a contemporary makeover, retaining the beams and country furniture but adding smart bathrooms, crisp linen and very comfortable beds. There are seven rooms in the main inn and two self-contained family suites in the adjoining buildings, which can accommodate up to four adults – one also has a kitchen and lounge. On-the-ball staff deliver quality bar meals (smoked sausage salad, salmon en croute, fell-bred steak, Herdwick lamb) and you can take in the sunsets in the beer garden and sink a pint of their exclusive own-brew beer. No smoking. Parking. ⑤, suites ⑦

🏃 **New House Farm** B5289, 1 mile south of Low Lorton ☎01900/85404, 🌐www .newhouse-farm.co.uk. Six hugely attractive rooms, either in the meticulously restored seventeenth-century farmhouse or its period outbuildings – the old dairy room (the largest) has an extraordinary carved four-poster bed and a stunning bathroom with freestanding bath and hanging tapestry. Seventeen surrounding acres include mown grass walkways, ponds, gardens and an outdoor hot tub, while the barn tearoom (closed Nov to mid-Feb) provides all-day meals and snacks – a set five-course dinner is available too, usually based around a proper English roast. The property is non-smoking and pet-friendly. Parking. ⑦, D,B&B ⑧

Old Vicarage Church Lane, Low Lorton ☎01900/85656, 🌐www.oldvicarage.co.uk. Wooded grounds surround this non-smoking Victorian property, and it's just as impressive inside where a mahogany staircase ascends to the rooms. There's also a family suite in an old coach house. Afternoon tea is served in the garden in good weather and the pub is only five minutes' walk away (they'll lend you a torch for evening visits). Dinner available (£30) if you prefer to stay put. Parking. ⑥

Wheatsheaf Inn Low Lorton ☎01900/85199, 🌐www.wheatsheafinnlorton.co.uk. Lorton's local pub has a pleasant beer garden, substantial bar meals (prices are very reasonable), Jennings' ales and jazz nights every week through the summer. Out the back, there's a campsite (closed Dec–Feb) with shower, toilet block and drying facilities (enquiries at the inn).

🏃 **Winder Hall** Low Lorton ☎01900/85107, 🌐www.winderhall.co.uk. There's been a house here on the banks of the River Cocker since the fifteenth century, though the hall has been extended and modernized over the years – there are now seven spacious rooms available, most filled with antiques (two have four-posters), though one is contemporary in style. A summerhouse overlooking the river meadow contains a Jacuzzi and sauna. Despite the undoubted elegance, it is friendly and informal, with Wainwright guides and maps provided, and children welcome. Breakfast incorporates their own free-range eggs and home-cured bacon, while room rates also include afternoon tea and dinner (not served Tues), though B&B might be possible at quieter times, for about £20 less per person. The pub is almost opposite. Parking. ⑧

Crummock Water and Buttermere

A glance at the map shows that **Crummock Water** and **Buttermere** – separated by only a half-mile of slightly elevated flood-prone land – were once joined as one lake. In the main, they're visited as one, with nearly all the day-traffic concentrated in and around **BUTTERMERE** village, a small settlement in the middle of the two lakes with an outlying church, two inns and the rest of the local facilities.

Loweswater & Cockermouth ▲   ▲ Newlands Valley & Keswick

Wood House ◉

Crummock Water

Bridge Hotel 🅿

Buttermere

Fish Hotel 🅿 Syke Farm

Buttermere YHA

Buttermere Moss

N

Scale Force & Loweswater

Scale Bridge

Long Crag

High Bank

Goat Crag

B5289

Sourmilk Gill

Red Pike

Burtness Wood

Dalegarth

Kirk Close

Buttermere

Muddock Crags

Bleaberry Tarn

High Stile

0   300 yds

B5289

Gatesgarth Farm ◉

© Crown copyright

Newlands Valley & Honister Pass

Honister Pass & Borrowdale

Haystacks ▼

The two lakes, however, have entirely different aspects: small Buttermere ("Boethar's lake") is ringed by crags and peaks, culminating in the desolate heights of Gatesgarthdale; more expansive Crummock Water ("crooked lake") is almost twice as long (at two and a half miles) and half as deep again, yet peters out in the gentle flat lands of Lorton Vale. It's a contrasting beauty that brought back that most obsessive of fell walkers, Alfred Wainwright, again and again. A plaque in the small parish **church of St James**, on a hillock above Buttermere village, asks you to pause and remember him and then lift your eyes to Haystacks, his favourite peak, where his ashes are scattered. In *Fellwanderer*, his account of the writing of his famous *Pictorial Guides*, he's typically and playfully brusque: "If, dear reader, you should get a bit of grit in your boot as you are crossing Haystacks in the years to come, please treat it with respect. It might be me."

The grandeur of the locality was well-known even before Wainwright gave it his seal of approval. With the Lakes in vogue amongst travelling men in the late eighteenth century, many made their way over the passes to what was then a remote hamlet with a reputation for good fishing in the twin lakes. A certain Captain Budworth – resident at the *Fish Inn*, the only inn in those days – waxed lyrical about the beauty of the landlord's daughter in his bestseller, *A Fortnight's Ramble in the Lakes*. Within a couple of years, curious sightseers – Wordsworth and Coleridge included – were turning up to view **Mary Robinson, the Maid of Buttermere**. One such visitor was Alexander Augustus Colonel Hope, Member of Parliament and brother to an earl. Flush with money and manners, he wooed and married Mary – only to be revealed as the bigamous impostor John Hatfield, whose whole life had been one of deception and fraud. Arrested and tried for forgery (franking letters as an MP without authority was a capital offence), Hatfield was hanged at Carlisle in 1802 – the entire scandal recorded for the *Morning Post* by Coleridge in investigative journalist mode.

Walks from Crummock Water and Buttermere

Many hikers have their fondest memories of the fells around Buttermere and Crummock Water, and one – Haystacks – is the final resting place of the greatest walker of them all, **Alfred Wainwright**. It's easy to gain height quickly around here for some terrific views, though the low-level circuits of the two lakes are also very rewarding.

Crummock Water and Scale Force

Any circuit of **Crummock Water** should include the diversion to the 170ft drop of **Scale Force**, among the most spectacular of Lake District waterfalls. You can then either regain the western shore and stick close to the lake for the rest of the circuit (8 miles; 4hr), or climb past the falls and follow the Mosedale valley path to Loweswater (where there's a pub, the *Kirkstile Inn*) before completing the circuit (10 miles; 5–6hr).

Around Buttermere

The four-mile stroll circling **Buttermere** shouldn't take more than a couple of hours – in wet weather, the waters tumbling a thousand feet down Sour Milk Ghyll are amazing. And you can always detour up **Scarth Gap** to **Haystacks** (see below) if you want more of a climb and some views. It's worth knowing that, in summer, there's usually an ice-cream van parked by Gatesgarth Farm at the southern end of the lake.

Red Pike to Haystacks

The classic Buttermere circuit (8 miles; 6hr 30min) climbs from the village up **Red Pike** (2479ft) and then runs along the ridge, via **High Stile** (2644ft), **High Crag** (2443ft) and **Haystacks** (1900ft), before descending to the lake – either by backtracking and heading down Scarth Gap or by picking your way down off Haystacks, rounding Inominate Tarn and descending via **Warnscale Bottom**. For a fuller experience, add another hour to the beginning of the hike by first climbing up Scale Force from Buttermere (see above) and working your way across to Red Pike from there.

See Basics, p.35, for general walking advice in the Lakes; recommended maps are detailed on p.42.

Mary became a cause célèbre, the subject of ballads, books and plays, before retiring from the public gaze at the *Fish* to become wife to a Caldbeck farmer. She died there, as Mary Harrison, in 1837.

Practicalities

There's a **car park** behind the *Fish Hotel* and another is 300 yards up the road to Crummock Water; other parking places are signposted on the Crummock Water lakeshore road. The direct **bus** service is the #77, which runs between April and October on a circular route from Keswick, via Whinlatter Pass and Lorton and then back through Borrowdale; the #77A comes the long way round, through Borrowdale first. There's also the summer Sunday and bank holiday #263 "Ennerdale Rambler" service, which connects Buttermere with Loweswater and Ennerdale Bridge and Water or Lorton and Cockermouth.

There's no tourist office in Buttermere, though Ⓦwww.buttermereweb .co.uk and Ⓦwww.buttermere-lorton.com gather together some useful local listings and **information**. The village also has no shops, but there are two **hotels**, the *Bridge* and the *Fish* (no TV reception in either), plus a **youth**

hostel and various local farms and houses offering **B&B** and **camping**. The popular bar and beer garden at the *Bridge* is the best place to eat, though there's a wide restaurant menu too. Alternatively, you could sit on the benches outside the *Croft House Café* and munch on filled rolls – and don't forget an ice cream from *Syke Farm* (closed Jan), made from the milk from their Ayrshire cows. *Dalegarth* campsite and B&B has **rowboats** for rent, and there are more available from *Wood House* on Crummock Water (Easter–Oct only), where the day-rate includes a fishing permit.

Hotels

Bridge Hotel Buttermere ℡017687/70252, Ⓦwww.bridge-hotel.com. As well as the stand-ard rooms – perfectly fine – there's a selection of cheerfully decorated superior rooms with large bathrooms, some with balconies; and there are south-facing, self-catering apartments avail-able across the beck (sleep 2–6, £300–680 per week). The room price includes afternoon tea and dinner, but you might be able to negotiate a B&B price. Non-guests can settle for filling Cumbrian specials (including home-made soups and casseroles) and Black Sheep beer in the oak-beamed Walkers' Bar. Two-night minimum stay at weekends. ❽

Fish Hotel Buttermere ℡017687/70253, Ⓦwww .fish-hotel.co.uk. The smaller *Fish Hotel* has history, romance and price on its side. Bar meals are avail-able at lunch and dinner (the beer here is Theak-ston's), while packed lunches cost £7. No advance bookings for single-night stays. ❺

B&Bs and campsites

Dalegarth Buttermere, 1.5 miles southeast of the village ℡017687/70233. The grounds at Dale-garth extend to the lakeside and you can walk off the property and on to the fells. The house has a Swiss-chalet look, with nine B&B rooms (not all en suite), plus camping on a grassy lawn (with the use of a shower-and-toilet block). Parking. Closed Nov–March. ❷, en suite ❸

Syke Farm Buttermere ℡017687/70222. The farm offers simple camping near the lake (toilet and shower block provided). No credit cards.

🏃 Wood House Crummock Water ℡017687/70208, Ⓦwww.wdhse.co.uk. Quite the nicest local choice is this attractive house in a serene setting on Crummock Water, just a few hundred yards from Buttermere village. Three elegant bedrooms and the drawing room enjoy marvellous views, while the gardens and surround-ing woodland harbour red squirrels and woodpeck-ers. There's a self-catering cottage in the grounds too (£360–540 a week). Packed lunches are £6, a good dinner £29. Closed Nov–Easter. Parking. No smoking. No credit cards. ❺

Youth hostel

Buttermere YHA Buttermere, 0.25 miles southeast of the village ℡0870/770 5736, Ⓔbuttermere@yha.org.uk. Overlooks the lake on the road to Honister Pass – it's one of the more popular YHA hostels in the Lakes. There's one two-bedded room, otherwise accommodation in this quiet lakeland slate house is in four or six-bedded dorm rooms. Evening meal served. Dorm beds £17.50–23, depending on season, includes breakfast.

Travel details

All timetables can be checked on Traveline ℡0870/608 2608. For Ravenglass & Eskdale Rail-way see p.178.

From Keswick

Bus #77 circular route to: Whinlatter Pass (15min), Lorton (25min), Buttermere (45min), Honister Pass (1hr) and through Borrowdale. Service operates April–Oct 4 daily.
Bus #77A circular route: through Borrowdale to

Honister Pass (40min), Buttermere (50min), Lorton (1hr 10min), Whinlatter Pass (1hr 20min). Service operates April–Oct 4 daily.

From Buttermere

Bus #263 "Ennerdale Rambler" to: Loweswater Waterend (25min), Ennerdale Bridge (45min) and Bowness Knott (50min); and to Lorton (15min) and Cockermouth (30min). Service operates July & Aug Sun & bank hol Mon 3 daily.

From Barrow-in-Furness

Furness coastal rail line to: Millom (25min), Silecroft (30min), Bootle (37min), Ravenglass (45min); and then via St Bees (1hr 5min) and Whitehaven (1hr 15min) to Carlisle (2hr 25min). There are connections from Manchester, and the Barrow-in-Furness to Carlisle service operates Mon–Sat 7 daily, though there is a limited Sunday Whitehaven to Carlisle service.

Ullswater

CHAPTER 6

Highlights

* **A steamer ride on Ullswater** Get off for some marvellous local walks or stay aboard for the round-the-lake cruise. See p.202

* **Striding Edge** There's no more exciting mountain walk than inching your way along Striding Edge, en route to the summit of Helvellyn. See p.204

* **Aira Force** Visit the romantic lakeland waterfall whose daffodil-strewn surroundings inspired Wordsworth to pen one of his most famous poems. See p.206

* **Pooley Bridge** Ullswater's prettiest village has a popular farmers' market and some excellent country-house accommodation nearby. See p.207

* **Dalemain** Successive generations of the same family have lived in this handsome stately home since 1679. See p.208

* **St Martin's, Martindale** This isolated stone chapel in a remote valley near Ullswater makes a fine target for a stroll. See p.211

△ Striding Edge, Helvellyn

6

Ullswater

W ordsworth declared **Ullswater** "the happiest combination of beauty and grandeur, which any of the Lakes affords", a judgement that still holds good. At almost eight miles long, Ullswater is the second-longest lake in Cumbria and much of its appeal derives from its serpentine shape, a result of the complex geology of this area. The glacier that formed the two-hundred-foot deep trench in which the lake now lies had to cut across a couple of geological boundaries, from granite in the south, through a band of Skiddaw slate, to softer sandstone and limestone in the north. The resulting fells are a dramatic sight, while the shores are stippled with woods of native oak, birch and hazel – one of the best surviving examples of pre-plantation lakeland scenery. Lake **steamer services** on Ullswater started in 1859, carrying passengers and cargo around the lake, and the same two vessels, *Lady of the Lake* and *Raven*, have been in operation for almost as long. Both were converted to diesel in the 1930s, and have since been joined by two other vessels, *Lady Dorothy* and *Lady Wakefield*, which between them run a year-round ferry and cruise service on Ullswater. On spring and summer days the A592 up the western side of the lake is packed with traffic, everyone looking for space in one of the few designated car parks. Twin lakeside settlements, **Patterdale** and **Glenridding**, less than a mile apart at the southern tip of Ullswater, soak up most of the visitors intent upon the local attractions: namely **cruises** from Glenridding, the falls of **Aira Force**, the Wordsworthian daffodils of **Gowbarrow Park** and the considerable heights of **Helvellyn**, the most popular of the four highest mountains in Cumbria. From **Howtown** on the lake's eastern side, much less-tramped walking routes run up glorious hidden valleys such as Fusedale and Martindale and along the High Street range. **Pooley Bridge** at the head of Ullswater is the last lakeshore stop before Penrith, though outlying sights might delay you further, such as the historic house at **Dalemain** or the attractive village of **Askham**, gateway to the rolling Lowther parklands.

The northeastern lakes finish with a flourish in the crinkled valleys between the southern foot of Ullswater and the desolate Shap Fells at the eastern edge of the National Park. The A592, heading south from Ullswater for the Kirkstone Pass and Ambleside, passes **Brothers Water**. Otherwise the only roads are the minor lanes south from Askham and west of Shap, which meet at **Haweswater**, easternmost and very possibly the least visited of all the lakes (and, with Thirlmere, the Lake District's other main reservoir).

Glenridding

A fast-flowing beck, flanked by stone buildings and cottages, tumbles through the centre of **GLENRIDDING**, which was formerly a mining village and is now the busiest of Ullswater's lakeside settlements. Although the village itself consists of little more than a couple of rows of cottages set back from the lake, there's also a huge car park, two or three tearooms, a general store, post office, outdoors store and a fair amount of accommodation. There are rowboats to rent and plenty of places to sit on the grass banks or wade into the water from the stony shore. If it sounds too popular for comfort it isn't particularly, since many visitors just park up for a day's walking and by early evening the lakeshore regains much of its peace and quiet.

If you're not here to climb Helvellyn, you can at least stretch your legs in the local valley and follow **Glenridding Beck** half a mile west as far as Rattlebeck Bridge. It's another mile up to the *Helvellyn* youth hostel, which sits amid old lead **mine workings**, which were first exploited in the seventeenth century and only ceased operation in the 1960s. The other way from the bridge, south and east, you can wind up to pretty little **Lanty's Tarn**, set in a grove of trees

GLENRIDDING

Petrol Station

ACCOMMODATION
Beech House	G
Gillside	D
Glenridding	E
Helvellyn YHA	B
Inn on the Lake	A
Moss Crag	F
Swirral Barn	C

Helvellyn, B & C ◄

A592

GREENSIDE ROAD

Helvellyn & D ◄

Glenridding Beck

General Store (ATM)

Ullswater Steamers

Howtown & Pooley Bridge ►

N

CAFÉS, RESTAURANTS & PUBS
Fellbites	2
Greystones	3
Travellers' Rest	1

0   200 yds

A592

St. Patrick's Well

▼ Lanty's Tarn   Patterdale, Troutbeck & Windermere ▼   © Crown copyright

and with nearby views from a knoll over Ullswater. The name is probably a corruption of "Lancelot", bestowed more in hope than accuracy on any romantically sited stretch of water that might conceal an Arthurian sword.

Practicalities

Buses #108 (from Penrith), #208 (from Keswick) and #517 (from Bowness/Windermere) stop on the main road (the A592) through the village. Pier House and the **steamer pier** are just five minutes' walk away on the lakeside. An **Ullswater Bus & Boat ticket** (from £12.80) is available for a day's travel between Penrith and Glenridding/Patterdale, using the #108 bus and the steamer service – buy the ticket on board the bus.

Ullswater lake services

The Ullswater Navigation & Transit Company (☎017684/82229, ⊛www.ullswater-steamers.co.uk) has four vessels operating **from Glenridding** to Howtown (£4.90 one-way, £7.90 return; 35min); and **from Howtown** to Pooley Bridge (£4.40 one-way, £7.20 return; 20min). Alternatively, you can buy a ticket between Glenridding and Pooley Bridge that effectively makes a two-hour round-the-lake cruise (£10.70).

Between April and mid-September, there are up to eight **daily departures** from Glenridding to Howtown and six daily as far as Pooley Bridge. For the rest of the year there's a reduced timetable though services still operate daily to both Howtown and Pooley Bridge – only Christmas Eve and Christmas Day have no sailings. There are also special cruises and activity weekends (like a Pirate Weekend and Santa Specials), with current details posted on the website.

There's a bar on board the steamers, plus parking, a café and picnic area at Glenridding's Pier House. At Pooley Bridge, a staffed café operates during the summer season.

There's an ATM inside the general store on the main road, and two or three other shops selling walking gear or supplies – you'll be able to put together a picnic easily enough. The **National Park Information Centre** (Easter–Oct daily 9.30am–5.30pm; Nov–Easter Sat & Sun 9.30am–3.30pm; ℡017684/82414) is sited on the edge of the **car park** and posts a daily weather report for walkers – you can buy all-day parking tickets inside the centre. Glenridding is only a small place, with everything just a few minutes' walk from the car park. Two big traditional slate **hotels** dominate the village, the *Inn on the Lake* and the *Glenridding Hotel*, and there are several cheaper **B&Bs**. Hikers make a beeline for the out-of-village youth hostel, campsite, bunkhouse and camping barn, all lying en route to the area's major peak, Helvellyn.

Hotels and B&Bs

Beech House On the main road ℡017684/82037, ⓦwww.beechhouse.com. Offers a cheery welcome and a spick-and-span base for local walks and excursions. Eight rooms (half share a bathroom), though small, are prettily furnished, and a couple sport inlet and fell views. Packed lunches cost £2 or £5. Parking. ❸, en suite ❹

Glenridding On the main road ℡017684/82228, ⓦwww.bw-glenriddinghotel.co.uk. Standard and lake-view rooms available (supplement charged for the latter), while family rooms and suites provide a bit more space. It's a three-star place with plenty of facilities, including an impressive indoor pool and sauna, and oak-panelled library with sun lounge. Walkers can borrow a map and a thermos flask. *Kilner's Coffee House* has Internet access and is open during the day, or there's dining at *Ratcher's*, which is both pub and restaurant combined. Parking. ❼

Inn on the Lake Ullswater lakeside ℡017684/82444, ⓦwww.lakedistricthotels.net/innonthelake. Rooms and public areas at this three-star hotel have been upgraded and decked in flowers, there are some splendid views, and fifteen acres of gardens stretching down to Ullswater. The *Ramblers' Bar* is the place for a beer, a bar meal and a game of pool, but there's also a more sophisticated lounge bar and lake-view restaurant (*table d'hote* menu £33, though D,B&B rates available), plus gym, sauna, Jacuzzi, croquet lawn and tennis court. Parking. ❽

Moss Crag On the south side of the beck near the shops ℡017684/82500, ⓦwww.mosscrag.co.uk. A genial B&B with half-a-dozen cottage-style rooms (four of them en suite, including a superior four-poster room) and an attached tearoom. Dinner available (£16). No smoking. Parking. ❹, four-poster ❺

△ Ullswater steamer

The climb to the summit of **Helvellyn** (3114ft) is among the region's most challenging. You are unlikely to be alone on the yard-wide approaches – on summer weekends and bank holidays the car parks below and paths above are full by 9am – but the variety of routes up and down at least offers a chance of escaping the crowds. The most direct route from Glenridding, via Striding Edge, returning via Swirral Edge and Red Tarn, is a good seven-mile (5–6hr) walk, while for any of the other variations you can count on being out all day.

Striding Edge

The most frequently chosen route to the summit is via the infamous **Striding Edge**. Purists negotiate the undulating ridge top of Striding Edge; slightly safer, but no less precipitous tracks follow the line of the ridge, just off the crest. However you get across (and some refuse to go any further when push comes to shove), there's a final, sheer, hands-and-feet scramble to the flat **summit** (2hr 30min from Glenridding). People do get into trouble on Striding Edge: if you're at all nervous of heights you'll find it a challenge to say the least, your mood probably not improved by the occasionally hovering rescue helicopters.

Swirral Edge and Red Tarn

The classic return from the summit is via the less demanding **Swirral Edge**, from where a straightforward route leads down to stunning **Red Tarn** – the highest Lake District tarn – then follows the beck down to Glenridding past the Helvellyn youth hostel. This is the best route *up* Helvellyn if you don't fancy Striding Edge, as Swirral Edge is far less exposed an approach (though there is still some hands-and-feet climbing). If you come up this way, then you can make your return circuit to the north instead (see next walk).

Raise and Sticks Pass

North from the Helvellyn summit there's an easy, obvious cairned route heading towards **Raise** (2897ft), with stupendous views away to the east over Red Tarn and down the valleys. The path then drops down to **Sticks Pass** for an interesting descent alongside Sticks Gill and down through the scars of the old mine workings. The route runs right past Helvellyn YHA for the final mile into Glenridding. Depending on the time and weather conditions, peak-baggers might make the decision at Sticks Pass first to tick off **Stybarrow Dodd** (2766ft), an easy twenty-minute diversion, and even **Watson's Dodd** (2589ft) beyond.

Grisedale

South from the Helvellyn summit, you can follow the flat ridge past **Nethermost Pike** (2920ft) and **Dollywagon Pike** (2810ft), after which there's a long scree scramble down to **Grisedale Tarn** and then the gentlest of descents down **Grisedale** valley, alongside the beck, emerging on the Patterdale–Glenridding road. This really is a fantastic walk, with a fine mix of terrain, a good six hours all told for the entire circuit.

See Basics, p.35, for general walking advice in the Lakes; recommended maps are detailed on p.42.

Campsite, hostel and camping barn

Gillside Caravan & Camping
①017684/82346, ⑩www
.gillsidecaravanandcampingsite.co.uk. In a

beautiful spot, en route to Helvellyn, a quarter of a mile up the valley behind the village – follow the path along the beck. There are also caravans for rent (from £40 a night, minimum two nights), a good bunkhouse with a modern kitchen (£8 a bed), though you need your own sleeping and cooking equipment, and a laundry. Milk and eggs are available from the family farm. No credit cards. Closed Nov–Feb.

Helvellyn YHA Greenside ☎0870/770 5862, ✉helvellyn@yha.org.uk. Walkers wanting an early start on Helvellyn stay at this dramatically sited hostel, 900ft and a mile-and-a-half up the valley road from Glenridding (the last half unmetalled, but suitable for vehicles if taken with care). There are lots of beds (and private rooms available), plus a full meals service and alcohol licence, while the nearest pub, the *Travellers Rest*, is only a mile away. The hostel is closed on occasional nights, and advance bookings are advised – call for availability. Closed Dec. Dorm beds from £12.95.

Swirral Barn ☎01946/758198. A hundred yards beyond the YHA, there's self-catering bunk-barn space in accommodation converted from former mine buildings. There are only eight beds and it's pretty basic (eg unheated, toilet in a separate building), but the hiking routes to Helvellyn go right past the door. Beds £6.

Cafés

Fellbites ☎017684/82664. The café in the car park – a handsomely converted lakeland barn – opens at 10am for walkers' breakfasts, after which it's light meals and drinks, and lunches and dinners using locally sourced lamb, beef and trout. Dinner is usually Thurs, Fri & Sat only; also closed 1 or 2 days a week from Nov–Easter. Moderate.

Greystones Coffee House and Gallery ☎017684/82392, ⊛www.greystones coffeehouse.com. Alongside the beck, cheery *Greystones* dishes up teas and cappuccinos and tasty bites such as ciabatta sandwiches, or beans on toast – a few outdoor tables catch the sun in summer. It's a venue for contemporary art installations and sculpture as well, while it's also a wi-fi zone. Daytime only. Nov–Jan open weekends and selected days only. Inexpensive.

Pub

Travellers' Rest ☎017684/82298. It's worth the 500-yard tramp up the hill from the village centre to this unpretentious pub, with fell and partial lake views from its outdoor terrace. Filling bar meals and cask ales available.

△ Red Tarn, Helvellyn

Patterdale

PATTERDALE, less than a mile south of Glenridding down the A592 (a path avoids the road for much of the way), lies at the foot of **Grisedale**, which provides access to a stunning valley hike up to Grisedale Tarn. St Patrick is supposed to have preached here (Patterdale is "Patrick's Dale") and the water in St Patrick's Well, on the road between Glenridding and Patterdale, was once thought to have miraculous powers. The saint's church, at the northern end of the village, is a nineteenth-century replacement of the medieval original, known for the locally made embroidered tapestries that hang inside.

The #108, #208 and #517 **bus** services stop in Patterdale. You're just off the lake in the village – though never very far away – but there's some reasonable **accommodation** strung along the road. Patterdale's only pub, the *White Lion* (℡017684/82214; ➌), has seven rooms available and Castle Eden beer on tap in the bar; sizzling steak platters are the house speciality, or try the trout with almonds. There's also a public bar at the large *Patterdale Hotel* up the road – it's no great shakes as a hotel, but the front beer garden fills up quickly on a summer's day. South, past the pub, on the bend in the road, *Old Water View* (℡017684/82175, Ⓦ www.oldwaterview.co.uk; ➍) is an attractive, non-smoking guesthouse with three rooms, private gardens and parking. They're used to walkers – even Alfred Wainwright stayed here on occasion. Just beyond lies Patterdale's popular ski-lodge-style **youth hostel**, *Patterdale YHA* (℡0870/770 5986; dorm beds from £14, Ⓔpatterdale@yha.org.uk; restricted opening Nov– March), on the banks of Goldrill Beck, with very comfortable beds, spacious public areas with open fire, Internet access and good food. There's **camping** at *Side Farm* (℡017684/82337; closed Nov–Easter) – the track to the farm is across from the church, with the campsite on the eastern shore of the lake – and the only other service is a small **village shop-post office** opposite the pub.

Aira Force, Dockray and Gowbarrow

To avoid the crowds trailing up the needle-carpeted woodland paths to **Aira Force**, three miles north of Glenridding (where the A5091 meets the A592), get there first thing in the morning or last thing in the evening. This is one of the prettiest, most romantic, of lakeland forces – a seventy-foot waterfall that's spectacular in spate and can be viewed from stone bridges spanning the top and bottom of the drop. It's only a thirty- to forty-minute round-trip from the car park, though you'll soon leave most of the visitors behind if you extend your walk further up the valley to High Force and on to **DOCKRAY** (where there's a pub with a beer garden, the *Royal*) and back – a three-mile, two-hour, circuit. Keep an eye out for red squirrels in the woods on the way. Back at the Aira Force car park there's an attractive **tearoom** (closed Nov–Easter) with an outdoor terrace; buses #108 and #208 stop nearby.

The falls flank the western side of **Gowbarrow Park**, whose hillside still blazes green and gold in spring, as it was doing when the Wordsworths visited in April 1802. Dorothy's sprightly recollections of the visit in her journal inspired William to write his "Daffodils" poem, though it was not until two years later that he first composed the famous lines (borrowing many of Dorothy's exact phrases). Despite its fame now, nothing much was thought of the poem at the time; it didn't even have a title on first publication in 1807 (in *Poems in Two Volumes*).

The walking is tougher going on adjacent **Gowbarrow Fell** (1579ft), which you can climb in an hour from Aira Force car park. The route runs via the viewpoint of Yew Crag and then up the boggy slopes to the cairn at the summit. From here you can descend to Dockray and the pub or, more directly, over the top to Green Hill and thence to Aira Force (2hr return). The National Park Authority is trying to cut the number of sheep grazing the fell in an attempt to lure back some of the wildlife, while every spring there's a battle of wits with visitors intent on picking the famous daffs.

Pooley Bridge and around

POOLEY BRIDGE, at the head of the lake, has a boulder-speckled shore with wonderful views south. The bridge itself is the sturdy example that crosses the River Eamont on the way into the village, evidence – along with the old village square, once used for markets – that this was a substantial settlement in past times. Its market charter was granted by King John in the twelfth century, the modern equivalent being the thriving **farmers' market** (last Sun of month, April–Sept, 10.30am–2.30pm) held behind the *Sun Inn*. Pooley Bridge itself is a cute retreat, rendered less so once the car parks on either side of the bridge are full, but it's still not a bad lunch or overnight stop, with a couple of tearooms and three pubs. Apart from the **steamer** (whose jetty is a couple of hundred yards from the bridge), there's a daily, year-round **bus service** (the #108) from Penrith to Pooley Bridge (and on to Glenridding/Patterdale), as well as a limited post bus from Penrith (not Sun), which continues on to Howtown and Martindale.

One of the shops on the square contains an informal visitor **information point** (Easter–Oct daily 9am–5pm). The best **accommodation** is listed below; in addition, a few local B&Bs advertise vacancies. Plenty of local **campsites** make the Pooley Bridge area popular with families. Those on the northeastern lake shore (listed below) are easiest to reach from the village. Another group of campsites lies two miles away on the northwest shore, behind **Watermillock**, but you'll need your own transport to reach these. The village pubs all provide **meals**, but the best food is either at *Sharrow Bay* country-house hotel (reviewed on p.208), to the south of the village, or at the two gastro-pubs just to the north, the *Queen's Head* at Tirril (see p.244) and the *Gate Inn* at Yanwath (see p.245).

Hotels and inns

Brackenrigg Inn Watermillock, A592, 2 miles southwest of Pooley Bridge ☎017684/86206, ⓦ www.brackenrigginn.co.uk. See chapter map for location. Traditional roadside inn with a varied choice of updated rooms, singles to family-sized suites, some with lake views. The best deals are the inclusive three-night breaks or a D,B&B rate, since the well-judged bistro-style food is worth the visit in any case, with an emphasis on locally sourced produce and fresh seafood. It's very easy-going – you can eat in the simple bar, the family dining area, the more formal dining room, or even out on the terrace in the sun – and choose from separate bar, *table d'hote* or *à la carte* menus. Parking. No American Express. ❺, D,B&B ❼

Pooley Bridge Inn ☎017684/86215, ⓦ www .pooleybridgeinn.co.uk. Just by the village square, this Alpine-style hotel seems to have been plucked out of a *Heidi* story. Breakfast in the wicker chairs on your own balcony is tempting, though standard rooms without a balcony are priced a category lower. Food is available in the rustic bar downstairs. Parking. Two-night minimum stay on summer weekends. ❺

Rampsbeck Country House Hotel Watermillock, A592, 2 miles southwest of Pooley Bridge ☎017684/86442, ⓦ www.hotel-lakedistrict .com. See chapter map for location. Victorian-era house with a magnificent lakeside location on the western shore – gardens run right down to the water's edge, and the terrace has sweeping views.

There's a rather comforting, old-fashioned feel within, abetted by hands-on family management; the twenty rooms vary in size but the best are very spacious and have uninterrupted lake views. The food is a hit, with an inventive *table d'hote* dinner (£47) served nightly in the candlelit dining room overlooking Ullswater. Parking. ❼, deluxe rooms ❽

🏃 **Sharrow Bay** 2 miles south of Pooley Bridge, on the Howtown road ☎017684/86301, ⓦwww.sharrowbay.co.uk. See chapter map for location. The special-occasion place par excellence, England's first country-house hotel (in business since 1948) offers a breathtaking setting, personal service and highly refined Michelin-starred food (dinner is included in the room rate). Needless to say, it's London prices in the country (from £350–420 a night) but there are few places anywhere in England that compare. A variety of lovely, antique-filled rooms available are in the main Victorian house, a garden annexe, the Edwardian gatehouse or in a converted, elevated Elizabethan farmhouse a mile away. Lake and fell views abound, there are acres of gardens and woods to wander in, and books and games in the rooms to pass the time when it pours. The dining room is open to non-residents; afternoon tea (£17.50) here is famous, while dinner (£52.50, reservations essential) is a classy, formal affair – desserts are renowned, notably the sticky toffee pudding, which the hotel claims as its own invention. Parking. ❾

Sun Inn ☎017684/86205, ⓦwww .suninnpooleybridge.co.uk. The best of the village pubs (100 yards up the road from the square) is the eighteenth-century *Sun*, with a carved, panelled bar and a beer garden to catch the rays. There are nine good-value rooms, with discounts for multi-night stays (midweek winter rates can be very good). It's a *Jennings'* pub, and bar meals are served. Parking. ❹

Campsites

Cross Dormont On the Howtown road ☎017684/86537, ⓦwww.crossdormont.co.uk. Family-run site on a working farm (raising Herdwick sheep on the local fells). You can launch dinghies and kayaks from the lakeside fields.

Hill Croft ☎017684/86363. The nearest site to the village, a family-run affair just 100 yards from the Howtown crossroads. Closed mid-Nov to Feb.

Park Foot On the Howtown road ☎017684/86309, ⓦwww.parkfootullswater.co.uk. Has its own lakeside access and club-house facilities, including a bar. Reservations essential during school holidays. Closed Nov–Feb.

Waterside House On the Howtown road ☎017684/86332, ⓦwww.watersidefarm -campsite.co.uk. Right on the water, on a working farm, this is a tent- and motorhome-only site, and has canoes, rowboats and bikes for rent. There's a small shop and children's playground. Closed Nov–Feb.

Cafés

Alpaca Centre Snuff Mill Lane, Stainton, A592 ☎01768/891440, ⓦwww.thealpacacentre.co.uk. A tearoom with a difference, sited on a working alpaca farm a couple of miles north of Pooley Bridge (just past Dalemain). Think llamas, and you're not far off – you can see the alpacas from the paddock or tearoom, and there's a craft shop and gallery selling clothes made from alpaca fibre, South American artefacts and jewellery, and hand-crafted furniture and ornamental wood. Daytime only. Inexpensive.

Granny Dowbekin's ☎017684/86453. Terraced riverside tea garden, by the bridge, serving soup and sandwiches, plus home-made cakes inspired by the recipes of the owner's great-great Lancastrian granny. Daytime only. Closed Jan. Inexpensive.

Dalemain

Two miles north of Pooley Bridge, up the A592, is the stately home of **Dalemain** (Feb half-term hol & Easter–Oct Mon–Thurs & Sun 11am–4pm, gardens & tearoom same days 10.30am–5pm; Nov to mid-Dec & early Feb–Easter gardens & tearoom only Mon–Thurs & Sun 11am–4pm; £6.50; gardens only £4.50; ☎017684/86450, ⓦwww.dalemain.com). Residence to the same family since 1679, it started life in the twelfth century as a fortified tower, but has subsequently been added to by every generation, culminating with a Georgian facade grafted on to a largely Elizabethan house. It's set in ample grounds – terraces, roses and Tudor gardens provide the main interest, best in late May and June – while the estate stretches west to encompass the fourteenth-century

▼ Cumberland and Westmorland wrestlers

Out and about in the Lakes

For such a small area, the Lake District packs in a fantastic
number of outdoor activities. Not surprisingly, most visitors
look to the lakes and mountains for their inspiration, but even
if you're not into scenic strolls or hardcore hiking there's
plenty on offer throughout the year. The special sections in
Basics on festivals and events, enjoying the mountains, water
sports or outdoor activities provide all sorts of contacts and
details, but for some general ideas – from family excursions
to lakeland adventures – read on.

On the water

Almost all the organized cruising, boating and water-sports facilities are concentrated on just four lakes – **Windermere** (England's largest lake) and **Coniston Water** in the south and **Derwent Water** and **Ullswater** in the north. Round-the-lake boat services on each offer short cruises, themed tours or ferry drop-offs for hikers and visitors, and the boats run year-round (with local variations) so there's no reason to miss out. It's hard to be selective, but if time is short and you have to pick just one lake trip, our vote would be for the **Keswick Launch** (p.150) which provides access to some great walks and dramatic scenery. If you're into dinghy sailing, windsurfing, kayaking or even dragon-boating – or just want to try it out – then the same four lakes have plenty of operators offering lessons, courses or simply rental by the hour or day. More details are given in the special "Boating and water sports" section on p.38.

Festival time

The region maintains its traditions in unique festivals, agricultural shows and rural events held throughout the old county lands of Cumberland and Westmorland (now Cumbria). Some – like the medieval rushbearings in churches at Grasmere and Ambleside – date back centuries, while others show a direct line from the very earliest informal shepherds' meets. Put a crowd of lakeland farmers together, plus their dogs and sheep, and it's not long before they're issuing challenges – at all the big summer agricultural "shows" and "sports" you'll see sheep-dog trials, hound-trailing, fell running and tugs-of-war, though for sheer spectacle it's hard to beat the hand-to-hand Cumberland and Westmorland wrestling. Traditional outdoor events have always been held in the summer – particularly August – but there's now a year-round calendar for all interests, from beer and film festivals to spring garden shows and Christmas markets. See p.31 for more on all annual events, including a full month-by-month festival calendar.

The best outdoor adventures

For organized courses and outdoor activities – mountain-biking to pony-trekking, fishing to 4WD expeditions – consult the suggestions on p.39. Meanwhile, the activities below are guaranteed to get your blood pumping.

1. **Go Ape** Make like a monkey on the high-adrenaline high-ropes course between the trees in Grizedale Forest. See p.130.
2. **Striding Edge** There's no more daredevil mountain route for walkers than this inch-by-inch clamber on the route to Helvellyn. See p.204.
3. **Eskdale T-Rail** Up Eskdale by narrow-gauge train, down by mountain bike, on this great day out on the Ravenglass & Eskdale Railway. See p.178.

▼ Ape high-ropes course, Grizedale Forest

4. **Whinlatter Forest Park** Mountain forest park with orienteering course, hiking and biking trails, and an adventure playground. See p.163.
5. **Coniston Water** Take out a kayak or learn to sail at the National Park's own Coniston Boating Centre. See p.118.
6. **Hit the trails at Staveley** Mountain-bike-hire centre, guided summer walks, hiker-friendly café and bar – Staveley village is all set up for a day in the hills. See p.81.

Wet-weather attractions

The skies are dark, the clouds are gathering and it's starting to pelt down – not so good if you're halfway up a mountain, not so bad if you're out and about and looking for an indoor attraction. At the **Aquarium of the Lakes** (p.66) you can learn all about lakeland river habitats without setting foot outside – even the otters and ducks are under cover. Museums, of course, are good wet-weather destinations, with two of the most diverting being Coniston's **Ruskin Museum** (p.116) and Kendal's **Museum of Lakeland Life and Industry** (p.221); both delve into the region's social and cultural history and you can easily spend a couple of hours in

▶ The Aquarium of the Lakes

either. You can also keep relatively dry at **Honister Slate Mine** (p.159), where daily hard-hat tours head deep underground to show you something of the region's mining history. Ambleside's **outdoors stores** (p.79) – including the UK's largest hiking superstore – are good for browsing and rain-dodging, and there are more shops, plus craft demonstrations and giant-screen movies at **Rheged** (p.246), just outside Penrith.

Top 6 family excursions

1. **Trotters World of Animals** An animal park with a difference – and where else in the Lakes are you going to see a troop of gibbons or a vulture in flight? See p.165.
2. **World of Beatrix Potter** No real fan – or anyone under 5 – will want to miss this, the entire Potter canon in 3D, with book characters, games, gifts and themed café. See p.58.
3. **Lake District Visitor Centre at Brockhole** The National Park's main visitor centre has something going on every day in season, and the excellent grounds are open all year round. See p.64.
4. **Muncaster Castle** You could easily spend all day here – from the haunted house to the spreading grounds, home to voles, herons and owls. See p.178.
5. **Fell Foot Park** Beautiful lawns and picnic areas, rowing boats, a nice café and launch rides across to the Lakeside and Haverthwaite Railway – and what's more, it's free. See p.68.
6. **Holker Hall** The famous gardens are a treat at any time of year, with plenty to explore for children of all ages. See p.227.

Holker Hall gardens, Cartmel ▶

Couch potatoes to mountain goats: ten walks for all abilities

- **High-altitude circuit** Keep your head in the clouds on the Coledale Horseshoe. See p.163.

- **Pub walk** Circle pretty Loweswater and stop off at the Kirkstile Inn. See p.191.

- **Mountain peaks** Langdale's most exciting walk is up Crinkle Crags and Bowfell. See p.106.

- **Round-lake** There are more famous lakes, but the long ramble around Haweswater gets you right off the beaten track. See p.212.

- **3000-footer** A must for list-tickers, England's highest mountain, Scafell Pike, tops out at 3205ft. See p.158.

- **Viewpoint** From Cat Bells – everyone's favourite scramble – you can see for miles. See p.153.

- **Waterfall hike**. Stock Ghyll force is dramatic in spate and an easy walk from Ambleside. See p.74.

- **Family stroll** There are woodland paths, glistening water and idyllic picnic spots at Tarn Hows. See p.128.

- **Only for experts** Early start, late finish, guts and stamina required – it's the gruelling Woolpack Walk. See p.180.

- **Into the valley** Strike off up glorious Grisedale from near Patterdale on Ullswater, with Grisedale Tarn your destination. See p.204.

▼ View from Scafell Pike

keep of Dacre Castle (no public access), which you can reach on a mile-long footpath from the house.

There are **guided tours** of the house in the mornings (the first at 11.15am), while in the afternoon it's self-guided. Rather remarkably, you're given the run of the public rooms, which the Hasell family still uses – hence the photographs and contemporary portraits alongside those of the ancestors. The house is heavy with oak, hewn from the estate's plantations, though lightened by unusual touches such as the eighteenth-century handpainted wallpaper in the Chinese Room. The servants' corridors and pantries offer a glimpse of life "below stairs", commanded from the Housekeeper's Room – at the rear of which was discovered a priest's hole. Outside, the medieval courtyard and Elizabethan great barn doubled as the schoolroom and dormitory of Lowood School in a TV adaptation of Charlotte Brontë's *Jane Eyre*. There's an agricultural and countryside collection in the great barn, and plenty of other displays and exhibits throughout the house, from dolls' houses and old toys to Gillows and Chippendale furniture and the family glassware. The **Medieval Hall** provides drinks, lunches and afternoon teas – you don't need a ticket to visit this.

Askham and Lowther Park

Three miles east of Pooley Bridge, and five south of Penrith, the serene little village of **ASKHAM** lies across the River Lowther from the rolling lands of **Lowther Park**, seat of the eighteenth-century coal-mining and shipping magnates, the Lowthers, creators of the Georgian port of Whitehaven. The most notorious family member, Sir James, employed Wordsworth's father as his agent but, when John Wordsworth died, refused to pay his back-salary to the Wordsworth children. Not that there was any shortage of Lowther money in those days, as attested to by an extravagantly built Gothic Revival castle in the estate grounds, though eventually its ruinous upkeep was too much, even for the Lowthers. The **castle** is now roofless and partly in ruins – there's no public access, but it's visible from the road – but you can catch a glimpse of the Lowther heritage at **St Michael's church**, just outside Askham, on a ridge above the river. Effectively the family chapel, this is filled with memorials to one Lowther or another – whose scions took the title Earl of Lonsdale – including a fine brass portraying a splendidly bewhiskered Henry Lowther. A later Lowther, the fifth Earl, Sir Hugh, was a keen sportsman, whose title at least is remembered in boxing's Lonsdale Belt, while the estate's **horse trials**, held here every August, are one of the region's major sporting events.

As well as the castle ruins, the Lowther estate includes two small villages, various farms and plantations and a deer park, through which you'll drive en route to the **Lakeland Bird of Prey Centre** (April–Oct daily 11am–5pm; £6; ☎01931/712746), just outside Askham. Here eagles, hawks, falcons and owls are put through their paces twice a day (call for current times), though they are also all on show in the aviaries set in the walled garden. There's a tearoom here, too.

Public transport to Askham is limited to the #111 "Haweswater Rambler" **bus** from Penrith, which runs year-round on Tuesdays and Saturdays and also on Sundays and bank holidays during the school summer holidays; however, there's no bus out to the bird of prey centre. Askham itself has a couple of local B&Bs and two traditional **inns**, at either end of a sloping village green. At the top, the *Queen's Head* (☎01931/712225) has been sympathetically renovated over the years – rooms and food have both been good in the past, but at the time of writing a change of landlord was in the offing. At the bottom, near the river, the eighteenth-century *Punch Bowl Inn* (℡01931/712443, Ⓦwww .punchbowlaskham.co.uk; ⑤) is the simpler of the two, with half a dozen straightforward rooms and a certain bygone charm in its ancient public bar – or you can eat and drink outside on the patio. The Lowther Estate maintains both the well-equipped *Lowther Holiday Park* (℡01768/863631, Ⓦwww.lowther-holidaypark.co.uk; closed Nov–March), for **camping** and caravans, signposted within the estate and from main roads nearby, as well as two superior **holiday cottages** (reservations on ℡01931/712577, Ⓦwww .lowther.co.uk), one in Askham village and one just to the south in the hamlet of Whale.

Howtown and Martindale

HOWTOWN – best reached by regular steamer services in summer from Glenridding – is tucked behind a little indented harbour, four miles south of Pooley Bridge. It's a popular spot that lies at the start of several fine walks. Many people cross to Howtown by boat and then walk back (6 miles; 3hr), following the shore of Ullswater around Hallin Fell to **Sandwick** and then through the woods and on around the bottom of the lake to Patterdale.

There are only a few houses in Howtown, huddled around the *Howtown Hotel* (℡017684/86514; no credit cards; closed Nov–March; ❼), which has a cosy wood-panelled and stained-glass snug bar around the back where hikers can revive themselves with a beer or a cup of coffee. Dinner is included in the

Walks from Howtown

For some of the nicest but least-vaunted walking in the Lake District, cross Ullswater on the steamer from Glenridding. Various routes radiate from Howtown, including the two described below.

Fusedale

A strenuous route (8 miles; 4–5hr) cuts past the *Howtown Hotel* and heads up lovely **Fusedale**, at the head of which there's an unrelenting climb up to the **High Street**, a broad-backed ridge that was once a Roman road. The path is clearly visible for miles and following the ridge south you meet the highest point, **High Raise** (2632ft) – two hours from Howtown – where there's a cairn and glorious views. The route then runs south and west, via the stone outcrops of **Satura Crag**, past **Angle Tarn** and finally down to the A592, just shy of Patterdale's pub and post office.

To Pooley Bridge

Time the steamer services from Glenridding right and you can cross to Howtown, walk to Pooley Bridge and catch the boat back. The most direct route (5 miles; 3hr) leaves Howtown pier and runs northeast under Austerstone Crag before cutting up to the **Stone Circle** on the Roman road, south of Roehead, a couple of miles from Pooley Bridge. But for the best views and most exhilarating walk climb up to High Street from Fusedale (see above) and then charge straight along the ridge to the Stone Circle (7 miles; 3–4hr).

See Basics, p.35, for general walking advice in the Lakes; recommended maps are detailed on p.42.

room rate, though non-guests can also take advantage of the moderately priced cold-table lunch or *table d'hôte* dinner available in the hotel dining room.

The minor road from Pooley Bridge runs south through Howtown and climbs up in switchbacks to a car park at the foot of **Martindale**. The road, in fact, continues another couple of miles up to Dale Head, but it's best to abandon the car and walk the ten minutes along to **St Martin's**, the most beautifully sited of all the Lake District's isolated churches. An Elizabethan stone chapel of great simplicity, all there is inside is a stone-flagged floor, a seventeenth-century altar table and lectern and rows of plain wooden benches. It's barely changed in centuries and, outside, the feeling of time immemorial is emphasized by the vast spreading yew tree, thought to be a thousand years old, whose gnarled branches shroud the tomb of Martindale's nineteenth-century curate George Woodley.

Brothers Water, Hartsop and Hayeswater

The car park at **Cow Bridge**, two miles south of Patterdale, is the jumping-off point for the short stroll along a quiet stretch of Goldrill Beck to **Brothers Water**. The Water itself (possibly taking its name from a corruption of the Norse name "Brothir") is a mere liquid scoop, but the path along the western shore takes you under the canopy of some of the Lakes' oldest oak woodlands. This was the way Dorothy Wordsworth came on Good Friday in April 1802, after her daffodil-spotting excursion of the previous day, and it's easy to trace her exact route from her journal: "I left William sitting on the bridge, and went along the path on the right side of the lake through the wood. I was delighted with what I saw. The water under the boughs of the bare old trees, the simplicity of the mountains, and the exquisite beauty of the path." When she got back to Cow Bridge, William was busy writing a poem, which he later entitled (mistakenly) "Written in March".

The path alongside Brothers Water runs a mile or so up to the 500-year-old **Hartsop Hall Farm**, standing on land which experts reckon has been farmed since the Bronze Age. You can press further on if you're in the mood for a decent hike – there are routes up Dovedale, for Dove Crag, Hart Crag and Fairfield – while local climbers and walkers all know about the beautifully sited *Brotherswater Inn* (℡017684/82239, 🌐www.sykeside.co.uk; ④) and associated *Sykeside Camping Park*, just to the east over by the A592. There are eight refurbished rooms in the inn, plus food available all day, while campers have their own shop and *Barn End* bar (open all summer and winter holiday weekends).

Back at the Cow Bridge car park, you cross the main road for the tiny hamlet of **Hartsop**, from where it's a mile-and-a-bit walk east up the valley to **Hayeswater**, a limpid little lake sitting under the High Street range. It's hard to believe now, but Hartsop was once a thriving mining and quarrying centre, the biggest in the region, and the track up to Hayeswater sits beneath crags riddled with old workings.

Haweswater

With the example of Thirlmere already set, there was less opposition when **Haweswater** was dammed in the 1930s to provide more water for the industrial northwest. The Lake District's easternmost lake became almost twice as long as a result (now four miles in length), while the water level rose by 100

Withnail and I: a location guide

"We've gone on holiday by mistake", bleats Withnail (Richard E. Grant) in cult film classic *Withnail and I* (1987), about two booze-and-pill-ridden unemployed actors who leave London for a trip to the country. The holiday in question is a disastrous stay in "Crow Cragg", a bleak, freezing, rain-sodden cottage belonging to Withnail's Uncle Monty. While the location is never specified, the "country" parts of the film are largely set on the eastern fringes of the Lake District between Shap and Haweswater. The cottage used in the film was Sleddale Hall overlooking **Wet Sleddale Reservoir**, two miles south of Shap, off the A6 (and 12 miles south of Penrith) – you can park at the reservoir and walk up to see the exterior but it's fairly dilapidated and access is often very muddy. The lake shown in the film isn't the Wet Sleddale reservoir but is the far larger **Haweswater** to the west – see below for a walk around that reservoir. Sadly, the **Penrith Tea Rooms** – scene of a desperate search for alcohol ("We want the finest wines available to humanity") – doesn't exist, or at least, not in Penrith. This and the Penrith pub scene were actually filmed in Stony Stratford, near Milton Keynes, though the old red telephone box used by Withnail to call his agent is the one in **Bampton** village, near Haweswater.

feet, completely drowning the village of Mardale. (It was visible in the hot summers of 1976, 1984 and 1995, when its deluged buildings emerged briefly from the depleted reservoir.) Such brutal dealings seem a long way off nowadays: the water company manages the valley and lake as a nature reserve, where woodpeckers and sparrowhawks inhabit Naddle Forest, and buzzards, peregrine falcons and the only pair of golden eagles in England swoop to the fells.

You can park at **Burnbanks**, at the northern end, near the dam wall, which is the best place to start the moderately strenuous **round-the-lake walk** (10 miles; 5hr), perhaps the best lakeside walk in the entire region – you'll usually be completely on your own on the way round. The path meanders above the water and through the woods on both sides of the lake, and if you walk anticlockwise you can reward yourself near the end with a drink at the extremely peaceful, nicely old-fashioned ⚓ *Haweswater Hotel* (☎01931/713235, ⓦ www.haweswaterhotel.com; ❸), built in 1937 to replace the inn at Mardale, lost when the valley was drowned. The terrace, dining room and bar all have magnificent views, as do the rooms, while the three at the front have lake-facing balconies (though these aren't en suite). Bistro-style meals are available at lunch; for dinner there's a two- or three-course *table d'hote* menu (£20/24).

The road ends at the southern foot of the lake where there's an official car park at **Mardale Head**: from here, walkers can climb south over the passes to Kentmere and Longsleddale or west up to High Street for Troutbeck, Patterdale or Howtown. The traditional circular day walk from Mardale Head (7 miles; 5hr) is up Riggindale to High Street (2719ft) and then south along the ridge to Mardale Ill Bell (2496ft) and Harter Fell (2539ft) before dropping down Gatescarth Pass back to the car park. On a clear day, the views for most of the way around are magnificent.

There are no other local facilities, save the *Mardale Inn* pub and a post office-store-café in the small village of **BAMPTON**, which is a couple of miles beyond the head of the lake (and four miles south of Askham). The #111 "Haweswater Rambler" **bus** runs from Penrith to Bampton and Burnbanks (all year, Tues & Sat only) and on to the foot-of-the-lake car park (mid-July to early Sept Sun & bank hols only).

Travel details

All timetables can be checked on Traveline
☎ 0870/608 2608; for Ullswater Steamers see p.202.

From Penrith

Bus #108, "Patterdale Bus" (4–5 daily) to: Pooley Bridge (18min), Aira Force (32min), Glenridding (40min), Patterdale (45min).

Bus #110 postbus to: Pooley Bridge (quickest journey time 25min), Howtown (40min) and Martindale (45min). Service operates Mon–Sat 2 daily. Of the two, the much quicker afternoon service (shown here, not Sat) is the only real option for most travellers.

Bus #111, "Haweswater Rambler" (2–3 daily) to: Askham (15min), Bampton (22min), Burnbanks (27min) and Mardale Head (1hr). Service operates Tues & Sat all year to Askham, Bampton and Burnbanks; and as far as Mardale Head on Sun & bank hols from mid-July to early Sept only.

From Glenridding/Patterdale

Bus #208, "Ullswater Connection" (5 daily) to: Aira Force (12min) and Keswick (38min). Service operates late-May to mid-July, Sat, Sun and bank hols; mid-July to Aug daily.

Bus #517, "Kirkstone Rambler" to: Brothers Water (10min), Kirkstone Pass Inn (25min), Troutbeck Queen's Head (35min), Windermere (47min) and Bowness (55min). Service operates Easter to mid-July & Sept–Oct Sat, Sun & bank hols 3 daily; mid-July to early Sept 3 daily.

From Bowness/Windermere

Bus #517, "Kirkstone Rambler" to: Brothers Water (45min), Patterdale (50min) and Glenridding (55min). Service operates Easter to mid-July & Sept–Oct Sat, Sun & bank hols 3 daily; mid-July to early Sept 3 daily.

7

Out of the
National Park

CHAPTER 7

Highlights

﹡ **L'Enclume, Cartmel** A cutting-edge gastronomic retreat in one of the region's prettiest medieval villages. See p.229

﹡ **Laurel and Hardy Museum, Ulverston** Picking over the life of Ulverston's finest son, Stan Laurel, provides a happy diversion from the lakes and fells. See p.229

﹡ **Furness Abbey** The romantic sandstone pillars and arcades of Cumbria's finest religious ruin lie only a few miles off the beaten track. See p.233

﹡ **Whitehaven** West Cumbria's most captivating town has a Georgian centre and revitalized harbour. See p.233

﹡ **Wordsworth House, Cockermouth** Wordsworth's childhood home has been enterprisingly restored as a working Georgian household. See p.237

﹡ **Rheged** A wet-weather attraction *par excellence*, Rheged visitor centre lures visitors with a giant-format cinema screen and Britain's national mountaineering museum. See p.245

△ Whitehaven harbour

7

Out of the National Park

When the Lake District National Park boundary was drawn around the lakes and fells, it excluded several peripheral Cumbrian towns, nearly all of the west Cumbrian coast and the southern Furness peninsulas. Most visitors to the Lakes will pass through at least one of these areas – indeed, the usual approaches to the Lake District make it hard to avoid Kendal or Penrith. And there's a case for aiming to see several other destinations not strictly within the National Park on any trip to the region. The distances help: it's not much more than thirty miles between Penrith and Cockermouth, and about the same around the west coast, making it easy to nip from lakeland valley to outlying town. This chapter highlights half a dozen of the most interesting destinations on the fringes of the National Park, all close enough to be considered part of the Lake District. You may well also pass through the largely industrial towns of the west coast – between Barrow-in-Furness and Maryport – and visit the county capital of Carlisle or the Morecambe Bay resort of Grange-over-Sands; but you won't find those places covered in this Guide. For these, you'll need to get hold of a copy of the *Rough Guide to England*.

The towns outside the National Park are all larger than those within, not least **Kendal**, in the southeast, once the county town of Westmorland and still an enjoyable market town with a pair of fine museums, an arts centre and other attractions. **Penrith**, to the north, is also an ancient commercial centre and, like Kendal, retains the ruins of the castle that defended it during the turbulent medieval border wars. It's a minor stop on the Wordsworth trail, while many pass through before or after seeing nearby **Rheged**, the Cumbrian visitor centre and film experience, which also houses the National Mountaineering Exhibition. Religious foundations established in the south at **Cartmel** and **Furness Abbey** had a lasting regional significance; the enterprising Furness monks could be said to have made early Cumbria an economic powerhouse well before the Industrial Revolution. Of the Cumbrian ports and towns that boomed in the eighteenth and nineteenth centuries, **Ulverston** still thrives as a market town (and claims comedian Stan Laurel as its own), while **Whitehaven**, on the west Cumbrian coast, has been rejuvenated by investment in its fine harbour and quayside. Here, and at nearby **Cockermouth** – yet another handsome market town – the Georgian well-to-do (including the young Wordsworth family) lived out their comfortable lives.

Map labels (within image):
- Carlisle, Carlisle, Newcastle
- Melmerby
- Maryport, A595
- Cockermouth
- Bassenthwaite Lake, A66
- Workington, Penrith
- Rheged, Brougham Castle
- Loweswater, A595, A5086, Keswick, A591, Appleby-in-Westmorland
- Crummock Water, Derwent Water, Thirlmere, Ullswater
- Whitehaven, Water, Buttermere, Glenridding
- Ennerdale, Helvellyn, Shap
- LAKE DISTRICT NATIONAL PARK, Haweswater, Orton, A685
- Wast Water, Scafell Pike, CUMBRIA
- Scafell, Grasmere, Ambleside, Tebay, A683
- N, Old Man of Coniston, Coniston, Windermere
- Devoke Water, A593, Coniston Water, Windermere, Kendal, A684
- A595, Sizergh Castle, A6, M6, A683
- Levens Hall, A590
- Ulverston, Cartmel, A590, A65
- Arnside, Kirkby Lonsdale
- Dalton-in-Furness, A5087, Grange-over-Sands, Holker Hall
- Barrow-in-Furness, Furness Abbey, Morecambe Bay, A693, A65, Settle
- OUT OF THE NATIONAL PARK, Morecambe, 0, 10 miles
- Heysham, Lancaster
- © Crown copyright, Manchester & Liverpool
- Scotch Corner (A1), Skipton & Leeds

All the places covered in this chapter are accessible by **public transport** and details are given where necessary. Cumbria's **Traveline** (℡0870/608 2608, 🌐www.traveline.org.uk.) can provide specific routes and timetables.

Kendal

The self-billed "Gateway to the Lakes" (though nearly ten miles from Windermere), limestone-grey **KENDAL** is the largest of the southern Cumbrian towns, with a population of 25,000. Upwardly mobile Norman barons created a medieval market town on the banks of the fast-flowing River Kent and built the first castle here, whose skeletal remains still stand. They also bequeathed to the town its most characteristic feature by establishing uniform building plots along a single main street in an attempt to increase their rents. This resulted in the layout visible today on both sides of Highgate and Stricklandgate: houses and shops to the fore, stables and workshops to the rear in the numerous "yards" and "ginnels". The town became known for its archers – who fought at Crécy and Poitiers in the Hundred Years War with France – and for its cloth, particularly the "Kendal green" (plant-dyed wool), which earned the town a mention in Shakespeare's *Henry IV*. No wonder that the town motto became the no-nonsense "Cloth is my bread". By the eighteenth century Kendal was a major European cloth distribution centre, while its tanneries (which grievously polluted the River Kent) laid the foundation for today's most important industry, shoe-making. However, you could be forgiven for thinking that **Kendal Mintcake** is what keeps the contemporary coffers filled. This solid, energy-giving block of sugar and peppermint oil, invented by accident in the mid-nineteenth century, has been hoisted to the top of the world's highest mountains and is on sale throughout the Lakes.

The Town

The old **Market Place** has long since succumbed to development, with the market hall now converted to the Westmorland Shopping Centre (off Strick-landgate), but traditional stalls still do business outside every Wednesday and Saturday and there's a well-established farmers' market on the last Friday of the month. The long main street – Stricklandgate and then Highgate – is backed by historic yards and alleys, many now tidily renovated and containing stores, businesses and shopping centres. Strolling along here will eventually take you down to the riverside, past restored almshouses, mullioned shop fronts and old trade signs, among them the pipe-smoking Turk outside the snuff factory on Lowther Street.

At Kirkland, by the river at the bottom of Highgate, the wide aisles of the Early English **Parish Church** house a number of family chapels, including that of the Parr family, who once owned the ruined **Kendal Castle** (free access) on a hillock to the east across the river. First erected in the early thirteenth century, it's claimed as the birthplace of Catherine Parr, Henry VIII's sixth wife, but the story is apocryphal – she was born in 1512, at which time the building was in an advanced state of decay. To reach the castle, follow the footpath from the end of Parr Street, across the footbridge just north of the church.

Kendal's other attractions – town museum, tapestry exhibition and the art gallery and museum at Abbott Hall – spread themselves along the River Kent, between the train station and the parish church.

Kendal Museum

The **Kendal Museum** on Station Road (hours may vary, but currently Thurs–Sat noon–5pm; £2.70; ☎01539/721374, ⓦwww.kendalmuseum.org.uk) is the repository of the district's natural history and archeological finds. Founded as early as 1796, what was essentially a gentleman's private collection was later given to the town and moved into an old wool warehouse in 1913, where it's been stationed ever since. It's far from dull, since as well as the usual flints and stuffed birds there are plenty of well-presented displays relating to the town's history and various pieces of ephemera – from a penny-farthing bicycle to a stuffed grizzly bear, shot by the Earl of Lonsdale. There are also finds from local Roman and Viking sites, including part of a tenth-century cross with similar Christian symbols to that of the more famous Gosforth cross. Later exhibits include a medieval coin hoard and even a key from the town castle. Kendal's former borough treasurer, Alfred Wainwright (see box on p.221) was honorary clerk at the museum between 1945 and 1974: his reconstructed office, various pen-and-ink drawings and a few of his personal effects are preserved, as well as many of the museum artefact labels written in his distinctive hand.

Quaker Tapestry

Just off the river, between New Road and Stramongate, one of Britain's larg-est Quaker Meeting Houses (built 1816) contains the 77 embroidered panels of the **Quaker Tapestry** (April–Nov Mon–Fri 10am–5pm, last admission

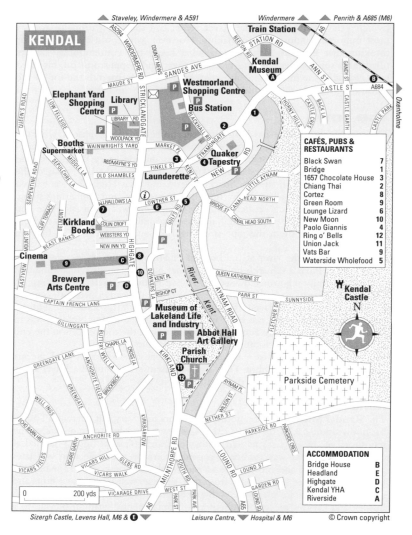

KENDAL

▲ Staveley, Windermere & A591   Windermere ▲   ▲ Penrith & A685 (M6)

Train Station

Kendal Museum Ⓐ

Elephant Yard Shopping Centre

Library

Westmorland Shopping Centre

Bus Station

Booths Supermarket

Quaker Tapestry ❹

Launderette

Kirkland Books

Cinema

Brewery Arts Centre

Museum of Lakeland Life and Industry

Abbot Hall Art Gallery

Parish Church

Kendal Castle

Parkside Cemetery

CAFÉS, PUBS & RESTAURANTS	
Black Swan	7
Bridge	1
1657 Chocolate House	3
Chiang Thai	2
Cortez	8
Green Room	9
Lounge Lizard	6
New Moon	10
Paolo Giannis	4
Ring o' Bells	12
Union Jack	11
Vats Bar	9
Waterside Wholefood	5

ACCOMMODATION	
Bridge House	B
Headland	E
Highgate	D
Kendal YHA	C
Riverside	A

0   200 yds

Sizergh Castle, Levens Hall, M6 & Ⓔ ▼   Leisure Centre, ▼ Hospital & M6   © Crown copyright

at 4pm, plus some Sats 11am–3pm; £4.90; ☏01539/722975, ⓦwww.quaker -tapestry.co.uk). This area of the southern Lakes was at the heart of early Quak- erism, beginning with the travelling ministry of George Fox (1652), a seeker after truth, whose followers were dubbed Quakers "because we bid them trem- ble at the Word of the Lord". The tapestry – produced by almost four thousand people gathered in embroidery groups between 1981 and 1996 – forms a narrative history of Quaker experience through the ages, with the delicately worked panels portraying historical subjects such as Elizabeth Fry's work in Newgate prison and the anti-slavery "underground railroad" in the USA, as well as contemporary Quaker campaigns for peace, relief work and reconciliation. Embroidery workshops and demonstrations are held throughout the year, while

If ever a person has changed the way others look at the Lake District hills it's **Alfred Wainwright** (1907–91), whose famous handwritten walking guides are studied with the intensity normally reserved for religious texts. Wainwright was born in Blackburn in Lancashire, left school at 13 and worked his way up through the Borough Treasurer's office, qualifying as an accountant in 1933. After a first visit to the Lake District in 1930 he became a keen walker and returned to the Lakes at every possible opportunity. So taken was he with the fells that he engineered a move to Kendal in 1941; he was Borough Treasurer from 1948 until his retirement in 1967.

His love of walking was taken to obsessional lengths; he set off alone at the crack of dawn every weekend to tackle distant fells, peaks and valleys. In 1952, dissatisfied with the accuracy of existing maps of the paths and ancient tracks across the fells, he embarked on a series of seven walking guides, each painstakingly handwritten with mapped routes and delicately drawn views. These *Pictorial Guides* to the Lake District were a remarkable undertaking, especially since the original idea was only for his own amusement. The first book, *The Eastern Fells*, was published in 1955 and was an unexpected success; six others followed by 1966, thus completing the task he had set himself of recording in detail 214 separate lakeland fells. The seven volumes have subsequently sold over two million copies. Many other titles followed: a *Pennine Way Companion* (1968), the *Coast-to-Coast* route he devised from St Bees to Robin Hood's Bay (1973), endless sketchbooks and guides to the Lake District, Scotland, Wales, the Yorkshire Dales and the Lancashire hills; fifty-odd books in all. His first wife, Ruth, left him in 1966, and in 1970 Wainwright married Betty McNally, with whom he'd corresponded (and secretly met on his walking trips) for years. He died in 1991, having given away most of his considerable earnings to animal rescue charities, and his ashes were scattered on Haystacks in Buttermere.

The effect his books have had is plain to see. People who don't normally consider themselves walkers are happy to follow his guidance through the Lake District, though others decry the books' popularity, which has led to the ravaging of the land he so adored, especially on his most trekked route, the Coast-to-Coast – much of Wainwright's original route (subsequently amended) was not on designated rights of way and often crossed sensitive wildlife areas and archeological sites. It's also wrong to treat Wainwright as gospel, as many do in their attempts to "bag" the 214 fells he recorded. The number was an entirely arbitrary figure – most of the Wainwright fells are over 1400ft high, but there are plenty of other crags and fells lower than that but just as spectacular, not to mention the lakes, tarns and valleys which he covered only in passing.

Wainwright allowed no revision of the *Pictorial Guides* to be made during his lifetime. However, although the hills themselves might seem largely unchanged in the fifty years since the books were first written, path routes have altered, walls have disappeared and the landscape has been affected by human activity. With a new publisher, and with the agreement of the Wainwright Estate, revised editions of all seven guides are now being undertaken by cartographer and Wainwright disciple Chris Jesty. Up-to-date news and views about this and other related subjects are observed by the **Wainwright Society** (⊛www.wainwright.org.uk), dedicated to the "Master Fellwalker" and his works.

there's a vegetarian café – in summer you can sit outside on the lawn. You can enter the Meeting House from either New Road or Stramongate.

Abbot Hall Art Gallery and Museum of Lakeland Life and Industry
The town's other two attractions – the Art Gallery and Museum of Lakeland Life and Industry – are found at the Georgian **Abbot Hall** (Mon–Sat: April–Oct

△ Abbot Hall

10.30am–5pm; Nov to mid-Dec & mid-Jan to March 10.30am–4pm; closed mid-Dec to mid-Jan; gallery and exhibitions £5, museum £3.75, combined ticket £7.50; ☎01539/722464, ⓦwww.abbothall.org.uk), by the river near the parish church. The main hall, painstakingly restored to its 1760s town-house origins, houses the **Art Gallery**, whose upper floors host temporary art exhibitions on varied themes. The lower-floor galleries are more locally focused, concentrating on the works of the eighteenth-century "Kendal School" of portrait painters, notably Daniel Gardner and, most famously, George Romney. Born in Dalton-in-Furness (and buried there), Romney set himself up as a portrait painter in Kendal in 1757, where he stayed for five years before moving to London to further his career. His society portraits are the pick of the gallery's collection, though you'll also find changing displays of works by those who came to the Lakes to paint, such as Constable, Ruskin, Turner and Edward Lear. Two large paintings of Windermere by Phillip James de Loutherbourg depict Belle Isle and its round house respectively beset by storms and becalmed. In addition, eighteenth-century chairs, writing desks and games tables designed and built by famed furniture-makers Gillows of Lancaster have all survived in Abbot Hall in excellent condition, and there's also a good **café** below the gallery.

A Barbara Hepworth sculpture, *Oval Form*, graces the grass between the hall and its former stables, which now house the **Museum of Lakeland Life and Industry**. Here, reconstructed house interiors from the seventeenth, eighteenth and nineteenth centuries stand alongside workshops that make a vivid presentation of rural trades and crafts, from mining, spinning and weaving to shoe-making and tanning. The museum also contains a room devoted to the life and work of the children's writer Arthur Ransome, whose widow donated his pipes, typewriter and other memorabilia to the collection after his death.

Sizergh Castle and Levens Hall

Three miles south of Kendal stands **Sizergh Castle**, tucked away off the A591 (Easter–Oct Mon–Thurs & Sun 1–5pm, gardens open same days from 11am;

£6.70, gardens only £4.50; NT; ☎015395/60070); take bus #555. Home of the Strickland family for eight centuries, the stately home owes its "castle" epithet to the fourteenth-century pele tower at its core – one of the best examples of these towers, which were built as safe havens during the region's protracted medieval border raids. The Great Hall underwent significant changes in Elizabethan times, when most of its rooms were panelled in oak with their ceilings layered in elaborate plasterwork. At nearby **Low Sizergh Barn** (daily 9.30am–5pm; ☎015395/60426, Ⓦwww.lowsizerghbarn.co.uk), four miles south of Kendal on the A591, there's a really good farm shop and craft gallery, while the tearoom has a viewing window onto the organic dairy herd's milking parlour (cows milked daily around 3.45pm).

Two miles south of Sizergh, **Levens Hall** (April to mid-Oct Mon–Thurs & Sun noon–5pm; gardens same days from 10am; £9.50, gardens only £6.50; Ⓦwww.levenshall.co.uk), also built around a medieval pele tower (1250–1300), is more uniform in style than Sizergh, since the bulk of it was built or refurbished in classic Elizabethan style between 1570 and 1640. House stewards are on hand to answer any questions and point out the oddities and curios – for example, the dining room is panelled not with oak but with goat's leather, printed with a deep-green floral design. Upstairs, the bedrooms offer glimpses of the beautifully trimmed topiary gardens (the world's oldest, according to *Guinness*), where yews in the shape of pyramids, peacocks, top hats, spirals and crowns stand adjacent to blooming bedding plants and apple orchards. The oldest ha-ha (sunken ditch and wall) in England allows views across the fields beyond, while on Sundays and bank holiday Mondays a showman's steam engine is put to work. You don't have to pay the admission

Walks from Kendal

Although Kendal isn't the most obvious hiking centre, you can in fact walk straight out of town and on to the nearby hills. There are no particularly dramatic heights to gain, but it's pretty countryside. The two moderate walks below offer a variety of scenery, while you're also only a short drive or train ride away from Staveley (p.81), the access point for Kentmere and its walks.

The River Kent to Staveley

Follow the path along the **River Kent** north out of Kendal (or jump the train one stop) to Burneside (the *Jolly Anglers* is a good pub), where you cut northeast up minor roads and farm tracks before climbing to **Gurnal Dubs** and **Potter Tarn**, two prettily sited tarns. The path skirts both before descending to Staveley (good café and pub), where you pick up the signposted Dales Way, which then meanders back down the River Kent through pastoral country to Burneside. From Burneside, this is a 7.5-mile (4hr) circular walk, though if you walk in and out of Kendal you can add another three miles (1hr) to this.

Scout Scar

The high limestone ridge known as **Scout Scar** is 3 miles southwest of Kendal and, on a clear day, provides some scintillating views. Again, you can walk out of Kendal if you want to make a day of it, though it's more usually climbed from either the Underbarrow road (north) or from Brigsteer (south) – there's parking at both places and a pub in Brigsteer.

See Basics, p.35, for general walking advice in the Lakes; recommended maps are detailed on p.42.

△ Milking parlour, Low Sizergh Barn

charge just to visit the plant centre and tearoom; and the #555 bus stops outside the hall.

Practicalities

Kendal's **train station** is the first stop on the Windermere branch line, just three minutes from the Oxenholme main-line station. By catching bus #41 or #41A (to the Town Hall) from Oxenholme (Mon–Sat every hour) you can avoid the wait for the connecting train. From Kendal station, head across the river and up Stramongate and Finkle Street to reach Highgate, a ten-minute walk. All buses (including National Express services) stop at the **bus station** on Blackhall Road (off Stramongate). Locally, the #599 (to Windermere, Bowness, Ambleside and Grasmere) and #555/556 (to Windermere, Ambleside, Grasmere and Keswick, or to Lancaster or Carlisle) are the main services. Driving in from the M6, take junction 38 (north) or 36 (south). There are signposted **car parks** all over town, including one at the Westmorland Shopping Centre (Blackhall Road) and several off Highgate, plus free unlimited parking on New Road by the river.

The **tourist office** (Mon–Sat 9am–5pm, Sun 10am–4pm; Nov–March closed Sun; ☎01539/725758, ⓦwww.kendaltown.org.uk) is in the Town Hall on Highgate (at the junction with Lowther Street). It has current details of the 90-minute **guided walks** organized by the local Civic Society and held on alternate Sundays from mid-June to mid-September (usually at 2pm; £2).

Accommodation

Kendal makes a reasonable overnight stop on the way to or from the Lakes, and can be a useful base for the southern region – though walkers should note that the central fells and valleys are all a good drive or bus ride away. There's not a massive amount of town centre accommodation, though there is a **youth hostel** and a handful of **pubs** offering rooms. Most of the local **B&Bs** lie along Windermere Road, north of the centre, and on Milnthorpe Road, to the south, while the most convenient campsite (and a few other good accommodation options) lies four miles northwest of town, near Staveley (see p.81). The celebrated *Punch Bowl Inn* at Crosthwaite (p.69) is also only five miles to the west.

B&Bs, guesthouses and hotels

Bridge House 65 Castle St ☏01539/722041, ⓦwww.bridgehouse-kendal.co.uk. Georgian family house, not far from the station (it was once the station master's residence), with just a couple of pretty rooms available. No smoking. No credit cards. ❸

Headlands 53 Milnthorpe Rd ☏01539/732464, ⓦwww.smoothhound.co.uk/hotels/headlands. The pick of the bunch on this popular road for guesthouses is this traditional stone house, five minutes' walk south of the centre. Good prices for the rooms, which are small but smart – the one at the top of the house, a family room with a couple of bunks, is the most spacious. There's a licensed lounge-bar and a pick-up service offered from the train or bus stations. No smoking. Parking. ❸

Highgate 128 Highgate ☏01539/724229, ⓦwww.highgatehotel.co.uk. Originally built for the town's first doctor, the rambling Georgian town house now conceals various spick-and-span rooms. There's a family room available (priced a couple of categories higher) and a small garden and patio, while you're

just yards from the town's pubs and restaurants. No smoking. Parking. ❸

Riverside Stramongate Bridge ☏01539/734861, ⓦwww.riversidekendal.co.uk. Kendal's leather industry bequeathed the town several old riverside tanneries, of which this is a prime example. The long rows of riverside windows let light into spacious, traditionally furnished rooms fitted with baths and showers, while a decent restaurant makes the most of the riverside setting. Also a leisure club on site with heated pool, spa, sauna and gym. Two-night D,B&B rates are a good deal. Parking. ❺

Youth hostel

Kendal YHA 118 Highgate ☏0870/770 5892, Ⓔkendal@yha.org.uk. Straightforward hostel accommodation in a building attached to The Brewery arts centre. The multi-bunked rooms are a bit barrack-like (though a few twin- and double-bedded rooms are available) and the hostel's tight on space, but the location's great and there's a lively arts centre bar next door. Evening meals by prior arrangement; bike rental available. Dorm beds from £14, includes breakfast.

Eating, drinking and entertainment

Kendal has the best selection of places to **eat and drink** in the south Lakes, so if you're moving on to the fells you'll want to get your cappuccinos and veggie specials while you can. There's also a huge new Booths **supermarket** in Wainwrights Yard. Many of the town-centre **pubs** have had unsympathetic makeovers, but there are still one or two traditional boozers left plus a few more stylish bars and coffee lounges ranged up and down the main street. However, the main focus of evening entertainment is the **Brewery Arts Centre**, 122 Highgate (☏01539/725133, ⓦwww.breweryarts.co.uk), with its foyer café-bar, restaurant, pub, cinema, theatre, galleries and concert hall. There's live music here throughout the year (including live outdoor concerts on summer Sundays), a special season of Christmas events, and a renowned annual **jazz and blues festival** every November. Other annual events in Kendal include the town's **Torchlight Procession** and **Westmorland County Show** (both Sept) and the **Mountain Film Festival** (Nov), which presents climbing and mountain-related films, events and speakers from around the world.

Cafés

1657 Chocolate House 54 Branthwaite Brow, Finkle St ☏01539/740702. Olde-worlde spot that sells hot chocolate in dozens of guises,

plus cakes, filled croissants and light meals. And don't miss at least a browse in the lovely choccie shop. Daytime only; closed Sun Jan–Easter. Inexpensive.

Union Jack 15 Kirkland ☎01539/722458. If you want veggie food but also crave chips and beans, this is the spot – a family-run diner where full breakfasts and mixed grills take their place on the menu alongside veggie grills, spicy bean burgers and other non-meat treats. Daytime only; closed Sun. Inexpensive.

Waterside Wholefood Gulfs Rd, bottom of Lowther St ☎01539/729743, ⓦwww .watersidewholefood.co.uk. A great place by the river for veggie and vegan wholefood snacks or meals – you can eat outside or grab a table in one of the homely little interior rooms. Soups, salads, bakes and cakes form the mainstay of the menu, but stuffed tortillas, wraps and other specials provide daily variation, and organic and Fair Trade ingredients are used where possible. Daytime only; closed Sun. Inexpensive.

Restaurants

Chiang Thai 54 Stramongate ☎01539/720387. Northern Thai dishes are the speciality in this intimate restaurant – such as *laab*, a spicy, minced-meat salad – but all the usual stir fries are available, alongside fragrant "mussaman" curries (with coconut, pineapple and peanuts) and delicate dishes like poached salmon and coconut soup. Dinner only. Moderate.

Cortez 101 Highgate ☎01539/723123, ⓦwww .cortezkendal.co.uk. A classy Spanish wine-bar and restaurant that tries hard to create an authentic feel. There's a daytime café (closed Sun), a good-value lunch menu, and tapas and full meals from 5pm, with the emphasis on contemporary Spanish cuisine – say, lentils with chorizo and black pudding, pan-seared tuna, or a char-grilled vegetable paella. Restaurant closed Sun lunch. Tapas and lunch moderate; restaurant expensive.

Green Room Brewery Arts Centre, 122 Highgate ☎01539/725133. The easy-going arts centre café-restaurant is a welcoming spot at any time of the day – open from 10am for coffee and cake, with a lunch menu served from 11.30pm (sandwiches, salads, classic dishes like bangers and mash, and the famous gourmet pizzas). The dinner menu is more elaborate and combines seasonal local produce with world flavours – spring rolls to king scallops, Cumbrian beef carpaccio to courgette gratin. Last orders are usually at 9pm, or 9.30pm for pizzas. Moderate.

New Moon 129 Highgate ☎01539/729254, ⓦwww.newmoonrestaurant.co.uk. Kendal's longest-serving foodie choice is a comfortable, contemporary bistro with a seasonally changing menu. Lunch sticks to things like panini, risottos, pastas and salads (£5–6), but at dinner (most mains £10–13) there's a Modern British take on locally sourced ingredients, like a rack of Cumbrian lamb served on garlic mash. There's always a good choice for fish-eaters and vegetarians too, and it's no-smoking throughout. Closed Sun & Mon. Expensive.

Paolo Giannis 21A Stramongate ☎01539/725858. Rustic Italian with tables placed cheek by jowl. No surprises on the menu – pizzas, pasta, grills – but it's a cheery place to dine, with a bargain happy-hour menu (noon–2pm & 5–6.30pm) when pizza or pasta is just £3.50. Moderate.

Pubs and bars

Black Swan 8 Allhallows Lane ☎01539/724278. A locals' local, with a roaring fire in winter to thaw the chilliest souls and a range of decent beers.

Bridge Hotel Stramongate ☎01539/724170. A classic old pub with well-kept beer and a small riverside beer garden. It's right at the bottom of Stramongate, by the bridge.

Lounge Lizard Yard 39, Tanners Yard, Highgate ☎01539/733905. Tucked down one of Kendal's central yards, this small bistro-bar serves fancy sandwiches, salads and meze/tapas-style snacks, and you can come in for coffee any time from 10am. But it's also a laid-back place for drinks and music, open until midnight during the week, 1am at weekends. Closed Sun & Mon.

Ring o' Bells 37 Kirkland ☎01539/720326. This pub, uniquely, stands on consecrated ground by the parish church, making it the bell-ringers' local. Does its holy location make the beer taste better? You decide.

Vats Bar Brewery Arts Centre, 122 Highgate ☎01539/725133. The Arts Centre hangout is more pub than a bar, with a selection of real ales avail-able – the huge "vats" provide circular booth seat-ing. You can eat well here too, as the menu (lunch and dinner) is the same as in the adjacent *Green Room* (see "Restaurants" above).

Listings

Banks and exchange ATMs at Barclays (9 High-gate); HSBC (64 Highgate); Lloyds-TSB (Finkle St); and NatWest (70 Stricklandgate). You can exchange travellers' cheques at the post office (see opposite).

Bookshop Kirkland Books, 11 Collin Croft ☎0800/011 2368, ⓦwww.kirklandbooks.biz (closed Sun). Offers an excellent selection of second-hand and antique books, and is especially strong on local interest, walking and topography.

Car rental Westmorland Vehicle Hire, Westmorland Business Park, Gilthwaiterigg Lane ☏01539/728532, ⓦwww.carhirecumbria.co.uk.

Emergencies Westmorland General Hospital, Burton Rd, Kendal ☏01539/732288.

Internet access Kendal Library, Stricklandgate (Mon & Tues 9.30am–5.30pm, Wed & Fri 9.30am–7pm, Thurs 9.30am–1pm, Sat 9am–4pm, Sun noon–4pm; ☏01539/773520).

Left luggage *Union Jack* café, 15 Kirkland, will look after your bags during the day for free; you should at least buy a cup of tea in return.

Pharmacies Boots, 10 Elephant Yard

☏01539/720180; Highgate Pharmacy, 41 Highgate ☏01539/720461; Lloyd's, Station Yd ☏01539/723988.

Police station Busher Walk ☏0845/330 0247.

Post office 75 Stricklandgate (Mon–Fri 9am–5.30pm, Sat 9am–12.30pm).

Swimming pool Lakes Leisure, Burton Rd ☏01539/729777, ⓦwww.lakesleisure.org .uk/kendal. Public admission usually lunchtime and evenings only during term-time, otherwise all day, but call or check the website for specific times; there's also a sauna, gym and squash court.

Taxis Blue Star Taxis ☏01539/723670; Crown Taxis ☏01539/732181.

Cartmel

CARTMEL grew up around its twelfth-century Augustinian priory and is still dominated by the proud **Church of St Mary and St Michael** (daily: Easter–Oct 9am–5.30pm, Nov–Easter 9am–3.30pm; church entrance free, tours Easter–Oct Wed 11am & 2pm, £2.50), the only substantial remnant of the priory to survive the Dissolution. A diagonally crowned tower is the most distinctive feature outside, while the light and spacious Norman-transitional interior climaxes at a splendid chancel, illuminated by the 45-foot-high East Window. The misericords are immaculate, carved with entwined branches, bunches of grapes, tools, leaves and crosses, while chief of the numerous sculpted tombs is the Harrington Tomb – the weathered figure is that of John Harrington, a fourteenth-century benefactor. Another patron of the church was one Rowland Briggs who paid for a shelf on a pier near the north door and for a supply of bread to be distributed from it every Sunday in perpetuity "to the most indigent housekeepers of this Parish". Before you leave, peruse the gravestones on the church floor, reminders of men and women swept away by the tide while crossing the sands – a short cut into the region from Grange-over-Sands to the south.

Everything else in the village is modest in scale, centred on the attractive **market square**, with its Elizabethan cobbles, water pump and fish slabs. Refreshment is at hand at any of the village's three pubs, all on, or close to, the square, and you can then walk down to the **racecourse** whose delightful setting by the River Eea deserves a look even if the races (held on the last weekend in May and August; ⓦwww.cartmel-steeplechases.co.uk) aren't in action. Given Cartmel's rather twee attraction, you'll not be surprised to find several antique, craft and gift shops, as well as weekly antiques fairs (April–Oct) held in the village hall. On the square, the **Cartmel Village Shop** is known to aficionados for the quality of its sticky-toffee pudding.

A couple of miles west of the village, on the B5278, one of Cumbria's most interesting and well-presented country estates, **Holker Hall** (April–Oct Mon–Fri & Sun 10.30am–5.30pm, last admission 4pm; £9.25, gardens only £5.95; ☏015395/58328, ⓦwww.holker-hall.co.uk), is still in use by the Cavendish family which has owned it since the late seventeenth century. Only the New Wing of the house – rebuilt after a devastating fire in 1871 – is open to the public (noon–4pm), where you can admire the beautiful wood panelling, the splendid cantilevered staircase and the library, which is stocked with more than three thousand leather-bound books, some of whose spines are fakes, constructed to hide electric light switches added in 1911. The highly impressive 23-acre **gardens** are the highlight for many, both formal and woodland, and featuring sweeping views from the surrounding meadows to the fells and estuary beyond. There's plenty to seek out – sunken garden, grotto, stone labyrinth and massive slate sundial – while a water cascade tumbles from a seventeenth-century marble Neptune down through the rhododendrons and oak trees. There's also a celebrated annual garden festival (June), and spring (April) and winter (November) markets held here, while you don't have to pay for entrance to visit the food hall-deli and café (see below), both of which are also open in March, November and December when Holker Hall is otherwise closed.

Practicalities

Cartmel lies a few miles inland of Morecambe Bay and just five miles south of Lakeside, the southern tip of Windermere. **Trains** stop at Cark-in-Cartmel, two miles southwest of the village (the station is a mile from Holker Hall); the #532 **bus** (not Sun) from Grange-over-Sands train station or from Cark runs to the village. The turn-off from the M6 is junction 36; the **car park** is by the racecourse.

There's no **information** office in Cartmel, but you might look at the local website, ⓦ www.cartmelvillage.com, for events and listings. Save for race meeting weekends, **accommodation** is easy to find, either in a local B&B or in one of the old pubs, while Cartmel boasts one of Britain's finest restaurant-with-rooms operations. Otherwise, the village **pubs**, all on and around the square, form the basis of the evening's entertainment – the two listed below also offer accommodation, though the *King's Arms*, with tables outside on the square, is the best bet for real ales and good-value bar meals. There's also an Indian restaurant on the square. Or drive out to Holker Hall, whose 🏃 *Courtyard Café* (opens daily 10.30am; closed Jan & Feb) is an excellent place for breakfast (until noon), lunch or tea, especially on nice days when you can sit outside in the courtyard. The adjacent **Holker Food Hall** (same times, ⓦ www.holkerfoodhall.co.uk) is a superior deli selling estate-produced beef and cheese, the local saltmarsh lamb, gourmet sausages, damson gin and all manner of other treats.

Accommodation and food

Bank Court Cottage Market Sq ☏ 015395/36593. Just through the arch off the square, this family-house B&B has one double and one single room available, with private use of the bathroom. No credit cards. ❸

Cavendish Arms Cavendish St ☏ 015395/36240, ⓦ www.thecavendisharms.co.uk. The most celebrated of Cartmel's inns – on the road through the gatehouse – is an atmospheric place that retains many of its original sixteenth-century features and an open fire in the public bar. It sits on the site of a monastic guesthouse and offers ten variously sized and furnished rooms (all fairly traditional, some a bit on the small side, some with four-posters, etc) – three-for-two-night deals (midweek, low season) are a really good deal. You can eat in the restaurant or bar – prices are moderate for things like

home-made steak-and-ale pie, braised lamb shank or baked salmon. Parking. ❸

🏃 **Howbarrow Farm** 2 miles west of Cartmel ☏ 015395/36330, ⓦ www.howbarrow organic.co.uk. Very peaceful and appealing B&B with one double and one twin room, with a shared bathroom down the hall (bathrobes provided). It's a fully certified organic farm and a really nice place to kick back and relax – there's a cosy lounge and farmhouse kitchen, a walking trail around the farm, and a shop selling organic produce (including everything you need for a picnic). Breakfast, from milk to bacon, is local and organic; fruit is from the farm and the bread's homemade. Dinner also available with advance notice (£19.50). From Cartmel Village Shop, take the road out alongside the racecourse, turn left at the signpost and follow the country lane for another mile. Parking. ❸

L'Enclume Cavendish St ☎015395/36362, ⓦwww.lenclume.co.uk. Seriously classy restaurant-with-rooms on the site of Cartmel's medieval blacksmiths (*enclume* is French for anvil). Seven highly individual rooms have been carved from the building, mixing antiques and contemporary furnishings and all featuring stylish fabrics, excellent bathrooms and flat-screen TVs. Chef Simon Rogan's food is simply extraordinary, with artfully constructed dishes presented in succession (think of it as designer tapas and you're not far off) – a single seared sea scallop on bacon polenta, or beef fillet with a fennel coulis, are typical examples, while other dishes are accompanied by intensely flavoured jellied cubes or mousses, or suffused with wild herbs, hedgerow flowers and exotic roots. It's Michelin-starred and very expensive (*á la carte* around £60 plus drinks and service), though a set lunch and set dinner menu are more affordable ways to enjoy the experience. Restaurant closed Mon; and whole place closed first two weeks Jan. Parking. ⑧

Market Cross Cottage Market Square ☎015395/36143, Ⓔdburgess@marketcross .freeserve.co.uk. Seventeenth-century cottage with simple guest rooms upstairs and oak-beamed tearoom downstairs, where you can sample Morecambe Bay potted shrimps and other traditional dishes. Tearoom closed Mon & Tues. No credit cards. ④

Royal Oak Market Sq ☎015395/36259, ⓦwww .theroyaloak.co.uk. Old pub on the square with a riverside beer-garden and smart modern rooms upstairs, decked out in country pine. No American Express. ④

Ulverston and around

The railway line winds westwards from Cartmel to **ULVERSTON** – eleven miles by road – a close-knit market town on the Furness peninsula that formerly prospered on the cotton, tanning and iron-ore industries. The cutting of Britain's shortest, widest and deepest canal in 1796 allowed direct shipping access into town and boosted trade with the Americas and West Indies, while exports from the heart of the Lake District (from wooden bobbins and linen to copper and slate) passed out through Ulverston and made it wealthy. It's still an attractive place today, enhanced by its dappled grey limestone cottages and a jumble of cobbled alleys and traditional shops zigzagging off the central Market Place.

The Town

What looks like a lighthouse high on a hill to the north of town is the **Hoad Monument**, built in 1850 to honour locally born Sir John Barrow, a former Secretary of the Admiralty. It's open on summer Sundays and public holidays (if the flag's flying) and the walk to the top grants fine views of Morecambe Bay, the town and – to the north – the lakeland fells. To get there, follow Church Walk from the end of King Street, past the parish church.

In town, stalls set up in **Market Place** and in the surrounding streets every Thursday and Saturday for the outdoor market, held since the thirteenth century – the granting of the town charter, by Edward I, is still celebrated here every autumn during Ulverston's Charter Festival. In addition, a **food fair** and farmers' market occupies Market Street on the third Saturday of every month. On all other days the **Market Hall** on New Market Street (9am–5pm; closed Wed & Sun) is the centre of commercial life.

Ulverston's most famous son is Stan Laurel (born Arthur Stanley Jefferson), the whimpering, head-scratching half of Laurel and Hardy. The duo are celebrated in a mind-boggling collection of memorabilia at the **Laurel and Hardy Museum** up an alley at 4C Upper Brook St (daily 10am–4.30pm; £3; closed Jan; ⓦwww.laurel-and-hardy-museum.co.uk), thirty yards off Market Place down King Street. The copy of Stan's birth certificate (June 16, 1890, in Foundry Cottages, Ulverston) lists his father's occupation as "comedian"

© Crown copyright

– young Arthur Stanley could hardly have become anything else. The eccentric showcase of hats, beer bottles, photos, models, puppets, press cuttings and props is complemented by a 1920s-style cinema, with almost constant screenings of Laurel and Hardy films.

It's also worth checking to see what's on at the **Lanternhouse**, on The Ellers (☎01229/581127, 🌐www.lanternhouse.org), just off the A590, at the bottom of Market Street and across Tank Square (a traffic roundabout). A group of multimedia artists known as Lanternhouse International occupies this award-winning conversion of an old school, presenting imaginative exhibitions, installations, concerts and community events relating to the "participatory arts".

The other main attraction in town is the **Lakes Glass Centre**, at Oubas Hill on the A590, behind Booths supermarket, where you can watch the crystal-making process from blowing to painstaking carving, either at Heron Glass (☎01229/581121, 🌐www.heronglass.co.uk) or Cumbria Crystal (☎01229/584400, 🌐www.cumbriacrystal.com). The two company factories are open Monday to Friday 9am to 4.30pm, and each also has a factory shop on site (Mon–Sat 9am–5pm, Sun 10am–4pm), and there's a café (daily 10am–4.30pm).

Conishead Priory and Bardsea

Just outside town, the dramatic Victorian Gothic mansion that is **Conishead Priory** stands on a site originally occupied by a twelfth-century Augustinian priory. Since being restored in the 1980s, it has served as a residential Buddhist centre, and the house and specially built **World Peace Temple** here are open for visits (weekdays by arrangement, weekends 2–5pm; closed last 2 weeks in May and mid-July to mid-Aug; admission free, weekend guided tours £2.50; ☎01229/584029, ⊛www.conisheadpriory.org), while several acres of woodland grounds (dawn to dusk; free) provide a peaceful place for a stroll. It's a couple of miles out of town on the A5087 coast road, or there's access from the Cumbria coastal footpath. Just beyond, at **Bardsea**, there's paddling when the tide is in, scenic views across Morecambe Bay, and a pub in the village for refreshments.

Practicalities

The turn-off from the M6 for Ulverston is junction 36; there are **car parks** off Market Street and at The Gill. Ulverston **train station**, serving the Furness and Cumbrian coast railway, is only a few minutes' walk from the town centre – walk up Prince's Street and turn right at the main road for County Square. **Buses** arrive on nearby Victoria Road from Cartmel, Grange-over-Sands, Barrow, Bowness, Windermere and Kendal. The **Cumbria Way**, the long-distance footpath from Ulverston to Carlisle, starts from The Gill, at the top of Upper Brook Street – a waymarker spire signals the start. The **tourist office** is in Coronation Hall on County Square (Mon–Sat 9am–5pm; ☎01229/587120, ⊛www.ulverston.net), and has a leaflet detailing a good 11-mile **circular walk** from town taking in the Hoad Monument, the canal, Conishead Priory and the local coast.

Accommodation

Ulverston is certainly worth a night of anyone's time and is particularly well-provided for at either end of the budgetary scale – boasting a superior "restaurant with rooms" as well as one of the region's most accommodating backpackers' hostels. The nearest YHA hostels are on the Duddon Estuary in Millom or in Coniston.

Bay Horse Canal Foot, 1.5 miles east of town ☎01229/583972, ⊛www.thebayhorsehotel.co.uk. Ulverston's best address for rooms and food, this old inn on the edge of the Leven estuary (30min walk) soothes you with water views and fine cooking. Most rooms open onto a terrace looking out over the estuary, while dinner is served in the candlelit conservatory. Non-guests are also welcome for coffee and shortbread or lunch (daily except Mon) in the public bar or at the outdoor tables. Dinner (reservations essential) sees a choice of two menus, a monthly changing *á la carte* menu (mains around £23) or a more bistro-style "seasonal" menu (mains around £17). From town, follow the A590 and turn off at the signpost for Canal Foot, running through an industrial estate to reach the inn, by the last lock on the Ulverston canal. Parking. **❼**

Dyker Bank 2 Springfield Rd ☎01229/582423. A welcoming family home just up from the train station, this Georgian house has three spacious rooms available, including one with views to the hills and another (actually two connecting rooms) suitable for families. Parking. No credit cards. **❷**

Trinity House Hotel Prince's St, junction with A590 ☎01229/588889, ⊛www.trinityhousehotel.co.uk. Half a dozen decently proportioned rooms in a handsome Georgian town house, once the rectory and still retaining its polished floors and impressive fireplaces. Two superior rooms offer a bit more space and a seating area. The staff here are all under training for the local hospitality industry (the hotel is in partnership with Windermere's four-star *Lakeside Hotel*), so the prices are fairly competitive and there's keen-as-mustard service. A good-value four-course dinner is also available, from £17.95. Parking. **❺**

Walkers' Hostel Oubas Hill, Canal Head ☎01229/585588, ⊛www.walkershostel .co.uk. Jan Nicholson's well-kept house is run on eco-friendly lines and sustains Cumbria Way walkers, backpackers, cyclists and outdoor types of all kinds. Beds are in small shared rooms (couples and families accommodated), with packed lunches (£4)

and four-course vegetarian evening meals (£10) also available. Plenty of local information to hand, including details of Ulverston's annual walking festival. The house is near the canal basin, east on the A590, at the foot of the Hoad Monument, a 15min walk from the centre (look for the "big boots" painted on the house). Parking. Beds £15, including breakfast.

Eating, drinking and entertainment

As befits a market town, there's plenty of choice when it comes to eating and drinking, and the best **cafés**, **pubs** and **restaurants** are listed below. Hartley's **beers**, a traditional Ulverston favourite, are available all over town (though the beer is no longer made here). For picnic food and local produce, you can't beat the markets, though there's also a good deli on King Street and a large Booths **supermarket** just out of the centre on the A590, at Canal Head, in front of the Lakes Glass Centre. Year-round entertainment – theatre, opera, music and other events – is provided at **Coronation Hall** in County Square (☎01229/587140, ⊛www.corohall.co.uk). The tourist office can provide details of the town's many annual **festivals** – Ulverston is trumpeted as "Festival Town" and there's a celebration of one kind or another almost every month.

Cafés and restaurants

Hot Mango 27 King St ☎01229/584866. The town's funkiest café has a typical daytime menu of cappuccinos, breakfasts, sandwiches, soups and similar, but rings the changes at night when a more adventurous menu mixes fusion flavours with traditional dishes, like spicy Thai soups, spaghetti or sea bass. Open daytime Mon–Sat, plus dinner Thurs–Sat (last orders 9pm). Moderate.

Rustique Off Brogden St ☎01229/587373, ⊛www.eatatrustique.co.uk. Very classy restaurant with a Modern European menu that changes every couple of weeks. Fish is a speciality, fashionably served with a truffle mash or in a spicy coconut broth among other ways; lunch is more bistro in character (fancy ciabatta sandwiches, Caesar salad, linguine with mushrooms), with dishes from around £5. Closed Sun & Mon. Expensive.

World Peace Café 5 Cavendish St ☎01229/587793, ⊛www.worldpeacecafe.org. An outlet of the Buddhist temple at nearby Conishead Priory, this relaxed veggie organic café serves bagel or rice-cake sandwiches, and a short list of hot daily dishes for a fiver. Also cosy armchairs and wireless Internet access, and meditation centre for

lunchtime and evening classes. Café open daytime only; closed Sun & Mon. Inexpensive.

Pubs

Farmer's Arms 3 Market Place ☎01229/584469. More wine bar and restaurant these days than pub, but it's still the best place in town for a convivial drink – there are half a dozen real ales, a good wine list and a cosy set of armchairs, plus outdoor tables with views down Market Street. It's known for its food, ranging from sandwich lunches and traditional bar meals to pricier blackboard specials, with fish always the best choice – expect things like a big bowl of mussels, clams and langoustines, or grilled plaice with a prawn and sweet chilli sauce.

Hope & Anchor Daltongate ☎01229/583934. Cracking little local pub featuring Hartley's beers, open fire, low beams, garden patio and good-value bar meals (not Sun).

Swan Inn Swan St ☎01229/582519. The real-ale choice – nine cask ales served at any one time, in a refurbished old pub on the edge of town. It's just off our map, 300 yards down the A590, on the left. Mon–Wed from 3.30pm, otherwise from noon.

Listings

Banks and exchange ATMs at Barclays (County Sq); HSBC (New Market St); Lloyds-TSB (Union St); NatWest (Queen St). You can exchange travellers' cheques at the post office (see opposite).
Bike rental Gill Cycles, The Gill (Mon–Sat 9am–5pm; ☎01229/581116).

Car rental Alan Myerscough (Ford), The Ellers ☎01229/581058.
Emergencies Local doctors are based at the Health Centre, Victoria Rd ☎01229/484050. Otherwise, the nearest full hospital is in Barrow-in-Furness (Furness General Hospital, Dalton Lane; ☎01229/870870).

Internet access At Ulverston Library, King's Rd
(Mon, Tues, Thurs & Fri 9am–6pm, Wed 9am–1pm,
Sat 9am–4pm; ☎01229/894151), and at the
World Peace Café, 5 Cavendish St (see "Cafés and
restaurants").
Pharmacies Boots, Market St ☎01229/582049;
J. Hewitt, 10 Market Place ☎01229/582003.
Police station Neville St ☎0845/330 0247.
Post office County Sq (Mon–Fri 9am–5.30pm, Sat
9am–12.30pm).

Swimming pool At Lakes Leisure Ulverston,
Priory Rd ☎01229/584110, ⓦwww.lakesleisure
.org.uk/ulverston. Public admission usually morning and evenings during term-time, otherwise
all day, but call or check the website for specific
times. There's also a gym and Cumbria's biggest
tennis centre.
Taxis DJs ☎01229/587110; Joe's
☎01229/586700; McKenna's ☎01229/582180.

Furness Abbey

Cumbria's wealth used to be concentrated at **Furness Abbey** (April–Oct daily 10am–5pm; Nov–March Thurs–Sun 10am–4pm; £3.50; EH; ☎01229/823420), which at the peak of its influence possessed much of southern Cumbria as well as land in Ireland and the Isle of Man. Founded in 1124, the Cistercian abbey had a remarkably diverse industry – it ran sheep farms on the fells, controlled fishing rights, produced grain and leather, smelted iron, dug peat for fuel and manufactured salt. By the fourteenth century it had become such a prize that the Scots raided it twice, though it survived until April 1536, when Henry VIII chose it to be the first of the large abbeys to be dissolved. The abbot and 29 of his monks, who had hitherto resisted (and, indeed, had encouraged the locals to resist Dissolution – a treasonable offence), were pensioned off for the sum of two pounds each.

Now one of Cumbria's finest ruins, the abbey's roofless red sandstone arcades and pillars lie hidden in a wooded vale north of Barrow-in-Furness. It's been a popular tourist diversion since the early nineteenth century, when a train station was built to bring in visitors, among them Wordsworth who was very taken with the "mouldering pile". Borrow an audio-guide from the reception desk to get the best out of the site, since there are no maps or explanatory signs. The transepts stand virtually at their original height, while the massive slabs of stone-ribbed vaulting, richly embellished arcades and intricately carved *sedilia* in the presbytery are the equal of any in England. A small museum houses some of the best carvings, including rare examples of effigies of armed knights with closed helmets and – as medieval custom dictated – crossed legs. Only seven others have ever been found intact. The *Abbey Tavern* at the entrance serves drinks at tables scattered about some of the ruined outbuildings.

The abbey lies a mile-and-a-half out of the industrial town of Barrow-in-Furness, on the Ulverston road (and about six miles from Ulverston). Local **buses** (including the hourly #X35) between Kendal, Ulverston, Dalton-in-Furness and Barrow pass by; details are available from Ulverston tourist office.

Whitehaven

Some fine Georgian houses mark out the centre of **WHITEHAVEN**, one of the few grid-planned towns in England and the most interesting destination on Cumbria's west coast. The economic expansion here was as much due to the booming slave trade as to the more widely recognized coal traffic. Whitehaven spent a brief period during the eighteenth century as Britain's third-busiest

WHITEHAVEN

N

Train Station

WAGON ROAD

North Harbour

Outer Harbour

Queens Dock

Inner Harbour

BULWARK QUAY

OLD QUAY

MILLENNIUM PROMENADE

Crow's Nest

LIME TONGUE

SUGAR TONGUE

South Harbour

The Beacon

WEST STRAND

QUAY STREET

STRAND STREET

NEW LOWTHER STREET

MARLBOROUGH STREET

STRAND STREET

DUKE STREET

KING STREET

NEW STREET

LOWTHER STREET

CHAPEL STREET

KING STREET

❶

LANGLEY STREET

SENHOUSE STREET

GEORGE STREET

WELLINGTON ROW

BRANSTY STATION ROAD

BRANSTY ROW

A, A5094, A595 & Rosehill Theatre

GEORGE STREET

QUEEN STREET

DUKE STREET

CHURCH STREET

QUEEN STREET

SCHOOLHOUSE LANE

SCOTCH STREET

LOWTHER STREET

CATHERINE STREET

A595 & B

❷

❸ Rum Story   St Nicholas

Michael Moon Bookshop

ROPER STREET

ⓘ

SWINGPUMP LANE

MARKET PLACE

ROSEMARY LANE

JAMES STREET

ROPER STREET

❹

QUEEN STREET

IRISH STREET

PRESTON ST.

HOWGILL STREET

CATHERINE STREET

Trinity Garden

0   100 yds

ACCOMMODATION
Corcickle   **B**
Fairladies   **C**
Fleatham House   **D**
Moresby Hall   **A**

CAFÉS, PUBS & RESTAURANTS
Courtyard   3
Espresso   4
John Paul Jones Tavern   1
Platform 9   5
Zest   6
Zest Harbourside   2

▼ B5345, Haven Cycles, ❺, ❻, Ⓒ & Ⓓ   © Crown copyright

port (after London and Bristol), making it a prime target for an abortive raid led by Scottish-born American lieutenant John Paul Jones. Disgusted with the slave trade he witnessed while ship's mate in America, Jones returned to the port of his apprenticeship to rebel, but, let down by a drunk and potentially mutinous crew, he damaged only one of the two hundred boats in dock and his mini-crusade fell flat.

The local history is covered entertainingly in **The Beacon** (admission fee charged; ☎01946/592302, ⓦwww.thebeacon-whitehaven.co.uk), an enterprising museum on the harbour that resembles a squat lighthouse. There are interactive exhibitions on all floors, on themes from slaving to smuggling, with a special emphasis on the local characters who have shaped the town. The museum was undergoing a major refit at the time of writing, but the new exhibitions will be open from the summer of 2007 – contact them for current opening hours and admission details. The **harbour** itself sits at the heart of a renaissance project that has spruced up the quayside and provided new promenades, sculptures and heritage trails. The **Crow's Nest**, a 130-foot-high tower, lit at night, is the dramatic centrepiece of the marina. The whole waterfront comes alive during the biennial **maritime festival** in June (next events 2007 and 2009).

For all the changes round the harbour, it's Whitehaven's Georgian streets and neatly painted houses that make it one of Cumbria's most distinguished towns. There's a **market** held here every Thursday and Saturday, which adds a bit of colour. Otherwise, stroll up Lowther Street to **The Rum Story** (daily 10am–4.30pm; £5.45; Ⓦwww.rumstory.co.uk), housed in the eighteenth-century shop, courtyard and warehouses of the Jefferson rum family. This is another place you could easily spend an hour or so, discovering Whitehaven's links with the Caribbean and learning all about rum, the Navy, temperance and the hideousness of the slaves' Middle Passage, amongst other matters. Across Lowther Street is the seventeenth-century church of **St Nicholas**, though all that stands is its tower (containing a café). The rest succumbed to a fire in 1971, but there's a lovely garden now surrounding the former nave – a further American connection with the town is that **George Washington's grandmother**, Mildred Gale, wife of a Whitehaven merchant, lies buried here. Also on Lowther Street, don't miss **Michael Moon's bookshop** at no. 19 (Ⓣ01946/599010; closed Wed Jan–Easter, & closed Sun all year), a bookworm's secondhand treasure trove.

On the cliffs above Whitehaven, you can get to grips with the industry that set the town on its way at the **Haig Colliery Mining Museum**, Solway Road, Kells (daily 9am–4.30pm; free; Ⓣ01946/599949, Ⓦwww.haigpit.com) – the footpath (10min walk) up and along the cliffs begins behind the Beacon Centre. Haig Colliery was Cumbria's last deep-coal mine (closed in 1986), and you can view the restored winding engines (operated every day) and learn about the dreadful living and working conditions that, in part at least, funded the elegant Georgian town below. A special walking tour (by arrangement, contact the

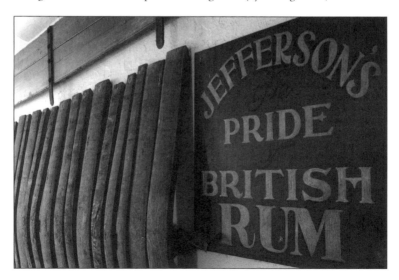

△ Rum Story, Whitehaven

museum) shows visitors the ruins of the early eighteenth-century Saltom Pit, the world's first undersea pit.

Five miles south of Whitehaven, the lighthouse on the sandstone cliffs of **St Bees Head** marks the start of Wainwright's 190-mile Coast-to-Coast walk. The beach below is one of the finest on the coast, wide and sandy, though a bit exposed on windy days. However, a massive car park and some rather unprepossessing buildings, including bucket-and-spade café and holiday park, don't do the beach any real favours – the quiet village of **St Bees**, half a mile inland, is often a more attractive prospect, set around its twelfth-century priory and with two or three old pubs. The bus from Whitehaven (see below) stops in the village and runs right to the beach, though the last one back is in the early afternoon; there are later services on the train.

Practicalities

Trains follow the coastal route south to St Bees, Ravenglass, Millom and Barrow, or north via Maryport to Carlisle. From the station you can walk around the harbour to The Beacon in less than ten minutes. **Buses** use a variety of stops around town – catch services going south from Duke Street, including to St Bees (#20, not Sun) and Gosforth, Ravenglass and Muncaster (#6/X6); or north from Lowther Street, including to Cockermouth and Carlisle (#600, not Sun). National Express services stop opposite the old bus station, just before Tesco's. There's limited-time disc zone **parking** in town (pick up a disc from local shops); for longer stays you're better off following signs to a central car park. The helpful **tourist office** is in the Market Hall on Market Place (Easter–Oct Mon–Sat 9.30am–5pm, plus Sun 11am–3pm in school holidays; Nov–Easter Mon–Sat 10am–4.30pm; ☎01946/598914, ⓦwww.rediscoverwhitehaven.com), just back from the harbour.

The Coast-to-Coast walk aside, Whitehaven itself is the start of the 140-mile **C2C cycle route** to Sunderland/Newcastle. A metal cut-out, protruding from the harbour slipway, marks the spot – it's traditional for C2C cyclists to dip their front wheel in the water before starting. Haven Cycles on Preston Street (☎01946/63263) is a park-and-hire outlet for bikes.

Hotels and B&Bs

Corcickle Guest House 1 Corcickle ☎01946/692073. Whitehaven's best B&B is the very comfortable *Corcickle*, five minutes' walk from the centre – keep on up Lowther Street, past Safeway and *McDonald's* to find the row of Georgian town houses. It's impeccably maintained, with a cheery welcome, and there's on-street parking outside. No American Express. ❸

Fairladies Barn Main St, St Bees ☎01946/822718, ⓦwww.fairladiesbarn.co.uk. Converted seventeenth-century sandstone barn with gardens, right in the centre of the old village, offering a variety of smart rooms. Parking. No credit cards. ❸

Fleatham House High House Rd, St Bees ☎01946/822341, restaurant ☎01946/822793, ⓦwww.fleathamhouse.com. Just five minutes from St Bees station (first left off Main St), this lovely house is set in its own secluded grounds – Tony Blair and family once stayed here on a rare UK holiday. It's very informal: tea and cakes are offered on arrival, there are six large rooms (three of them singles, two overlooking the gardens) and a good breakfast. And, unlike most places, weekends have the cheapest rates, when rooms are £10 less. The restaurant at the house (Mon–Sat dinner only; open to non-residents; *table d'hote* from £18.95) has a good Modern British menu, anything from chilli-and-lime kangaroo to lakeland lamb shank. Parking. ❺

Moresby Hall Moresby, 2 miles north of Whitehaven ☎01946/696317, ⓦwww.moresbyhall.co.uk. Medieval in origin, the hall provides quality B&B in an attractive Grade I listed building with walled gardens, and sea and fell views. Dinner is available (£25, advance booking required). Parking. ❻

Cafés and restaurants

Courtyard Café In *The Rum Story*, Lowther St ☎01946/592933. Serves wraps, sandwiches, baked potatoes and snacks under a glass roof in a converted stables. Daytime only. Inexpensive.

Espresso 22 Market Place ℡01946/591548. A classic espresso bar of the old school, dishing up frothy coffees, fry-ups and grills for forty years. Daytime only. Inexpensive.

Platform 9 Station House, Main St, St Bees ℡01946/822600, ⓦwww.platform9.co.uk. The railway-themed bistro at the station is great for a date, and comes complete with Edwardian-style furnishings, a replica Pullman carriage and elegantly set tables. There are good-value *table d'hote* menus, plus *à la carte* steaks, fish, grills and veggie dishes, and Thai food is available on selected evenings. Bar and gardens open from noon for drinks, lunch and teas, dinner from 6.30pm. Moderate.

Zest Harbourside West Strand ℡01946/66981. Harbourside café-bar doing mix-and-match tapas-style bowls and dishes, plus wraps and sandwiches, pasta, salads and more. Food served until 9.30pm, 10pm at weekends. Moderate.

Zest Low Rd, B5349, ℡01946/692848. The sister restaurant is three-quarters of a mile out of the centre on the Whitehaven–St Bees road. It's a stylish stop for Modern British cuisine, and bookings are recommended as it's Whitehaven's classiest night out. Wed–Sat dinner only. Expensive.

Pub

John Paul Jones Tavern Duke St ℡01946/690916. You can get a decent pint here, in a modern pub that delivers a nod to the father of the American Navy by modelling its interior on that of a sailing ship.

Theatre

Rosehill Theatre 1 mile north of Whitehaven, signposted off A595 ℡01946/692422, ⓦwww.rosehill theatre.co.uk. Enterprising local venue for classical and contemporary music, drama and art-house films. Rosehill Barn in the theatre grounds is the venue for the fortnightly Folk in the Barn gigs (alternate Fridays; ⓦwww.folkinthebarn.net), putting on the best national and international folk acts.

Cockermouth

COCKERMOUTH, midway between the industrial coast and Keswick at the confluence of the Cocker and Derwent rivers, dominates the flat vales that leach out of the northwestern fells, an obvious strategic stronghold. Its Norman castle was at the heart of the medieval border skirmishes, but the town later thrived as a market centre – market day is Monday. Cockermouth tries hard to please, with its impressive Georgian facades, tree-lined streets and riverside setting, but after the dramatic fellside approaches from the south and east it can fall a little flat. However, there's no shortage of local attractions, not least the logical first stop on the Wordsworth trail – the house where the future poet was born.

The Town

The single, long, Main Street crosses the River Cocker and runs parallel to the Derwent through the town. At the western end is the **Wordsworth House** (Easter–Oct Tues–Sat 11am–4.30pm, admission by timed ticket; £4.90; NT; ℡01900/824805, ⓦwww.wordsworthhouse.org.uk), a handsome, terracotta-hued Georgian building that was the birthplace of all five Wordsworth children, including William (1770) and Dorothy (1771). It's a house suitable for the professional man that Wordsworth's father was, though he only rented it from his employer, Sir James Lowther, for whom he spent much of his time away on business. The children, too, though happy in the house, were often sent to their grandparents in Penrith, and when Wordsworth's father died in 1783 – with the children already either away at school or living with relations – the family link with Cockermouth was broken. The building has been beautifully restored, but rather than a pure period piece it's presented as a functioning eighteenth-century home – with a costumed cook willing to share recipes in the kitchen and a clerk completing the

CAFÉS, PUBS & RESTAURANTS

Bitter End	5	Old Stackyard	
Merienda	4	Tearooms	7
Norham Coffee		Quince & Medlar	1
House	3	Royal Yew	8
Number XVII	6	Thyme	2

COCKERMOUTH

ACCOMMODATION

Cockermouth YHA	G
Croft House	D
Manor House	C
Old Homestead	E
Shepherd's	F
Six Castlegate	A
Trout	B

Lakeland Sheep & Wool Centre, A66, **F**, ▼ **7** & **8** ▼ **G**

© Crown copyright

ledger with quill and ink. Many of the fittings and furnishings are of the period (though actual Wordsworth relics are few), while others – kitchen equipment to carpets – have been specially commissioned. In around half the rooms you're encouraged to touch the items on display – children can dress up in one of the bedrooms – or lend the servants a hand, while the walled kitchen garden beside the river has been planted with fruit, vegetables and herbs that would have been familiar to the Wordsworths. It's an education, in the best sense, and a really excellent visit.

Various rainy-day attractions occupy the historic buildings and yards ranged along the Main Street – including small museums of minerals and fossils, printing, toys and models, and motoring – while if you follow your nose you're likely to stumble upon **Jennings Brewery** on Brewery Lane by the river confluence. Jennings have been brewers in the town since 1874 and you don't have to step far to sample their product, available in any local pub. For those sufficiently interested in the brewing process, take the hour-and-a-half-long **brewery tour** (July & Aug 2 daily; March–June, Sept & Oct Mon–Sat 2 daily; Nov–Feb Mon–Sat 1 daily; £4.50; ☎0845/129 7190, Ⓦ www.jenningsbrewery.co.uk); it's advisable to book, and note that there's a free tasting at the end. Also, it's always worth checking to see what's on at **Castlegate House** (Mon & Fri–Sat 10.30am–5pm, Sun 2.30–4.30pm; free; ☎01900/822149, Ⓦ www.castlegatehouse.co.uk), a Georgian mansion on Castlegate, opposite the entrance to Cockermouth Castle – itself a private residence and closed to the public. The house and sculpture garden supports a changing programme of contemporary art displays, specializing in the work of accomplished local artists.

Less rarefied lakeland affairs are dealt with in the out-of-town **Lakeland Sheep and Wool Centre** (daily 9am–5.30pm; closed for two weeks in Jan;

☎01900/822673, ⊛www.sheep-woolcentre.co.uk), a mile south of town on the Egremont road (A66/A5086 roundabout), where various exhibits introduce visitors to the complexities of country life. Most come to the centre for the entertaining indoor sheepdog trials and sheep-shearing displays (March–Oct; 4 shows daily Mon–Thurs & Sun; £4.50), during which you'll learn how to be able to spot a Herdwick sheep, the most characteristic lakeland breed, and watch sheepdogs handle a flock of unruly geese. On Fridays and Saturdays, when there are no shows scheduled, you'll be able to see the centre's video introduction to the region instead. Access to the visitor centre, video show, shop and café is free.

Practicalities

All **buses**, including National Express services, stop on Main Street, from where you follow the signs east to the **tourist office** in the Town Hall, off Market Place (April–Oct Mon–Sat 9.30am–4.30/5pm, July–Sept also Sun 10am–2pm; Nov–March Mon–Fri 9.30am–4pm, Sat 10am–2pm; ☎01900/822634); there's **online information** at ⊛www.cockermouth.org.uk. Driving in, the A66 (from Keswick or Workington) bypasses the town to the south; turn in on either the B5292 (Whinlatter Pass road) or A5086 (from Loweswater and Ennerdale). The **car park** in front of the tourist office is the best place to park, since parking on Main Street is limited to an hour (and you need to display a disc in your car, available from local shops).

Herdwick sheep

The hardiest of indigenous British sheep breeds is the **Herdwick**, its name derived from the "herdwyck" (or sheep pasture) on which it was raised in medieval times. Other sheep breeds are more numerous but it's the grey-fleeced (black when young), white-faced Herdwick that's most characteristic of the Lake District – and which, in many ways, echoes the enduring struggle of lakeland hill farmers. The sheep, bred over the centuries to withstand the local terrain, live out on the inhospitable fells for almost the whole year – most are so good at foraging they never require additional feed. They are territorial, knowing their own "heafs" or particular grazing areas on the fells, and are historically concentrated in the central and western fells of Borrowdale, Buttermere, Langdale, Ennerdale, Wasdale, Eskdale and the Duddon Valley. The National Trust has been instrumental in maintaining the breed on its own farms by obliging tenants to keep Herdwicks. Beatrix Potter was also a keen sheep farmer and encouraged the breed on the farms she left to the Trust on her death.

Partly, the emphasis on maintaining the numbers of Herdwicks is to do with heritage: much of the existing lakeland landscape has been created for and around them, from the intensively grazed fields of the valley bottoms to the dry-stone walls further up the fells. But there's also an economic imperative not to let upland sheep farmers (guardians of much of the landscape) go to the wall without a fight. Even before the foot and mouth crisis of 2001, which saw many flocks destroyed, lakeland sheep farmers found it tough to make a living. While the medieval sheep were bred for their wool, the fleeces today are barely worth clipping as wool prices are so low, and it's as high-quality meat that the farmers are attempting to position their flocks. To see the sheep at their best, visit one of the Lake District's summer agricultural shows, when the Herdwick Sheep Breeders' Association hands out prizes to the healthiest and best-looking sheep. There's more information on the Herdwick Sheep Breeders' Association website ⊛www.herdwick-sheep.com.

Accommodation

Cockermouth makes a handy base for the western Lakes – not far from Loweswater, Ennerdale Water and Buttermere – and there's a good range of accommodation. The best are picked out below, or the tourist office posts a list of other local options outside its office. The **youth hostel** is reasonably central, while the two local **campsites** are around a mile out of town, off the Lorton (B5292) road.

In Cockermouth

Croft House 6–8 Challoner St ☎01900/827533, ⓦwww.croft-guesthouse.com. A stylish revamp of a Georgian town house on a quiet residential street. It's decidedly chintz-free – maplewood floors throughout, contemporary furnishings and bed linen – while the owners offer veggie and vegan alternatives for breakfast as well as Fair Trade coffee and tea. Six rooms available, one (with bunks) suitable for families. Parking. Closed Jan. ❸

Manor House Crown St ☎01900/828663. A favourite mid-range choice, the small family-run hotel spreads thirteen rooms across several floors of a tidy, Georgian-style detached house, complete with rotunda and spiral staircase. Space is at a bit of a premium inside the rooms, though most have a bath as well as a shower. Parking. ❺

Six Castlegate 6 Castlegate ☎01900/826749, ⓦwww.sixcastlegate.co.uk. The period-piece house has been completely refurbished under new owners. The lofty Georgian proportions, impressive staircase and panelling remain, but the half-dozen smartly furnished rooms now have power showers and flat-screen TVs. Parking available nearby. No smoking. No American Express. ❹

Trout Crown St ☎01900/823591, ⓦwww.trouthotel.co.uk. On the banks of the Derwent, this is the top choice in Cockermouth, well known among the fishing fraternity. It's a comfortable base, retaining something of its traditional aspect with its ornate staircase, panelled bar and silver-service restaurant, but the rooms are large and modern, with comfortable beds and good bathrooms, and there's a contemporary bar and bistro, *The Terrace*, with courtyard seating. Rates vary – river and garden views are pricier – but special two-night weekend deals (including dinner) and other special offers can be a real bargain. Parking. ❼

Around Cockermouth

🏃 **Old Homestead** Byresteads Farm, Hundrith Hill Rd, off B5292, 2 miles southeast ☎01900/822223, ⓦwww.byresteads.co.uk. Wake

to the sight of pedigree sheep grazing outside your window on this 180-acre farm, whose original farmhouse (from 1624) has been impressively and authentically restored using traditional lime plaster, cobbles, oak and stone. Rooms are spacious (some are king-sized) and up to date, with underfloor heating, walk-in showers, carved pine beds and sweeping views down the Lorton valley. The breakfast room was where the animals were once kept, and there's a huge inglenook fireplace in the lounge. It's only a quick drive into town, though there are bar meals a couple of hundred yards' walk away at the *Hundrith Hill Hotel*. No smoking. Parking. ❹, king/4-poster rooms ❺

Shepherd's At the Lakeland Sheep and Wool Centre, Egremont Rd, A66/A5086 roundabout, 1 mile south ☎01900/822673, ⓦwww.shepherdshotel.co.uk. Good-value modern motel-style rooms on the edge of town (including four family rooms) – and definitely the only hotel in Britain with its own "live sheep show". There's a bar and restaurant. Parking. ❷

Youth hostel

Cockermouth YHA Double Mills ☎0870/770 5768, ⓔcockermouth@yha.org.uk. Housed in a seventeenth-century watermill down a track by a bend in the River Cocker: the double wheels (that lend the mill its name) and grindstones are still *in situ* and it's in a very peaceful spot – fifteen minutes' walk south from Main Street, along Station Rd and then Fern Bank. There's limited parking here. Usually closed for individuals Nov–March, though call the day before for availability. Dorm beds from £13.

Campsites

Graysonside Off the B5292 Lorton Rd ☎01900/822351. Small site with space for just a few tents, but with good fell views. Closed Oct–March.

Violet Bank Simonscales Lane, off B5292 Lorton Rd ☎01900/822169. Holiday park for caravans and RVs, with plenty of tent space. Closed Dec–Feb.

Eating, drinking and entertainment

You'll find most of the **cafés and restaurants** in town spread along Main Street and up Market Place. There are lots of **pubs**, too – this is the home ground of Jennings brewery, remember — and if you're in the mood, Cockermouth provides the hostelries for one of the more bizarre pub-crawls-of-the-rich-and-famous. Soccer manager Sir Matt Busby, cricketer Ian Botham and (strange but true) crooner and fisherman Bing Crosby have all had a drink in the bar of the *Trout Hotel*, while Robert Louis Stevenson plus local lad (and father of atomic theory) John Dalton frequented the front bar of the *Globe Hotel* on Main Street.

Cafés and restaurants

Merienda 7A Station St ☎ 01900/822790, 🖰 www.merienda.co.uk. Bright, contemporary café-bar — it's Spanish for "snack" — with an arty feel, offering breakfasts, sandwiches and light meals, with the emphasis on locally sourced and Fair Trade products. Also open Friday nights for tapas and music. Daytime only, though Fri until 10.30pm; closed Sun. Inexpensive.

Norham Coffee House 73 Main St ☎ 01900/824330. Trades on its history — it was formerly the home of John Christian, grandfather of *Mutiny on the Bounty*'s Fletcher Christian — and its courtyard seating. Daytime only; closed Sun. Inexpensive.

Number XVII 17 Station St ☎ 01900/822622. Amiable deli with café seating at the back, for brunch, lunch, salads, wraps and sandwiches. The eagle-eyed will notice it's a sister café to the one in Keswick — which, spookily, is also located at 17 Station St. Closed Sun. Inexpensive.

Old Stackyard Tearooms Wellington Farm, off A66/A5086 roundabout, 1 mile southwest of town ☎ 01900/822777, 🖰 www.wellingtonjerseys.co.uk. The Stamper family farm on the edge of town has a fine tearoom — not only are there great views from the terrace and home-made food, but there's also award-winning ice cream made from the milk from the farm's pedigree Jerseys. Dubbs Moss wetland and woodland reserve is only a short walk away, so you can park up for a stroll. At the roundabout, take the exit signposted for "Mitchell's" agricultural market and the farm. Daytime only. Inexpensive.

Quince & Medlar 13 Castlegate ☎ 01900/823579, 🖰 www.quinceandmedlar.co.uk. Gourmet vegetarian dishes served in a wood-panelled, candlelit Georgian house. Reservations advised. Dinner only; closed Sun & Mon. Expensive.

Thyme 7 Old Kings Arms Lane ☎ 01900/821223, 🖰 www.thymerestaurantandbar.com. Enjoy a bit of metropolitan chic in this sleek-looking restaurant and bar, which serves a mix of classic and up-to-the-minute tastes, from rib-eye steak to Thai green curry. Menus change weekly, but the service and food are assured. Tues–Sat dinner only, also open Sun lunch; closed two weeks Jan. Expensive.

Pubs

Bitter End 15 Kirkgate ☎ 01900/828993, 🖰 www.bitterend.co.uk. The nicest, cosiest pub in town also contains Cumbria's smallest brewery, producing ales like "Farmers'", "Cockersnoot" and "Cuddy Lugs", or there's a long list of imported bottled beers. The bar food is really popular — get here early if you want to eat.

Royal Yew Dean, 5 miles south of Cockermouth ☎ 01946/861342. The best destination for a drive out to a country pub, a traditional inn with a handsome yew tree outside and good food and beer within.

Arts centre

Kirkgate Centre Kirkgate ☎ 01900/826448, 🖰 www.thekirkgate.com. The converted Victorian school offers a wide-ranging programme of theatre, cinema, music and the arts.

Listings

Banks and exchange ATMs at Barclays (30 Main St); HSBC (1 Main St); Lloyds-TSB (50 Main St); NatWest (23 Station St).
Emergencies Cockermouth Cottage Hospital, Isel Rd ☎ 01900/822226.
Internet access Cockermouth Library, Main St (Mon–Wed & Fri 10am–7pm, Thurs & Sat 9am–noon; ☎ 01900/325990).
Laundry DIY Wash & Dry, Meadow Bank, Windmill Lane (daily 8.30am–6.30pm; ☎ 01900/827219).
Pharmacies Allison, 31 Main St ☎ 01900/822292; Boots, 56–58 Main St ☎ 01900/823160.

Police station Main St ☎ 0845/330 0247.
Post office Lowther Went, Main St (Mon–Fri 9am–5.30pm, Sat 9am–12.30pm).
Swimming pool Cockermouth Leisure Centre, Castlegate Drive ☎ 01900/82359, 🖰 www .carlisleleisure.com/cockermouth. There's a gym and climbing wall, as well as a pool; public admission hours vary; check the website or call for exact times.
Taxis A. & K. Taxis ☎ 01900/823665; Cockermouth Taxis ☎ 01900/826649; L. & M. Taxis ☎ 01900/825339.

Penrith

PENRITH – four miles from Ullswater and sixteen east of Keswick – has a long pedigree and an historic significance greater than anywhere else in the Lakes. Probably Celtic in origin, it was the capital of the independent kingdom of Cumbria until 1070, a thriving market town on the main north–south trading route from the thirteenth century onwards and harried by the Scots until the sixteenth century. Its castle, built as a bastion against raids from the north, was one of the northern headquarters of Richard III. It still prospers today as an important local market centre and has positioned itself as one of the main gateways to the Lake District; reasonable enough given that it's a stop on the London–Scotland train route and lies off the M6 motorway and A66 to Keswick. It does, however, suffer from undue comparisons with the improbably pretty settlements of the nearby Lakes, and certainly its brisk streets, filled with no-nonsense shops and shoppers, have more in common with the towns of the North Pennines than the stone villages of south Cumbria.

The Town

Come on market day, Tuesday, if you want to get to grips with the local economy. The narrow streets, arcades and alleys off **Market Square**, the old **Corn Market**

© Crown copyright

PENRITH

▲ M6 & Carlisle

0   100 yds

▼ A66, Rheged, Keswick & Ullswater

Hospital, Eamont Bridge, Brougham Castle, **⑥** & **ⓒ** ▼

and the open space of **Great Dockray** provide traditional shopping for stalwart Cumbrian families, in the butchers' shops, fishmongers, outfitters, tobacconists and agricultural feed merchants. There's a really good **farmers' market**, too, held in Market Square on the third Tuesday of every month. **St Andrew's Church** (possibly designed by Nicholas Hawkmoor) sits back from the square in a spacious churchyard surrounded by Georgian houses. The so-called "Giant's Grave" is actually a collection of pre-Norman crosses and "hogsback" tombstones. If you walk back round to the square and up Devonshire Street to the **George Hotel** – where Bonnie Prince Charlie spent the night in 1745 – you'll pass Arnison's, the drapers and milliners. The shop stands on the site of the town's old Moot Hall, owned in the eighteenth century by Wordsworth's grandparents. The young William and Dorothy often stayed here and their mother died in the house in 1778 (she's buried in St Andrew's churchyard, though the grave isn't marked).

At the far end of Middlegate, the tourist office shares its seventeenth-century schoolhouse premises with a small local **museum** (Mon–Sat 10am–5pm, plus April–Oct Sun 1–5pm; free). After a quick review of the town's history, you'll want to climb up to the immaculately kept sandstone ruin of **Penrith Castle** (daily: Easter–Sept 7.30am–9pm; Oct–Easter 7.30am–4.30pm; free), opposite the train station, whose warm colour is at its best at sunset. Traditionally, warnings of attack or – in Napoleonic times – of possible invasion came from the north side of town, from the site of the sandstone beacon tower on **Beacon Hill**. To get there, head up Sandgate and Fell Lane to Beacon Edge (15min), turn left and follow the signposted right turn up through the woods. It takes about an hour, there and back, though the best views of Penrith and the fells beyond are on the way up rather than from the tree-shrouded summit.

The more impressive local fortification is actually that of **Brougham Castle** (April–Sept daily 10am–6pm; Oct Mon & Thurs–Sun 10am–4pm; £2.80; EH), a mile and a half south of Penrith in a pretty spot by the River Eamont. You can climb the towering sandstone keep, in which you'll find remnants of Roman tombstones used as building material, plundered from an earlier Roman fort on this site. Coming back (follow the B6262), you can detour past **Brougham Hall**, an unusual fourteenth-century fortified country house now in service as a crafts centre and numbering a smokehouse, chocolate and truffle-maker, and small café among its businesses. Devoted stone-chasers can also track down the minor standing stones in the vicinity, known as **King Arthur's Round Table** and **Mayburgh**, just south of Eamont Bridge.

Practicalities

Trains from Manchester, London, Glasgow and Edinburgh pull into Penrith station, five minutes' walk south of Market Square and Middlegate. The bus station is on Albert Street, behind Middlegate, and has regular services to Patterdale, Keswick, Cockermouth and Carlisle. Driving in off the M6, take junction 40 – there's disc parking on town-centre streets (discs available from the tourist office and elsewhere), a large **car park** off Brunswick Road and others signposted around town, though spaces are hard to come by on Tuesdays (market day). The **tourist office** is on Middlegate (Easter–Oct Mon–Sat 9.30am–5pm, Sun 1–4.45pm, though daily until 6pm in July and Aug; Nov–Easter Mon–Sat 10am–4pm; ☎01768/867466, ⓦwww.visiteden.co.uk).

Accommodation

Penrith itself isn't overly blessed with **accommodation** and if you're aiming for the Lakes themselves it doesn't make much sense to stop, with Ullswater and

Keswick both under half an hour away. But there's enough choice if you fancy a town stopover, and some very nice options in the surrounding countryside. The bulk of the standard B&Bs line noisy Victoria Road, the continuation of King Street, two minutes' walk south of Market Square. Portland Place has a rather more refined row of guesthouses.

In Penrith

Brooklands 2 Portland Place St ⓣ01768/863395, ⓦwww .brooklandsguesthouse.com. A very handsome town house of the 1870s that's been well restored. Seven colour-coordinated rooms have pine furniture, one has a four-poster; those at the rear overlooking the churchyard are the quietest. It's non-smoking, and there's on-street parking outside. ❹

George Devonshire St ⓣ01768/862696, ⓦww .lakedistricthotels.net/georgehotel. The traditional choice in Penrith is this atmospheric old coaching inn right in the centre. Refurbishment has brought most of the rooms up to three-star standard and, though some can be a bit of a squeeze, the gloriously old-fashioned public areas compensate – there are cosy wood-panelled lounges with roaring fires, rustic bric-a-brac and armchairs you could hibernate in. Also a decent bar and restaurant – the sort of place where Cumbrian ladies-who-lunch come to take tea and sip sherry. Parking. ❻

Around Penrith

Crake Trees Manor Crosby Ravensworth, 15 miles southeast of Penrith, A6 via Shap or M6 junction 39 ⓣ01931/715205, ⓦwww .craketreesmanor.co.uk. It takes more effort to reach than most, but this gorgeous barn conversion B&B in the nearby Eden Valley is emphatically worth it. There are two rooms in the stylish, galleried family home, three round the courtyard, all with slate floors, antique beds, serious showers and thick towels. It's a working farm set in beautiful surroundings, and there are self-guided walks available right off the property. Help yourself to hot drinks and home-made biscuits in the house, where a fantastic breakfast (and evening meals, £25, by arrangement) are taken around an enormous oak table. There's a local pub or it's a 10min drive to Shap (on the A6) and the excellent bar meals at the *Greyhound*, or 25min to Penrith. Closed Jan & Feb. No smoking. Parking. ❺

Queen's Head Tirril, B5320, 2.5 miles southwest of Penrith ⓣ01768/863219, ⓦwww.queensheadinn.co.uk. The traditional village inn certainly looks the part, with its oak beams and stone flags, while half a dozen charming rooms upstairs have solid furniture and decent bathrooms. It's known for its food (most mains £9–12), which is on the traditional side – sausage and mash, home-made pies – though daily blackboard specials offer veggie, fish and other choices. And the beer is from its own brewery, bolstered by guest ales and forty malt whiskies. Parking. ❺

Eating, drinking and entertainment

The best of the **cafés and restaurants** are highlighted below, while for picnic food and local produce the fantastically stocked J. & J. Graham's deli-grocery in Market Square (closed Sun) can't be beaten. Penrith **pubs** are a bit of a disappointment, save perhaps the *Agricultural Hotel*, at the top of Castlegate, near the castle, which has a good selection of real ales. The local **cinema**, the Alhambra, is on Middlegate (ⓣ01768/862400), next to the tourist office.

Penrith is the regional arts and music hub. **Penrith Playhouse** on Auction Mart Lane at the top of Castlegate (box office information from the tourist office) puts on theatrical productions throughout the year and also hosts regular rock, folk and blues **gigs** sponsored by Plug & Play (ⓦwww.plug-play.co.uk). A three-day annual music festival, **Edenfest**, takes place each summer (usually Aug) in the Deer Park, off the A6 at Brougham, with separate days devoted to jazz/blues, indie and family/tribute bands. The sixty-year-old **Penrith Music Club**, meanwhile, hosts monthly classical concerts and recitals (Sept–April) in town. **Eden Arts** (ⓣ01768/899444, ⓦwww.edenarts.co.uk) has details of other events in town and throughout the region – one of the more unusual shows is **Potfest in the Pens** (ⓦwww.potfest.co.uk), an annual exhibition (August) of ceramics in the sheep and cattle auctions mart, just outside town on the A66.

Costa's 9 Queen St ☎ 01768/895550. Tapas bar and Spanish restaurant where you can just snack and drink, or tuck into charcoal-grilled meat and fish specials. Dinner only; closed Mon. Moderate.

⚒ Gate Inn Yanwath, B5320, 2 miles south of Penrith ☎ 01768/862386, ⍾ www .yanwathgate.com. Trading as an inn for over 300 years, and looking very much the part, the *Gate* has reinvented itself as a gastro-pub *par excellence*. Lunch might be a wild venison burger or a bowl of seafood chowder, while dinner combines locally sourced ingredients with more than a dollop of imagination – say native oysters dressed with soy and spring onion, or bubble-and-squeak and wild mushrooms served with Cumbrian cheese. Add regional beers and a choice of a dozen wines by the glass, and you've got the best informal dining for many miles. Lunch moderate, Dinner expensive.

Listings

Bookshops Bluebell Bookshop, Angel Sq ☎ 01768/866660, is a great local bookshop with coffee and cakes upstairs.
Bike rental Arragon's Cycle Centre, Brunswick Rd ☎ 01768/890344, ⍾ www.arragonscycles.com.
Car rental Westmorland Vehicle Hire, Ullswater Rd Garage ☎ 01768/864546, ⍾ www.carhirecumbria .co.uk.
Emergencies Penrith New Hospital, Bridge Lane, Penrith ☎ 01768/245300.
Internet access At Penrith Library, Devonshire Arcade ☎ 01768/242100 (Mon, Tues & Fri 9.30am–7pm, Wed 9.30am–1pm, Thurs 9.30am–5pm, Sat 9.30am–4pm).

Grant's of Castlegate 54 Castlegate ☎ 01768/895444. Wine bar-bistro that's attracting a loyal local following for its casual ambience and range-the-world menu (savoury pancakes to Thai-style prawns). There's a shorter, simpler, cheaper menu at lunch (mains £5–7), otherwise dinner dishes average £11–15. Closed Mon & Tues. Moderate.
Number 15 15 Victoria Rd ☎ 01768/867453. The food's very good in this stripped-wood, veggie-friendly café and gallery – there's a Mediterranean-style menu, which uses local organic produce where possible. Daytime only. Inexpensive.
Villa Bianca Corney Sq ☎ 01768/862221. Italian restaurant in characterful cottage surroundings. Friendly service and decent prices for pizza (the "Villa Bianca" comes with rocket and Parma ham) and pasta make this a good choice for fill-me-up dining. Moderate.

Laundry The Dolly Tub, 5 West Lane (daily 8am–7pm ☎ 01768/868081).
Pharmacies Boots, 3 Grahams Lane ☎ 01768/862735; Lightfoot's, 8 Middlegate ☎ 01768/862695.
Police station Hunter Lane ☎ 0845/330 0247.
Post office Crown Sq (Mon–Fri 9am–5.30pm, Sat 9am–12.30pm).
Swimming pool Penrith Leisure Centre, Southend Rd ☎ 01768/863450, ⍾ www.leisure-centre.com. Also has a climbing wall, gym, bowling and café. Public admission hours vary; check the website or call for details.
Taxis A. Taxis ☎ 01768/863354; Express ☎ 01768/890890; Lakeland ☎ 01768/865722.

Rheged

Rheged (daily 10am–5.30pm; general admission and parking free; ☎ 01768/868000, ⍾ www.rheged.com) – a Cumbrian "visitor experience", just outside Penrith – is a good place to bring children, especially if it's pouring down outside. Sited in a disused limestone quarry, and billed as Europe's largest earth-covered building, it's designed to blend in with the surrounding fells, which it does admirably – from the main road you wouldn't know it was there. It's at Redhills, on the A66, half a mile west of the M6 (junction 40); bus #X4/X5 (between Penrith and Keswick/Cockermouth) calls at the centre.

It takes its name from the ancient kingdom of Cumbria, which once stretched from Strathclyde in Scotland as far south as Cheshire. Inside, an impressive atrium-lit underground visitor centre fills you in on the region's history by way of a giant-format cinema screen showing a specially commissioned film (*Rheged: The Lost Kingdom*). Most visitors try to coincide with this or one of the other films (see p.246), but there are plenty of other distractions, all aiming to showcase

△ Rheged

the best of Cumbria, so you'll also find souvenir shops, galleries displaying arts and crafts, seasonal exhibitions and events, workshops, demonstrations and play areas. There's a farmer's market here, too, held on the last Sunday of the month throughout winter.

Anyone even remotely interested in mountaineering shouldn't miss the separate **National Mountaineering Exhibition** at Rheged, celebrating British mountaineering achievement from the very early days. Its centrepiece is an exhibition on the 1953 Everest climb, while other displays home in on historic artefacts (including the ice axe belonging to the first person to climb the Matterhorn) or the development of climbing equipment. Local characters are remembered too, none more important in advertising the early sport than the Abraham brothers of Keswick, whose 1897 camera and tripod are on display. If you think the equipment looks cumbersome to operate on the level, bear in mind they had to carry it up the fells to get their pictures. Your ticket gets you a sit-down in the tent-like Summit Theatre to watch a film about the Hillary and Tensing expedition of 1953, complete with howling wind and dropping temperatures in the theatre just to get you in the mood.

For a different view of Everest, you can also buy a ticket to see the thrilling large-format film, *Everest*, a staple of IMAX theatres around the world and shown throughout the day on the Rheged big screen. There are presentations of this, and half a dozen other films (*Vikings*, the *Grand Canyon* and so on), throughout the day on the hour from 11am. **Admission** to one film or entrance to the National Mountaineering Exhibition costs £5.95, while seeing each extra film costs £4. There's an atrium **café** for soups, sandwiches, pizza and grills, though the finer dining is at the horseshoe bar of the contemporary "food hall" known as *Taste*, which specializes in regional Cumbrian foods and dishes. If you can't find something here to take home (sticky-toffee pudding, smoked venison, Cumbrian cheese, damson gin), you're not trying.

Contexts

Contexts

History

The Lake District remained a land apart for centuries, its features – rugged and isolated – mirrored in the characteristics of its inhabitants. Daniel Defoe thought it "eminent only for being the wildest, most barren and frightful of any that I have passed over" – and, as he went on to point out, he'd been to Wales so he knew what he was talking about. Two factors spurred the first waves of tourism: the reappraisal of landscape brought about by such painters as Constable and the writings of Wordsworth and his contemporaries, and the outbreak of the French Revolution and its subsequent turmoil, which put paid to the idea of the continental Grand Tour. Later, as tourism to the Lakes was cemented by the arrival of the railway, Wordsworth – while bemoaning mass travel – wrote in his *Guide to the Lakes* that he desired "a sort of national property, in which every man has a right and interest who has an eye to perceive and a heart to enjoy". His wish finally came to fruition in 1951 when the government established the Lake District as England's largest national park. It's subsequently become one of the most visited parts of England.

Early times

Although human habitation is relatively recent, geologically speaking the Lake District is extremely old. The rocks which make up the Skiddaw and Blencathra massif consist of 500-million-year-old slate, while 100 million years later occurred the immense volcanic activity which shaped the high central mountains. The granite outcrops visible at Ennerdale and Eskdale were formed 350 million years ago. Later still, a tropical sea covered the region (320 million years ago) whose shell remains formed the ubiquitous limestone and sandstone.

At the heart of the region is Scafell, the remnant of a volcanic dome that had already been weathered into its present craggy shape before the last **Ice Age**, when glaciers flowed off its flanks to gouge their characteristic U-shaped valleys. As the ice withdrew, moraines of sediment dammed the meltwater, creating the main lakes, all of which radiate from Scafell's hub – Wordsworth, in a famous image, described them as immense spokes. The gentler terrain to the south was formed after this main burst of activity, with subsequent mini ice ages (the last around 12,000 years ago) gouging out smaller tarns, flattening the valley bottoms and modifying the shape and scale of the mountains. Consequently, the Lake District as it appears today comprises a huge variety of terrains and geological material within a compact region.

The first humans

Human interaction has also played a significant part in the shaping of the Lake District. Before **Neolithic peoples** began to colonize the region around 5000 years ago, most of the now bare uplands were forested with pine and birch, while the valleys were blanketed with thickets of oak, alder, ash and elm. As these first settlers learned to shape flints into axes, they began to clear the upland forests for farmland – remnants of shaped stone axes have been found in so-called "factory" sites on Pike of Stickle (in Langdale) and on the slopes of Scafell. During the later **Stone and Bronze ages**, the subsistence existence of Lake District settlers is unlikely to have changed much. Their hunter-gatherer lifestyle was augmented by early stock-rearing and planting, though evidence of their lives is sketchy. Bronze tools and weapons have been found (around Ambleside, Keswick and St John's in the Vale), though few burial or settlement sites have been pinpointed. The **stone circles** at Castlerigg (near Keswick), Melmerby (near Penrith) and at Swinside (near Duddon Bridge) are the region's most important sites and even the purpose of these is unclear. Some have suggested they had a time-keeping function or were used for religious purposes; others that the circles were a commercial focus or meeting place. What's clear is the high degree of cooperation between people required to erect the stones in the first place.

By the third century BC, **Celtic peoples** from the south and east were pushing into the region. From their hillfort settlements (like that on Carrock Fell) they exploited the local metal deposits and employed advanced farming techniques. Sophisticated religious practices (including burial) and basic systems of law and communal defence (against raiders from the north) were established features of their lives by the time the Romans arrived in Britain in 55 BC.

The Romans and Celts

The **arrival of the Romans** in the north of England after 69 AD led to the first large-scale alteration of the region's landscape. **Hadrian's Wall**, from the Tyne to the Solway Firth – marking the northern limit of the Roman Empire – was completed by 130 AD. Associated with the wall were roads, forts and supply routes which cut through the heart of the Lakes. There are the remains of fortresses still to be seen at Hardknott Pass and at Waterhead, near Ambleside, while Roman roads can be traced between Kendal and Ravenglass and, most obviously, from Troutbeck to Brougham (near Penrith) along the ridge known as High Street.

The roads and forts were principally a means of subduing the local population. Throughout the Roman period the Lake District was essentially a **military zone**, policed by auxiliaries (recruited from all parts of the Roman Empire) rather than true legionnaires. However, around the bases grew **civilian settlements** as at Ambleside – which formed the basis of later towns and villages. Lead-mining was first practised during Roman times, while upland forests continued to be replaced by agricultural land as cereal crops were planted to supply the various permanent settlements. At Ravenglass, on the Cumbrian coast, are the extant remains of a bathhouse, part of a fort which survived in Ravenglass until the fourth century.

In the face of constant raids and harassment, England had become irrevocably detached from what remained of the Roman Empire by the start of the fifth century AD. The original **Celtic inhabitants** of the northwest had never fully abandoned their traditions and practices in the face of Roman might, and surviving Celtic place names (Derwent, Blencathra) indicate strong local ties. Indeed, from the Celts comes the word they used to describe themselves – *Cymry* – from which derives the modern place name Cumbria. **Christianity** secured an enduring toehold in the region too. St Kentigern (or Mungo), the Celtic missionary, founded several churches in the region, passing through Crosthwaite in Keswick in 553 AD.

The Saxon and Norse invasions

The **Saxon invasion** of England's south and east during the sixth century initially had little impact on the Lake District, which slowly fell under the control of the newly established **kingdom of Northumbria**. However, place-name evidence does suggest that Saxon farmers later settled on the lakeland fringes – names ending in "ham" and "ton" betray a Saxon influence, as does the suffix "-mere" attached to a lake.

A greater impact was made by **Norse (ie Norwegian) Vikings** during the ninth and tenth centuries. Although they eventually supplanted much of the native lakeland population, it would be wrong to see the Norse arrival as a violent invasion. Unlike the Danes, who had sacked Lindisfarne on the east coast in 793, the Norse invasion was less brutal, with Viking settlers (rather than warriors) gradually filtering into the Lake District from their established bases in Scotland, Ireland and the Isle of Man. They farmed the land extensively and left their indelible mark on the northern dialect – dale, fell, force, beck, tarn and the suffix "-thwaite" (a clearing) all have Norse origins. Physical remains are scarce, the finest example being the splendid Norse cross in the churchyard at Gosforth, which combines Pagan and Christian elements in a style reminiscent of similar crosses in Ireland and the Isle of Man. By the end of the eleventh century, wherever they originated, Lakelanders were living in small farming communities in recognized shires, or administrative districts, whose names survived for the next nine hundred years: Cumberland and Westmorland.

However, the region began to be disputed in a burgeoning number of turf wars between rival kingdoms. **Dunmail**, a Cumbrian warlord, was defeated in battle in 945 by the Saxon **King Edmund**, who granted control of the region to the kings of Scotland. This heralded six hundred years of political manoeuvring, between Scottish kings keen to push the border south and, after the Conquest, Norman rulers intent upon holding the line at Carlisle. The Lakes themselves, and their farming communities, were largely left alone as the opposing armies marched north and south, but the northern and western lowlands became a cross-border battleground. Castles at Cockermouth, Penrith and Kendal attest to the constant political threat, while raiding "**reivers**" or local clans made the borderlands ungovernable.

Medieval and Elizabethan times

By medieval times, most of the Lake District's **traditional industries** had been firmly established. The native breed of sheep, the Herdwick (black, with white faces), had proved itself a hardy species since at least Roman times, surviving harsh winters on the fells, while in summer cropping the hills of their wild flowers and preventing the regeneration of the woodland. **Religious houses** bordering the Lake District, such as Furness Abbey in the south, Carlisle in the north and St Bees in the west, came to hold large rural areas, establishing outlying farms – or "granges" – which further exploited the land. The **wool** produced found its way into markets throughout Europe and beyond, with **packhorse routes** meandering across the region to and from market towns such as Kendal, Keswick, Penrith and Cockermouth. The monks also maintained woods, or **coppices**, whose timber they used to produce charcoal (for iron-smelting) and bark (used in tanneries). The **dissolution of the monasteries** in 1536 had little effect on these industries. The new crown tenants and the emerging "**statesman" farmers**, who bought their own small-holdings, merely continued the age-old practices, denuding the uplands further with every passing year.

Mining was also altering the contours of the land. Plumbago, or graphite, had been discovered in Borrowdale and in 1564 Elizabeth I gave royal assent to an Anglo-German venture to exploit the ore – invaluable for pencil-making, glazing, black-leading iron weapons (to stop them rusting) and making casting moulds for cannon bore and shot. German miners settled in Keswick, while locals found employment in providing lodging, transport and charcoal. Later, copper mining took hold in the Keswick and Coniston areas, while slate quarrying in Borrowdale had always taken place on a local basis and was to boom in later centuries. For most people, though, **domestic life** probably altered very little for three hundred years – clothes were still produced locally, while primitive agricultural methods and poor land kept yields relatively low. The general diet was largely unchanged since Viking times, based around oatmeal cakes or porridge, bread and cheese – potatoes weren't widely cultivated until the eighteenth century. Increasingly, however, houses were being built of durable stone (rather than turf and timber) and many of the Lake District's farms and cottages – including notable examples such as Townend at Troutbeck – can trace their origins back as far as the seventeenth century.

The Picturesque and the Romantic

Until the eighteenth century, it was difficult to persuade the wider world – or at least fashionable England – that the Lake District had anything to offer. Indeed, the old county of Cumberland (containing the northern part of the Lake District) was viewed as a dangerous, unstable corner of the kingdom, too close to lawless Scotland for comfort. William, Duke of Cumberland, the "butcher" son of George II, put down the Jacobite rebellion of 1745, and the fortified towers and castles on the lakeland periphery tell their own story of border raids and skirmishes.

A sea change occurred with the advent of the so-called **Picturesque Movement** in the late eighteenth century, when received notions of beauty shifted from the classical to the natural. Vivid, irregular landscapes were the fashion amongst writers and artists, and it was with a palpable sense of excite-ment that the era's style arbiters discovered such landscapes on their doorstep. The poet **Thomas Gray** made the first of two visits in 1767 and recorded his favourable impressions in his journal (published in 1775), while in 1778 **Thomas West** produced the first guidebook dedicated solely to the region, waxing lyrical about the "Alpine views and pastoral scenes in a sublime style". These, and a dozen other books or treatises touching on the Lake District published during the 1770s, merely reinforced the contemporary Romantic view that contact with nature promoted artistic endeavour and human develop-ment. **Thomas Gainsborough, J.M.W. Turner** and, later, **John Constable** were all eager visitors to the Lakes, and all drew inspiration from what they saw. The first visitors were encouraged to view the mountains and lakes in a methodical manner – from particular "stations" (ie viewpoints) and through a "claude glass" (or convex mirror) to frame the views.

The pre-eminent Romantic, **William Wordsworth**, was born in Cockermouth in 1770, moving to Dove Cottage outside Grasmere in 1799 and, in 1813, to nearby Rydal Mount. He became the centre of a famous, if fluctuating, literary circle – not only one of the so-called **Lake Poets** with **Samuel Taylor Coleridge** and **Robert Southey**, but also friend of the critic, essayist and opium eater **Thomas De Quincey** and of the writer **John Wilson** ("Christopher North" of *Blackwood's Magazine*). Wordsworth's own *Guide to the Lakes* – a mature distillation of all his thoughts on nature and beauty – was first published in 1810 and had gone through four further editions by 1835.

The eighteenth and nineteenth centuries

The **Industrial Revolution** didn't so much pass the Lake District by as touch its periphery. Carlisle was a cotton manufacturing town of some repute, while the coastal ports became important shipping centres and depots for nearby coal and iron industries. Georgian Whitehaven was Britain's third-busiest port for a time in the late eighteenth century; Barrow-in-Furness is still an important shipbuilding town.

Within the Lakes themselves, sheep farming remained the mainstay of the economy. Textile production still tended to take the form of homespun wool, as it had for centuries. However, the manufacture of wooden **bobbins** for the northwest's cotton mills later became an important local industry. There were also improvements in farming as turnips were introduced widely as a crop, which meant that cattle and sheep could be kept alive throughout the winter. Meanwhile, the French Revolution and the ensuing **Napoleonic Wars** (1803–15) not only precluded European travel (in part explaining the growing popularity of the Lakes with the English gentry) but also pushed food prices higher. As a consequence, farmers began to reclaim the once-common land of the hillsides, a tendency sanctioned by the General Enclosure Act of 1801. Most of the region's characteristic dry-stone walls were built at this time.

Copper mining at Coniston became increasingly important, as did **slate quarrying** at Honister Pass and around Elterwater. The still-visible scars, shafts and debris on the Old Man of Coniston and at Honister Pass are evidence of these booming trades.

Transport and communications improved slowly. Roads and packhorse routes that had been barely altered since Roman times saw improvement following the passing of the Turnpike Acts in the 1750s. High passes opened up to the passage of stagecoaches, while England's burgeoning canal system reached Kendal in 1819. The **railway age** arrived late, with early railway lines associated with the mining and quarrying industries. The first passenger line, in 1847, connected Kendal with Windermere – and prompted a furious battle with the elderly Wordsworth who, having spent years inviting appreciation of the Lake District by outsiders, now raged against the folly of making the region easier to visit. Not only was it easier to visit, but after 1869 the Lake District even had its very own indigenous candy to sweeten the tooth of visitors – **Kendal Mintcake**, a peppermint candy that's been the mainstay of climbing expeditions ever since. It's still made in Kendal today.

With the passing of Southey (1843) and Wordsworth (1850), the mantle of local literary endeavour passed to writer **Harriet Martineau**, who lived at Ambleside between 1845 and 1876, and to social philosopher and critic **John Ruskin**, who settled at Brantwood near Coniston in 1872. Meanwhile, a seemingly endless succession of men and women of letters continued to visit or take a house, pronounce upon and then write about the region – **Sir Walter Scott**, **Percy Bysshe Shelley**, **Matthew Arnold**, **Alfred (Lord) Tennyson**, **Thomas Carlyle**, **George Eliot**, **Charlotte Brontë**, **Ralph Waldo Emerson** and **Nathaniel Hawthorne** all spent various periods in the Lake District. **Charles Dickens** and **Wilkie Collins** came together and climbed Carrock Fell, a trip recounted in Dickens' *Lazy Tour of Two Idle Apprentices* (1857).

The twentieth century: protecting the Lake District

Some of those who made a career of boosting the Lake District were also among the first to notice that two thousand years of farming and two hundred years of industrialization were taking their toll. Ruskin's unsuccessful campaign to prevent the damming of Thirlmere was just one example of an increased **environmental awareness** which manifested itself most obviously in the **creation of the National Trust** in 1895. Ruskin's disciple, Octavia Hill, and a Keswick clergyman, Canon Rawnsley, were the Trust's co-founders (with Rawnsley its first secretary) – Brandlehow Woods on Derwent Water's western shore was the Trust's first purchase in the Lakes (1902). The Trust is now the largest landholder in the Lake District, gaining early impetus from the generous bequests of **Beatrix Potter**, who has probably done more than anyone – after Wordsworth – to popularize the region through her children's stories.

The **formation of the Forestry Commission** in 1919 presented another threat to the natural landscape as afforestation gathered pace, turning previously bare valleys and fellsides into thick conifer plantations. Successful environmental battles in the 1930s limited the scope of the plantations, but afforestation is still an emotive subject today.

Similarly, **water extraction** had long fuelled fears for the landscape. The Lake District has been used as a water source for northwestern England since Thirlmere was dammed in 1892. Construction at Haweswater in the 1930s raised the water level there by ninety feet – and drowned a village in the process. (Ennerdale Water still supplies the coastal towns and as late as 1980 there were serious proposals to raise levels there and at Wast Water in an attempt to drain more water for industrial use.)

Legal protection of the Lake District was, therefore, long overdue by the time of the establishment in 1951 of the **Lake District National Park**, spreading over 885 square miles. For the first time, there was to be direct control over planning, building and development within the Lake District, as well as systematic maintenance of the footpaths, bridleways, dry-stone walls, open land and historic monuments. The widely recognized National Park emblem – the outline of Great Gable – was adopted in 1953, and the Queen made the first royal visit to the park in 1956.

The National Park: the first fifty years

The establishment of the National Park didn't, of course, end the threats to the social and natural environment of the Lake District, but it did provide the framework to defend the region from mass commercialism and development. Even so, many of the current problems facing the National Park were signalled in its earliest years.

As rationing ended and the privations of the postwar years were reduced, the number of leisure visitors increased dramatically. The first dedicated car park, at Tarn Hows, was established in 1954, while traffic in the National Park doubled in the five years until 1959. The number of caravan sites increased and there were early worries about litter on the fells and other obtrusive irritants. In the 1960s, speed restrictions were imposed on Derwent Water, Ullswater and Coniston for the first time and the first full-time park warden was employed as tourism to the Lakes became a year-round phenomenon. The house at **Brockhole**, near Windermere, was acquired in 1966 and opened in 1969 as the country's first National Park Visitor Centre. Meanwhile, in 1974, centuries of tradition were abandoned when local government reorganization resulted in the scrapping or reduction of the old counties of Cumberland, Westmorland and Lancashire: the Lake District became part of the new county of **Cumbria**.

During the 1970s and 1980s, **conservation** became the new watchword as visitor numbers steadily increased, fuelled in part by the extension of the M6 motorway to Penrith. Car park charges were introduced for the first time, to provide revenue and deter drivers; meanwhile, footpath erosion had become a major problem in many areas. Attempts were made to educate visitors about the impact of their presence on the lakes and landscape – information centres were opened at Keswick, Bowness Bay and Seatoller among others, while 10mph limits were imposed on craft using Derwent Water, Ullswater and Coniston. Cars were kept out of ancient villages such as Hawkshead, whose centre became pedestrianized, and the centre of Ambleside became the Lakes' first formal conservation area.

However, the underlying fragility of the park's ecosystem was exposed in 1986, after the accident at the nuclear power station at Chernobyl in the Soviet Union. Radioactive fallout contaminated Cumbrian soil, acting as a reminder – if one were needed – of the danger on the Lakes' own doorstep presented by the presence of the **Sellafield nuclear-reprocessing plant**, near Ravenglass, symbol of all that threatens the local environment.

Great strides were made during the 1990s to address some of the most fundamental problems facing the National Park. Coordinated traffic management and erosion control schemes were formulated, which began to have a significant effect on the environment. In 1993, Bassenthwaite became the first lake in Britain to be declared a National Nature Reserve and, in the same year, the Lake District Environmentally Sensitive Area (ESA) was established to protect traditional buildings and landscapes. Upland farmers – struggling with the downturn in their industry, and affected by the BSE crisis and other health scares – were given grants to maintain dry-stone walls and hedgerows, renovate traditional buildings and stock wildflower meadows.

The Lakes today

The National Park celebrated its half-centenary in 2001, with its successes balanced equally against its numerous challenges. There's no doubt that it's been a force for good – for example, defending the lakes from over-exploitive water extraction and preventing mass development in scenic areas. But, at times, it seems as if it's fighting a losing battle with the wider problems facing rural England as a whole.

Hill farming everywhere is in crisis, with farmers unable to turn a profit on their animals. In the Lake District, the unproductive nature of much of the land means that hill farming is basically undertaken at subsistence level, and would hardly be possible at all without European Union and central government subsidies. Prices for sheep and cattle halved in the late 1990s, and just when it looked like things couldn't get any worse, Cumbria was hardest hit of all English counties by the **foot and mouth crisis** of 2001. As their animals were burned on pyres, farmers watched their incomes disappear – along with the tourists who were asked to keep away from infected areas as footpaths and farms were closed. Related businesses – rural accommodation, cafés, local attractions and activity centres – all suffered a drastic loss in trade. Although many Cumbrian farms subsequently restocked, replacing the many thousands of animals slaughtered in the government's programme to contain the disease, not all businesses survived. The truth is, there were probably too many farms trying to make a living in inauspicious economic circumstances (a deep-rooted problem for British farming as a whole) and no amount of diversification – from camping barns to pony rides – could save some businesses from going under.

In a region where **hunting with hounds** dates back to Norman times, local concern about the fate of agriculture also manifested itself in solid support for the pro-hunting "Countryside Alliance" cause. The government's 2005 ban on hunting foxes and other wildlife with dogs caused much anger in Cumbria though, despite dire warnings at the time, none of the local hunts has closed. The hunts instead now meet – within the law – for trail-hunting, though as they generally use fox urine as the trail scent (rather than aniseed), it's clear that hounds in England are being kept accustomed to fox scent in the event of the ban being overturned (either by the European Court of Human Rights or a future change of government). Hardly surprisingly, there are constant reports of foxes being "accidentally" killed by hunts that flush them out in the course of their trail-hunt.

Another flash point is the necessary **development restrictions** imposed by the National Park Authority, the National Trust (which owns a quarter of the land) and the district councils, which – to many locals – seem only to conspire against people from making a living on "their" land. At the same time, second-homers from the towns and cities ("off-comers" in the local parlance) push up **housing** prices, thus forcing the lakeland youth away from home and from the land – in line with other rural British holiday regions, it's estimated that a fifth of all Lake District houses are second or holiday homes. The situation was exacerbated by the council-house sales of the 1980s which further reduced the availability of affordable housing stock. But housing pressure has been a constant problem since the inception of the National Park, when early planning applicants first submitted plans to convert old barns into accommodation.

Indeed, the National Park faces its own pressures since, as a destination, it's simply too successful for its own good. At its first meeting in 1951, the authority dealt with fifteen planning applications. Today, it deals with over 1200 a year. A local population of just 42,000 is swamped by annual **visitor numbers** topping twelve million, with all the traffic and environmental pressure that that entails – it's estimated that 89 percent of visitors currently arrive in the National Park in a private motor vehicle. Expanded bus services, the promotion of cycling and an integrated **transport strategy** are starting to have some effect, but it's a long haul to persuade people to leave their cars at home. Around 350 **voluntary wardens** help manage the environment (patrolling lakeshores, maintaining footpaths, planting trees, restoring hedgerows and rebuilding stone walls), but they are faced with an exponential increase in leisure activities which impinge directly upon the Park's habitats – such as mountain biking, ghyll scrambling, four-wheel-drive safaris and water sports. The long-running and contentious saga of speed restrictions, on Windermere presented the park authorities with the classic dilemma of balancing business needs with those of the environment. Water-sports companies and related businesses fought a long campaign against the restriction but since 2005 powered craft on England's largest lake has been restricted to 10mph.

On the land, the 2005 CRoW Act, giving a statutory "right to roam" across open countryside, has provided new rights for the public while safeguarding the landscape and wildlife. Over fifty percent of the National Park area is open for public access: more than two thousand miles of **paths and bridle ways** are virtually all clear of obstructions and some have been made suitable for wheelchair users and pushchairs. Erosion control is well in hand on all the most popular walking routes. **Employment** initiatives are working to provide more opportunities for local people, not just in tourism and hospitality, but also in the retail, small business and technology industries.

Projects designed to preserve some of the Lake District's most **threatened species** (such as the red squirrel, otter and the water vole) are under way and new native woodlands are being established. **The Lake District Environmentally Sensitive Area** (ESA), set up in 1993 and covering almost the entire National Park, provides the supportive framework for traditional farm buildings to be restored, hedges and orchards replanted, and moorland and riverbanks protected. Over one hundred Sites of Special Scientific Interest (SSSIs) cover another sixteen percent of the Park, and there are eight National Nature Reserves (NNRs), and another eighty-odd Regionally Important Geological Sites. Conservation, at last, is being made fundamental to the National Park's wellbeing; the future challenge is to extend the same protection to lakeland traditions and the way of life.

Books

We've highlighted a selection of books below which will give you a flavour of Lake District life, past and present, as well as the impressions of the visitors, writers and poets who have toured and settled in the region. As a glance in any bookshop will show you, there are hundreds of Lake District titles available. We've concentrated on titles of interest to the general reader (which discounts most of the academic literary criticism of the Lake Poets) and those most useful to the non-specialist visitor – for rare historical monographs, mountain-climbing guides, lavish limited-edition pop-up Beatrix Potter books and other arcana, consult a specialist bookshop or the comprehensive website of the Internet bookseller **Amazon**: ⓦwww.amazon.co.uk in the UK, ⓦwww.amazon.com in the US. **Books Cumbria** (ⓦwww.bookscumbria.com) is a very handy source for locally published, out-of-print, rare or otherwise esoteric books about the Lake District and Cumbria. Two useful **publishers** are Frances Lincoln (ⓦwww.franceslincoln.com), now responsible for all the Wainwright walking guides, plus other lakeland titles, and Cicerone (ⓦwww.cicerone.co.uk), who specialize in walking, climbing, scrambling and cycling guides. Books marked o/p are **out of print**, though many of those covered below are available in secondhand and antiquarian bookshops in the region.

Lakeland life, history and nature

Richard Askwith *Feet in the Clouds*. If you've ever been passed on a mountain by wiry people running uphill, very quickly, and wondered quite how barmy they must be – here's your answer. Askwith's painful and obsessive quest to join the ranks of the hardest-of-the-hard fell runners manages to be both insightful and funny at the same time. It's a sports book, certainly, but only in the same way as *Fever Pitch* or *Touching the Void*.

Hunter Davies *A Walk Around the Lakes; London to Loweswater; Strong Lad Wanted for Strong Lass*. The journalist, biographer and author Davies takes every opportunity to plug the Lakes in print. His account of a walk around the region is an entertaining mix of anecdote, history and reportage, while in *London to Loweswater* (and inspired by J.B. Priestley's *English Journey* of 1934) Davies spends a year travelling from London to his Lake District home, reflecting on his own past and the

state of the nation. *Strong Lad Wanted for Strong Lass*, meanwhile, is his wry account of growing up in Carlisle in the 1950s.

A.H. Griffin *A Lifetime of Mountains*; *The Coniston Tigers*; and others. The veteran lakelander climber, writer, journalist and *Guardian* newspaper country diarist, Harry Griffin (1911–2004) produced a dozen volumes that range around the fells with a keen eye for nature and tradition. Although the early books, written in the 1960s and 1970s, are mostly out of print (*Inside the Real Lakeland*, *In Mountain Lakeland*, *Pageant of Lakeland* etc), the best of his *Guardian* diary pieces are collected in *A Lifetime of Mountains* while *The Coniston Tigers* (1999) is a climbing and walking memoir recalling seventy years of mountain adventure.

Grevel Lindop *A Literary Guide to the Lake District*. Poet and critic Lindop's well-received guide to the Lakes presents five routes for walkers

258

and drivers, covering places associated not just with the Lake Poets, Beatrix Potter and the rest but literary visitors from Hardy to Lawrence. First published in 1993 but a revised edition appeared in 2005.

Norman Nicholson *The Lakers*; *Portrait of the Lakes* (o/p); *The Lake District: An Anthology* (o/p). Cumbria's best-known poet turned to prose with his informed, sympathetic studies of lakeland life, history, geology and people. The comprehensive *Anthology* is a joy, with extracts from writings of every period since the first visitors, and incorporating dialect verse, legends, letters and journals.

John Pepper *Cockley Beck*. Pepper happened upon a farm cottage in the Duddon Valley in the early 1980s, and spent several winters there, later writing a lyrical tribute to the countryside and local community which was first published in 1984 (with a new edition in 2006). Inspired in parts by Henry David Thoreau's account of a solitary rural retreat in *Walden*, it's a reflective, philosophical book that soon attracted the epithet "classic".

Nikolaus Pevsner *Cumberland and Westmorland*. The regional edition of Pevsner's renowned architectural guide to the old counties of England. First published in 1967 (when there was still a Cumberland and Westmorland, rather than Cumbria) and detailing every church, hall, house and cross worth looking at.

William Wordsworth *Guide to the Lakes*. The old curmudgeon's guide to the Lakes went through five editions between 1810 and 1835. This facsimile of the last, and definitive, edition is full of his prejudices (on the "colouring" of buildings, the shape of chimneys, forestation, the railway, the great unwashed) and timeless scenic observations.

John Wyatt *The Shining Levels*. Billed as "the story of a man who went back to nature", this was originally published in 1973 (and later reissued in 1993). John Waytt was brought up in industrial Lancashire but disowned city life to become a forest-worker, living in a woodsman's hut in the Lakes (he was later Head Warden for the National Park). Sleeping by the fire, coppicing, rabbit-hunting, searching for wild berries and nuts, adopting a roe deer – three decades later it reads as a heartfelt rural lament.

Landscape and photography

Bill Birkett *A Year in the Life of…the Langdale Valleys; Borrowdale; the Duddon Valley*. Birkett is well-known as a climber and walker (see "Walking guides" p.260), but he's also a respected mountain writer and photographer. Here he turns his camera on the lakeland valleys in his own backyard to provide stunning photographic essays of the seasonal landscapes, interspersed with features on local history, heritage, farming and nature.

John Boardman *Classic Landforms of the Lake District*. A thin volume (one of a series) published by the Geographical Association (@www.geography.org.uk) and aimed at explaining the landscape to general observers, covering topics like lakeland geology and valley formation.

Gilly Cameron Cooper *Beatrix Potter's Lake District*. A beautifully produced coffee-table book, presenting Potter as naturalist, farmer and conservationist, as well as seeking out the places that inspired her stories. The excellent photography is from the National Trust (with map references to help you track down the locations), and there are also reproduced Potter watercolours and illustrations, plus images from the 2007 *Miss Potter* film about her life.

Jim Watson *Lakeland Towns*; *Lakeland Villages*; *Lakeland Panoramas*. The first two titles are coffee-table format books covering all the lakes and towns and villages in chatty, anecdotal fashion, with the text accompanied by black-and-white pen-and-ink drawings and detailed hand-drawn maps. Not guidebooks as such (though walks and viewpoints are included), more background information and observations by the Penrith-born artist and cartoonist. His *Lakeland Panoramas* are Wainwright-style drawings presenting the widescreen view from the top of 49 easy-to-get-to viewpoints.

Walking guides

Bill Birkett *Complete Lakeland Fells*; *Lakeland Fells Almanac*; *Exploring the Lakes and Low Fells*. The *Complete* edition is the definitive, modern fell-walking reference guide from a leading Cumbrian mountain writer and photographer; classic walks to the top of 541 separate fells for all levels of walker. The *Almanac* distils the *Complete* fells into 129 circular walks taking in the tops, with maps, times and route details. Less adventurous walkers can tour the lake perimeters, tarns, valley bottoms, viewpoints and low fells in his company, too, using eighty easy-to-follow, half-day circular routes laid out clearly over two small-format hardback volumes of *Exploring the Lakes and Low Fells.*

Ian and Krysia Brodie *The Cumbria Coastal Way*. The first available guidebook to the 150-mile Cumbria Coastal Way (Morecambe Bay to the Solway Firth), which runs around the southern lakeland peninsulas and up the west Cumbrian coast to the Scottish border. Essential for day-walkers (the route can be walked in sections) and long-distance hikers alike.

Anthony Burton *The Cumbria Way*. This is the best guide to pack for the 72-mile Cumbria Way (Ulverston to Carlisle), which cuts right through the heart of the Lake District National Park. Durable format, clear walking instructions, Ordnance Survey map extracts, plus history and anecdotes.

Frank Duerden *Best Walks in the Lake District*. First published in 1986, but thoroughly revised in 2006, the forty well-conceived walks in this hefty pocket guide range from easy strolls to major full-day hikes in every area of the Lakes, complete with historical and descriptive background notes. Only sketch maps are included, but the walking instructions are very detailed, and it's particularly good on the dozen or so strenuous "horseshoe" routes that are among the Lake District's finest walks.

Eileen and Brian Evans *Short Walks in…North Lakeland*; *South Lakeland*; *West Lakeland*. A three-volume series of informative, nicely produced, pocket-sized walking guides which cover fifty half-day (four- to eight-mile) walks in each lakeland region, concentrating on the lower fells, valleys and woodlands. Some classic routes are included, but the emphasis is more on out-of-the-way tracks and secluded areas.

John and Anne Nuttall *The Tarns of Lakeland, Vol.1 (West)* and *Vol. 2 (East)*. Wainwright walked fells, the Nuttalls tackle tarns (mountain lakes), the little specks of blue in their own words – hundreds of them, across the Lake District, linked by forty walks in each volume that range from easy to hard. Obsessive? Clearly so, but you'll soon be seduced by the clear, hand-drawn route maps and walk details, handsome line drawings and interesting asides and anecdotes.

Pathfinder Guide *Lake District Walks; More Lake District Walks.* The best general guides for the day-pack: two slim volumes of walks, graded from short-and-easy to challenging, with useful accompanying text and clear Ordnance Survey map extracts.

W.A. Poucher *The Lakeland Peaks.* First published in 1960 and updated intermittently, Walter Poucher's classic guide for fell-walkers and peak-baggers has almost as many fans as the Wainwright volumes. The pocket-sized guide details 142 routes up fourteen separate mountain groups, accompanied by Poucher's impressive black-and-white landscape photographs (on which are superimposed the various summit routes).

Jim Reid *Tour of the Lake District.* A unique trekking guide to the Lakes that proposes a one- or two-week circular tour taking in the region's scenic valleys, passes and bridleways, rather than conquering peaks for their own sake.

Colin Shelbourn *Rocky Rambler's Wild Walks.* Put the children in charge of the route with this delightful ring-bound family walking guide, aimed at 6- to 14-year-olds. It contains ten colourfully illustrated short walks concentrated in the main tourist areas between Windermere, Coniston, the Ravenglass and Eskdale Railway, and Keswick. There are rhymes and riddles, and things to spot, and "grown ups can help but don't let them become a nuisance".

Graham Thompson *The Backpacker's Guide to the Lake District.* Covers forty two-day walks in the Lake District, an ideal companion for weekend hikers who want to experience the high fells. The walks are either circular or point-to-point, backed up by useful planning information and some fine photography.

A. Wainwright *A Pictorial Guide to the Lakeland Fells (7 vols); Lakeland Sketchbooks (5 vols); In the Valleys of Lakeland; On the Lakeland Mountain Passes; Favourite Lakeland Mountains; Fellwalking with Wainwright.* Wainwright's *Pictorial Guide* is his masterpiece: seven beautifully produced small-format volumes of handwritten notes and sketches (written between 1952 and 1966) guiding generations of walkers up the mountains of the Lake District. Wainwright refused any revision during his lifetime and the originals still stand as remarkable works, though all seven volumes are now being revised and updated to take account of changing routes and landscapes – volumes 1–4 are already complete. There are also five volumes of pen-and-ink lakeland sketchbooks, from the late 1960s and early 1970s, while later spin-off publications (most with superb photography by Derry Brabbs) include Wainwright in elegiac mood, holding forth on the majesty of lakeland mountains, passes and valleys.

Jim Watson *The Cumbria Way and the Allerdale Ramble.* Single-volume walking guide to the two long-distance trans-Lakes footpaths; in particular it's the best guide to the less-walked fifty-mile Allerdale Ramble (from Seathwaite in Borrowdale to the Solway Firth). It's a useful map-pocket-sized book and Watson's hand-drawn maps keep you company every step of the way.

Melvyn Bragg *Without A City Wall*; *The Silken Net*; *The Second Inheritance*; *For Want of a Nail*; *The Maid of Buttermere*; *The Cumbrian Trilogy*; *The Soldier's Return*; *A Son At War*; *Crossing the Lines*. The writer, broadcaster, professional Cumbrian (born in Wigton) and butt of Dame Edna Everage – "don't write any more, Melvyn dear, or we'll never catch up" – Bragg is at his historical best in *The Maid of Buttermere*, a fictionalized romantic tragedy involving one of the Lakes' most enduring heroines. *The Soldier's Return* and its sequels, *A Son At War* and *Crossing the Lines*, all very moving portraits of small-town life in the years after World War II, draw heavily on the experiences of his own family in Wigton. Other novels also lovingly explore the Cumbrian past and present, notably *The Cumbrian Trilogy* (comprising *The Hired Man*, *A Place in England* and *Kingdom Come*), which traces the lives of four generations of a Cumbrian family through the twentieth century.

Sarah Hall *Haweswater*. In the 1930s, as the remote village of Mardale is destined to be flooded to create Haweswater reservoir, all kinds of passions are released. Hall's lyrical first novel delves graphically into the lives and loves of a simple farming community attempting to come to terms with progress.

Reginald Hill *The Stranger House*. Prolific crime-writer Hill – creator of book and TV detective duo Dalziel and Pascoe – goes back to his native Cumbria in a hugely entertaining thriller. Two strangers arrive in the remote village of "Illthwaite" in "Skaddale", pursuing personal histories but soon becoming enmeshed in a web of past religious intrigue, child abuse, ghosts and murder. Hill claims the inn at the heart of the novel, the Stranger House, isn't based on any particular

Guidebooks

The first guidebook to the Lake District was written in the late eighteenth century and dozens more followed as the region opened up to people of leisure. Most of the earliest guides are long out of print, but a trawl through the stock in any local second-hand/antiquarian bookshop throws up old copies of other classic publications. They make interesting souvenirs, while you'll often find that the landscapes described have hardly changed in more than a century.

The earliest lakeland writings were contained in the journal of the poet **Thomas Gray**, first published as part of **Thomas West's** *Guide to the Lakes in Cumberland, Westmorland and Lancashire* (1778). In 1810, **William Wordsworth** wrote down his own observations, appearing in the most complete form as his *Guide to the Lakes* (1835), which, alone of all the historic guides, is still in print. His friend in later life, the writer and political observer **Harriet Martineau** of Ambleside, produced her own *Complete Guide to the English Lakes* (1855). Fifty years later, **W.G. Collingwood's** *The Lake Counties* (1902) set new standards of erudition, while **Canon H.D. Rawnsley** (founder of the National Trust) also found time to produce a multitude of lakeland volumes: *Round the Lake Country* (1909) is typical. Between 1904 and 1925, in the days before cheaply available colour photography, landscape watercolourist **Alfred Heaton Cooper** illustrated guidebooks for A. & C. Black; the Lake District titles are fairly easy to come by, as are the four lakeland books illustrated by his son **William Heaton Cooper**, starting with *The Hills of Lakeland* (1938). *The Lake Counties* (1937) volume in **Arthur Mee's** classic "King's England" series is widely available too.

hostelry, but the setting is clearly the western valleys of Eskdale and Wasdale, with their isolated churches, old halls, mountain tarns and Viking crosses.

Val McDermid *The Grave Tattoo*. What if Bounty mutineer Fletcher Christian didn't die on Pitcairn Island, but returned in secret to his native Lake District? And what if he told his tale to his childhood friend William Wordsworth – both were born in Cockermouth – who produced an epic poem on the subject, never yet found but potentially worth millions? Psychological thriller writer McDermid takes a few literary and historical facts and mixes them up with a dollop of speculation, intrigue and forensic science to produce a contemporary Lake District mystery that never quite shifts into top gear.

Magnus Mills *All Quiet on the Orient Express*. Strange goings-on in an unnamed lakeland community as the outsider-narrator is slowly sucked into the confused relationships of the hard-to-fathom locals. Great, and increasingly sinister, fun.

Hugh Walpole *Rogue Herries*; *Judith Paris*; *The Fortress*; *Vanessa*. Largely forgotten now, Walpole was a successful writer by the time he moved to the Lake District in 1923. He immersed himself in the local history to produce these four volumes covering two hundred years of the rip-roaring lives and loves of the Herries clan – too flowery for today's tastes but full of lakeland lore and life.

Children's books

Beatrix Potter *The Tale of Peter Rabbit*; *The Tale of Jemima Puddle-duck*; *The Tale of Squirrel Nutkin*; and many more. Rabbits, pigs, hedgehogs, mice and ducks in lakeland stories of valour, betrayal, adventure and romance. The original 23 titles (available individually or as *The Complete Tales* box set) have been ruthlessly merchandised since Potter's day – as colouring books, pop-up books, foam-filled fabric books, wallpaper, board games, diaries, calendars, etc – while the recent Renee Zellweger-Ewan McGregor biopic *Miss Potter* (about her life and the writing of the first book, *The Tale of Peter Rabbit*) has spawned even more spin-offs, from commemorative movie editions to audio CDs.

Arthur Ransome *Swallows and Amazons*; *Swallowdale*; *Winter Holiday*; *Pigeon Post*; *The Picts and the Martyrs*. Ransome's innocent childhood stories of pirates and treasure, secret harbours and outdoor camps, summer holidays and winter freezes still possess the power to entrance. The series starts with *Swallows and Amazons* (first published 1930), and there's no better evocation of the drawn-out halcyon days of childhood.

People

Juliet Barker *Wordsworth: A Life*. A very readable book by an author who gets right to the emotional heart of her subject's life and loves. Barker manages to make the irascible man of letters seem more human, even more likeable, as a consequence, and the evenly paced account of his quiet death, which came in 1850, is a moving read.

John Batchelor *John Ruskin: No Wealth But Life*. This book provides the best background material yet on Ruskin's life for the non-academic

263

reader. The subtitle is Ruskin's own evaluation of "wealth" and Batchelor conveys well Ruskin's journey from precocious child to visionary and moralist.

Hugh Brogan *Signalling From Mars: The Letters of Arthur Ransome.* Ransome's biographer adds flesh and bones to a fascinating man – Ransome was a journalist and Russian political expert before he was a children's writer – and gets to the bottom of the books' influences. The edited letters chart Ransome's life, marriages, sailing and writing career – a useful counterweight to Brogan's *The Life of Arthur Ransome* (o/p) and Ransome's own *Autobiography* (o/p).

A.S. Byatt *Unruly Times.* Authoritative, insightful study of Wordsworth and Coleridge "in their times", which charts their relationship, ideas, work and family situation against a lively backdrop of contemporary politics, society and culture.

Hunter Davies *Wainwright: The Biography; William Wordsworth.* Davies turns his informal, chatty style upon two of the Lake District's biggest enigmas. Hard biographical detail aside, there's not much to learn about the character of either man that a close reading of their respective works won't tell you already – but then that's not Davies's fault.

Richard Holmes *Coleridge: Early Visions; Coleridge: Darker Reflections.* The supreme account of the troubled genius of Coleridge, who emerges from Holmes's acclaimed two-volume biography as an animated intellectual and creative poet in his own right as well as the catalyst for Wordsworth's poetic development.

Linda Lear *Beatrix Potter: A Life in Nature.* Potter's is a life that's been largely overlooked by serious biographers, possibly down to snobbery about the perceived literary value of her works. But as this definitive biography (published 2007) makes abundantly clear, not only was she a pioneer children's writer (one of the first to see the potential in tie-in merchandising) but also an accomplished scientist, innovative farmer, businesswoman and conservationist. Lear argues that Potter reinvented herself several times over, moving from her early botanical drawings to children's books and finally to the farm, but always conscious of her "life in nature".

Kenneth R. Johnston *The Hidden Wordsworth.* For "hidden" read "young", as Johnston's controversial book focuses on the creation of the poet by examining his early life and work in exhaustively researched detail. The book ends in 1807 with more than half of Wordsworth's life yet to run, but the argument is that "his young life was his most important life". And along the way are sprinkled the controversies, with Wordsworth variously touted as lover, rebel and – most contentiously – spy.

Kathleen Jones *A Passionate Sisterhood.* Welcome feminist take on the lives of the sisters, wives and daughters of the Lake Poets, whose letters and journals reveal not quite the rustic idyll we've been led to expect by the poetry.

Thomas De Quincey *Confessions of an English Opium-Eater; Recollections of the Lakes and the Lake Poets.* Tripping out with the best-known literary drug-taker after Coleridge – "Fear and Loathing in Grasmere" it isn't, but neither is the *Confessions* a simple cautionary tale. The famous *Recollections* collected together magazine features De Quincey wrote in the 1830s, providing a highly readable, often catty, account of life in the Lakes with the Wordsworths, the Coleridges and Southey.

Mark Storey *Robert Southey: A Life*. Generally eclipsed by the shining lights of Coleridge and Wordsworth, Southey's reputation is somewhat rehabilitated by this biography. Although he's little known now, in his day Southey was a major man of letters, author of 45 books, and expert on Brazil, Portugal and Spain (not to mention surrogate father and husband to the Coleridge brood). In his own time, he was thought of primarily as a poet, his reputation established by *Joan of Arc* and subsequent epics and by his appointment as Poet Laureate. Despite his poetry, however, what has endured most is his clear, plain prose style – thought "perfect" by Byron – and his biographical history of Nelson. As Southey himself recognized, "I have done enough to be remembered among poets, though my proper place will be among the historians."

Andrew Wilson *An American President's Love Affair with the English Lake District.* The president in question is Woodrow Wilson (1865–1924), whose mother was born in Carlisle. He visited the Lake District five times between 1896 and 1908, cycling along Ullswater, staying in local inns and hotels, paying his respects at the literary shrines and discovering his Cumbrian roots. This definitive account traces Wilson's Cumbrian heritage and records his local tours and friendships, and is a handy companion if you want to retrace the presidential steps.

Dorothy Wordsworth *The Grasmere Journals*; *Home at Grasmere*. Was she a poet in her own right? Judge for yourself from the sharply observed descriptions of nature and day-to-day Grasmere life contained in the *Journals*. *Home at Grasmere* lets you see the debt Wordsworth owed his sister by placing journal entries and completed poetry side by side.

Poetry

Samuel Taylor Coleridge *Selected Poems*; *The Complete Poems*; *Critical Edition of the Major Works*. Final texts of all the poems in varying editions: the Penguin *Selected* (edited by his biographer Richard Holmes) also includes extracts from Coleridge's verse plays and prefaces; the Penguin *Complete* edition includes unfinished verses.

Norman Nicholson *Collected Poems*. The bard of Cumbria – who lived all his life in Millom, on the coast – produced five books of verse by the time of his death in 1987, collected here. He writes beautifully and movingly of his country, its trades, its past and its people.

William Wordsworth *The Prelude*; *Lyrical Ballads*; *Poetical Works*; *Selected Poems*. There are dozens of editions of the works of Wordsworth on the market, but these are the current pick. The major poems, sonnets and odes are all collected in *Selected Poems* (Penguin), which has the advantage of being a cheap, pocket-sized edition. For the full text of major works, you'll need *Lyrical Ballads* and *The Prelude* (both Penguin) – the latter presenting the four separate texts of 1798, 1799, 1805 and 1850. (Wordsworth revised his original, 1798, text three times, the last published after his death.) *Poetical Works* (OUP) contains every piece of verse ever published by Wordsworth.

Habitats of the Lake District

The Lake District National Park covers 880 square miles, or half a million acres – approximately one percent of Britain's land area. For such a relatively small region it has a highly varied landscape, geology and climate, and possesses a unique combination of spectacular mountains, rugged fells, pastoral and wooded valleys, and tarns, lakes and rivers. These physical aspects – climate, soil type, topography and altitude – influence the habitats for a rich selection of plants and animals, though other determining factors are at work too, including human and economic influences. This section gives a general introduction to the various habitats of the Lake District, including a rundown of the threats posed by modern agricultural methods and human encroachment. Each habitat description includes brief details of the flora and fauna found there, while some of the more prominent nature reserves in the National Park are also covered. For more information about local habitats and wildlife, don't miss the interesting exhibits at the Lake District Visitor Centre at Brockhole (see p.64).

Whichever habitat you encounter, it's crucial to realize that the landscape you see today bears little resemblance to that which has endured for most of the time since the last Ice Age. Five thousand years ago, for example, nearly all of Britain was covered in woodland. Over time, people began to clear selected fell areas for settlement and **agriculture**, which created new habitats as the previously almost unbroken tracts of forest were opened up. The process gained speed during the Norse settlement of the Lake District – place names ending in "thwaite" (signifying a clearing in the forest) are a clue to the changing landscape – and again during monastic times, with the rapid development of sheep farming. Since then, a "semi-natural" pattern of habitats has evolved, reflecting the area's strong history of farming. Indeed, in the absence of grazing and other management regimes, much of the land in the Lake District would revert to oak woodland – the so-called "climax vegetation".

Today's landscape and habitats within the Lake District National Park are heavily protected and maintained for future generations. There are currently eight **National Nature Reserves** (NNR), over a hundred **Sites of Special Scientific Interest** (SSSI), three **RAMSAR** sites (an internationally important wetland designation), two **European Special Protection Areas** (SPA) and 23 candidate **Special Areas of Conservation** (cSAC). In addition, in an attempt to combat the threat of agricultural intensification the Lake District National Park was designated an **Environmentally Sensitive Area** (ESA) in 1993. By providing them with financial incentives, farmers are encouraged to reduce chemical inputs such as fertilizers and pesticides; to safeguard and restore hedges, dry-stone walls, traditional farm buildings and archeological remains; and to take care of wildlife habitats such as flower-rich hay meadows, heather moor, wetlands and native woodland. At the same time, the National Park Authority works closely with organizations such as the **Cumbria Wildlife Trust** (@www.wildlifetrust.org.uk/cumbria), **Friends of the Lake District** (@www.fld.org.uk), **Natural England** (@www.naturalengland.org.uk), the **National Trust** (@www.nationaltrust.org.uk) and the **Royal Society for the Protection of Birds** (@www.rspb.org.uk) to monitor important habitats and ensure they are protected and maintained for future generations.

Woodland and forest

There is more **native woodland** in the Lake District than in any other upland National Park in Britain. The most widespread type, sessile-oak woodland, occurs on the acid rocks that make up most of the Lake District, with birch, rowan, hazel and holly also present alongside the dominant oaks. On limestone it's ash woodland that dominates, though elm, hazel, silver birch, yew and rowan might also be present. The woodlands provide food, shelter and breeding sites for many different birds such as buzzard, pied flycatcher, warbler and tawny owl, and animals including deer, badger, fox, bat, wood mouse, weasel, shrew and stoat. As for ground flora, plants common on limestone – but found in other types of woodland too – include bluebell, primrose, wood anemone, cowslip and wild daffodil. Shrubs such as blackthorn and buckthorn are typical. In more acidic soil, bilberry, wavy hair and other grasses, ferns and bracken are common, shrubs less so. Woodlands in **Borrowdale** are particularly important for their lichens and their rich moss and liverwort communities, which depend upon high rainfall and humidity.

There's little, if any, true natural forest, or "wildwood", remaining in the Lakes – most had already been cleared by Roman times. However, there are sites that have been continually wooded for at least the past four hundred years, which are known as **ancient semi-natural woodland**. The continuity of woodland cover over such a long period of time has allowed a rich flora and fauna to develop. **Roudsea Wood NNR**, on the southern fringes of the National Park (a mile southwest of Haverthwaite village), is a good example of this kind of habitat, featuring a large variety of trees, ferns and woodland birds. East of Windermere, near Staveley, **Dorothy Farrer's Spring Wood** shows the continuing benefit of coppicing (cutting trees, often hazel, back to a stump) in ancient semi-natural woodland. The tree canopy is periodically opened up, allowing more light to reach the woodland floor and encouraging the growth of plants and fungi. The National Park also contains the highest-altitude woodland in England and Wales, including the **Eskdale and Birkrigg woods** in the Newlands Valley, which are both thought to be descended from original wildwood.

Conifer plantations occupy large areas of the Lake District. They often contain fast-growing, non-indigenous, tree species such as spruce and pine, which are favoured by commercial timber growers but support only a limited range of wildlife. They are, however, used by several birds of prey, including the sparrowhawk, goshawk and merlin, and provide refuge, feeding and nesting areas for the native red squirrel. Recent moves towards more varied planting and felling patterns are producing a mosaic of smaller stands of different-aged trees, seen for example in plantations at **Thirlmere** and in **Grizedale Forest**. These are more botanically diverse and of much greater value to wildlife. For example, young plantations often harbour small mammals such as voles and mice which, in turn, are a food source for kestrels and owls. Other coniferous plantations worth visiting include **Dodd Wood**, four miles north of Keswick (harbouring red squirrel and various birds of prey), **Ennerdale Forest** (roe deer, red squirrel and badger) and **Thornethwaite Forest** (buzzard and sparrowhawk).

Overgrazing by stock and deer is perhaps the greatest cause of decline in the natural regeneration of broad-leaved woodlands. A diverse age structure within a woodland is vital to ensure the long-term survival of the habitat and its associated species. In some areas where regeneration is not occurring naturally, woodland management (providing stock-proof fencing or undertaking coppicing and so on) is being practised. Other threats are posed by the **ornamental species** introduced by the Victorians, such as rhododendron and laurel, which have escaped from the private gardens for which they were intended and spread into surrounding woodland. Their dense canopy prevents light from reaching the woodland floor, while the roots produce toxic chemicals that prevent other plants from growing. This makes the surrounding soil very acidic and reduces the species diversity of woodlands.

Grassland

The National Park has many different kinds of grassland, reflecting the diversity of rocks, climate and topography. Before people began to clear the forests for agriculture and settlement, open grassland was a rare feature below the tree line. Most grasslands have been created by humans and grazing animals. Some areas have been drained, ploughed and re-seeded with "improved" grass mixtures for agriculture and so have limited wildlife value. Others remain as unimproved pasture, which supports a greater diversity of plants and animals.

Acid grassland is common on upland sheep pasture where high rainfall, coupled with a long history of burning and grazing, has favoured this relatively species-poor habitat. However, the invertebrate species associated with grasslands provide a vital food source for birds such as skylark and meadow pipit, along with small mammals such as mouse and vole. Acid grasslands often contain small areas of richer habitat in the form of wet flushes, springs and mires where many interesting plants, such as the insectivorous sundew and butterwort, can be found.

Calcareous grassland occurs on the limestone outcrops in the Lake District, which were formed during the last Ice Age when huge glaciers scoured the bedrock. In limestone areas this created a smooth, flattened surface, which is characteristic of **limestone pavements**. Weathering and runoff from rainwater widened and deepened any cracks in the rock, giving rise to a complex pattern of solid blocks called **clints**, separated by fissures (sometimes several feet deep) known as **grikes**. These habitats form distinctive niches for a range of plants and animals. For instance, rare ferns thrive in the deep grikes, while above you may catch a glimpse of the Duke of Burgundy or other rare butterflies.

The flattened area of limestone known as limestone pavement is a nationally rare habitat of international importance and, outside Britain, it's found in only a few other areas of Europe. Limestone, of course, has been extracted for decades, to build walls, gateposts and decorative rockeries. Commercial exploitation of limestone pavement has led to large-scale destruction of this fragile habitat and, today, most pavement in England is protected. Cumbria holds 36 percent of Britain's limestone pavement and examples at **Whitbarrow NNR** are some of the finest in Britain. Here, just to the southeast of Cartmell Fell and Bowland Bridge in the Winster Valley, the limestone ridge of Whitbarrow Scar is dominated by the rare blue moor grass, but also contains the hart's tongue fern, dog's mercury, yellow rockrose and limestone bedstraw, as well as the rarer dropwort, dark-red helleborine and rigid buckler fern. Uncommon orchids and distinctive plants, such as crested hair-grass, can also be seen, along with four species of fritillary butterfly, plus the grayling, northern brown argus and common blue butterfly.

Further south, near Witherslack village, a very different mix of grassland flora occupies the small reserve of **Latterbarrow**. Grazing has cleared much of the ancient woodland here, allowing over 150 flowering plant species to be recorded, including numerous orchids.

Hay meadows support a rich variety of wild flowers and tall-growing grasses, and provide nectar for invertebrates. Their richness is maintained by the fact that plants can flower and set seed before mowing, enabling them to be dispersed during summer hay-making. Unfortunately, many hay meadows have been lost over recent years due, in part, to the intensification of agriculture. The move away from hay-making towards silage production (which requires an earlier cut and often relies on the input of artificial fertilizer) has led to a considerable loss of species diversity on many grasslands or pastures. However, under the Environmentally Sensitive Area scheme, farmers are now being encouraged to take care of traditional hay meadows, which can sometimes support over a hundred different species of flowering plants.

Upland heath

Heathland is an open habitat dominated by dwarf shrubs such as heather. It is thought that such areas were originally cleared for agriculture, but their poor acidic soils made them unsuitable for farming. This enabled the acid-tolerant heather to colonize the land. These open habitats are particularly important for insects, and over 170 species of butterfly and moth have been identified at **Rusland Moss NNR** in the south of the National Park (three miles north of Haverthwaite village), along with numerous spiders, flies, beetles, birds and reptiles.

Large areas of upland heath have traditionally been managed as shooting estates. A diverse age structure of vegetation is maintained through systematically burning strips of heather to promote seed germination and encourage the growth of new shoots. This practice ensures a constant food supply for birds, such as the red grouse (found only in Britain), and provides an important breeding ground for the short-eared owl as well as Britain's smallest bird of prey, the merlin.

Heathland needs careful management to prevent it reverting to woodland. This is commonly achieved through stock grazing. However, if stocking densities are too high, the regeneration of heather cannot keep pace with the consumption of young shoots by the sheep, and the heather dies back. This continues to be a problem in the Lake District, although financial incentives aimed at tackling overgrazing have been introduced as part of the Environmentally Sensitive Areas scheme.

Mires

The cool, wet climate of the Lake District provides ideal conditions for the development of peat, and the area is considered to be of national importance for both the extent and quality of its **mires**. Peat is characteristic of waterlogged conditions and consists of partially decomposed plant material. In areas where soil micro-organisms cannot complete their natural breakdown processes due to highly acidic conditions and a lack of oxygen, organic remains accumulate as peat. Many mires are nutrient-poor ecosystems, unsuitable for farming. The vegetation depends almost entirely on dilute nutrient supplies present in rainwater and atmospheric dust. Mosses and liverworts flourish, along with many species of lichen and dwarfed forms of heathers and sedges.

Blanket mire (ie where there's a blanket covering of peat) is a scarce habitat, particularly important for breeding moorland birds such as red grouse, golden plover and merlin. Many sites have become impoverished through burning, grazing and drainage, but extensive areas remain on some of the flatter fell tops within the National Park. Here you'll find cross-leaved heath, purple moor grass, cotton grass, bog asphodel, sundew and sphagnum mosses. Small fragments of **raised mire** (flattish, boggy areas of deep peat) also occur within the National Park, such as **Meathop Moss SSSI** – one of the best remaining examples in southern Cumbria – which supports a wide range of plants, over two hundred species of moth and butterfly (including the large heath butterfly), and several species of dragonfly and damselfly. At **Roudsea Mosses NNR** (a mile southwest of Haverthwaite village in the southern Lakes), a raised mire provides a breeding site for over fifty species of bird including woodcock, curlew, greater spotted woodpecker and reed bunting. **Dubbs Moss**, a small reserve just to the southwest of Cockermouth, is a mostly wet mixture of mire, fen, meadow and woodland, with plenty of mosses and ferns in evidence.

Like many wildlife habitats, mires were once more numerous and extensive, but vast tracts have disappeared over the last century, mainly as a result of reclamation for agriculture and horticulture. Artificial drainage of sites, coupled with the increased demand for peat by gardeners, has led to a widespread decline of this wetland habitat. To try to reverse this situation, attempts are being made to raise gardeners' awareness of alternatives for soil conditioning (such as homemade compost), and steps are being taken to protect and manage existing mires more sympathetically. A few have been rewetted and are managed by controlling water levels. In areas where rare plants such as the bog orchid have been found, grazing has been controlled.

Lakes, tarns and rivers

Lakes and tarns make a vital contribution to the identity and beauty of the National Park and support an exceptional variety of aquatic plants and animals. They were formed in the last Ice Age by huge glaciers gouging out depressions, which were later filled by meltwater and rain. They vary considerably in their size, depth and nutrient status. Some lakes in particular have a long tradition of recreational use, while others are valued for their tranquil and relatively undisturbed atmosphere.

The deep, cold, clear lakes of **Buttermere**, **Ennerdale** and **Wast Water** provide habitats for a restricted range of plants and animals, but these include some rare crustaceans specifically adapted to nutrient-poor environments. In contrast, lakes such as **Windermere** and **Bassenthwaite** support a more diverse range of species. Their more wooded shorelines, with shallow bays and areas of reedbed, provide valuable nesting haunts for swans, grebes, ducks, geese and other birds. **Esthwaite Water** is the most nutrient-rich of the lakes, supporting white and yellow water lilies and rare pondweeds as well as nesting grebes, plus wild rainbow and brown trout. Windermere is of national importance for wintering wildfowl, while Bassenthwaite Lake is very rich in aquatic plants (including the scarce floating water plantain) and is one of only two lakes in Britain known to support the rare fish, vendace – the other, **Derwent Water**, also attracts various wintering wildfowl, including the pochard and tufted duck. In 2001, the first pair of ospreys to nest in northern England for 150 years bred near the shores of Bassenthwaite Lake, and ospreys continue to return – three chicks were reared for the first time in 2006. However, recreational use of some lakes can sometimes conflict with nature conservation interests. The lakeshore habitat is a fragile "soft shore" environment that is highly susceptible to erosion. The trampling action of feet, coupled with grazing by livestock and waves created from passing boats, can lead to soil and organic material being washed away. Over time the reedy shoreline may begin to resemble a pebble beach, which contains only a fraction of the invertebrate species and little or no aquatic vegetation.

Many of the **rivers** within the National Park are of considerable ecological importance. The significant populations of fish, together with other species such as native crayfish, freshwater pearl mussel, water vole and otter, reflect the generally high standards of water quality. The fast-flowing upland streams provide ideal conditions for birds such as dippers and yellow and grey wagtail.

Rock and scree

Glacial activity has produced a wide variety of crags, knolls, ledges and other rock features. In some places, steep-sided **gills** cut deeply into the fellsides. These ravines provide a damp, sheltered environment and are largely inaccessible to grazing animals, which enables them to support many unusual plants. Steep rocky cliffs, known locally as **crags**, support a mixture of lowland plant species and the more distinctive arctic-alpine flora (including yellow, purple and mossy saxifrage and alpine lady's mantle). Sheltered **rock ledges** and **screes** provide a habitat for tall herbs and ferns (including the parsley fern, common in the Lake District, but fairly rare elsewhere) along with many mosses, liverworts and flowering plants.

Crags and ledges also provide a habitat for a varied range of bird species, including stonechat, wheatear and ring ouzel, and nest sites for the buzzard, raven, peregrine falcon and golden eagle. The population of peregrine falcons, in particular, suffered a huge decline during the 1950s and 1960s due to widespread use of pesticides and illegal persecution. Their numbers dropped to just six pairs in Cumbria, though over the last twenty years they have made a considerable recovery and the Lake District today supports the highest density of peregrines anywhere in Europe. Golden eagles are far less numerous; in fact, the only pair in England have been seen on the outcrops and open fells above **Haweswater**, along with buzzards and peregrine falcons. The very high fells (particularly in Langdale) are also the only place you'll spot the mountain ringlet butterfly, Britain's only true alpine butterfly.

Cliff, rock and scree habitats are, of course, highly vulnerable to the activities of climbers, walkers and scramblers. Many agencies are working in partnership to promote responsible use of the countryside and seasonal access restrictions to crags with nesting birds are negotiated annually. Walkers should always keep to marked paths and trails, since going "off trail" – even just stepping off a marked path – can spoil a fragile habitat.

Coastal environments

Coastal environments include areas of shingle, dune, grazing marshes, coastal heath, mudflats and the banks of tidal rivers. Five sites of international importance for nature conservation are located on the coast of the National Park, while on its southern boundary the National Park encompasses small parts of the **Duddon Estuary** and **Morecambe Bay**. These extensive areas support huge numbers of breeding and wintering birds for which they are awarded special European protection – RAMSAR status. Depending on the time of year, you're likely to see flocks of knot, dunlin and oystercatcher, plus grey and ringed plover, curlew, greenshank, spotted redshank, mallard, shelduck and wigeon.

In the west, the National Park's coast stretches from **Drigg Local Nature Reserve** (SSSI) for twelve miles south to **Silecroft**. Large numbers of the natterjack toad are found here along with the palmate, great crested and smooth newt, and the common lizard, while other important species include the adder and the slowworm. Over two hundred plant species are found in the coastal habitats, from sea campion, sea beet and sea kale established on the shingle beaches to typical saltmarsh plants such as glasswort and sea arrowgrass. On the dunes, marram grass and lyme grass help stabilize the sand, while in the hollows, or "slacks", of the dune systems (sometimes filled with fresh or sea water) rarer species such as creeping willow, marsh pennywort and various other marsh orchids can often be found. Shingle and dune habitats also provide breeding areas for five species of tern and large colonies of gulls. The **Hodbarrow** nature reserve, near Millom – a habitat fashioned from a former iron-ore mining site – sees a huge variety of coastal bird species, including great crested grebe, tufted duck, shelduck, oystercatcher and ringed plover, as well as birds of prey such as the kestrel, sparrowhawk and barn owl.

This feature is based on literature kindly provided by the Lake District National Park Authority.

Climbing in the Lake District

Two centuries ago, no one climbed rocks for fun. That's not to say that people didn't go up mountains, but they would never have thought of themselves as climbers or what they were doing as a sport. Shepherds, soldiers and traders ventured onto high ground, but only with good reason. Mountains were the stuff of myth and legend – useless to farmers, dangerous to travellers, largely unknown and often feared. Daniel Defoe, writing of the Lake District in the 1720s, thought the region's mountains "had a kind of inhospitable terror in them"; and Dr Johnson, some fifty years later, was "astonished and repelled by this wide extent of hopeless sterility". But revolution was afoot in the late eighteenth century, as much in man's perception of the natural world as in politics, and two new influences were making themselves felt upon the landscapes of Europe: Romanticism and the urge for scientific discovery.

Early steps

In August 1786, Mont Blanc in the French Alps (the highest summit in Western Europe) was climbed for the first time by a young Chamonix doctor, **Michel-Gabriel Paccard** and his porter **Jacques Balmat**. The pair made notes and collected botanical and geological specimens as they went – and picked up a substantial prize in addition, offered by the Swiss scientist and explorer Horace-Benedict de Saussure for the first successful ascent. Given that only eighty years previously a serious attempt had been made to seek out and classify "alpine dragons", Paccard's climb was both a mountaineering *tour de force* and a triumph of scientific rationalism over superstition.

In England it was the artistic, rather than the scientific, community which began to influence the general attitude towards the Lake District's own, lesser, mountain range. **The Picturesque Movement**, precursor of Romanticism, had made the depiction of landscape fashionable and, by the 1760s, various English artists were making good money out of the developing public taste for mountainous scenery. Idealized prints of Derwent Water by Thomas Smith and William Bellers proved both popular and profitable, while in 1783 the renowned artist Thomas Gainsborough visited the Lakes and produced three well-received works (including one of the Langdale Pikes).

Capturing the prevailing Romantic spirit, other visitors published successful accounts of their lakeland expeditions, and in the writings of **William Gilpin**, **Thomas West** and novelist **Mrs Ann Radcliffe** are found the first descriptions of mountains as objects to be climbed (primarily for the "picturesque" views from the top). But the relatively easy ascent of Skiddaw aside (which could be conquered on horseback), most Lake District mountain tops were still well off-limits. It took the energy and vision of an opium-riddled, rheumatic poet to transform the way people regarded lakeland crags and cliffs.

Coleridge and the birth of rock climbing

If Wordsworth was the great walker in the Lake District, then **Samuel Taylor Coleridge** was the pioneer of rock climbing. In August 1802, setting off from his home in Keswick, he made a nine-day solo tour – which he dubbed his "circumcursion" – taking in the peaks and valleys of the central and western Lakes in a hundred-mile circuit. Coleridge was escaping a troubled marriage and an ebbing literary career and, recording his travels in his journal and in a series of letters to his beloved "Asra" (Wordsworth's sister-in-law, Sara Hutchinson), he became the sport's first great writer. ,

Coleridge had no time for most contemporary visitors to the Lakes, who tended to follow the same routes set down by early guidebook writers, viewing picturesque beauty spots from predetermined stations and idling in boats. Coleridge's was a wilder spirit and it was with a real sense of exhilaration that he found himself on the top of **Scafell** on the fifth day of his tour. In a famous passage from his journal he records his hair-raising descent, dropping down the successive ledges of **Broad Stand** by hanging over them from his fingertips. In this manner, he soon found himself in a position where: ". . . every Drop increased the Palsy of my Limbs . . . and now I had only two more to drop down, to return was impossible – but of these two the first was tremendous, it was twice my own height, and the Ledge at the bottom was so exceedingly narrow, that if I dropt down upon it I must of necessity have fallen backwards and of course killed myself". A moment's reflection brought respite: "I know not how to proceed, how to return, but I am calm and fearless and confident."

This ability to overcome the body's response to fear is a quality all climbers must possess, and Coleridge's breathless account marks him out as a true mountaineer. His descent of Broad Stand may have been accidental but his reasons for being on the fells, and his response to them, would be understood by any modern climber. He revelled in the activity for its own sake and in his "stretched and anxious state of mind" he discovered calm and an escape from the cares of home.

Others followed Coleridge onto the fells. The description of Ennerdale's **Pillar Rock** as "unclimbable" by a guidebook writer, John Otley, in 1825, led to a competition among local dalesmen to ascend the only sizeable summit in the area that could not be gained by walking alone. It was duly scaled in 1826 by a shepherd, **John Atkinson**. By 1875, some fifty annual ascents were being recorded, amongst them that of the first woman, a Miss Barker of Gosforth, and a 14-year-old boy, Lawrence Pilkington, later a pioneering Alpine climber (and the founder of the famous glass company).

Wasdale and the Victorian climbers

For the most part, the Lake District crags were largely ignored by daring English gentlemen climbers and their professional guides. Mountaineering meant Alpine glaciers and snow ridges, and most Alpinists regarded lakeland rock climbers as mere "chimney sweeps" and "rock gymnasts". But change was in the air. A handful of more broad-minded climbers began to gather for winter practice at **Wasdale Head**, from where Coleridge had set off for Scafell in 1802. On the whole they were professional men from the industrial cities or academics, with the time and energy to indulge their passion for the mountains. From their ranks came the Cambridge classicist and unlikely sporting revolutionary **Walter Parry Haskett Smith**. Having been introduced to the high fells at Wasdale in 1881, Haskett Smith returned the following year and set out to discover challenging routes up the gullies and chimneys that cleave their way through the rocks. Climbing for the sheer thrill of it, Haskett Smith began to record his routes, guiding those who might choose to follow his footsteps and handholds. The visitor's book at the **Wastwater Hotel** (now the *Wasdale Head Inn*) became the lakeland climber's bible, and the hotel doubled as the rock climbers' clubhouse.

An almost chivalrous code developed amongst the climbers: comradeship tempered the excesses of competition and bar-room bragging was not tolerated. These men found in climbing an escape from the demands of their professions, families and society, and a few days spent at Wasdale each year was an excuse for the sort of behaviour not usually associated with the staid lives of Victorian gentlemen. After a hard day on the crag, there were often evening gymnastic revelries: the "billiard room traverse" – circling and leaving the room without touching the floor – or the "passage of the billiard table leg", completed by climbing beneath the table and around a table leg. Boyish games, certainly, but by the end of the century these supple lakeland climbers were pioneering routes unmatched anywhere else in the country.

In 1886, Haskett Smith made the first ascent of **Napes Needle**, that slender pillar of rock that rises on the southern flank of Great Gable. This was no simple gully scramble, nor could it be rationalized as merely an alternative route to a fell top. This was climbing pure and simple, and climbing for its own sake at that. If one climb set the standard for a new sport, this was it. The route is short, but exposed, and is still many a novice's first lakeland climb. Haskett Smith did it alone, unroped and in nailed boots, at the end of a full day in the hills. (He later repeated this pioneering climb on its fiftieth anniversary, when he was a sprightly 76-year-old.)

Haskett Smith's exploits didn't go unnoticed. **Owen Glynne Jones**, the son of a Welsh carpenter, was teaching at the City of London School when, in 1891, he saw a photograph of Napes Needle in a shop on the Strand and within a fortnight had climbed it during his Easter holidays. He was a bold, brash man ("The Only Genuine Jones", as he called himself), who climbed ferociously well and pioneered several physically demanding routes, eagerly taking up the right of first ascenders to name new climbs (a tradition that remains to this day) – "Jones's Route Direct" on Scafell owes its name to him.

Jones came to dominate lakeland climbing in the 1890s, doing much to publicize the new sport in the process. In 1897, his book, *Rock Climbing in the English Lake District*, was published, including thirty magnificent full-page photographs by Keswick brothers and photographers **George** and **Ashley Abraham** – examples of these pictures still hang in Keswick shops and pubs, and in the *Wasdale Head Inn*. Jones's accompanying descriptions of the routes included **grades** allocated according to the difficulty of the climb – from Easy to Severe. This was the first attempt to put some order into what had been, until now, a sport without classification, and Jones's basic grading framework still stands, although there are now some twenty intermediate and additional grades (to accommodate the huge rise in standards over the last century).

Danger and progress on the fells

Jones was killed in a fall in the Alps in 1899 and his death highlighted the dangers facing the early climbers. Their **specialist equipment** was basically limited to nails arranged in varying patterns on the sole or around the edge of the boot to help grip the rock. Heavy hemp ropes (as used when crossing crevasse-strewn Alpine glaciers) were of dubious benefit on lakeland crags. Two or more climbers might rope themselves together but, as the rope itself was not attached to the rock (as it is today), the chances of surviving a fall were slim. Put bluntly, it was "one off, all off" and the tragic results can be seen in St Olaf's graveyard at Wasdale Head, where three headstones mark the graves of a roped party who fell together from the Pinnacle Face of Scafell in 1906.

Some measure of organization came to lakeland rock climbing with the establishment in 1907 of the **Fell and Rock Climbing Club (FRCC)** of the English Lake District. Ashley Abraham became its president, with honorary memberships granted to Haskett Smith, Cecil Slingsby (a great lakeland climber on Scafell and Gable, and probably the first Englishman to learn the art of skiing) and Norman Collie (an experienced climber in Skye, the Alps, the Rockies and the Himalayas, who also found time to discover the gas neon and develop the first practical application of the X-ray). The Fell and Rock, as the club came to be known, not only promoted safer climbing techniques but helped usher the sport out of the Victorian age with its revolutionary acceptance of women members (something the more established Alpine Club didn't do until after World War II).

Meanwhile, lakeland climbers continued to push at the boundaries of possibility. **Siegfried Herford** (Welsh-born but with a German mother) began climbing in 1907, and his eventual ascent of **Central Buttress** on Scafell in the spring of 1914 was a landmark climb, requiring a new grade to be added to the grading framework – it was so tough, no one else repeated the climb for seven years.

A democratic sport

By the **mid-1930s**, climbing had become a popular, rather than a specialist, pastime. Partly, this was because it was now a safer sport than it had been: rubber-soled gym shoes were worn in dry weather rather than nailed boots, and rope techniques had improved markedly. But, more importantly, what had once been the preserve of daring gentlemen was now open to all – better road access, more holiday time and the establishment of youth hostels and rambling clubs all brought new faces (known as "crag rats") onto the crags.

Jim Birkett, a quarryman from Langdale, and **Bill Peascod**, a Workington coal miner, were typical of the new breed of climber. Birkett was a reserved man and a traditionalist, who kept climbing in nailed boots long after his contemporaries had abandoned them. On May 1, 1938, he pioneered his first classic route on **Scafell East Buttress**, calling it "May Day". This was followed by "Gremlin's Groove" on the same face and two other classics on **Esk Buttress** ("Afterthought" and "Frustration"), before Birkett turned his attention to **Castle Rock** in Thirlmere, climbing what was then known as the Lakeland Everest in April 1939 by a route he called "Overhanging Bastion". Meanwhile, the more extrovert Peascod was making similar advances in **Buttermere**, with routes such as "Eagle Front", climbed in June 1940, followed by nine other new routes of a similarly severe standard in 1941.

Popularity and professionalism

By **the 1960s**, thanks to the conquest of Everest, climbing rode high in the public conscience. Men like **Joe Brown** and **Chris Bonington** became household names – although they were better known for their achievements in the Alps and Himalayas than for any of the notable lakeland routes they had also created. Other British climbers were also branching out from the Lakes, not only to Scotland and Wales but to the warmer rocks of France, Spain and Morocco. However, fashions come and go and the Lake District has always attracted climbers back, drawn by the huge variety of rock faces crammed into such a tightly packed mountain range.

By **the 1970s**, an increasing number of professional climbers were taking a new approach to their sport, training as hard as any top athlete in order to push the boundaries still further. Typical of this single-minded athleticism were the exploits of the Yorkshireman **Pete Livesey**, whose great lakeland season came in 1974. In **Borrowdale** alone he put up four routes of such a magnitude that many at first thought them impossible without using "aid" (pitons, ropes or other artificial help on the rock). But Livesey maintained the tradition of so-called "free climbing" (whereby equipment is used only to provide safety in the event of a fall), thus proving it was simply another psychological barrier that had to be broken. Soon others were climbing even more "impossible" routes than Livesey. **Bill Birkett** – son of the Langdale climber, Jim – undertook some audacious climbing in the Patterdale area, most notably on **Dove Crag**, in the 1970s and 1980s. And today, **Dave Birkett**, Bill's cousin, is creating a new standard right back in the heart of Langdale: on Pavey Ark, his "Impact Day" (graded Extreme 9) is about as tough as it gets in the Lakes.

Modern equipment and challenges

Climbing equipment has developed alongside the athletic professionalism. Nailed boots and gym shoes have given way to specialized climbing shoes, first developed in the 1950s by the French climber Pierre Allain (and known by his initials as PAs). Where Haskett Smith would have climbed in tweeds, modern climbers don multicoloured Lycra leggings: chalk bags hang from belts, ready to dry sweat-dampened fingers, along with a battery of safety chocks and slings, placed in the rock to give the nylon rope a secure anchor point in the event of a fall. Despite the severity of today's climbing, accidents are few and far between, since a securely placed sling or "runner" (through which the rope is clipped) holds anyone whose ambition out-runs their ability. There was a move towards "**aid climbing**" in the Lakes in the 1960s, when pitons and screws were used to assist an ascent, but it was largely frowned upon and today nearly all lakeland climbers climb "**free**"; that is, by their own efforts alone. It's a technique championed by Cumbria's latest young gun, Leo Houlding, a climber with rock-star looks and boundless confidence – one of a bunch of young British climbers (including Ian Parnell, Andy Kirkpatrick and Airlie Anderson) scaling crags and peaks from Yosemite to Patagonia.

The number of climbers on the Lake District's crags has increased to such an extent that queues now form on popular routes in the summer. But there are still **challenging routes** to be discovered alongside the classics on Gable and Scafell. Hikers, meanwhile, have the history of climbing all around them. Take a walk up from the *Wasdale Head Inn* and the very names of the features around the Great Napes on Great Gable – Sphinx Ridge, Needle Gulley and Napes Needle itself – are all attributable to the pioneer climbers. You may not know it, and it will not be listed by the Ordnance Survey, but on Scafell Crag you could pass by "Botterill's Slab" (1903, F.W. Botterill), "Pegasus" (1952, A. Dolphin & P. Greenwood) or "The White Wizard" (1976, C.J.S. Bonington & N. Estcourt), and find climbers on each. All are finding something different in the challenge of hand and foot on rock, and all are, in their own way, conquering the impossible. In that, nothing has changed.

William Wordsworth: A Life

Wordsworth was of a good height, just five feet ten, and not a slender man . . .
Meantime his face . . . was certainly the noblest for intellectual effects that, in
actual life, I have seen.

Thomas De Quincey, *Recollections of the Lake and Lake Poets*

William Wordsworth and the Lake District are inextricably linked, and in the streets of Grasmere, Hawkshead and Cockermouth, and the fells surrounding Ullswater, Borrowdale and the Duddon Valley you're never very far away from a house or a sight associated with the poet and his circle. His birthplace, houses, favourite spots and final resting place are all covered in the Guide, together with anecdotes about, and analysis of, his day-to-day life, his poetry and personal relationships. Below, a general biographical account of Wordsworth's life is provided to place the various sites and accounts in context.

Childhood, school and university

William Wordsworth was **born in Cockermouth** (April 7, 1770), the second eldest of four brothers and a sister, Dorothy. His father, John, was agent and lawyer for a local landowner, Sir James Lowther, and the family was comfortably off, as the surviving Wordsworth home in Cockermouth attests. The children spent much time with their grandparents in Penrith – William even attended a school there – and when their mother Ann died (she was only 30) in 1778, the family was split up: Dorothy was sent to live with relations in Halifax in Yorkshire, while William and his older brother Richard began life at the respected **grammar school in Hawkshead**, lodging with **Ann Tyson** and going back to Penrith or Cockermouth in the holidays. On his father's death in 1783, William and the other children were left in relative poverty as the Lowthers refused to pay John Wordsworth's long-owed salary (indeed, it was almost twenty years before the debt was honoured).

At school in Hawkshead, Wordsworth (now supported by his uncles) flourished, storing up childhood experiences of ice-skating, climbing, fishing and dancing that would later emerge in his most celebrated poetry. In 1787, finished with school and clutching new clothes made for him by Ann Tyson and the already devoted Dorothy, Wordsworth went up to **St John's College**, **Cambridge**, where his uncles intended that he should study to become a clergyman. His academic promise soon fizzled out. Despite a bright start – to his evident amusement, De Quincey later recalled that Wordsworth briefly became a "dandy", sporting silk stockings and powdered hair – he abandoned his formal studies and left in 1790 without distinction and with no prospect of being ordained. His uncles were furious, but Wordsworth had other plans for his future.

In France

A walking tour through **France and the Alps** in the summer of 1790 excited the young, idealistic Wordsworth who had grand thoughts of being a poet. His interest was fired by the contemporary revolutionary movements of Europe. The Bastille had fallen the previous year and Wordsworth's early republicanism flowered. ("Bliss was it in that dawn to be alive, but to be young was very Heaven!") He returned to France in 1791 where he met one **Annette Vallon**, with whom he fell in love – she became pregnant, giving birth to their child, Caroline, in December 1792. But by this time, Wordsworth had returned to England, to oversee the publication, in 1793, of his first works, *Descriptive Sketches* (inspired by his revolutionary travels) and the lakeland reverie *An Evening Walk*. When war broke out between England and France in 1793 Wordsworth was unable to return to France or to Annette; they didn't meet again until 1802.

Depressed by the events of the Terror in France, which rather dented his revolutionary enthusiasm, Wordsworth alternated between fretting and idling in London and making walking tours around England. He thought he might become a teacher and shared Dorothy's oft-expressed dream of setting up home together and devoting his life to poetry – something that at last seemed possible when a small, but unexpected, bequest from the dying **Raisley Calvert**, the brother of an old schoolfriend, gave him just enough to live on.

Becoming a poet: the Lyrical Ballads and Germany

William and Dorothy moved to **Dorset** in 1795 (where they'd been offered a house), and William became acquainted with a fiery, widely read, passionate young critic and writer. **Samuel Taylor Coleridge** had read and admired Wordsworth's two published works and, on meeting Wordsworth himself, was almost overcome with enthusiasm for his ideas and passions. There's no doubt that they inspired each other and the Wordsworths moved to **Somerset** to be near Coleridge – "three people, but one soul", as Coleridge later had it. Here they collaborated on what became the **Lyrical Ballads** (1798), a work which could be said to mark the onset of English Romantic poetry and which contained some of Wordsworth's finest early writing (quite apart from Coleridge's "The Rime of the Ancient Mariner"): not just the famous "Lines Written above Tintern Abbey", but also snatches later incorporated into *The Prelude* (Wordsworth's great autobiographical work, unpublished during his lifetime – Wordsworth only ever knew it as the "Poem on my own Life"). It's hard to see today quite how unusual the *Lyrical Ballads* were for their time: conceived as "experiments", the mixture of simple poems with a rustic, natural content and longer narrative works flew right in the face of contemporary classicism. Sales and reviews were universally poor.

Wordsworth, Dorothy and Coleridge went to **Germany** in 1798, during which time their joint idea for a long autobiographical, philosophical work began to gel in Wordsworth's mind. He produced a first version of *The Prelude* in Germany, along with the affecting "Lucy" poems (including "Strange fits of passion have I known"), which some say pointed to an unnatural passion for his sister. It was certainly an unusual relationship: Dorothy devoted herself entirely to William (her favourite brother since childhood) and his work; she kept house for him, walked with him, listened to his poems, transcribed and made copies of them, and he wrote passionate poems about nameless women who could be no one else but Dorothy. But there's no evidence – to be blunt – that she slept with him, despite the claims of some critics.

Grasmere

In 1799 William and Dorothy moved to **Grasmere** (and Coleridge followed), in the search both for conducive natural surroundings in which Wordsworth's work could flourish and for somewhere they could survive on a restricted budget. William was to spend the last two-thirds of his life in and around the village.

Brother and sister first moved into **Dove Cottage** where they remained until 1808, a period in which Wordsworth established himself as a major poet. A new edition of the *Lyrical Ballads* (1801) appeared, including some of the poems he'd written in Germany together with his first major Grasmere poems, such as "The Brothers" and "Michael", based on local stories and characters. This edition also included its famous **preface** expounding his theories of poetry (against "inane phraseology"; for simple, natural, emotive language), which many critics found arrogant. Wordsworth was at his most productive in the years to 1805, resulting in the publication of *Poems in Two Volumes* (1807), containing the celebrated odes to "Duty" and "Immortality", the Westminster Bridge sonnet, the "Daffodils" poem (untitled when first published) and a hundred other new poems and sonnets. A third edition of *Lyrical Ballads* appeared, and he had also found time to expand and complete a second version of *The Prelude*. All this early work set new standards in poetry: questioning the nature of perception, challenging contemporary prejudices and orchestrating a highly original vision of the human soul within nature.

Dorothy, meanwhile, kept a **journal** recording life at Dove Cottage which has become a classic in its own right. Her skilled observations of the local people and landscape prompted some of William's best-known work, most famously the "Daffodils" stanzas – Wordsworth relied heavily on her journal for the famous images of the flowers dancing and reeling in the breeze.

Marriage and money

Wordsworth's dire financial position slowly improved. His sales and reviews weren't getting any better (Byron trashed most of *Poems in Two Volumes*) but the Lowthers finally stumped up the debt owed to William's long-dead father. This allowed him to marry an old childhood friend from Penrith, **Mary Hutchinson**, in 1802, having first travelled with Dorothy to France to make amends with his first love Annette; Wordsworth later provided an annuity for Annette and their young daughter. Outwardly, the **marriage to Mary** seemed precipitous and passionless and scholars have speculated about Wordsworth's motives, though letters between William and his wife (discovered in the 1970s) tend to scotch the myth that he was marrying out of duty. **Children** followed – John, Dorothy (always known as Dora), Thomas, Catherine and William – though Catherine and then Thomas, both infants, succumbed to mortal illnesses in the same tragic year of 1812.

Dove Cottage became too small for comfort as the family grew. His wife's sister, Sara Hutchinson, was a permanent fixture, as was Coleridge (by now separated from his wife) and his visiting children. The Wordsworths moved to other houses in Grasmere (Allan Bank and the Old Rectory), and then in 1813 finally settled on **Rydal Mount**, a gracious house two miles south of the village. Here William lived out the rest of his life, supported for some years by his salaried position as **Distributor of Stamps for Westmorland** (good fortune, caused, as De Quincey noted, by the current incumbent distributing "himself and his office into two different places"). It was hardly a sinecure – he had to travel through the county, collecting dues and granting licences, work which he undertook assiduously – but it brought him in £200 a year.

The Rydal years

Wordsworth may have already written his finest poetry, but after the move to Rydal he was at the peak of his fame. Over the years, the literary world made its way to his door, a procession recorded in detail by the critic and essayist **Thomas De Quincey** who first made the pilgrimage to Grasmere to meet his hero in 1807. After a long friendship interrupted by disagreements, De Quincey's frank series of articles on Wordsworth and his family in 1839 (later published as *Recollections of the Lakes and the Lake Poets*) caused an irreparable rift. **Coleridge**, too, was *persona non grata* after a falling-out in 1810, though the two old friends did come to some kind of an accommodation in later life, and *The Prelude* remained dedicated to him.

There were family setbacks. The death of William's brother, John, in 1805 had affected him deeply (and led later to a burgeoning religious faith); after 1828, his beloved sister Dorothy suffered a series of depressive illnesses, which incapacitated her mind for most of the rest of her long life; and his wife's sister, Sara Hutchinson – who had so besotted Coleridge and who had lived with them for thirty years – died of the flu in 1835.

Wordsworth continued to be productive, at least in the early Rydal years. The *Excursion* (1814), long enough in itself, was conceived as part of an even longer philosophical work to be called "The Recluse", which he never completed. His first *Collected Poems* appeared the following year, together with *The White Doe of Rylstone*; but it wasn't until *Peter Bell* (1819) and *The River Duddon sonnets* (1820) that sales and reviews finally flourished. His *Vaudracour and Julia* (1819) also had deep significance: a tale of seduction, it was a fictionalized account of his affair with Annette.

As Wordsworth grew older he lost the radicalism of his youth, becoming a loud opponent of democracy, liberalism and progress. Political developments in France and the threat of the mob and the Reform Bill at home appalled him. His views on nature and the picturesque had led him to produce his own descriptive **Guide to the Lakes** ("for the minds of persons of taste"), at first published anonymously (1810) to accompany a book of drawings; its later popularity (a final, fifth edition, appeared in 1835) did much to advertise the very charms of the region he was keen to preserve. In the end, fulminating against the whitewashed houses and fir plantations he thought were disfiguring the Lakes, Wordsworth retreated to his beloved garden at Rydal Mount.

Apart from the rare crafted sonnet or couplet, Wordsworth's later work was largely undistinguished. The third major revision of *The Prelude* had been completed in 1838; the poem didn't see the light of day until after his death, when Mary gave it a name and handed it over for publication. But in 1843, on the death of Robert Southey and at the age of 73, Wordsworth's position as Grand Old Man of the literary establishment was confirmed by his appointment as **Poet Laureate**.

After his **death in 1850**, William's body was interred in St Oswald's churchyard in Grasmere, to be later joined by Dorothy (1885) and by his wife Mary (1889).

Travel store

Kenya
Marrakesh **D**
Morocco
South Africa, Lesotho
& Swaziland
Syria
Tanzania
Tunisia
West Africa
Zanzibar

Travel Specials
First-Time Africa
First-Time Around
the World
First-Time Asia
First-Time Europe
First-Time Latin
America
Travel Health
Travel Online
Travel Survival
Walks in London
& SE England
Women Travel
World Party

Maps
Algarve
Amsterdam
Andalucia
& Costa del Sol
Argentina
Athens
Australia
Barcelona
Berlin
Boston & Cambridge
Brittany
Brussels
California
Chicago
Chile
Corsica
Costa Rica
& Panama
Crete
Croatia
Cuba
Cyprus
Czech Republic
Dominican Republic
Dubai & UAE
Dublin
Egypt

Florence & Siena
Florida
France
Frankfurt
Germany
Greece
Guatemala & Belize
Iceland
India
Ireland
Italy
Kenya & Northern
Tanzania
Lisbon
London
Los Angeles
Madrid
Malaysia
Mallorca
Marrakesh
Mexico
Miami & Key West
Morocco
New England
New York City
New Zealand
Northern Spain
Paris
Peru
Portugal
Prague
Pyrenees & Andorra
Rome
San Francisco
Sicily
South Africa
South India
Spain & Portugal
Sri Lanka
Tenerife
Thailand
Toronto
Trinidad & Tobago
Tunisia
Turkey
Tuscany
Venice
Vietnam, Laos
& Cambodia
Washington DC
Yucatán Peninsula

**Dictionary
Phrasebooks**
Croatian
Czech
Dutch
Egyptian Arabic
French
German
Greek
Hindi & Urdu
Italian
Japanese
Latin American
Spanish
Mandarin Chinese
Mexican Spanish
Polish
Portuguese
Russian
Spanish
Swahili
Thai
Turkish
Vietnamese

Computers
Blogging
eBay
iPhone
iPods, iTunes
& music online
The Internet
Macs & OS X
MySpace
PCs and Windows
PlayStation Portable
Website Directory

Film & TV
American
Independent Film
British Cult Comedy
Chick Flicks
Comedy Movies
Cult Movies
Film
Film Musicals
Film Noir
Gangster Movies
Horror Movies
Kids' Movies
Sci-Fi Movies
Westerns

Lifestyle
Babies
Ethical Living
Pregnancy & Birth
Running

Music Guides
The Beatles
Blues
Bob Dylan
Book of Playlists
Classical Music
Elvis
Frank Sinatra
Heavy Metal
Hip-Hop
Jazz
Led Zeppelin
Opera
Pink Floyd
Punk
Reggae
Rock
The Rolling Stones
Soul and R&B
Velvet Underground
World Music
(2 vols)

Popular Culture
Books for Teenagers
Children's Books,
5-11
Conspiracy Theories
Crime Fiction
Cult Fiction
The Da Vinci Code
His Dark Materials
Lord of the Rings
Shakespeare
Superheroes
The Templars
Unexplained
Phenomena

Science
The Brain
Climate Change
The Earth
Genes & Cloning
The Universe
Weather

Visit us online
www.roughguides.com
Information on over 25,000 destinations around the world

- **Read** Rough Guides' trusted travel info
- **Access** exclusive articles from Rough Guides authors
- **Update** yourself on new books, maps, CDs and other products
- **Enter** our competitions and win travel prizes
- **Share** ideas, journals, photos & travel advice with other users
- **Earn** points every time you contribute to the Rough Guide community and get rewards

BROADEN YOUR HORIZONS

"The most accurate maps in the world"

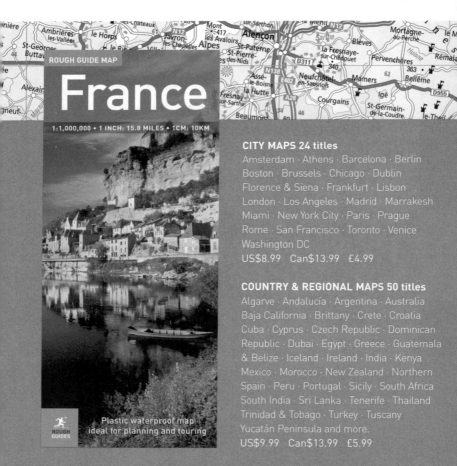

ROUGH GUIDE MAP

France

1:1,000,000 · 1 INCH: 15.8 MILES · 1CM: 10KM

Plastic waterproof map
ideal for planning and touring

CITY MAPS 24 titles

Amsterdam · Athens · Barcelona · Berlin
Boston · Brussels · Chicago · Dublin
Florence & Siena · Frankfurt · Lisbon
London · Los Angeles · Madrid · Marrakesh
Miami · New York City · Paris · Prague
Rome · San Francisco · Toronto · Venice
Washington DC
US$8.99   Can$13.99   £4.99

COUNTRY & REGIONAL MAPS 50 titles

Algarve · Andalucía · Argentina · Australia
Baja California · Brittany · Crete · Croatia
Cuba · Cyprus · Czech Republic · Dominican
Republic · Dubai · Egypt · Greece · Guatemala
& Belize · Iceland · Ireland · India · Kenya
Mexico · Morocco · New Zealand · Northern
Spain · Peru · Portugal · Sicily · South Africa
South India · Sri Lanka · Tenerife · Thailand
Trinidad & Tobago · Turkey · Tuscany
Yucatán Peninsula and more.
US$9.99   Can$13.99   £5.99

ROUGH GUIDES

waterproof • rip-proof • amazing value

BROADEN YOUR HORIZONS

Avoid Guilt Trips

Buy fair trade coffee + bananas ✓

Save energy – use low energy bulbs ✓

– don't leave tv on standby ✓

Offset carbon emissions from flight to Madrid ✓

Send goat to Africa ✓

Join Tourism Concern today ✓

Slowly, the world is changing.
Together we can, and will, make a difference.

Tourism Concern is the only UK registered charity fighting exploitation in one of the largest industries on earth: people forced from their homes in order that holiday resorts can be built, sweatshop labour conditions in hotels and destruction of the environment are just some of the issues that we tackle.

Sending people on a guilt trip is not something we do. We know as well as anyone that holidays are precious. But you can help us to ensure that tourism always benefits the local communities involved.

Call 020 7133 3330
or visit **tourismconcern.org.uk** to find out how.

A year's membership of Tourism Concern costs just £20 (£12 unwaged) – that's 38 pence a week, less than the cost of a pint of milk, organic of course.

Small print and
Index

A Rough Guide to Rough Guides

Published in 1982, the first Rough Guide – to Greece – was a student scheme that became a publishing phenomenon. Mark Ellingham, a recent graduate in English from Bristol University, had been travelling in Greece the previous summer and couldn't find the right guidebook. With a small group of friends he wrote his own guide, combining a highly contemporary, journalistic style with a thoroughly practical approach to travellers' needs.

The immediate success of the book spawned a series that rapidly covered dozens of destinations. And, in addition to impecunious backpackers, Rough Guides soon acquired a much broader and older readership that relished the guides' wit and inquisitiveness as much as their enthusiastic, critical approach and value-for-money ethos.

These days, Rough Guides include recommendations from shoestring to luxury and cover more than 200 destinations around the globe, including almost every country in the Americas and Europe, more than half of Africa and most of Asia and Australasia. Our ever-growing team of authors and photographers is spread all over the world, particularly in Europe, the USA and Australia.

In the early 1990s, Rough Guides branched out of travel, with the publication of Rough Guides to World Music, Classical Music and the Internet. All three have become benchmark titles in their fields, spearheading the publication of a wide range of books under the Rough Guide name.

Including the travel series, Rough Guides now number more than 350 titles, covering: phrasebooks, waterproof maps, music guides from Opera to Heavy Metal, reference works as diverse as Conspiracy Theories and Shakespeare, and popular culture books from iPods to Poker. Rough Guides also produce a series of more than 120 World Music CDs in partnership with World Music Network.

Visit www.roughguides.com to see our latest publications.

Rough Guide travel images are available for commercial licensing at www.roughguidespictures.com

Rough Guide credits

Text editor: Helena Smith
Layout: Umesh Aggarwal
Cartography: Alakananda Bhattacharya
Picture editor: Nicole Newman
Production: Aimee Hampson
Proofreader: Jan McCann
Cover design: Chloë Roberts
Photographer: Helena Smith
Editorial: **London** Kate Berens, Claire
Saunders, Ruth Blackmore, Polly Thomas,
Richard Lim, Alison Murchie, Karoline Densley,
Andy Turner, Keith Drew, Edward Aves, Nikki
Birrell, Alice Park, Sarah Eno, Lucy White, Jo
Kirby, Samantha Cook, James Smart, Natasha
Foges, Roisin Cameron, Joe Staines, Duncan
Clark, Peter Buckley, Matthew Milton, Tracy
Hopkins, Ruth Tidball; **New York** Andrew
Rosenberg, Steven Horak, AnneLise Sorensen,
Amy Hegarty, April Isaacs, Ella Steim, Anna
Owens, Joseph Petta, Sean Mahoney
Design & Pictures: **London** Scott Stickland, Dan
May, Diana Jarvis, Mark Thomas, Jj Luck, Harriet
Mills, Chloë Roberts; **Delhi** Ajay Verma, Jessica
Subramanian, Ankur Guha, Pradeep Thapliyal,
Sachin Tanwar, Anita Singh, Madhavi Singh,
Karen D'Souza

Production: Katherine Owers
Cartography: **London** Maxine Repath, Ed
Wright, Katie Lloyd-Jones; **Delhi** Jai Prakash
Mishra, Rajesh Chhibber, Ashutosh Bharti,
Rajesh Mishra, Animesh Pathak, Jasbir
Sandhu, Karobi Gogoi, Amod Singh, Athokpam
Jotinkumar
Online: **New York** Jennifer Gold, Kristin
Mingrone; **Delhi** Manik Chauhan, Narender
Kumar, Rakesh Kumar, Amit Kumar, Amit Verma,
Rahul Kumar, Ganesh Sharma, Debojit Borah
Marketing & Publicity: **London** Liz Statham,
Niki Hanmer, Louise Maher, Jess Carter,
Vanessa Godden, Vivienne Watton, Anna
Paynton, Rachel Sprackett; **New York** Geoff
Colquitt, Megan Kennedy, Katy Ball; **Delhi**
Reem Khokhar
Special Projects Editor: Philippa Hopkins
Manager India: Punita Singh
Series Editor: Mark Ellingham
Reference Director: Andrew Lockett
Publishing Coordinator: Megan McIntyre
Publishing Director: Martin Dunford
Commercial Manager: Gino Magnotta
Managing Director: John Duhigg

SMALL PRINT

Publishing information

This fourth edition published May 2007 by
Rough Guides Ltd,
80 Strand, London WC2R 0RL
345 Hudson St, 4th Floor,
New York, NY 10014, USA
14 Local Shopping Centre, Panchsheel Park,
New Delhi 110017, India
Distributed by the Penguin Group
Penguin Books Ltd,
80 Strand, London WC2R 0RL
Penguin Group (USA)
375 Hudson Street, NY 10014, USA
Penguin Group (Australia)
250 Camberwell Road, Camberwell,
Victoria 3124, Australia
Penguin Books Canada Ltd,
10 Alcorn Avenue, Toronto, Ontario,
Canada M4V 1E4
Penguin Group (NZ)
67 Apollo Drive, Mairangi Bay, Auckland 1310,
New Zealand

Cover concept by Peter Dyer.

Typeset in Bembo and Helvetica to an original
design by Henry Iles.

Printed and bound in China

© Jules Brown 2007

No part of this book may be reproduced in any
form without permission from the publisher except
for the quotation of brief passages in reviews.

304pp includes index

A catalogue record for this book is available from
the British Library

ISBN: 978-1-84353-805-9

The publishers and authors have done their
best to ensure the accuracy and currency of
all the information in **The Rough Guide to The
Lake District**, however, they can accept no
responsibility for any loss, injury, or inconvenience
sustained by any traveller as a result of
information or advice contained in the guide.

3   5   7   9   8   6   4   2

Help us update

We've gone to a lot of effort to ensure that the
fourth edition of **The Rough Guide to The Lake
District** is accurate and up to date. However,
things change – places get "discovered", opening
hours are notoriously fickle, restaurants and
rooms raise prices or lower standards. If you
feel we've got it wrong or left something out,
we'd like to know, and if you can remember the
address, the price, the time, the phone number,
so much the better.
We'll credit all contributions, and send a copy of
the next edition (or any other Rough Guide if you

prefer) for the best letters. Everyone who writes
to us and isn't already a subscriber will receive
a copy of our full-colour thrice-yearly newsletter.
Please mark letters: "**Rough Guide The Lake
District Update**" and send to: Rough Guides,
80 Strand, London WC2R 0RL, or Rough Guides,
345 Hudson St, 4th Floor, New York, NY 10014.
Or send an email to **mail@roughguides.com**
Have your questions answered and tell others
about your trip at
www.roughguides.atinfopop.com

Acknowledgements

The author would like to thank the following organisations for invaluable information, advice and assistance: Cumbria Tourism, Lake District National Park Authority, Youth Hostels Association, English Heritage and National Trust. Thanks are also due in particular to Melanie Clarkson, Ellis Butcher, Paul Fearn, Barney Hill and Allan King, and to the various tourist information centres, sights, museums and attractions who responded willingly to my endless questions and requests. I am also grateful to Helena for her patient editing, Matt and Marta for their hospitality, mum and dad for road-testing and research, and Mark for climbing the Pikes in a storm.

Readers' letters

Thanks to all the readers who have taken the time to write in with comments and suggestions (and apologies if we've inadvertently omitted or misspelt anyone's name):

Lois Blackburn, Mrs T.A. Bradley, Margaret Gallery, David Gibson, Lionel Major, Hilary Patrick, Helen Reynolds, Rosalind Riley, Laura Smith, Liz Thomas

SMALL PRINT

Photo credits

Selected images from our guidebooks are available for licensing from:

ROUGHGUIDESPICTURES.COM

Index

Map entries are in colour

INDEX

Map symbols

maps are listed in the full index using coloured text

―――	Chapter division boundary	⚠	Campsite
‑‑‑‑‑	National park boundary	▲	Mountain peak
▭▭▭	Motorway	⌃⌃	Hills/mountains
═══	Major road	⩶	Pass
――――	Minor road		Waterfall
‑ ‑ ‑ ‑	Path		Rocks
―•―	Railway	∴	Ruin
― ―	Ferry route	★	Bus stop
――――	Waterway	P	Parking
▪▪▪▪	Wall		Petrol station
≍	Bridge	◉	Accommodation
♜	Castle	ⓘ	Tourist office
⾕	Stately home	@	Internet access
⌂	Abbey	✉	Post office
⚓	Church (regional maps)		Building
♦	General point of interest	⊞	Church
⊥	Gardens	⊤	Cemetery
⚜	Viewpoint		Park
◓	Cave		Marsh